Selected One-Act Plays of
HORTON FOOTE

Selected
One-Act
Plays of
HORTON FOOTE

Edited by

Gerald C. Wood

Southern Methodist University Press

Inquiries on all rights (except as indicated below) should be addressed to the Lucy Kroll Agency, 390 West End Avenue, New York, New York 10024.

Stock and amateur production rights to the following plays are controlled exclusively by the Dramatists Play Service, Inc., 440 Park Avenue South, New York, New York 10016: *The Old Beginning*, *A Young Lady of Property*, *The Oil Well*, *The Death of the Old Man*, *John Turner Davis*, *The Midnight Caller*, *The Dancers*, *The Man Who Climbed the Pecan Trees*, *The Roads to Home (A Nightingale*, *The Dearest of Friends*, *Spring Dance)*, *Blind Date*, and *The Road to the Graveyard*. No stock or amateur performance of these plays may be given without obtaining in advance the written permission of the Dramatists Play Service, Inc., and paying the requisite fee.

Library of Congress Cataloging-in-Publication Data

Foote, Horton.
    Selected one-act plays of Horton Foote.

    1. Wood, Gerald C.   II. Title.
PS3511.0344A6   1988b   812'.54   88-42635
ISBN 0-87074-274-4
ISBN 0-87074-275-2 (pbk.)

For Mary Hunter Wolf
with affection and gratitude

Contents

Author's Preface

My first encounter with the one-act play, or a play of any kind for that matter, was as an actor in high school. Unfortunately, I don't remember the name of the author, but I do remember that it dealt with narcotics addiction among college students—hardly a typical subject for high school production in those days. We entered the play in the state one-act play contest, and our director/teacher told us it was its first production anywhere. I remember too that the playwright strictly observed the unities of time, place and action. I know now that part of the impact of the play came from the author's skillful use of these unities, giving it a force and impact that I didn't find later in the three-act plays I was given to act in. Many, many years later I was to see Laurence Olivier perform *Oedipus*, which, of course, is the greatest and most profound use of the classic one-act form.

When I went to New York to begin a career as a professional actor, the one-act play seemed to be everywhere. There was a one-act play magazine, edited by William Kozlenko; one-act play anthologies; one-act play contests; and William Kozlenko, again, with Emjo Basshe and Alfred Kreymborg, founded a one-act play theater. They rented the Hudson, a Broadway theater now torn down, and chose three one-act plays for their opening bill. I was cast in two of them: *The Red Velvet Goat,* by Josephina Niggli, and *The Coggerers,* by Paul Vincent Carroll.

Later I joined the American Actors Company, a group of actors with varying degrees of experience. In our seasons we always included an evening of one-acts. We produced one-act plays by Thornton Wilder, E. P. Conkle, Paul Green and Lynn Riggs. It was while working as an actor with this company that I began writing plays. My first was a one-act called *Wharton Dance.* It was directed by Mary Hunter, a gifted and generous woman who was to have a profound influence on my work as a writer, as she has had on the work of many others: writers, directors, dancers, composers. For the American Actors I also wrote four related one-acts that I named *Out of My House.* All of these plays were an exploration of a town and its people that I was to continue over the years. I began by using the name of the Texas town I was born in, but the literalness of it was too confining to me, so I renamed it Harrison, and much of my writing life in my three-act, two-act and one-act plays has been spent in this mythical town.

Gradually, the one-act play seemed, at least in New York, to lose favor. No one wanted to produce one-acts and it seemed futile to write them. There were exceptions, of course. Tennessee Williams arrived in New York with a number of them. They were read and admired, published, given productions outside of New York, and many an actor worked on them in acting classes.

Around this time I had begun working with dancers to try to combine dance and speech in plays, and I was commissioned by the Neighborhood Playhouse to write a one-act play that would combine the different disciplines taught there: dance, speech, music, acting. I called the play *The Lonely,* and Martha Graham, head of the dance department, choreographed it, and Louis Horst, head of the music department, did the score. Later that year I was again commissioned by the Playhouse and I wrote *Good-bye to Richmond.* In both these plays I abandoned the unities of time and place that I had imposed on my earlier one-acts, and they had many scenes and a much more complicated time scheme. I continued this approach in the plays I did for television in the 1950s.

Some of the most effective theater I have ever seen has been in the one-act form: Sartre's *No Exit* and *The Respectful Prostitute*, Beckett's one-act plays and the one-acts of Tennessee Williams, David Mamet and Lanford Wilson.

Today in New York and all over America there are many theaters again producing one-acts and giving opportunities to young writers. I have had recent productions of my one-acts at the HB Playwrights Foundation, the Ensemble Studio Theatre and Manhattan Punch Line Theatre. Ensemble Studio Theatre and Manhattan Punch Line now have an annual festival for these plays.

I have been writing one-act plays now for many years and I continue to be devoted to the form because it allows me to explore material that would not be effective in any other length.

Introduction

There seems to be a kind of order in the universe, in the movement of the stars and the turning of the earth and the changing of the seasons, and even in the cycle of human life. But human life itself is almost pure chaos. . . . We don't really know what is going to happen to us, and we don't know why. . . . the work of the artist—the only thing he's good for—is to take these handfuls of confusion and disparate things, things that seem to be irreconcilable, and put them together in a frame to give them some kind of shape and meaning.

—Katherine Anne Porter[1]

Since the early 1940s the plays of Horton Foote have been praised for the truthfulness of their language and characterization, for their realistic portrait of the Coastal Southeast Texas he knows so well. They have been favorably compared with the dramas of Strindberg, Ibsen and Chekhov, and with the fiction of Flannery O'Connor, Katherine Anne Porter and William Faulkner. Now, as the deeply personal and universal qualities of the plays are being discovered, Foote's work is taking its rightful place "near the center of our largest American dramatic achievements."[2] He has been acclaimed as "America's greatest playwright" and "a national treasure."[3] Although he is well known for his two Academy Awards for screenwriting and for his work in American independent filmmaking (as writer, co-director and producer), the theater has been Foote's abiding love.

Throughout his long career he has been continually attracted to the economy and simplicity of the one-act. The first eight plays in this collection, which exemplify the nature and achievement of his early work in the form, were written between 1952 and 1954, an extremely productive time for the young playwright. In those three years more than a dozen of Foote's plays appeared on the stage or on television; among them were three longer works—*The Chase, The Trip to Bountiful* and *The Traveling Lady*—which were eventually made into films. Though none of the eight short plays of the fifties included in this volume became movies, all were produced on television, airing on shows like Goodyear Theatre, Philco Television Playhouse and Gulf Playhouse. Now often called the Golden Age of Television, it was a period in which the work of young writers like Foote, Paddy Chayefsky, Gore Vidal, Rod Serling and Reginald Rose was respected and supported. Foote had especially fertile collaboration with producer Fred Coe and directors Delbert Mann, Vincent Donehue and Arthur Penn. Also included in this creative circle producing Foote's plays on television were such actors as E. G. Marshall, James Broderick, Dorothy and Lillian Gish, Joanne Woodward and Kim Stanley.

Despite Horton Foote's active participation in early dramatic television, there are few differences between the stage versions of the one-acts, which are collected in this volume, and the versions produced on television. For the most part, even in the early days of live drama, Foote did not write specifically for television. The medium was just one more place to present his plays. When writing them, he never thought about commercial breaks, for example. He had a general sense of the greater mobility available from the television camera, but he also felt that most cinematic techniques had already been absorbed into the craft of playwriting. In fact, since the technology of early television usually limited its action to three sets and two cameras, staging was very similar in the two media. In every case, even the two tele-

plays written as commissioned experiments in point of view—
The Death of the Old Man and *The Tears of My Sister*—he wrote
his teleplays as "long one-act plays."

The eight plays which open this collection demonstrate
that by the fifties Horton Foote had developed a psychological
realism similar to, yet subtly different from, his most recent work.
In *John Turner Davis*, for example, little remains of the writer's
tendency in the early 1940s to rely on real names and events
(what he calls "reporting"). In this play, as in the other early
plays collected here, he uses language and conflicts to develop a
subtext more suggestive of essential emotional needs and dep-
rivations than specific people and situations. Similarly, Foote
uses the setting of *John Turner Davis* expressively; the Texas landscape has become part of the writer's personal mythology, in
which the endless search for connectedness, order and contentment is the primary reality, not literal places. These television
and stage plays from 1952–54 already have the Horton Foote
signature.

At the same time, the characters in the plays of the early
1950s are sometimes quite articulate about their emotional lives
and confident of their powers to change themselves and others in
definitive ways. Consequently, many of the earlier plays tend to
be a shade more affirmative than the later ones. And, though
Foote's work is never exactly didactic, the conflicts in the dramas
of the fifties tend to be more clearly defined for both characters
and audience than is the case in his later work. The endings also
offer more resolution and closure than is typical of his recent
writing. First-time readers of his plays of the 1950s may be surprised to find that the playwright's work has not always been
quite as understated and inconclusive as it is in his nine-play
cycle *The Orphan's Home* or in his Academy Award–winning
screenplay for *Tender Mercies*.

Although Foote never consciously avoided the one-act form,
some twenty-five years passed between the writing of the first eight
plays in this collection and the appearance of the last nine. They
were years of experimentation and change. He continued to
write a few more television plays in the late fifties, but with the
increasing commercialization of that medium, Foote gradually

moved away from TV. In the sixties he became an active and successful screenwriter. When the work in film expressed his vision
or he felt sympathetic to the material—as was the case with *To
Kill a Mockingbird, Baby, the Rain Must Fall* and *Tomorrow*—he
found it enjoyable; it was, he felt, personal writing. But when he
tried commissioned writing—as was the case with *Hurry Sundown* and *The Stalking Moon*—he found the work less rewarding,
too often formulaic and uninspiring. He was no happier writing
for Hollywood in the sixties than he had been during the summer
he spent there in the mid-forties.

Worst of all, from the mid-sixties until late in the seventies,
Foote's first love—theater—was disinterested in plays like his. In
those times of political and racial unrest, subtle, realistic drama
of personality tended to be ignored; iconoclastic theater of ex-
plosive rhetoric and simple, cartoonish surfaces was the rage. But
Foote, having moved from New York to New Hampshire in the
mid-sixties, continued to write, personally and faithfully. He
adapted two short stories for PBS: Flannery O'Connor's "The
Displaced Person" (1977) and William Faulkner's "Barn Burning"
(1980). More significantly, by the end of the seventies he had
written or was reworking more than a dozen plays; he was writing
more drama than at any time since the fifties. Eventually, by the
time the eighties began, he had returned to one-acts as well.

These new plays, like those he wrote nearly three decades
before, are both light and dark. They range from a charming
story of adolescents finding their own way (*Blind Date*) to a bru-
tal portrait of murder (*The One-Armed Man*) and an enervating
vision of emotional isolation (*Spring Dance*). Like the earlier
plays, they are about going away and coming home, finding a
place and moving on. These characters, like those of the fifties,
long for sustaining connections with the deep rhythms of life,
which they sometimes find. But they are often pursued by an
even more disturbing sense of physical and emotional dislocation
than that in the earlier plays. In the *Roads to Home* trilogy and
The Land of the Astronauts, for example, there is a horrible confusion and disorientation, a profound loss of identity and meaning
that haunts the characters. They are not only away from home;

they are looking for a way back to a place that no longer exists. Or at least it is nothing like the place they remember. In a few of the plays—like *The One-Armed Man* and *Spring Dance*—this pervasive sense of darkness transforms Foote's otherwise realistic theater into a mental, impressionistic one. The poetic, visionary impulses of his work, for the most part checked and muted in the fifties, are dramatically present in the eighties.

In all these one-act plays—from the fifties and from the eighties—Horton Foote reveals himself as a writer with a place. The home of his creativity and renewal has always been Wharton, Texas. Born in that small Gulf Coast town in 1916, he lived there until he was sixteen years old. It was there that he first saw the ancient pecan trees, the Victorian houses with their large galleries, the courthouse square and the other primary images of his writing. Surrounding Wharton he also found prairies and rich bottomlands farmed by diverse groups of people: blacks, whites, Mexicans, Czechs. In the conversation of these people—his relatives and neighbors—he heard a few useful colloquialisms (such as "swanny" or "in a little"), but he was most attracted to the rhythms and nuances of the local speech. For Horton Foote, the simple, direct Southeast Texas vernacular expressed the dignity and probity he has always cherished. Naturally, the good talkers from Wharton, Texas, told interesting stories, some of which Foote used as sources for the plays in this collection.

Over fifty-five years after Horton Foote left Wharton to pursue an acting career, his homeplace still guides and supports his writing. By remembering the voices of Wharton's gifted story-tellers, he connects with his place and similar ones throughout the South. Once his imagination has taken him home again, the local muses present him with the images, characters and stories he needs for his writing. And, always thankful for such gifts, he is true to his place. Almost as if protecting its integrity, he carefully establishes authentic settings and precise historical moments in his dramas; he allows himself little sentiment and no condescension. As a result of this process, he writes what Katherine Anne Porter calls "real fiction." Like her stories, the plays in this volume are "made up of thousands of things that did happen to living human beings in a certain part of the country, at a certain time . . . things that are still remembered by others as single incidents."[4]

But as much as his writing relies on the details and specific instances of a natural place, Foote does not write local color. And he is not sentimental about the past. Instead he uses his Wharton materials to create the Harrison, Texas, of his imagination. In order to meet the demands of this fictional place he redesigns real stories so that they take the shape and nature of myth. He crafts them into tales of going away and coming home, grief and rebirth, despair and healing—tales for all places and times. His love of order leads Foote to create patterns of feeling and experience which connect one person with another, one place with another. In the process, his place gives birth to stories that are both from their place and beyond it. They are the artist's gift to a broken, chaotic world.

Foote's vision grows from his ability to see the characters and themes in these stories from many points of view. He works a small patch of creative ground, always assuming there is another way of seeing, another side to the story he tells. *The Dancers* and *Blind Date*, for example, are both about adolescence, but the first is a play of the fifties about the natural power of intimacy, the second a work of the eighties about the joy of identity. *John Turner Davis* and *Spring Dance* are both orphan plays; one about the need to connect, the other about the horror of dislocation. Because Foote writes to discover new ways of knowing a limited number of experiences (which he calls "my stories"), no single play—or script—expresses his complete vision.

But read together, these plays reveal life as essentially a mystery. There are no formulas here; there are only primary feelings and human events. These primitive needs control the life of Harrison just below its serene, quiet surface. Unfortunately, the characters usually are not fully aware of their longings, and the needs change from one play to another. In *John Turner Davis* connectedness is called for; in *The Midnight Caller* it's autonomy. In *The Old Beginning* leaving home is a virtue, but in *The Death of the Old Man* finding a new home is just as valuable. Hope is cherished one time; it must be abandoned the next. There are no assurances, no evils, no simple solutions in any of these dramatic situations.

Most sobering of all, Foote's antagonists are not evil people. They are forces for the most part beyond the understanding and control of even the best of the characters. Broken families, economic and racial injustice, alcoholism and death pass relentlessly through these plays. The strongest characters face themselves and their life situations with grace and learn to love others. But even then contentment may not last; everything changes and happiness cannot always be trusted. So Foote's people endlessly pursue healing ties to the land, their families, loved ones, even work. Finally they are faced with the terrible reality that each must live and die, to some degree, alone. They are all orphans searching for an elusive sense of identity in a storm of circumstance.

Why some of them are able to find themselves while others cannot is never fully explained in Foote's work. But that is because he writes to discover, not to preach. Rather than lecture to his readers, he investigates with them the "great mystery" about the sources of courage and personhood:

> I do understand, and do appreciate the fact, that I am able to some measure to be enough in control of my emotions and my physical being that I can make some choices. I think there is a great mystery here, and I don't know why some people have this ability and some don't. But I think that is part of what I am trying to write about.[5]

In the face of such an eternal mystery, the fact of present courage is explanation and reward enough. As Foote has said, "My God, people have a lot of courage in facing all the things they're asked to meet."[6]

But courage is only one of many topics in these plays. Foote is more generally interested in what he calls the "patterns . . . in people," only one of which is their capacity for courage:

> I think what has been increasingly interesting to me (And I suppose, you see, I'm in touch with six or seven generations

living in Wharton. The seventh generation has begun.) is trying to bring order out of disorder . . . to try to make sense out of what sometimes seems just total confusion. And if you see the patterns . . . in people . . .[7]

The uncovering of these patterns is, as he explains it, his means of bringing "order" and making "sense." Like Katherine Anne Porter before him, he is using art as a "frame to give . . . shape and meaning" to the otherwise "almost pure chaos" of human life. The Texas voices, characters and stories in his work are Foote's tools in his quest for continuity and tradition. But the goals of his search are not just particular and regional. He wants to discover the roots of courage, the peace of identity, and the healing power of our myths and legends. For an artist who commits himself to the eternal struggle of order against disorder, nothing less will satisfy.

I would like to thank Lillian and Horton Foote for their support of this project. They have happily answered questions, kindly pointed out errors and gracefully encouraged me when that too was needed. They also were superb hosts when my wife and I visited Wharton in the summer of 1987. At Carson-Newman, Roy A. Dobyns, vice-president and academic dean, has fostered this project from the beginning, and Jeff Daniel Marion has offered his flawless advice and criticism along the way. Lynda Hill has rescued me from more than one deadline. Terry Barr, of Presbyterian College, has been a good friend and companion over the last several years. Thanks, Terry, for listening and sharing your work. The Appalachian College Program, under the capable direction of Alice Brown, has twice supported this project under the James Still Fellowship Program. Jane Harris and the Lucy Kroll Agency have been most prompt and thorough in providing background information on the plays. And I want to thank Suzanne Comer, senior editor at Southern Methodist University Press, for her many contributions to this collection; her response to the first draft of the introduction was especially wise. Finally, thanks to my wife, Barb, and our children, Tim and Sarah, for sharing much of this experience, and for tolerating the rest.

Gerald C. Wood
Carson-Newman College

Notes

1. Barbara Thompson, "Katherine Anne Porter," in *Writers at Work: The "Paris Review" Interviews, Second Series* (New York: Viking, 1965), 150–51, 161–62.

2. Reynolds Price, "Introduction," in *Courtship, Valentine's Day, 1918: Three Plays from "The Orphans' Home Cycle,"* by Horton Foote (New York: Grove Press, 1987), xiii.

3. Marian Burkhart, "Horton Foote's Many Roads Home," *Commonweal,* 26 February 1988, 110; Jim Lehrer, quoted in *Roots in a Parched Ground, Convicts, Lily Dale, The Widow Claire: The First Four Plays of "The Orphans' Home Cycle,"* by Horton Foote (New York: Grove Press, 1988), n.p.

4. Katherine Anne Porter, *The Collected Essays and Occasional Writings of Katherine Anne Porter* (New York: Dell, 1973), 468–69.

5. Horton Foote, telephone conversation with English 490 class, Carson-Newman College, 9 October 1986.

6. Horton Foote, quoted in publicity brochure for *The Trip to Bountiful.*

7. Gerald C. Wood and Terry Barr, "'A Certain Kind of Writer': An Interview with Horton Foote," *Literature/Film Quarterly* 14, no. 4 (1986): 227.

Besides these sources, I have also made use of other information gathered in personal interviews with Horton Foote on 18 July and 24 October 1985 and in a telephone interview with the writer on 23 July 1987. In preparing this introduction and the headnotes to the plays in this volume I have found useful the following works:

"Christianity Today Talks to Horton Foote." *Christianity Today,* 4 April 1986, 30.

Darnton, Nina. "Horton Foote Celebrates a Bygone America in '1918.'" *New York Times,* 21 April 1985.

Davis, Ronald L. "Roots in Parched Ground: An Interview with Horton Foote." *Southwest Review* 73, no. 3 (Summer 1988): 298–318.

Foote, Horton. "Introduction." *Roots in a Parched Ground, Convicts, Lily Dale, The Widow Claire: The First Four Plays of "The Orphans' Home Cycle."* New York: Grove Press, 1988.

———. "On First Dramatizing Faulkner" and "*Tomorrow:* The Genesis of a Screenplay." In *Faulkner, Modernism, and Film: Faulkner and Yoknapatawpha,* edited by Evans Harrington and Ann J. Abadie. Jackson: University Press of Mississippi, 1979.

———. "Preface." *Harrison, Texas: Eight Television Plays by Horton Foote.* New York: Harcourt, Brace and Company, 1956.

———. "The Trip to Paradise." *Texas Monthly,* December 1987, 140–49, 182–83.

———. "The Visual Takes Over." In *Tomorrow and Tomorrow and Tomorrow,* edited by David G. Yellin and Marie Connors. Jackson: University Press of Mississippi, 1985.

Freedman, Samuel G. "From the Heart of Texas." *New York Times Magazine,* 9 February 1986.

Hachem, Samir. "Foote-Work." *Horizon,* April 1986, 39–41.

Hunter, Mary. "Foreword." In *Only the Heart,* by Horton Foote. New York: The Dramatists Play Service, 1944.

Neff, David. "Going Home to the Hidden God." *Christianity Today,* 4 April 1986, 30–31.

Skaggs, Calvin. "Interview with Horton Foote." In *The American Short Story,* edited by Calvin Skaggs. New York: Dell, 1977.

Young, Stark. "Foreword." In *The Traveling Lady,* by Horton Foote. New York: The Dramatists Play Service, 1955.

Chronology

March 14, 1916   Born Wharton, Texas, to Albert Horton
                  and Hallie Brooks Foote.
1932   Graduated from high school, Wharton,
                  Texas. Studied elocution in Dallas,
                  Texas.
1933–35   Studied acting at Pasadena Playhouse in
                  California. In March 1934 saw Eva Le
                  Gallienne production of Ibsen and "be-
                  came totally dedicated to the theater."
1936–44   Worked as an actor in New York City and
                  at summer theaters (1936–42).
                  Trained at Tamara Daykarhanova school for
                  acting in New York City (1937–39).
                  First plays written for American Actors
                  Company, under direction of Mary
                  Hunter: *Wharton Dance* (1939–40),
                  Texas Town (1940–41), *Out of My House*
                  (1942), *Only the Heart* (Off-Broadway
                  production, 1943; Broadway production,
                  1944).
                  Wrote briefly for Universal Studios in

Hollywood (1944). After three months returned to New York City, convinced formula writing not his style.

Wrote *Daisy Lee* (1944), a dance play choreographed and performed by Valerie Bettis.

For Neighborhood Playhouse wrote *Miss Lou, The Lonely* (a dance play choreographed by Martha Graham) and *Good-bye to Richmond* (all 1944).

June 4, 1945   Married Lillian Vallish.

1945–49   Moved to Washington, D.C. Taught acting and wrote and directed *Homecoming, People in the Show, Themes and Variations* and *Good-bye to Richmond* (also performed at the Baltimore Museum of Art and at Hunter College in New York City).

1949   Moved from Washington, D.C., to New York City.

1951–54   Wrote for "The Gabby Hayes Show." Also for television, wrote *Ludie Brooks* (1951), *The Travelers* (1952), *Expectant Relations* (1953), *The Trip to Bountiful* (1953) and *The Shadow of Willie Greer* (1954). Completed first eight plays in this volume.

Wrote ballet-with-words for Jerome Robbins musical *Two's Company* (1953).

Important stageplays: *The Chase* (1952), *The Trip to Bountiful* (1953), *The Traveling Lady* (1954; later performed on television).

1955–65   Continuing work in television, often commissioned: *The Roads to Home* (1955; not the trilogy of the eighties), *Flight* (1956), *Drugstore, Sunday Noon* (1956), *A Member of the Family* (1957), *Old Man* (1960),

Tomorrow (1960), *The Shape of the River* (1960), *The Night of the Storm* (1961; precursor to *Roots in a Parched Ground*), *The Gambling Heart* (1964).

Moved from New York City to Nyack, New York, in 1956.

First screenplay: *Storm Fear* (1956).

Publication of *Harrison, Texas: Eight Television Plays by Horton Foote* and the novel *The Chase* (both 1956).

Many teleplays also staged: *A Young Lady of Property, The Midnight Caller, John Turner Davis, The Dancers.*

Academy Award and Writers Guild of America Award for adaptation of Harper Lee's novel *To Kill a Mockingbird* (1962).

Screenplay for *Baby, the Rain Must Fall* (1964), from his play *The Traveling Lady.*

1966–77   Moved from Nyack, New York, to New Hampshire (1966).

Non-personal work in film adaptation: *Hurry Sundown* (1966), *The Chase* (1966; additional work on Lillian Hellman screenplay), *The Stalking Moon* (1969).

HB Playwrights Foundation production of *Tomorrow,* adapted from a short story by William Faulkner, in New York City (1968).

Adaptation of *Gone with the Wind* as stage musical, in London and Los Angeles (1971–73).

Major work for film produced during this period: *Tomorrow* (1972).

Wrote *The Orphans' Home Cycle* (1974–77).

HB Playwrights Foundation production of A

Young Lady of Property (1976).
Wrote *The Habitation of Dragons* and *Night Seasons*.

1977–81   Period of renewed production of his works.
Adaptations for PBS of Flannery O'Connor's short story "The Displaced Person" (1977) and Faulkner's short story "Barn Burning" (1980).

Returned to New York City to work with Herbert Berghof at HB Playwrights Foundation. Taught acting at HB Studio, 1978–79.

HB Playwrights Foundation productions of *Night Seasons* (1977), *In a Coffin in Egypt* (1980), *Arrival and Departure* (1981). Three plays of *The Orphans' Home Cycle—Courtship* (1978), *1918* (1979), *Valentine's Day* (1980)—produced under playwright's direction.

1982 to present   *The Roads to Home* presented by Manhattan Punch Line Theatre (1982).

Staged reading of *The Widow Claire*, from *The Orphans' Home Cycle*, off-Broadway (1982).

HB Playwrights Foundation production of *The Old Friends* (1982).

Academy Award and Writers Guild of America Award for original screenplay of *Tender Mercies* (1983). Also received the Christopher Award for best film of 1983.

Teleplay for *Keeping On: A Drama of Life in a Mill Town* (PBS, 1983).

HB Playwrights Foundation productions of *Blind Date, The Prisoner's Song, The One-Armed Man* (all 1985).

Ensemble Studio Theatre production of *The Road to the Graveyard* (1985).

Ensemble Studio Theatre Founders Award
(1985).
Publication of *Tomorrow and Tomorrow and
Tomorrow* (1985; Faulkner short story,
Foote teleplay and screenplay).
Academy Award nomination for screenplay
of *The Trip to Bountiful* (1985). Also,
Independent Film Award and Luminas
Award.
Workshop production of *The Habitation of
Dragons* in New York City (1986).
Ensemble Studio Theatre production of
Blind Date (1986).
Last nine plays in this volume written; also,
Talking Pictures and *Dividing the Estate*.
Beginning of independent film production:
1918 (1985), *On Valentine's Day* (1986),
Courtship (1987). The three films re-
edited and shown on PBS as *The Story of
a Marriage* (1987).
Off-Broadway productions of *The Widow
Claire* and *Lily Dale* (1986–87).
Publication of *Courtship, Valentine's Day,
1918: Three Plays from "The Orphans'
Home Cycle"* (1987)
The Widow Claire included in *The Best Plays
of 1986–1987* (The Burns Mantle The-
ater Yearbook, 1988).
Ensemble Studio Theatre productions of
The Man Who Climbed the Pecan Trees
and *The Land of the Astronauts* (both
1988).
Publication of *Roots in a Parched Ground,
Convicts, Lily Dale, The Widow Claire: The
First Four Plays of "The Orphans' Home
Cycle"* (1988).
Film work in progress: adaptation of Bette B.

Lord's novel *Spring Moon* for Alan J. Pakula; production of four films from *The Orphans' Home Cycle* (*Roots in a Parched Ground, Convicts, Lily Dale, The Widow Claire*).

Agrees to adapt Flaubert's novel *Madame Bovary* for television (a Roland Joffe production for HBO and BBC).

First production of *The Habitation of Dragons*, Pittsburgh Public Theater (September–October 1988), directed by the author.

Compostela Award (1988).

Selected One-Act Plays of
HORTON FOOTE

The Old Beginning

The Old Beginning is the first of many plays in this collection which take place in the fictional Harrison, Texas. Harrison, a small Gulf Coast town, was a community serving the cotton industry and its plantation society before World War I. That earlier Harrison had many crosses to bear, including racism and a rigid patriarchy. But the innocent Harrison of the early twentieth century was also a stable place where connections by blood, history and duty grew naturally and never died. Identity came with the territory.

This orderly past haunts Horton Foote's postwar Harrison, but *The Old Beginning*, like the plays that follow in this volume, is not simply nostalgic for the old days. The drama of *The Old Beginning* is created by the tension between old and new, and shaped by the invisible forces of change which few of Harrison's people understand. H. T. Mavis, for example, appears in a number of these plays as an agent and prophet of the new capitalism. In Harrison, as old buildings are torn down and new oil wells are erected, as new money buys old furniture, Mavis is taking over. Tommy Mavis, in quiet imitation of his father, explains the method: "We buy and we rent, but we don't sell." The new breed of lawyers and real estate developers, like Mavis, are quick to shed

I

the static hierarchy of the old cotton society for the "forward-looking" style of the chain stores and the legalistic call to "read the contract." The Harrison of The Old Beginning is taking its first steps into the modern age of shopping centers, subdivisions and the breathless pace of a new, upwardly mobile generation.

Readers familiar with only Horton Foote's most recent plays and screenplays will probably be surprised by The Old Beginning. This play is, for one thing, funnier than The Orphans' Home Cycle or Tender Mercies. The humor ranges from Tommy's all-too-human choking fit following his declaration of independence to the compulsive interest of Mrs. Mavis and Mrs. Nelson in taxes and parties of the first and second part.

But the humor is probably less surprising to most readers than is the dramatic construction. Horton Foote has become known for his subtle, open-ended plots which rely on understatement. Compared to his more recent work, The Old Beginning has a well-defined plot constructed around clear external tensions. For example, Tommy's agreement with Lee Johnson is quickly called into question by the appearance of Mr. Scott, and Mrs. Nelson's problems with her home act as a kind of chorus, under-lining the conflict by reminding the audience of H. T.'s rigidity and hidden aggression. The whole play is unified by Tommy's need to establish his independence from his father, a motive which is clear to both Tommy and the audience throughout the play. In The Old Beginning, written in 1952, leaving home is just as necessary to Tommy Mavis and Julia Thornton as returning home will be to Carrie Watts a year later in the first production of The Trip to Bountiful.

The Old Beginning is also about one of Horton Foote's favor-ite subjects: work. In many of his plays, like The Traveling Lady and Old Man, work creates an elemental bond between the otherwise lonely outsider and his or her community. Without the ritual of work it is easy for many of Foote's characters to slide into violence and self-destruction. With healthy, healing work come feelings of connection—to the land, a profession, other people and the community—which give the characters a sense of per-sonal worth and purpose. But The Old Beginning, like Only the

Heart before it (a three-act play of 1943), is a study of the dark side of work. For Lester and for H. T. Mavis, work has become compulsive. As Roberta innocently declares, "H. T. just loves this business. He eats it, lives and sleeps it." Here, as in Foote's other plays on destructive work, H. T.'s business gives him an illusion of control over himself and others that, sadly, keeps him from understanding and empathizing with his son. Typically, H. T. can offer Tommy only a check or another building rather than the messy intimacy that he needs for emotional growth. And so, like Elizabeth Vaughn in *Courtship*, Tommy leaves one home to make another. It is a new experience for Tommy, but countless other stories describe the same pattern. It is an old beginning.

The Old Beginning was first produced on the Goodyear Theatre on November 23, 1952.

The Old Beginning

CAST

Tommy Mavis   Mrs. Nelson
Lester   Roberta Mavis
Rose   H. T. Mavis
Lee Johnson   Mr. Scott
Julia Thornton   Sheriff
              Second Man

Place: Harrison, Texas
Time: 1950

The lights are brought up D. R. *on part of a sidewalk. The sidewalk area runs the length of the* D. S. *area and up the* C. *of the stage, dividing the areas* L. *and* R. *There are entrances to the areas* L. *and* R. *at the* C. *of each area. The area* R. *is part of a drugstore. The area* L. *is the office of* H. T. MAVIS. *Depending on the style of production, doors could be used marking the entrances to the two areas. When the* R. *area is in use the* C. *sidewalk becomes part of that area, and when the* L. *area is in use the* C. *sidewalk becomes part of it.*

At rise, LESTER, *a man in his middle years, is standing on the sidewalk* D. R. *He seems to have no particular reason for being there.* TOMMY *enters sidewalk* D. L.

LESTER. Hello, Tommy.

TOMMY. Mornin', Lester.

LESTER. How goes it?

TOMMY. Great. Just great. How goes it with you?

LESTER. All right. On my vacation, you know.

TOMMY. Going anyplace?

LESTER. Nope. Wanted a real rest this time so thought I'd stay home. I'm not gettin' any rest though. Been off work three days and don't know what to do with myself. I thought by staying home I'd get lots of sleep. But doggone it I can't sleep later than seven o'clock to save my life. My wife is tired of me hanging around the house, so thought I'd come on downtown and see what's doing. Hear your dad is going on a trip. . . .

TOMMY. That's right.

LESTER. Is that so? Well, I never would have believed it if I hadn't heard it from your lips.

TOMMY. It's true. See you around.

(TOMMY *goes up sidewalk* C., *opens the door* L. C. *of drugstore area and goes in. A table with three chairs represents our drugstore. Behind the table is a pinball machine.* TOMMY *sits at the table and* ROSE, *a sleepy-looking waitress, comes in from* R. C. *and goes up to him.*)

TOMMY. Hi, Rose.

ROSE. Hi, Tommy. Down early this morning.

TOMMY. Yep. Cup of coffee, please.

ROSE. O.K. Anything with it?

TOMMY. No, thank you. Just coffee.

ROSE. Light?

TOMMY. That's right.

(ROSE *goes off* R. C. *to get the coffee.* LEE JOHNSON *enters sidewalk* D. L., *comes into the drugstore* L. C. *He is a middle-aged man.*)

LEE. Hello, Tommy. (*Sitting at table.*) Sorry I'm late.

TOMMY. It's all right. I just got here myself. Cup of coffee?

LEE. Thanks.

TOMMY. (*Calling to* ROSE, *offstage* R.) Make that two, Rose.

ROSE. (*Calling from offstage.*) That black, Mr. Lee?

LEE. That's right, Rose. What did you want to see me about, Tommy? I'm sorry that I couldn't meet you at my place of business, but I have to be over at the other side of town before nine to look at some furniture.

TOMMY. I won't take much of your time. I wanted to talk to you about renting a building. I understand they're tearing the place you're in down.

LEE. That's right. Putting up a filling station. I've been talkin' to John Taylor about renting that old tin building of his.

(ROSE *comes in* R. C. *with the coffee.*)

TOMMY. Wouldn't that be awful hot in the summer?

LEE. It sure will be. And it'll be torn down in another year or so. But it's cheap. About all a business like mine can afford.

TOMMY. What are you paying now?

LEE. You won't believe it when I tell you. Twenty a month. They're asking thirty-five for the tin building.

TOMMY. Do you know that building of Dad's two doors down from the post office?

LEE. The one that had the flower shop in it?

(ROSE *goes off* R. C.)

TOMMY. Yeah. You know it's been vacant a year.

LEE. What's your dad asking for it?

TOMMY. It isn't Dad's any longer. He gave it to me last night.

LEE. Is that so?

TOMMY. Yes sir. I spent most of last night trying to figure what kind of a business would make a go of it in there. All of a sudden I thought of you, Mr. Lee.

LEE. How much do you want for it?

TOMMY. Let me finish what I have to say before we talk price.

LEE. It's no point in wasting your time if I think I can't afford it, son.

TOMMY. But I have an idea I wish you'd let me tell you about before we discuss price.

LEE. All right. Walk me down the street. I have to meet a customer at my store in ten minutes.

TOMMY. Yes sir. (TOMMY *leaves twenty cents on the table. They start walking slowly out* L. C. *of the area. They walk* D. S., *stopping every few feet to talk, and go out* D. R. *along the sidewalk.*) You handle some antiques along with your secondhand furniture, don't you?

LEE. Yes. I always have. I've never tried to push them though.

TOMMY. Why not?

LEE. Well, I don't know. I've just always had my biggest turnover in secondhand furniture. The antiques were always there for anyone that was interested.

TOMMY. A lot of money in this town now. Sometimes I think we're all too close to Harrison to realize how it's changing that way. Women here are buying lots of antiques. Do you know a lot of people don't even know you're handling them stuck way off where you've been?

LEE. Is that so?

TOMMY. My mother didn't. I asked her last night. She said she'd forgotten it if she ever knew. She said she bet that none of her friends knew. And she buys a lot of antiques. Now that's why I think my store is the place for you. You can display your things well. You have to admit it's a pretty store. Most of the women in town will have to pass by you going to the post office. I bet if you started to emphasize your antiques you'd find lots of new customers. . . .

LEE. How much is the rent?

TOMMY. I'm asking sixty a month.

LEE. Sixty? I can't do it, son. That's three times what I pay now.

TOMMY. But I guarantee you'll get three times the business. You know what I'd do? I'd even call myself an antique shop. I know my mother said she'd be glad of a place in town to go to. She said you'd be bound to get people from all the little towns around here. Trade that now goes into San 'tonia an' New Orleans. I bet if you don't do it, somebody is gonna think of the idea and open up a shop.

LEE. You think so?

TOMMY. I'm convinced of it. Why, Mr. Lee, I'm convinced . . .

(*As they disappear* D. R., *the lights are brought down on the drugstore area and brought up* L. *on the* MAVIS *office. The office is small and crowded. It has a desk, with a phone on it, two file cabinets and three chairs. There is a door* L. C. *leading to another office. The phone is ringing as the lights come up.* TOMMY MAVIS *comes hurrying in* D. R. *He is whistling, carrying some mail. He hears the phone ring in the office.* TOMMY *breaks into a run, hurrying up the sidewalk* C. *until he reaches office entrance. He grabs his keys out of his pocket and hurriedly unlocks the office door. He runs inside the office to the phone.*)

TOMMY. (*On phone.*) H. T. Mavis and Son. Oh, hello, Dad. Yes, I just got here. I know but it's only three minutes after eight. Yes sir.

(*He puts the phone down. He throws some mail on the desk. He goes to the desk, sits and takes out some leases and starts working on them as the lights are brought down. The lights come up again, an hour later.* TOMMY *is reading the mail. The phone rings again. He answers it.*)

TOMMY. H. T. Mavis and Son. No. This is the son. Yes. No. Nothing to sell. No. We buy and we rent, but we don't sell.

(*He puts the phone down. A handsome girl in her early twenties comes in* R. *alongside walk, up* C. *sidewalk to office entrance* R. C. *She is* JULIA THORNTON, TOMMY'S *fiancée.*)

JULIA. Hello, Tommy.

(TOMMY *scrambles out of his chair and goes to her.*)

TOMMY. Hello, Julia. (*Gives her a kiss.*) Congratulate me.

JULIA. On what?

TOMMY. First of all for having the good luck of having the prettiest girl in Harrison agree to marry me.

JULIA. (*Laughing.*) Who is that?

TOMMY. Who is the prettiest girl? Or who has agreed to marry me? They're the same person. . . . I'll kiss her so you'll know. (*He goes toward* JULIA *to kiss her again.*)

JULIA. (*Laughing.*) You silly thing. Stop it. This is a place of business.

TOMMY. Is that so?

JULIA. (*Laughing.*) If your father walked in and saw you act like this, you'd find out quick enough it's so. Now sit down and act sensible.

TOMMY. You sit down and you act sensible. I couldn't act sensible even if I wanted to. I'm in love.

JULIA. (*Laughing.*) Tommy, what has gotten into you?

TOMMY. I'm a free man. I'm drunk with my own independence.

JULIA. Honey, what are you talking about?

TOMMY. I've made a decision by myself.

JULIA. You have?

TOMMY. Yes ma'm. I'm twenty-three years old and I have just done the second thing in my life that I ever did without consulting my father. Do you know what the first was?

JULIA. Asking me to marry you?

TOMMY. Yes. And that turned out so well it gave me courage for the second. You know I was sore at you yesterday. Awfully sore.

JULIA. I thought you must have been. And I was sorry, but I felt I had to say those things, Tommy.

TOMMY. I was sore because I knew you were so right. Anyway, after I left you I marched up to Dad and I said I wanted to talk to him. I told him I thought he was bossing me around too much and that I didn't have a mind of my own.

JULIA. And what did he say?

TOMMY. Well . . . he took it pretty well. He said he knew he wasn't easy to work with. He explained he was used to doing everything himself and having things his own way. And then he said he thought it might be better if he gave me something of my own to handle, and he said he would give me one of his brick buildings.

JULIA. My goodness. Which one?

TOMMY. The one two doors from the post office.

JULIA. Oh.

TOMMY. Well, it doesn't seem like so much, I know. But I decided to accept it as a real challenge and I went right to work and I found myself a tenant this morning. I rented it all by myself. I made my own deal, drew up my own leases and here they are waiting to be signed.

JULIA. Oh, Tommy, that's wonderful. Who did you rent it to?

TOMMY. Lee Johnson. He's moving his secondhand store there. I sold him on the idea of featuring antiques. He agreed to pay fifty dollars a month. It's not the highest rent in town, but it's not the lowest.

JULIA. I should say not. Did you tell your father?

TOMMY. Nope. Not yet, but I'm going to tell him. This calls for a celebration, doesn't it? Will you have lunch with me?

JULIA. Sure.

(LEE JOHNSON *comes in* D. L., *crosses sidewalk to* C. *sidewalk and up that to entrance of office* R. C.)

LEE. Hello, Julia.

JULIA. Hello, Mr. Lee.

(TOMMY *goes to desk and picks up the leases he has been working on.*)

TOMMY. Here is everything for you to look over.

LEE. Fine. I'll get them back sometime this afternoon.

TOMMY. That's O.K.

LEE. You still want it kept a secret?

TOMMY. Yep. Until I get a chance to tell Dad this morning.

LEE. O.K. He's a fast operator, Julia.

JULIA. Is that so?

LEE. I guess he told you I was renting his store for an antique shop.

JULIA. Yes, and I think it's a wonderful idea.

LEE. It better be. I've burned my bridges now. I just turned down the tin building, Tommy. They've rented it to somebody else.

TOMMY. You'll never regret this, Mr. Lee.

LEE. I'm sure not. (*He starts out of the office, then pauses.*) When's your dad leaving on the trip?

TOMMY. Tomorrow morning.

LEE. How did you get him out of town?

TOMMY. I didn't. That was Mother's work.

LEE. Well, I'll believe it when he goes. They were kidding him down at the drugstore about it yesterday afternoon. But he vowed he was going. Well, he works hard. He needs a vacation if any man does.

TOMMY. That's right.

LEE. I'll see you.

(*He goes out the door* R. C. *and starts* L. *down the* C. *sidewalk.* MRS. NELSON *comes up the sidewalk from* R. *toward the office. She is a small, nervous woman in her late fifties.*)

MRS. NELSON. Good morning, Lee.

LEE. How are you, Mrs. Nelson?

MRS. NELSON. Mad. Mad enough to snatch somebody bald-headed. I've been paying my good rent to H. T. Mavis for a rat trap so long and I'm tired of it. (*She marches past* LEE *and goes into the office* R. C. LEE *continues down the sidewalk and off* L.) Hello, Thomas.

TOMMY. Hello, Mrs. Nelson.

MRS. NELSON. Where's your father?

TOMMY. He's out someplace, Mrs. Nelson. He's getting ready for a trip he's taking tomorrow.

JULIA. Hello, Mrs. Nelson.

MRS. NELSON. Oh, hello, Julia. I didn't see you. What time do you expect your father back, Thomas?

TOMMY. I don't know, but it shouldn't be long. Won't you have a seat?

MRS. NELSON. Thank you. (*She goes to a chair.*) I've come in to complain about the way our house is leaking. It needs new shingles. The rain has stained all the ceiling paper. The wall-paper in the living room is in tatters. The paint on the doors and woodwork is peeling.

(ROBERTA MAVIS, TOMMY's *mother, enters sidewalk* D. R., *comes up* C. *sidewalk and enters office. She is a nervous, high-strung woman in her late forties.*)

ROBERTA. Hello, Sonny. (*She goes over and kisses* TOMMY.) Hello, Julia. Hello, Mrs. Nelson.

TOMMY. Hello, Mother.

JULIA. Hello, Mrs. Mavis.

MRS. NELSON. Hello, Roberta.

ROBERTA. Tommy, where is your father?

TOMMY. He went over to the courthouse to look up some deeds. He said he'd be right back.

JULIA. I have some things to tend to down the street. I'll meet you at the drugstore in fifteen minutes. Good-bye, everybody.

ROBERTA. Good-bye, Julia.

TOMMY. 'Bye, honey.

MRS. NELSON. (*Nods.*) Good-bye.

(JULIA *goes out* R. C. *and down the sidewalk exiting out* R. TOMMY *picks up a paper and starts glancing through it.*)

ROBERTA. Isn't Julia working this morning, Tommy?

TOMMY. Yes, she is. We're gonna have lunch together.

ROBERTA. Did you know Julia and Tommy were engaged, Mrs. Nelson?

MRS. NELSON. Yes. I heard.

ROBERTA. We think she's mighty sweet. She isn't the prettiest girl in the world, but she's mighty sweet.

TOMMY. I think she's the prettiest girl in the world.

ROBERTA. I'm glad you do, Sonny. Anyway, Daddy and I think she's mighty sweet. I'm just worn out. I've been running all morning. Did you hear I was getting H. T. on a vacation, Mrs. Nelson?

MRS. NELSON. (*Looking at her watch impatiently.*) No. I didn't.

ROBERTA. Well, I am. His first in twenty-five years. The last and only time he left Harrison was when we started for Colorado on our honeymoon. We drove as far as El Paso and he was worrying so over his business we turned right around and came home.

MRS. NELSON. Where are you going?

ROBERTA. Mexico City. We're driving. He gave me a new Cadillac for our anniversary. And I asked him one morning why didn't we drive to Mexico City. I thought he would refuse like he's always done, but no. This time he said he would. I still can't believe it. Can you, Tommy?

TOMMY. No ma'm. (TOMMY *has gone back to reading the paper.*)

ROBERTA. H. T. just loves this business. He eats it, lives and sleeps it. Doesn't he, Tommy?

TOMMY. Yes ma'm.

ROBERTA. His father was the same way. So was mine, Lord knows. But Tommy is more like me. He's more of a dreamer. Aren't you, Sonny?

TOMMY. (*Reading the paper.*) I suppose.

ROBERTA. How are you, Mrs. Nelson?

MRS. NELSON. Pretty well, thank you.

ROBERTA. You look well.

MRS. NELSON. Thank you. I was hoping I wouldn't have to spend the whole morning in here.

ROBERTA. What did you want, dear?

MRS. NELSON. I wanted to make a complaint about that house I rent.

ROBERTA. Sonny, can't you take care of Mrs. Nelson's complaint?

TOMMY. Well, Daddy usually likes to handle the complaints.

ROBERTA. You go ahead. You're going to be in charge now while we're gone.

TOMMY. All right. I'll write everything down, Mrs. Nelson. Now let me have the story again.

MRS. NELSON. Well, first of all the house isn't fit to live in.

ROBERTA. Why, dear?

MRS. NELSON. Because it leaks.

ROBERTA. Then it should be fixed.

TOMMY. Wait a minute, Mother.

ROBERTA. Tommy, you heard Mrs. Nelson. We have to fix her house, honey, it leaks.

TOMMY. But Dad says we can't afford to fix the property any longer.

ROBERTA. Oh, that's right. I'd forgotten.

MRS. NELSON. What do you mean you can't afford to fix it?

ROBERTA. Taxes, honey. It is all to do with taxes. They just keep Mr. Mavis poor. Don't they, Tommy?

TOMMY. Mother, you're getting it all mixed up. You see . . .

ROBERTA. They do too. I've heard him complain many times. Why, Mrs. Nelson . . .

TOMMY. Mother, are you going to handle this or am I?

ROBERTA. (*Ignoring him.*) Why, would you believe it, Mrs. Nelson, H. T. was saying just the other day . . .

TOMMY. Mother, I tell you, you don't know what you're talking about.

ROBERTA. I certainly do know what I'm talking about. Now just let me finish. Your father was saying just the other day . . .

TOMMY. Mother, please.

ROBERTA. Just let me finish, Son. I can explain the whole thing to Mrs. Nelson. Why, Mrs. Nelson, do you know that Mr. Mavis has to pay the most enormous taxes? I can't quote you the exact amount, of course, but they're just enormous. Why, I didn't have the heart to buy anything for a whole week after I'd heard what they were. . . .

(TOMMY *gives up and goes back to his paper.* H. T. MAVIS *comes bustling in* R. *He walks across sidewalk, up* C. *sidewalk, and enters his office. He is heavyset and in his middle fifties. He chews a cigar nervously.*)

MAVIS. (*Sharply.*) Tommy.

(TOMMY *puts his paper down. He seems embarrassed and ill at ease at his father finding him reading the paper.*)

TOMMY. Yes sir.

MAVIS. Never read during business hours. It doesn't look businesslike.

TOMMY. Well, I was just waiting . . .

MAVIS. No excuses, Son. No excuses. (*He kisses his wife.*) Hello, Roberta. Hello, Mrs. Nelson.

ROBERTA. Poor Mrs. Nelson's house leaks and we can't afford to fix it. Isn't that too bad?

MRS. NELSON. Somebody had better fix it. I'm not going to. The roof is just going to fall in if it isn't fixed.

MAVIS. Did you read your contract, dear lady?

MRS. NELSON. The house needs painting. The paper is hanging in shreds.

MAVIS. Read the contract, dear lady. All of these problems are carefully taken care of in our contract. Tommy, get Mrs. Nelson a copy of the contract.

TOMMY. Yes sir. (*He jumps up. He goes over to the file cabinet.*)

MAVIS. Under N, Tommy. Hurry. (TOMMY *begins looking through the file cabinet.*) Hurry, Son. Hurry.

ROBERTA. H. T., stop making the boy nervous. How can you ex-pect him to do anything if you shout at him that way?

TOMMY. Are you sure this is the right file cabinet? (MR. MAVIS *is busy looking at papers on his desk and doesn't answer.*) Dad, where is it? I can't see it.

MAVIS. Now where would it be, Son? Think carefully. Think.

TOMMY. It should be under N, but it isn't.

MAVIS. Then look again. It's bound to be under N.

ROBERTA. Oh, H. T., stop teasing the boy and help him to find it. I'm in a hurry.

MAVIS. He's twenty-four, Roberta. I'm leaving him in charge of my business. It's time he learned to think things through for himself. Have you found it, Tommy?

(TOMMY looks through the files.)

TOMMY. I tell you it's not here.

MAVIS. Then you have the wrong file cabinet.

TOMMY. O.K. But you said . . .

MAVIS. Never argue with your father in front of customers, Son, just look in the other one.

TOMMY. All right. (He starts for the next one.)

MAVIS. You must have had the wrong file cabinet.

TOMMY. I didn't have the wrong one. You told me to look there.

MAVIS. Quickly, Son, never keep a customer waiting.

(TOMMY gives him a look and goes to the other cabinet.)

ROBERTA. Help him, H. T. We have so much to do this afternoon.

MAVIS. Now, Roberta. Let me handle this. Tommy is twenty-four. He has to learn about things. By the time I was twenty-four, Mrs. Nelson, I had saved twenty thousand dollars.

ROBERTA. Tommy is twenty-three, H. T. He is not twenty-four.

MAVIS. Well, do you think he's going to save twenty thousand dollars in the next year?

ROBERTA. He might surprise us.

TOMMY. (Quietly and desperately.) Dad, if it's here I can't find it.

MAVIS. I find that difficult to believe, Tommy. (He goes to the file cabinet. He begins to search. He finds it.) Right here, boy. Right here where it was supposed to be.

TOMMY. You said it was under N. You got it from under T.

MAVIS. Where's your initiative, boy? If a thing isn't under N, look elsewhere. You know it hasn't got legs to get up and walk out of the file cabinet. (*He hands the contract to* MRS. NELSON.) My boy is a dreamer, Mrs. Nelson, just like his mother. But he'll learn. We just have to all be patient. Now, my dear lady, do me the honor of reading this contract. Read carefully and slowly and then I'll let you tell me what it says about papering and painting.

ROBERTA. I was explaining to her, H. T., it has all to do with taxes.

MAVIS. Taxes have nothing to do with it, Roberta.

ROBERTA. It hasn't? I thought you said . . .

MAVIS. Nothing at all. It is a matter of principle, that's all. Tommy, show Mrs. Nelson into the other office so she can read quietly and calmly.

TOMMY. Yes sir. Come on, Mrs. Nelson. (*He goes out the door* L. C. *She follows him.*)

MAVIS. I get very discouraged with Tommy sometimes, Roberta.

ROBERTA. Now you have to be patient. It wasn't under N. You kept shouting at him to look under N.

MAVIS. It should have been under N. He probably moved it. I hate to think of what those file cabinets will look like when I get back. I wonder if I'm not being hasty going on this trip. After all, the boy . . .

ROBERTA. He's twenty-three years old, H. T.

(TOMMY *comes back in.*)

MAVIS. Tommy, sit down and let's go over carefully everything that has to be done while I'm away.

ROBERTA. H. T., can't you do that tonight? We have to go shopping this afternoon.

MAVIS. Now, Roberta. Business . . .

ROBERTA. You promised me you would. I'm just not going any-place with you until you get a new suit. And that's my final word.

MAVIS. All right. Give me half an hour to straighten things up here. Can you get your lunch in half an hour, Son?

TOMMY. Well . . . I . . . I could ordinarily, but you see I made a date with Julia . . .

MAVIS. (*Shaking his head slowly.*) Oh, I don't know, Son. I swear I don't know. Now why would you make a lunch date on the very day I'm going to leave? Well, you'll just have to explain to Julia and get back in half an hour.

TOMMY. O.K.

ROBERTA. You tell her that your father is leaving tomorrow for his first vacation in twenty-five years, and he's very nervous. She'll understand.

TOMMY. O.K.

(*He goes out the door* R. C. *and down the sidewalk, exiting* R. MRS. NELSON *comes in* L. C.)

MRS. NELSON. Who's the party of the first part?

MAVIS. What?

MRS. NELSON. Who's the party of the first part?

MAVIS. (*Wearily.*) Read the contract, dear lady. It's all explained in the contract.

MRS. NELSON. Yes sir.

(*She goes back through the door* L. C. MAVIS *is looking through the papers on his desk. The lights are brought up* R. *on the drugstore area.* JULIA *comes in* L., *walks along the sidewalk, up the* C. *sidewalk and into the drugstore. She sits at the table.*)

ROSE. (*Enters* R. C.) Hello, Julia.

JULIA. Hello, Rose.

ROSE. Ready to order?

JULIA. No. I'm waiting for Tommy.

ROSE. All right.

(*She goes out* R. C. TOMMY *comes in from* R. *He walks along side-walk, entering drugstore* L. C. *He seems very depressed.*)

TOMMY. Sorry I'm late.

JULIA. I just got here.

TOMMY. Did you order?

JULIA. Not yet. What do you like?

TOMMY. Oh, nothing much. I'm not very hungry. What are you going to have?

JULIA. Tuna fish sandwich and a Coke.

(ROSE *comes up to them from* R. C.)

TOMMY. Two tuna fish sandwiches and two Cokes.

ROSE. All right. (*She goes out* R. C. *of drugstore area.*)

JULIA. Tommy, what's the matter?

TOMMY. Nothing.

JULIA. There is too. You were in such good spirits when I left you. Now you act as if the world had come to an end.

TOMMY. I'm furious. I'm furious. Doggone it.

JULIA. Why?

TOMMY. After my big talk with Dad he comes into the office like nothing had happened and starts pushing me around in front of Mother and Mrs. Nelson and I just gulped and took it.

JULIA. Well, why do you let him do it?

TOMMY. Because he makes me feel inferior. Oh, I'm so mad at myself I could bust. Maybe I am inferior. I know I am when he's around. I can't think fast, I act clumsy and awkward . . .

JULIA. Tommy Mavis . . .

TOMMY. And don't lecture me, honey. I feel depressed enough as it is. It's always been this way. He can think faster than I can, do things quicker.

(ROSE *comes back in from* R. C. *with the food. She puts it on the table.*)

ROSE. Your father just phoned, Tommy. He said not to forget you're to be back in half an hour.

TOMMY. O.K.

(ROSE *goes out* R. C.)

JULIA. Why do you have to be back in half an hour?

TOMMY. Because he's nervous about that darned old trip tomorrow. He thinks the office is going to pot when he's gone. And maybe it will. He gives me such a complex I know I'll never get anything right.

JULIA. Didn't you tell him about renting the building?

TOMMY. No. I was afraid to. I was afraid he'd find fault with that some way. (*He suddenly pounds his fist on the table.*) You know, I'm going to stop this. I'm just plain going to stop this. I'm going to stand up to Dad and have my own independence and self-respect or else I'll leave the Abstract Company and go on my own. I will not be back from lunch in half an hour just because he is nervous about leaving town. Every man is entitled to an hour lunch.

JULIA. Oh, Tommy. That's the spirit. That's the way I like to hear you talk.

TOMMY. I'm going to have him understand I know how to do everything around that office and that he needn't tell me fifty-five different times.

JULIA. Oh, that's wonderful, Tommy. That's great. Stick to that. Just stick to that.

(*She takes his hand and squeezes it. She gives him a smile. He returns it and starts eating his sandwich vigorously and forcefully. . . . He suddenly chokes.* JULIA *runs over and pats his back as the lights are brought down. The lights are brought up on the* MAVIS *office.* H. T. *is looking at his watch.*)

MAVIS. He should be here in seven minutes. Did you call the drugstore to remind him?

ROBERTA. Yes, dear, I did. Now put that watch away. He's a grown boy. He certainly has enough sense of responsibility to get back from the drugstore in half an hour.

(MAVIS *puts his watch away. He taps the desk with his fingers impatiently.*)

MAVIS. Go outside and see if you see him coming.

ROBERTA. All right. But please try to keep calm.

MAVIS. Keep calm. Do you realize all that has to be done?

(ROBERTA *doesn't answer him. She goes outside the office. She stands looking down the street.* MR. SCOTT, *an energetic man in his early thirties, comes up the sidewalk from* D. L. *He passes* ROBERTA *and tips his hat.*)

MR. SCOTT. Good morning. (ROBERTA *nods her head as one does in recognizing the greeting of a stranger.* MR. SCOTT *goes inside the office. He walks over to* MAVIS *at his desk.*) Good morning, sir.

MAVIS. Good morning. And what can I do for you?

SCOTT. Are you Mr. Mavis?

MAVIS. That's right, sir.

SCOTT. Scott is the name. Mandell Scott.

MAVIS. It's an honor, sir. Won't you be seated? (ROBERTA *comes back inside the office.*) Mr. Scott, my wife.

SCOTT. How do you do, Mrs. Mavis?

ROBERTA. Just fine, thank you.

SCOTT. Mr. Mavis, I represent, I am proud to say, one of the most forward-looking firms in the whole of the Gulf Coast area. We have sixteen branches of the parent firm all serving with pride the good people of this glorious state.

(MRS. NELSON *comes back in from door* L. C.)

MRS. NELSON. Excuse me, who is the party of the second part?

MAVIS. You are, my dear lady. You are.

MRS. NELSON. Thank you. (*She holds up the lease.*) This is all just as clear to me as Chinese. (*She goes back inside the* L. C. *room.*)

MAVIS. You were saying, Mr. Scott?

SCOTT. After a great deal of thought our officers have decided that right here in the town of Harrison with its forward-looking citizenry should be our next branch of the Good Deal supermarkets. Before coming over here I went over your pretty and prosperous town and looked at all the vacant buildings. I have one picked out. If we can agree on the rent, of course. It's two or three doors from the post office, and it's vacant at present.

MAVIS. I know the building. You couldn't pick a better location. Technically, it now belongs to my son. I made him a present of it last night.

SCOTT. Oh, I see. Where could I find your son?

MAVIS. Oh, I make all the business arrangements for him. He's only a youngster. He leaves all business details to me.

SCOTT. I see. Very wise of him, I'm sure.

MAVIS. What was your firm prepared to offer?

SCOTT. Seventy-five dollars a month.

MAVIS. I'm sorry, Mr. Scott. I couldn't have my son consider that. We are asking at least a hundred and seventy-five.

SCOTT. A hundred and seventy-five? You must be joking, Mr. Mavis.

MAVIS. That's our price, Mr. Scott.

SCOTT. Eighty-five.

MAVIS. I'm sorry, sir.

SCOTT. Ninety-five . . .

MAVIS. Mr. Scott . . .

SCOTT. A hundred and fifteen. And that's my top price, Mr. Mavis.

MAVIS. I'm very sorry.

SCOTT. And I'm sorry. Good day, sir. (SCOTT *starts out* R. C.)

MAVIS. Mr. Scott. Just a moment. As a special favor to you, I'll let it go at a hundred and twenty-five.

SCOTT. That's a deal, sir.

MAVIS. Fine. Fine. Sit down, sir.

SCOTT. Thank you.

MAVIS. Now. (*He takes some forms out of the desk drawer.*) How shall I make out the lease?

SCOTT. Good Deal Stores, Inc.

MAVIS. (*Writing.*) Good Deal Stores, Inc. . . .

(*The phone rings.* ROBERTA *answers it.*)

ROBERTA. Yes? Oh, hello, Tommy. What? What? (*She hangs the phone up. She looks puzzled.*) That was Tommy. He said he was not coming back in half an hour. And then he hung up. Now I wonder why he's acting like that, H. T.?

(MAVIS *doesn't even hear what she's saying. He is too busy writing out the lease as the lights are brought down. The lights are brought up.* TOMMY *comes in* L., *walks to* C. *of stage and goes up sidewalk to the entrance of the office,* R. C. *He is very angry and he charges into the office.* MAVIS *is at the desk working away.* ROBERTA *is seated in one of the chairs.*)

TOMMY. Dad, I want you to understand exactly why I was half an hour late.

MAVIS. Sit down, Son. Sit down. Don't bother me. I'm very busy.

TOMMY. Dad, I insist.

MAVIS. Shh, Tommy, shh . . .

(TOMMY *starts to speak again. Then he thinks better of it. He goes to a chair. He glares at his father.*)

ROBERTA. Why were you late? Not that it matters. Your father couldn't have gone out anyway.

TOMMY. I did it to show that I cannot be humiliated and intimidated by telephone messages at drugstores.

ROBERTA. Who was trying to humiliate you?

TOMMY. My father. And it's going to stop.

ROBERTA. Oh. He is not trying to humiliate you. He just knows how absentminded you are, that's all.

TOMMY. I am not absentminded. I have as much sense of responsibility as he has or anyone else. He and I are going to have a long talk about this once and for all.

ROBERTA. Oh, Tommy. Now let's all just be happy this last day. You never know what will happen when we go off in a car like this. You know your daddy is going to insist on doing all the driving and he's a very nervous driver.

TOMMY. I'm sorry, Mother. This is a matter of principle. (MAVIS *has finished what he is doing and turns around in his chair.*) Dad. I want to say here and now . . .

MAVIS. Just a minute, boy. Just a minute. Now about the store I gave you last night. Frankly, Son, I gave it to you to teach you a little lesson in humility. To show you how hard it is to earn a dollar of your own. I thought it was the last place in town that would ever rent, but I was fooled. I just finished renting it for you.

TOMMY. You rented it?

MAVIS. Yes sir, and got an excellent price, if I do say so myself.

TOMMY. Who did you rent it to?

MAVIS. Good Deal Stores, Inc. Fine, forward-looking firm. I could have rented them another building, but I decided to give my boy a break.

TOMMY. Thank you, Dad, but I'm sorry . . .

(MAVIS *hands* TOMMY *some papers.*)

MAVIS. Now take these over to the courthouse right away. These are the papers turning the building over to you. I want them filed before I leave.

TOMMY. Dad, I'm sorry. But I rented the building this morning.

MAVIS. You what?

TOMMY. I rented the building this morning.

MAVIS. What do you mean renting something without consulting me first? I swear, Tommy. Sometimes I just don't know.

TOMMY. But you gave me the building, Dad. The whole point of it was . . .

MAVIS. Naturally I expected to be consulted. You haven't the experience, boy. Have you signed anything yet?

TOMMY. No. But I've agreed to it.

MAVIS. Who did you rent to?

TOMMY. Lee Johnson. He's moving his secondhand store over there.

MAVIS. How much have you agreed to rent for?

TOMMY. Fifty a month.

MAVIS. Well, call him up and tell him the whole thing is off.

TOMMY. Dad . . .

MAVIS. Hurry up, Son, and call him. I haven't much time. I have a suit to buy. I have gotten you a fine price for the building. A hundred and twenty-five dollars.

TOMMY. Dad, I don't want to do it this way.

MAVIS. What's the matter, are you afraid? Then I'll call him.

(MRS. NELSON *comes out the door* L. C. *She has the contract. She goes over to* MAVIS.)

MRS. NELSON. (*Handing him the contract.*) Here.

MAVIS. Did you read it?

MRS. NELSON. Yes, and I couldn't understand a single word of it. Now look, Mr. Mavis, all I want to know is . . .

MAVIS. It's very simple to understand, my dear lady. Among other things, it says all repairs are the sole responsibility from now on of the tenants. You, my dear lady, are the tenant in this case. . . .

MRS. NELSON. That means you're not going to fix my house.

MAVIS. That is absolutely correct.

MRS. NELSON. I can't afford to fix it.

MAVIS. Then it doesn't get fixed.

MRS. NELSON. It leaks like a sieve.

MAVIS. Most unfortunate.

MRS. NELSON. Every other landlord in this town fixes their houses. You used to.

MAVIS. I don't any longer. If you're dissatisfied, maybe you'd better move someplace else, my dear lady. Now if you'll pardon me . . .

MRS. NELSON. Don't think I wouldn't like to. I would move someplace else if I could find a house. I want to tell you just what I think of you, Mr. H. T. Mavis . . .

ROBERTA. Now, Mrs. Nelson. Let's not get excited. Remember, we're all ladies and gentlemen. . . .

MRS. NELSON. No. I won't get excited, but I'm going to tell him what I think of him. I have rented his houses for fifteen years. I have always paid my rent on time, and I've never bothered him. I can't afford to fix my house, and I can't find another one. But someday I will and I'll move. And so will everyone else that rents from you, because you're the most disliked person in this whole town. (*She marches out the entrance* R. C. ROBERTA *and* MAVIS *look embarrassed.*)

MAVIS. That's gratitude for you.

ROBERTA. Maybe you should fix her house, honey.

MAVIS. No, Roberta. I have made a stand. I will have to stick to it. A principle is a principle.

ROBERTA. But, H. T., if other people like she says . . .

MAVIS. I didn't get my property by acting like other people.

ROBERTA. I know, honey, but . . .

MAVIS. Sticks and stones may break my bones, but the words of Mrs. Nelson can never harm me. The subject is closed. Tommy, will you please call Lee Johnson?

TOMMY. I'm not going to call him, Dad.

MAVIS. And why not?

TOMMY. Because I don't want to.

MAVIS. Very well then, I'll call him myself.

TOMMY. And I don't want you calling him either.

MAVIS. And why not?

TOMMY. Because it's my building. The first thing in my life that ever belonged to me, and I'm going to do with it as I please.

MAVIS. (*Sarcastically.*) And what do you please to do with it? Rent it at seventy-five dollars loss a month?

TOMMY. I don't know what I'll do yet. But I'm making up my own mind.

MAVIS. Look, Tommy . . .

TOMMY. And that's final.

MAVIS. Very well. Then I guess I will just have to take my building back.

ROBERTA. Now you're both just getting too excited. Let's everybody just keep calm.

MAVIS. I won't keep calm. I have a numbskull for a son.

TOMMY. Thank you. Thank you very much. (*He jumps up and goes out the door* L. C. *to the other office.*)

ROBERTA. (*Calling after him.*) Tommy, come back here. (*A pause.* TOMMY *doesn't return.*) H. T., you go to that boy and apologize.

MAVIS. I won't apologize. I have nothing to apologize for.

ROBERTA. Now, honey. You called him a numbskull. Your own son.

MAVIS. I got excited. I didn't mean that exactly.

ROBERTA. But you said it. And it hurt his feelings. Now you call him back here and apologize.

MAVIS. Now, Roberta . . .

ROBERTA. Call him back here and apologize. I want us to leave tomorrow feeling happy and at peace, and you know you won't enjoy the trip and I won't enjoy it unless you make up with him.

MAVIS. All right. I'll apologize for calling him a numbskull, but he's not going to rent that building at a seventy-five-dollar loss.

ROBERTA. Well, then, for goodness sake, try talking to him nicely. He'll give in to you. He always does, but just be nice about it.

MAVIS. All right. (*He calls into the other room.*) Tommy . . .

TOMMY. (*Calling back.*) What do you want?

MAVIS. Come in here.

(TOMMY *comes out of the other office.*)

TOMMY. What do you want?

MAVIS. Now you listen to me . . .

TOMMY. Look, Dad . . .

MAVIS. Now don't interrupt me, Son. I want to say, first of all, I'm sorry I called you a numbskull. I didn't mean that.

TOMMY. That's not why I got sore, Dad. I . . .

(MR. SCOTT *enters sidewalk* D. L., *crosses* R. *and up on* C. *sidewalk, opens the door* R. C. *and comes in.*)

SCOTT. Is the lease ready?

MAVIS. Oh, yes, Mr. Scott. Sit down, won't you? Mr. Scott, my boy, Tommy. He's the junior partner here in the business.

SCOTT. How are you, Tommy? A great pleasure, I'm sure. (*He extends his hand.* TOMMY *takes it.*)

TOMMY. How do you do. (TOMMY *goes out of the room to the other office* L. C. MAVIS *goes over to the desk to get the lease.*)

MAVIS. Here's your lease, Mr. Scott. Everything just as we discussed. (*He hands the lease to* SCOTT, *who glances over it, hurriedly.* MAVIS *goes to the desk and gets some keys.*) Everything satisfactory, Mr. Scott?

SCOTT. Perfectly. Perfectly. Here's my check. (*He gives the check to* MAVIS.)

MAVIS. Thank you so much. (SCOTT *walks to the desk and signs the lease. He hands it to* MAVIS.) Thank you so much. (MAVIS *gives* SCOTT *the keys to the building.*) Here are your keys, sir. You can get in anytime now.

SCOTT. Thank you. (*He takes the keys and puts them in his pocket.*) Good day, Mrs. Mavis.

ROBERTA. Good day, Mr. Scott. (*She gets up from her chair and goes offstage* L. C. *into the other office.*)

SCOTT. (*Holding out his hand to* MAVIS.) Mr. Mavis.

MAVIS. (*Shaking* SCOTT'S *hand.*) It's been a pleasure, Mr. Scott.

SCOTT. Same here, sir. Say good-bye to your son for me.

MAVIS. I will indeed.

(MR. SCOTT *goes out the door* R. C., *down* C. *sidewalk and off* D. L. ROBERTA *comes back into the room from the other office.*)

ROBERTA. I wonder where Tommy went to.

MAVIS. Isn't he in there?

ROBERTA. No. (TOMMY *comes into the office from the outside entrance* R. C.) Oh, Tommy. We were wondering where you were.

MAVIS. Mr. Scott was asking for you. Wanted to say good-bye.

TOMMY. You rented the building to him?

MAVIS. Yep. Here's your check, Son. Let me endorse it over to you. (*He takes out his pen and goes to the desk to endorse it.*) This is the easiest money you will ever make in your life.

ROBERTA. I hope we're gonna all be happy now. I was telling your father that it would just have ruined my vacation if . . .

TOMMY. Dad, I beg you not to do this to me. . . .

MAVIS. Do what to you?

TOMMY. Rent this building over my head.

MAVIS. I swear, Tommy, sometimes you talk like a crazy man. Now let's not talk anymore about it or I'm gonna get mad. Here, take the check and forget about it. . . .

TOMMY. I don't want the check. I don't want the building.

MAVIS. Take the check, Son.

TOMMY. I don't want it. You keep it. I think it's much more important to you.

MAVIS. Oh, you do. Well, maybe it is. (*He takes the check.*) Maybe I better keep it. I don't think you're ready for it yet. You know I think the trouble with you, Tommy, is that you've had everything too easy. You've never made a dime of your own. You don't know how hard it is to come by.

TOMMY. I think I work pretty hard here.

MAVIS. Frankly, you do nothing but get in my way and make things just twice as tough as they would be ordinarily. That's what you do. Now I put up with you, because you're my son, but I'm not gonna have a little two-bit kid that hasn't sense enough to come in out of the rain telling me what to do and what not to do.

TOMMY. I'm not trying to tell you what to do or what not to do. I just don't want you to give me something and then tell me . . .

MAVIS. I'll tell you anything I please as long as you're working for me, and you'd better get that straight. Now if you want to do with a thing as you like then go out and get a job and earn your brick building.

(*He gets up and exits into the other office* L. C. *There is a silence. Suddenly* TOMMY *jumps up and runs to the entrance* L. C. *He stands screaming in to his father.*)

TOMMY. Now let me tell you what I think of you. I think you're domineering and egotistical and cold-blooded and ruthless. All you care about is getting your own way. From this moment on, I'm through. I wouldn't work for you now if you got down on your knees and begged me to.

ROBERTA. Tommy, don't talk to your father like that. . . .

TOMMY. (*Turning to her.*) And you've helped him be that way, Mother. You've spoiled him and given in to him. Well, I'm not going to any longer. You both think money can buy anything. Well, it can't buy me. I'm through.

(*He walks out of the office* R. C. *He slams the door after he goes. He walks down sidewalk and off* L. *A pause.* . . . MAVIS *comes out* L. C. *He looks embarrassed.*)

MAVIS. Where did he go?

ROBERTA. I don't know. He just marched out.

MAVIS. Well, let him walk around for a while. He'll cool off. (*A pause.*) Well, I guess he got us told.

ROBERTA. I guess he did.

MAVIS. I guess I talked pretty rough too.

ROBERTA. Yes, you did.

MAVIS. What do you think I ought to do? Do you think I ought to go after him and apologize, or do you think I ought to give him a chance to calm down?

ROBERTA. I don't know what to say.

MAVIS. Frankly, I didn't know the kid had that much spirit. Did you know that Tommy had that much spirit?

ROBERTA. No, I didn't.

MAVIS. He's got a temper. That's one thing.

ROBERTA. Yes, he has.

MAVIS. Well, I guess things like this are pretty common between a father and a son. I guess we're lucky it hasn't happened before. Jim Brandell and his son had a disagreement just last week. Right in Draper's law office. They made up.

ROBERTA. And Thurman May and Stanley had one and they've never spoken again since.

MAVIS. All right. Go ahead. Look on the gloomy side of things. That's just like you, Roberta.

ROBERTA. Well, have they spoken?

MAVIS. No, but they're both stubborn fools. That's the reason. (A pause.) What did I say exactly? I was so mad I've forgotten.

ROBERTA. You said he was in the way here, and he had no sense. You talked awful to him.

MAVIS. Well, I was mad. (A pause.) We were both mad, doggone it. Well, I'm not going to apologize. I'm definitely not going to do that. We were both in the wrong. . . . Do you think I ought to apologize? . . .

ROBERTA. I don't know. I'm scared, H. T.

MAVIS. What are you scared about?

ROBERTA. You were both so angry. I've never seen either of you so angry. Maybe I'd better go out and see if I can find him.

MAVIS. No. He'll come back. I'm sorry I lost my head, but you can't let a boy run over you. Can you?

ROBERTA. I guess not. (*A pause.*) Do you think he'll come back?

MAVIS. There you go dwelling on the gloomy side of things. What do you think he'll do, jump off the river bridge?

ROBERTA. Now, H. T., don't be funny. This is no time for humor.

MAVIS. Of course he'll come back. He's gonna feel very sorry when he thinks of the ugly things he said to me. (*She goes to the phone.*) Who are you going to telephone at a time like this?

ROBERTA. I thought maybe he was with Julia.

MAVIS. Now don't call her. Why do you want to drag Julia into it?

ROBERTA. All right. It was just a thought. (ROBERTA *cries.*)

MAVIS. Now why are you getting yourself all upset? I know he's coming back.

ROBERTA. It's too late now. My trip is ruined.

MAVIS. Now, Roberta.

ROBERTA. Well, it is. It's just ruined. I've waited twenty-five years for a vacation and now all the pleasure's gone. All because of seventy-five dollars. It isn't as if we needed the money. If we did, I could understand, but to fight, a father and a son, over seventy-five dollars . . . (*She is crying.*)

MAVIS. Now, Roberta. I'll make it up. You see . . . Anyway, I wasn't fighting over seventy-five dollars. I was fighting over a principle.

(JULIA *enters sidewalk* D. R., *goes up* C. *sidewalk to office and comes in the door* R. C. *of office.*)

JULIA. Hello.

MAVIS. Hello, Julia.

JULIA. Where's Tommy?

MAVIS. He's out, Julia.

JULIA. Where did he go?

MAVIS. To the bank for me.

JULIA. I'll wait for him. Did he tell you about renting his building?

MAVIS. Yes. Yes, he did.

JULIA. Weren't you proud of him?

MAVIS. Yes, I was.

(ROBERTA *is crying again.*)

JULIA. Why, Mrs. Mavis, what on earth's the matter?

MAVIS. It's nothing, Julia. Don't be alarmed. She always gets this way when she is going away from home. She gets over it. It always makes her very depressed, but she recovers.

JULIA. Oh, I'm sorry.

(LEE JOHNSON *enters sidewalk* D. L., *goes up* C. *sidewalk and comes in office entrance* R. C. *with a lease.*)

LEE. Hello, folks.

MAVIS. Hello, Lee.

LEE. They told me over at my place that Tommy had been looking for me. I guess he was wondering why I hadn't brought the lease back. Well, here it is. I've signed it. All it needs now is his signature. Here's my check. (*He puts the check down on the desk.*)

MAVIS. Oh . . . er . . . Tommy didn't find you, Lee?

LEE. No. I was gone for almost an hour and he said he'd be back, but then I figured I'd catch him over here.

MAVIS. Too bad Tommy didn't find you, Lee. He got a better offer for the building right after you left and he decided to take it. . . .

LEE. I don't understand that. I might have been able to go a little higher if it was a question of money. . . . This leaves me in an awful hole. Tommy knows that I turned down another place this very morning. . . . A place with a very attractive rent . . .

MAVIS. Well, to be perfectly frank about it, Lee, *I* thought it was a great deal more than you could afford to pay.

LEE. But I turned another building down. Places I can afford don't turn up that often. I'm having to move from my place in two weeks. . . .

MAVIS. Sorry, Lee. You shouldn't count on a thing until it's signed. Business is business, you know.

LEE. (*Obviously annoyed.*) Oh. Well . . . I'll take my check back then. (*He picks the check up and walks out of the office* R. C., *down* C. *sidewalk and off* D. L.)

JULIA. I don't understand. I thought . . .

ROBERTA. There's no use trying to conceal this from you any longer, Julia. Tommy and H. T. had a disagreement over that building and it led to a terrible fight. Tommy left in a fury. Personally, it's taken all the heart out of the trip for me.

JULIA. Oh. Well, excuse me. I think I'd better go try to find Tommy. . . . (*She goes out* R. C., *down sidewalk and off* D. L.)

MAVIS. Now what did you want to go and tell her all that for? I thought you weren't going to tell her.

ROBERTA. What difference does it make? He'd tell her anyway. (*A pause.*) Well, I guess I might as well go home.

MAVIS. I guess the trip's off for tomorrow. (*A pause.*) Oh, well. One day more won't make any difference. We'll just come back home a day later, that's all. Did you go by the filling station and get the car?

ROBERTA. No. I forgot all about it in the confusion.

MAVIS. I'll get it on the way home.

(*The* SHERIFF *enters sidewalk* D. L., *goes up* C. *sidewalk and comes in office* R. C.)

SHERIFF. Hello, Mr. Mavis.

MAVIS. Good afternoon, Sheriff.

SHERIFF. Mrs. Mavis . . .

ROBERTA. Hello, Sheriff. . . .

SHERIFF. Did a man named Scott come in here this afternoon by any chance?

MAVIS. Why, yes. He was here twice.

SHERIFF. Says he wanted to rent something for the Good Deal supermarkets?

MAVIS. Yes. He rented my brick building over by the post office. Gave me his check.

SHERIFF. Well. You're the third person in town he's given one of those checks to. . . . Pitiful case. He's off his rocker.

MAVIS. I find that hard to believe, Sheriff. He seemed like . . .

SHERIFF. I know. Everyone says the same thing. But the firm just wired me and asked me to be on the lookout for him. You see, he used to work for them and had a nervous breakdown, and now he goes all over the state saying he represents them and making all kinds of wild leases in their name.

MAVIS. You don't say?

SHERIFF. Oh, yes. Isn't that pitiful?

MAVIS. Yes, it is.

SHERIFF. You'd better give me the check and I'll tear it up.

MAVIS. Oh, yes.

(*He hands the check to the* SHERIFF. . . . *The* SHERIFF *tears it up and puts it in a wastebasket.*)

SHERIFF. He got away from town before I got on to him. But I imagine they'll catch him over in Blessing before tonight. (*He starts out.*) You folks going on a trip tomorrow I hear. . . .

MAVIS. Tomorrow or the next day, Sheriff. Tomorrow or the next day. . . .

SHERIFF. Have a good time.

MAVIS. Thank you. (*The* SHERIFF *goes out* R. C. *There is a pause.*) Well, it just goes to show you, Roberta, that you never can tell. . . . (*A pause.*) I . . . I'm sorry . . . I don't know what to say. . . .

ROBERTA. There's nothing to say. I'm going home now.

MAVIS. It's a pretty good joke on me. Isn't it?

ROBERTA. I guess. If you're in the mood for joking. I'm not.

(*She gets up and goes out* R. C., *down* C. *sidewalk and off* D. R. MAVIS *sits at his desk. He seems pathetic and lonely. . . . He is chewing frantically on his cigar. The lights are brought down on office and up on drugstore area.* LESTER *is standing on sidewalk* D. R. *with another man.* TOMMY *comes in* D. L.)

LESTER. Heh again, Tommy.

TOMMY. Hi. (*He rushes past them up to* C. *sidewalk and into drugstore.*)

SECOND MAN. He's in a fine mood. I thought he was gonna knock you down for speaking to him. (*They follow up* C. *sidewalk and peer into drugstore.*) Look yonder. (LESTER *looks in to where he's pointing.* TOMMY *is at pinball machine.*) First time I ever heard of a Mavis foolin' with a pinball machine. (*They exchange glances and go inside the drugstore. They walk over to* TOMMY, *who is playing the pinball machine furiously.*) When did you take up shootin' the pinball machine, Tommy?

TOMMY. Didn't. I'm thinking.

(ROSE *comes over to the group from* R. C.)

ROSE. I didn't notice you come in, Tommy. Your dad just called. He said if I saw you to ask you to wait here for him, he was coming right over. He wanted to talk to you.

TOMMY. Thanks.

(*He turns and walks out, goes down* C. *sidewalk. The two men exchange glances and hurriedly follow him out. They stand on the sidewalk watching him exit* D. L.)

LESTER. He's going someplace in a hurry.

SECOND MAN. Real big hurry. (MAVIS *comes in from* L. *He is walking very fast. He starts to pass the men to enter the drugstore.*) Oh, H. T. Looking for your boy? Rose gave him your message and he said, "Thank you," and turned around and walked out as fast as he could.

MAVIS. Which way did he go?

LESTER. That way!

MAVIS. Thank you.

(*He starts out after* TOMMY. *The two men exchange glances. The lights are brought down on the drugstore. The lights are brought up* D. L. *A chair has been placed there, and a suitcase, closed but not locked, is on top of the chair.* TOMMY MAVIS *comes in* L. *and starts to lock his suitcase. A knock is heard offstage.*)

TOMMY. (*Calling.*) Come in.

(ROBERTA *enters* D. L. TOMMY *continues locking his suitcase.*)

ROBERTA. Oh, Tommy. I thought I heard someone come in the front door. Where have you been, Son? We've all been so worried.

TOMMY. Well . . . I . . .

(*She sees for the first time that he is packing.*)

ROBERTA. Tommy, what are you doing?

TOMMY. I'm moving out, Mother.

ROBERTA. (*Crying.*) Oh, Tommy.

TOMMY. It's the only thing to do, Mother.

ROBERTA. Don't say that, Tommy. Don't say that.

TOMMY. I should have done it all a long time ago.

ROBERTA. Are you leaving because of what your father said to you today?

TOMMY. Partly that. It brought it all to a head anyway.

ROBERTA. Oh, honey. I know he didn't mean it. He gets so excited. Please, Tommy. Why don't you wait until tomorrow?

TOMMY. No, Mother. I've made up my mind what I want to do. I'm not going to work with Dad any longer.

ROBERTA. Oh, Tommy. Now you don't mean that. You've just gotten all upset.

TOMMY. I do mean it, Mother. I'm not blaming anyone, you understand. I should have done this a long time ago, that's all. I'm not angry with Dad anymore. Only I can't work with him. He wants everything his way and maybe he's right. Anyway I know I'll never be able to stand being bossed the rest of my life.

ROBERTA. But if you'd only talk to him frankly. I know he would . . .

TOMMY. I did. Yesterday. He said he understood. Only, he didn't. He gave me that building to teach *me* a lesson. You heard him. He hadn't understood anything. I'll never be able to change him. So I'd better go.

ROBERTA. Where are you going to, Tommy?

TOMMY. I'm going to the hotel. Until I find a room.

ROBERTA. What will you do?

TOMMY. I'll find me a job. There are plenty around.

(*She is crying again.*)

ROBERTA. To think that a father and a son can't get along.

TOMMY. It happens all the time, Mother. We'll all be much happier this way.

ROBERTA. No. I really don't think he'd care one way or the other.

(MAVIS *comes in from* D. L.)

MAVIS. Tommy, Son.

TOMMY. Hello, Dad.

(ROBERTA *is crying again.*)

ROBERTA. He's leaving us, H. T. He's moving away from home.

TOMMY. Now, Mother. I'll see just as much of you as before.

MAVIS. Tommy, I looked all over town for you. I went down to the drugstore.

TOMMY. I came on here to pack.

MAVIS. I think we both got excited today. That's what I think.

TOMMY. I guess we did.

MAVIS. It's all a good joke on me, anyway. Did your mother tell you that?

TOMMY. No.

MAVIS. Didn't you tell him what a good joke the whole thing was on me, Roberta?

ROBERTA. No.

MAVIS. Well, tell Tommy. We all need a good laugh.

ROBERTA. I don't know what you're talking about.

MAVIS. About Mr. Scott!

ROBERTA. Oh. Well . . . you see . . . (*She is crying again.*)

MAVIS. Now, Roberta. You're acting like this is a funeral. Tommy and I just had a little misunderstanding. That's all in the world.

(*A pause. They all three look miserable.*)

TOMMY. What was the joke, Dad?

MAVIS. Oh. Yes. Well. That man turned out to be crazy.

TOMMY. Which man?

MAVIS. Mr. Scott. Yes sir, he turned out to be crazy. He sure had me fooled. Of course, I should have figured that only a crazy person would offer me a hundred and twenty-five dollars for that old building. . . . (*He laughs but not very successfully.*) Isn't that a pretty good joke on your old dad?

TOMMY. (*Gives a weak smile.*) Yeah . . .

MAVIS. And you'll be glad to hear that I went over to Lee Johnson, myself, and squared everything with him. He's taking the building just the same. He was real nice about it. We both had a good laugh over my being taken in that way by a crazy man.

(*A pause.* TOMMY *picks up his suitcase.*)

TOMMY. Well . . . I guess this is it. . . .

(H. T. *grabs his arm. He holds on to* TOMMY.)

MAVIS. Tommy, Son. Listen to me. I wouldn't have given it to that man in the first place if I . . . I didn't think you'd go this far . . . I . . . Tommy, I have waited so long to have you come into the business. And I've worked hard too, all because of you, Tommy . . . just because of you. . . .

TOMMY. I know you have, Dad.

MAVIS. Then why are you going? Because of that old building? I've admitted I was wrong about that. . . .

TOMMY. No, Dad. . . .

MAVIS. It's yours now forever to do as you please.

TOMMY. No, Dad.

MAVIS. And I'll give you another one besides. Two brick buildings. . . . That's quite a lot for a young fellow your age. Come on, Tommy. . . . Forgive me. Forgive your old dad. . . .

TOMMY. Dad, I'm not angry. There's nothing to forgive you now. Only I'm not staying here. And I'm not going to work for you any longer. It's not fair to you and it's not fair to me. You made your money, and you should do with it what you want. I'm going out now and make mine, or not make it, but anyway, I'm gonna try. That's the only way I'll feel free to do what I want. (*He picks up his suitcase.*)

MAVIS. Tommy, please. Just stay for the three weeks we're gonna be gone on our trip, and then if you want to still go work someplace else, I swear I won't stand in your way.

TOMMY. Dad . . . I . . .

MAVIS. I've worked hard, Son. I've never had a vacation. I promised it to your mother. And I'd hate so to disappoint her.

TOMMY. Well . . . I thought you said that you'd rather close your office up . . .

MAVIS. Now you know I didn't mean that. Will you stay for these three weeks?

TOMMY. Well . . .

MAVIS. Promise me.

TOMMY. Dad . . . I . . . I . . .

MAVIS. Don't let me down. Don't do that to your dad. I've tried never to let you down.

TOMMY. (*Reluctantly.*) All right. If you put it that way.

MAVIS. Wonderful, Son. Wonderful! He's gonna stay, Roberta.

ROBERTA. Oh, I'm so glad.

MAVIS. I told you I'd make it up with my boy. I've got the finest boy in the world.

ROBERTA. Of course you have.

MAVIS. Unpack Tommy's bag for him, Roberta.

(*She gets the bag and starts to unlock it.* TOMMY *stops her.*)

TOMMY. No, Mother. That won't be necessary. I'll go on and go to the hotel. There's no need to change that.

MAVIS. Nonsense, boy. Why spend all that money for a room? You have your room here.

TOMMY. I've made my plans about that, Dad . . . and I . . .

MAVIS. That's the most ridiculous thing I ever heard of. You'll stay right here. I have to go over everything with you one last time tonight if we're to get away tomorrow.

TOMMY. But, Dad, that isn't necessary. I understand everything.

MAVIS. Oh, you think you do, Son. But I would feel better if we went over every little detail. After all, our bread and butter is right here in this office.

TOMMY. All right. I'd better call Julia. I was going to meet her.

MAVIS. All right. You call her, Son. I'll meet you downstairs. We'll work on the dining room table. Roberta, you unpack his things.

ROBERTA. All right, H. T. But let's don't stay up all night. I want to get an early start.

MAVIS. Now we're having to go do business, Roberta. You can't rush a thing like that.

ROBERTA. All right, honey. All right.

MAVIS. Now you call Julia, Son, and I'll meet you downstairs.

(*He starts out of the area* D. L. TOMMY *calls to him:*)

TOMMY. Dad.

(MAVIS *stops.*)

MAVIS. Yes, Son?

TOMMY. Dad, I'm sorry. I'm terribly sorry, but it's wrong.

MAVIS. What are you talking about?

TOMMY. We're going right back on the same old merry-go-round.

MAVIS. We are?

TOMMY. I don't want the ride again. Do you?

MAVIS. Did I say anything to offend you? What did I say, Son? I swear to my Maker, if I said anything to offend you . . .

TOMMY. No. You said nothing to offend me.

MAVIS. Then I don't understand.

TOMMY. I think it's best if you just close the office for these three weeks.

MAVIS. But I don't understand. You just said a moment ago . . . (*A pause.*) Speak out, boy. If you've got something to say . . .

TOMMY. I have spoken out. I think we better call it quits. I think it's better for you, and better for me.

MAVIS. Tommy . . .

(TOMMY *holds out his hand.*)

TOMMY. Good-bye, Dad. . . .

(*His father takes his hand and shakes it.*)

MAVIS. Tommy. I'm just as puzzled. . . . Why? Why?

TOMMY. I don't know. But it won't work. Will it? I'm different and you're different. . . . (*He goes to his mother and kisses her good-bye.*)

ROBERTA. (*Crying.*) Tommy . . .

(*But he is out of the area, exiting* D. L. *before she can finish. A pause.*)

MAVIS. Well, we've done all we can do. If he wants to go ahead and make a fool of himself, we can't stop him. But he'll be back. You mark my words. He'll be back. (ROBERTA *continues crying.*) Now what in heaven's name is the matter with you?

ROBERTA. He's never coming back. He never will.

MAVIS. That's right. Go ahead and look on the gloomy side of things. Go ahead.

(*But she is crying so loud she doesn't hear him. The lights are brought down as he walks off* D. L. *and she follows after him. The lights are brought up on the sidewalk* D. R. JULIA *is standing there.* TOMMY *comes in* D. R.)

TOMMY. Sorry I'm late.

JULIA. That's all right. I had to eat something. The drugstore just closed up.

TOMMY. I've checked in at the hotel. I'll start looking for a new job tomorrow.

JULIA. I'm glad, Tommy. Did they take it hard?

TOMMY. It wasn't easy on them. Or on me. I wish it hadn't had to happen this way. I won, but there was no pleasure in winning. I wish they could understand why I had to win.

JULIA. I expect they will someday, honey.

TOMMY. Do you think so?

JULIA. I'm sure they will.

(*He takes her arm and puts it through his. They start walking* L. *along the sidewalk as the lights fade.*)

A Young Lady of
Property

A *Young Lady of Property* is an excellent example of Horton
Foote's writing in the very productive 1952–54 years. In this
play, as in many of his early plays, characters explain their feelings and intentions in more detail than do any of the later characters Foote has created. For example, after Wilma starts to
understand her real motives for wanting to run off to Hollywood,
she tells Arabella, "Maybe I was going to Hollywood out of pure
lonesomeness. I felt so alone with Mrs. Leighton getting my
daddy and my mama having left the world." Wilma and the
others in A *Young Lady of Property* discuss their actions so glibly
because they are more self-aware and seemingly more in control
of their destinies than are later characters in Foote's work; furthermore, this play has more definitive choices and a stronger
sense of closure than do the writer's more recent plays. As in *The
Old Beginning,* here the main dramatic tension reaches a neat cli-
max that leads to a clean, satisfying conclusion. In the first play,
H. T.'s renter is revealed to be a fraud; in A *Young Lady of Property,* Delafonte turns out to be a crook.

But if Horton Foote over the years has tended to leave behind some of the self-assurance and completed action of these

early plays, the drama of attachment in A *Young Lady of Property* has remained his central theme as an artist. In *The Old Beginning* Tommy Mavis needs to go away from home in order to gain his autonomy and, hopefully, his identity. He is a pilgrim. But Wilma Thompson's desire to "get rich and famous" is a flight from failed intimacy. Early in the play the loss of her mother and her jealousy over her father's relationship with Sybil Leighton overwhelm her and Wilma retreats into fantasies of Hollywood stardom much like the dreams of the "land of the astronauts" which will mesmerize the inhabitants of Harrison in Foote's 1983 play. Wilma finally triumphs over her illusions by remembering that she "belongs" to Harrison; she cares for the house and recognizes the pecan tree in its yard as a link between her life and that of her dead mother. She almost loses her connection to the place that helps her know who she is, but she resists the temptation and is ready once again to fill her house with life.

As he explained in a recent interview in *Literature/Film Quarterly*, writing black characters has become difficult, if not impossible, for Horton Foote. Most of his plays take place in a time when blacks were servants who held menial jobs in white households. Today many black actors do not want to play characters in such positions, even if the roles have dignity. And there is, for Foote, the persistent belief that authenticity is best achieved by having people, or a people, tell their own stories. Now maybe only blacks can tell black stories with authenticity and authority.

Fortunately for readers of Foote's work, A *Young Lady of Property* was written in a more innocent, less self-conscious time in the author's career. After the social change of the last thirty-five years this play remains one of the few records of Horton Foote's view of the integral role played by blacks, here represented by Minna Boyd, in the social and moral history of Harrison. More than any of the other adults, Minna is consistently the voice of responsibility and order; it is she who repeatedly reminds Wilma of her studies and other duties, she who urges Wilma's aunt to seek legal help to reclaim the girl's property. Despite the economic and political realities outside the household, within the home Minna is Wilma's confidante and the character who reminds Gert, Wilma and even Lester of their responsibilities to the family and community. Minna Boyd speaks on behalf of reason, realism and the law in the Thompson family, and in *A Young Lady of Property*.

A *Young Lady of Property* was first produced on Philco Television Playhouse on April 5, 1953. The production featured Kim Stanley, to whom Foote dedicated the play, in the role of Wilma Thompson, and Joanne Woodward in the role of Wilma's friend Arabella Cookenboo. Fred Coe was producer; Vincent J. Donehue, director.

A Young Lady of Property

CAST

Miss Martha Davenport   Lester Thompson
Mr. Russell Walter Graham   Mrs. Leighton
Wilma Thompson   Minna Boyd
Arabella Cookenboo   Miss Gert
               Man

Place: Harrison, Texas
Time: Late spring, 1925

The stage is divided into four areas. Area one, directly across the front of the stage, is a sidewalk. Area two, just above the sidewalk L. of C., is part of a kitchen. A table, with a portable phonograph on it, and four chairs are placed here. Area three is above the sidewalk R. of C. It has a yard swing in it. Area four is directly U. C. In it is a post office window.

The lights are brought up on the post office window. It is attended by two people, MISS MARTHA DAVENPORT, *who is inside the window, and* MR. RUSSELL WALTER GRAHAM, *who is leaning on the outside ledge of the window. It is about three-thirty of a late spring day.* MISS MARTHA *and* MR. RUSSELL WALTER *look very sleepy. Two girls around fifteen come in with schoolbooks in their arms. They are* WILMA THOMPSON *and* ARABELLA COOKENBOO. WILMA *is a handsome girl with style and spirit about her.* ARABELLA *is gentle looking, so shy about growing into womanhood that one can't really tell yet what she is to look like or become. She is* WILMA's *shadow and obviously her adoring slave. They go up to the window.* MR. RUSSELL WALTER *sees them and punches* MISS MARTHA.

RUSSELL. Look who's here, Miss Martha. The Bobbsey twins.

(MISS MARTHA *gives a peal of laughter that sounds as if she thought* MR. RUSSELL WALTER *the funniest man in five counties.*)

MISS MARTHA. (*Again giggling.*) Now, Mr. Russell Walter, don't start teasing the young ladies. How are you, girls?

WILMA *and* ARABELLA. Fine.

RUSSELL. Can I sell you any stamps? We have some lovely special deliveries today. Our one's and two's are very nice too.

MARTHA. (*Giggling.*) Isn't he a tease, girls?

WILMA. Mr. Russell Walter, when's the next train in from Houston?

RUSSELL. Why? Going on a trip?

MARTHA. (*Rolling at his wit.*) Now, Mr. Russell Walter, stop teasing the young ladies. The next mail doesn't come in on the train, dear ones, it comes in on the bus. And that will be at six. Although the Houston mail is usually very light at that time, there are a few special deliveries. Do you think your letter might come by special delivery, Wilma?

WILMA. No ma'm. Regular.

MARTHA. Oh. Well, in that case I don't hold out much hope for it on that delivery. It's usually mostly second-class mail. You know, seed catalogues and such. The next Houston mail heavy with first-class is delivered at five tomorrow morning.

RUSSELL. Which she knows better than you.

MARTHA. (*Giggling.*) Now, Mr. Russell Walter, stop teasing the young ladies.

WILMA. Arabella and I were discussing coming here from school, Mr. Russell Walter, that the mail sometimes gets in the wrong box.

RUSSELL. Rarely, Miss Wilma. Rarely.

WILMA. Arabella says that once a Christmas card meant for her got put by mistake in Box 270, instead of her box which is 370, and she didn't get it back until the third of January.

RUSSELL. Well, if that happens, nothing we can do about it until the person whose box it got into by mistake returns it.

WILMA. Yes sir. (*A pause.*) I don't suppose any mail has been put in my box since my Aunt Gert was here last.

RUSSELL. Well, seeing as she was here just a half hour ago, I don't think so.

MARTHA. Who are you expecting a letter from, young lady?

WILMA. Somebody very important. Come on, Arabella. (*They start out. They pause. She goes back to the window.*) Mr. Russell Walter, once I had a movie star picture, Ben Lyons I think, that was addressed to Wilma Thomas instead of Thompson, and if you remember, Mr. Peter was new at the time and put it into General Delivery, and it wasn't until two weeks later that you discovered it there and figured it belonged to me.

RUSSELL. Well, Mr. Peter isn't new here now.

WILMA. But I thought maybe accidentally someone put my letter in General Delivery.

RUSSELL. Nope.

MARTHA. Oh, Mr. Walter. Go ahead and look. It won't hurt you.

RUSSELL. Now, Miss Martha . . .

MARTHA. Now just go ahead . . . (*She hands him a stack of letters.*)

RUSSELL. All right. . . . Anything to please the ladies. (*He goes over the letters and starts looking into them.*)

MARTHA. Wilma, I saw your daddy and Mrs. Leighton at the picture show together again last night. Maybe you'll be having a new mother soon.

WILMA. Well, I wouldn't hold my breath waiting if I were you.

MARTHA. I was saying to Mr. Russell Walter I see the tenants have left the Thompson house. Maybe they were asked to leave so Mr. Thompson might move in with a bride.

WILMA. They were asked to leave because they were tearing it to pieces. They had weeds growing in the yards and had torn off wallpaper. My Aunt Gert asked them to leave. . . .

MARTHA. Oh, of course. They didn't take any pride in it at all. Not like when your mother was living. Why, I remember your mother always had the yard filled with flowers, and . . . (*The phone rings.*) Excuse me. (MISS MARTHA *answers it.*) Post office. Yes. Yes. She's here. Yes, I will. (*She puts the phone down.*) That was your Aunt Gertrude, Wilma. She said you were to come right home.

WILMA. All right.

MARTHA. Found any mail for Wilma, Mr. Russell Walter?

RUSSELL. Nope, Miss Wilma. No mail, and no female either.

MARTHA. (*Giggling.*) Isn't he a sight? You come back at six, Wilma. Maybe we'll have something then.

WILMA. Yes ma'm. Come on, Arabella.

(*They go outside the area and walk directly down the* C. *of the stage and pause at the apron looking up and down. They are now on the sidewalk area.*)

WILMA. I'd like to scratch that old cat's eyes out. The idea of her saying old lady Leighton is going to be my mother. She's so nosy. I wonder how she'd like it if I asked her if Mr. Russell Walter was going to ask her to marry him after she's been chasing him for fifteen years.

ARABELLA. Well, just ignore her.

WILMA. I intend to.

ARABELLA. What are you going to do now, Wilma?

WILMA. Fool around until the six o'clock mail.

ARABELLA. Don't you think you ought to go home like your aunt said?

WILMA. No.

ARABELLA. Have you told your Aunt Gert about the letter you're expecting yet?

WILMA. No.

ARABELLA. When are you going to tell her?

WILMA. Not until it comes. I think I'll go over and see my house. Look at how those tenants left it. I may have to sell it yet to get me to Hollywood. . . .

ARABELLA. Wilma, is that house really yours?

WILMA. Sure it's mine. My mother left it to me.

ARABELLA. Well, do you get the rent for it and tell them who to rent to like Papa does his rent houses?

WILMA. No. But it's understood it's mine. My mother told Aunt Gert it was mine just before she died. Daddy had put it in her name because he was gambling terrible then, and Aunt Gert says Mama was afraid they'd lose it. I let Daddy rent it and keep the money now. Aunt Gert says I should as he is having a very hard time. His job at the cotton gin doesn't pay hardly anything. Of course, I feel very lucky having my own house.

ARABELLA. Well, I have a house.

WILMA. Do you own it yourself?

ARABELLA. No. But I live in it.

WILMA. Well, that's hardly the same thing. I own a house, which is very unusual, Aunt Gert says, for a girl of fifteen. I'm a young lady of property, Aunt Gert says. Many's the time I thought I'll just go and live in it all by myself. Wouldn't Harrison sit up and take notice then? Once when I was thirteen and I was very fond of my Cousin Neeley I thought I'd offer it to him to get through law school. But I'm glad I didn't since he turned out so hateful. (*A pause.*) Do you remember when I used to live in my house?

ARABELLA. No.

WILMA. Well, it's a long time ago now, but I still remember it. My mama and I used to play croquet in the yard under the pecan trees. We'd play croquet every afternoon just before sundown and every once in a while she'd stop the game and ask me to run to the corner without letting the neighbors know what I was doing, to see if my father was coming home. She always worried about his getting home by six, because if he wasn't there by then she knew it meant trouble. My mother always kept me in white starched dresses. Do you remember my mother?

ARABELLA. No. But my mother does. She says she was beautiful, with the disposition of a saint.

WILMA. I know. Her name was Alice. Isn't that a pretty name?

ARABELLA. Yes. It is.

WILMA. There's a song named "Sweet Alice Ben Bolt." Aunt Gert used to sing it all the time. When Mama died, she stopped. My mama died of a broken heart.

ARABELLA. She did?

WILMA. Oh, yes. Even Aunt Gert admits that. Daddy's gambling broke her heart. Oh, well. What are you gonna do about it? Boy, I used to hate my daddy. I used to dream about what I'd do to him when I grew up. But he's sorry now and reformed, so I've forgiven him.

ARABELLA. Oh, sure. You shouldn't hate your father.

WILMA. Well, I don't know. Do you know something I've never told another living soul?

ARABELLA. What?

WILMA. Swear you won't tell?

ARABELLA. I swear.

WILMA. I love him now. Sometimes I think I'd give up this whole movie star business if I could go back to our house and live with Daddy and keep house for him. But Aunt Gert says under the circumstances that's not practical. I guess you and everybody else knows what the circumstances are. Mrs. Leighton. She's got my Daddy hogtied. Aunt Gert says she isn't good enough to shine my mother's shoes, and I think she's right.

(MISS MARTHA *comes out of the post office area* U. C. *She walks half-way down the* C. *of the stage.*)

MARTHA. Are you girls still here?

WILMA. Yes ma'm.

MARTHA. Minna called this time, Wilma. She said you were to come home immediately. (MISS MARTHA *goes back inside the post office area and into her window* U. C.)

ARABELLA. Now come on, Wilma. You'll just get in trouble.

WILMA. All right. (*They start off* R. WILMA *stops. She looks panicky.*) Wait a minute, Arabella. Yonder comes my daddy walking with that fool Mrs. Leighton. I just as soon I didn't have to see them. Let's go the other way. (*They turn around and start* L. *A man's voice calls in the distance:* "Wilma, Wilma." WILMA *and* ARABELLA *stop.* WILMA *whispers:*) That's the kind of luck I have. He saw me. Now I'll have to speak to old lady Leighton.

ARABELLA. Don't you like her?

WILMA. Do you like snakes?

ARABELLA. No.

WILMA. Well, neither do I like Mrs. Leighton and for the same reason.

(LESTER THOMPSON *and* MRS. LEIGHTON *enter from* D. R. LESTER *is a handsome, weak man in his forties.* MRS. LEIGHTON *is thirty-five or so, blonde, pretty and completely unlike* WILMA's *description. There is a warmth about her that we should wish that* WILMA *might notice.* LESTER *goes over to* WILMA.)

LESTER. (*As he leaves* MRS. LEIGHTON.) Excuse me, Sibyl. Wilma . . .

WILMA. Yes sir.

LESTER. Say hello to Mrs. Leighton.

WILMA. (*Most ungraciously.*) Hello, Mrs. Leighton.

MRS. LEIGHTON. (*Most graciously.*) Hello, Wilma.

LESTER. What are you doing hanging around the streets, Wilma?

WILMA. Waiting to see if I have a letter.

LESTER. What kind of letter, Wilma?

WILMA. About getting into the movies. Arabella and I saw an ad in the *Houston Chronicle* about a Mr. Delafonte who is a famous Hollywood director.

LESTER. Who is Mr. Delafonte?

WILMA. The Hollywood director I'm trying to tell you about. He's giving screen tests in Houston to people of beauty and talent, and if they pass they'll go to Hollywood and be in the picture shows.

LESTER. Well, that's all a lot of foolishness, Wilma. You're not going to Houston to take anything.

WILMA. But, Daddy . . . I . . .

LESTER. You're fifteen years old and you're gonna stay home like a fifteen-year-old girl should. There'll be plenty of time to go to Houston.

WILMA. But, Daddy, Mr. Delafonte won't be there forever.

LESTER. Go on home, Wilma.

WILMA. But, Daddy . . .

LESTER. Don't argue with me. I want you to march home just as quick as you can, young lady. I'm going to stand right here until you turn that corner and if I ever catch you hanging around the streets again, it will be between you and me.

WILMA. Yes sir. Come on, Arabella.

(*She and* ARABELLA *walk out* L. LESTER *stands watching.* SIBYL LEIGHTON *comes up to him.*)

MRS. LEIGHTON. Have you told her we're getting married, Lester?

LESTER. No, I'm telling Gert tonight.

MRS. LEIGHTON. Aren't you going to tell Wilma?

LESTER. No. Gert's the one to tell her. Wilma and I have very little to say to each other. Gert has her won over completely.

MRS. LEIGHTON. They must be expecting it. Why would they think you're selling your house and quitting your job?

LESTER. I don't think they know that either. I'll explain the whole thing to Gert tonight. Come on. She's turned the corner. I think she'll go on home now.

(*They walk on and off. The lights are brought up* D. L. *in area 2. It is part of the kitchen in* GERTRUDE MILLER's *house.* MINNA BOYD, *a thin, strong Negro woman in her middle forties, is seated at the table. She has a portable hand-winding Victrola on the table. She is listening to a jazz recording.* WILMA *and* ARABELLA *come in* U. C. *of the kitchen area.*)

MINNA. Well, here's the duchess. Arrived at last. Where have you been, Wilma? What on earth do you mean aggravating us this way? Your Aunt Gert was almost late for her card party worrying over you.

WILMA. You knew where I was. You called often enough. I was at the post office waiting for the mail.

MINNA. How many times has Miss Gert told you not to hang around there? Where's your pride? You know Mr. Russell Walter called and told her you were about to drive them crazy down at the post office. He said when you got your letter he's gonna be so relieved he'll deliver it in person. Your aunt says you're to get right to your room and study.

WILMA. We're just going. Come on, Arabella.

MINNA. And without Arabella. I know how much studying you and Arabella will do. You'll spend your whole time talking about Hollywood and picture shows. Clara Bow this and Alice White that. You go in there and learn something. The principal called your auntie this morning and told her you were failing in your typing and shorthand.

WILMA. (*Very bored.*) Well, I don't care. I hate them. I never wanted to take them anyway.

MINNA. Never mind about that. You just get in there and get to it. (WILMA *pays no attention. She goes deliberately and sits in a chair, scowling.*) Wilma . . .

WILMA. What?

MINNA. Now why do you want to act like this?

WILMA. Like what?

MINNA. So ugly. Your face is gonna freeze like that one day and then you're gonna be in a nice how-do-you-do.

ARABELLA. I'd better go, Wilma.

WILMA. All right, Arabella. Someday soon I'll be established in my own house and then you won't be treated so rudely.

MINNA. You come back some other time.

ARABELLA. Thank you, I will.

WILMA. I'll never get out of the house again today, Arabella, so will you check on the six o'clock mail?

ARABELLA. All right.

WILMA. Come right over if I have a letter.

ARABELLA. All right. Good-bye.

(ARABELLA *goes out* U. C. *of the kitchen area and goes offstage.* WILMA *plunks an imaginary guitar and sings, in an exaggerated hill-billy style,* "Write me a letter. Send it by mail. Send it in care of Birmingham jail.")

MINNA. Wilma, what is that letter about you're expectin'? Have you got a beau for yourself?

WILMA. Don't be crazy.

MINNA. Look at me.

WILMA. I said no, and stop acting crazy. I'm expecting a letter from Mr. Delafonte.

MINNA. Mr. who?

WILMA. Mr. Delafonte, the famous movie director.

MINNA. Never heard of him.

WILMA. Well, I wouldn't let anyone know if I was that ignorant. The whole world has heard of Mr. Delafonte. He has only directed Pola Negri and Betty Compson and Lila Lee and I don't know who all.

MINNA. What are you hearing from Mr. Delafonte about?

WILMA. A Hollywood career.

MINNA. What are you going to do with a Hollywood career?

WILMA. Be a movie star, you goose. First he's going to screen-test me, and then I'll go to Hollywood and be a Wampus baby star.

MINNA. A what?

WILMA. A Wampus baby star. You know. That's what you are before you are a movie star. You get chosen to be a Wampus baby star and parade around in a bathing suit and get all your pictures in the papers and the movie magazines.

MINNA. I want to see Miss Gert's face when you start parading around in a bathing suit for magazines. And what's all this got to do with a letter?

WILMA. Well, I read in a Houston paper where Mr. Delafonte was in Houston interviewing people at his studio for Hollywood screen tests. So Arabella and I wrote him for an appointment.

MINNA. And that's what your letter is all about? No gold mine. No oil well. Just Mr. Delafonte and a movie test.

WILMA. Yes. And if you be nice to me, after I win the screen test and sell my house I might take you out with me.

MINNA. Sell your what?

WILMA. My house.

MINNA. Wilma . . . why don't you stop talking like that? . . .

WILMA. Well, it's my house. I can sell it if I want to.

MINNA. You can't.

WILMA. I can.

MINNA. That house wasn't give to you to sell. A fifteen-year-old child. Who do you think is gonna let you sell it?

WILMA. Haven't you told me the house was mine? Hasn't Aunt Gert?

MINNA. Yes, but not to sell and throw the money away. And besides, it looks like to me the house is gonna be having permanent visitors soon.

WILMA. Who?

MINNA. What you don't know won't hurt you.

WILMA. If you mean my daddy and old lady Leighton, I'd burn it down first.

MINNA. Wilma.

WILMA. I will, I'll burn it down right to the ground.

(MISS GERT comes in D. L. of the kitchen area. She is in her forties, handsome and tall.)

MINNA. Hello, Miss Gert. . . .

GERT. Hello, Minna. Hello, Wilma.

MINNA. How was the party?

GERT. All right. Minna, Neeley is going to be away tonight so don't fix any supper for him and we had refreshments at the party so I'm not hungry. (She suddenly bursts out crying and has to leave the room. She goes running out D. L. of the kitchen area.)

WILMA. Now what's the matter with her?

MINNA. Sick headache likely. You stay here, I'll go see.

WILMA. All right. If she wants any ice, I'll crack it.

(MINNA *goes out* D. L. *of the kitchen area.* WILMA *turns on the phonograph and plays a popular song of the 1920s.*)

MINNA. (*Comes back in.*) We better turn that off. She's got a bad one. First sick headache she's had in three years. I remember the last one.

WILMA. Does she want any cracked ice? . . .

MINNA. No.

WILMA. Did she hear any bad news?

MINNA. I don't know.

WILMA. Can I go in to see her?

MINNA. Nope. You can please her, though, by getting into your studying.

WILMA. If you won't let me sell my house and go to Hollywood, I'll just quit school and move over there and rent out rooms. Support myself that way.

MINNA. You won't do nothin' of the kind. You go in there now and study.

WILMA. Why do I have to study? I have a house . . . and . . .

MINNA. Wilma, will you stop talking crazy?

WILMA. I'm not talking crazy. I could think of worse things to do. I'll rent out rooms and sit on the front porch and rock and be a lady of mystery, like a lady I read about once that locked herself in her house. Let the vines grow all around. Higher and higher until all light was shut out. She was eighteen when the vines started growing, and when she died and they cut the vines down and found her she was seventy-three and in all that time she had never put her foot outside once. All her family and friends were dead. . . .

MINNA. I know you're crazy now.

WILMA. Minna . . . Minna . . . (*She runs to her.*) I'm scared. I'm scared.

MINNA. What in the name of goodness are you scared of?

WILMA. I'm scared my daddy is going to marry Mrs. Leighton.

MINNA. Now . . . now . . . (*Holds her.*)

WILMA. Minna, let me run over to my house for just a little bit. I can't ever go over there when there's tenants living in it. I feel the need of seeing it. I'll come right back.

MINNA. Will you promise me to come right back?

WILMA. I will.

MINNA. And you'll get right to your studying and no more arguments?

WILMA. No more.

MINNA. All right, then run on.

WILMA. Oh, Minna. I love you. And you know what I'm going to do? I'm going to be a great movie star and send my chauffeur and my limousine to Harrison and put you in it and drive you all the way to Hollywood.

MINNA. Thank you.

WILMA. H.O.B.

MINNA. H.O.B.? What's H.O.B.?

WILMA. Hollywood or bust! . . . (*She goes running out* U. C. *of the kitchen area.* MINNA *calls after her:*)

MINNA. Don't forget to get right back.

(*We hear* WILMA's *voice answering in the distance:* "All right." *The lights are brought down. The lights are brought immediately up in the kitchen, a half-hour later.* AUNT GERT *comes in* D. L. *of the area. She has on a dressing gown. Twilight is beginning. She switches on a light. She looks around the room. She calls:*)

GERT. Minna, Minna. (*A pause. She calls again:*) Minna. Minna.

(*In comes* ARABELLA U. C. *of the area. She is carrying two letters.*)

ARABELLA. Hello, Miss Gertrude.

GERT. Hello, Arabella.

ARABELLA. Where's Wilma?

GERT. I don't know. The door to her room was closed when I went by. I guess she's in there studying.

ARABELLA. Yes'm. (*She starts out of the room* D. L. *of the area.*)

GERT. Arabella.

(ARABELLA *pauses.*)

ARABELLA. Yes'm.

GERT. Wilma's gotten behind in her schoolwork, so please don't ask her to go out anyplace tonight, because I'll have to say no, and . . .

ARABELLA. Oh, no ma'm. I just brought her letter over to her. She asked me to get it if it came in on the six o'clock mail and it did.

GERT. Is that the letter she's been driving us all crazy about?

ARABELLA. Yes ma'm, I got one too. (*She holds two letters up. Puts one on the table.*)

GERT. Oh. Well . . . (ARABELLA *starts out again* D. L. *of the area.*) Arabella, what is in that letter?

ARABELLA. Hasn't Wilma told you yet?

GERT. No.

ARABELLA. Then you'd better find out from her. She might be mad if I told you.

GERT. All right. (ARABELLA *starts out of the room.*) You didn't see Minna out in the backyard as you were coming in, did you?

ARABELLA. No.

GERT. I wonder where she can be. It's six-fifteen and she hasn't started a thing for supper yet.

(ARABELLA *goes out* D. L. *of the area and looks out an imaginary window* R. C. *She comes back in the room.*)

ARABELLA. Wilma isn't in the bedroom.

GERT. She isn't?

ARABELLA. No ma'm. Not in the front room either. I went in there.

GERT. That's strange. Isn't that strange? (MINNA *comes in* U. C. *of the area. She has a package in her hand.*) Oh, there you are, Minna.

MINNA. I had to run to the store for some baking soda. How do you feel? (MINNA *puts the package on the table.*)

GERT. Better. Where's Wilma?

MINNA. You don't mean she's not back yet?

GERT. Back? Where did she go?

MINNA. She swore to me if I let her go over to her house for a few minutes she'd be back here and study with no arguments.

GERT. Well, she's not here.

MINNA. That's the trouble with her. Give her an inch and she'll take a mile.

GERT. Arabella, would you run over to Wilma's house and tell her to get right home?

ARABELLA. Yes ma'm.

(*She picks the letter up off the table and takes it with her as she goes out* D. L. *of the area. A knock is heard offstage.*)

GERT. (*Calling.*) Come in. (MISS MARTHA *comes in* U. C. *of the area.*) Oh, hello, Miss Martha.

MARTHA. Hello, Gert. Hello, Minna.

MINNA. Hello, Miss Martha. . . .

MARTHA. I thought you'd be back here. I knocked and knocked at your front door and no one answered, but I knew somebody must be here this time of day, so I just decided to come on back.

GERT. I'm glad you did. We can't hear a knock at the front door back here. Sit down, won't you?

MARTHA. I can't stay a second. I just wanted to tell Wilma that her letter arrived on the six o'clock bus.

GERT. She knows, thank you, Miss Martha. Arabella brought it over to her.

MARTHA. Oh, the address on the back said the Delafonte Studio. I wonder what that could be?

GERT. I don't know.

MINNA. I knows. It's the moving pictures. She wrote about getting into them.

GERT. I do declare. She's always up to something.

MARTHA. Well, I never heard of moving pictures in Houston. I just heard the news about Lester. Was I surprised! Were you?

GERT. Yes, I was.

MARTHA. When's the wedding taking place?

GERT. I don't know.

MARTHA. Oh, I see. Well, I have to run on now.

GERT. All right, thank you, Miss Martha, for coming by. I know Wilma will appreciate it.

MARTHA. I'll just go out the back way if you don't mind. It'll save me a few steps.

GERT. Of course not.

MARTHA. Good night.

GERT. Good night, Miss Martha. (*She goes out* U. C. *of the area.*)

MINNA. What news is this?

GERT. Oh, you must know, Minna. Lester and Mrs. Leighton are getting married at last. That's why I came home from the party all upset. I had to hear about my own brother's marriage at a bridge party. And I know it's true. It came straight from the county clerk's office. They got their license this morning.

MINNA. Well, poor Wilma. She'll take this hard.

GERT. She's going to take it very hard. But what can you do? What can you do?

(*They both sit dejectedly at the table. The lights fade in the area* D. L. *as they come up on the area* D. R. WILMA *comes in from* U. C. *of the* D. R. *area. It is the yard of her house. She sits in the swing rocking back and forth, singing "Birmingham Jail" in her hillbilly style.* ARABELLA *comes running in* R. C. *of the yard area.*)

WILMA. Heh, Arabella. Come sit and swing.

ARABELLA. All right. Your letter came.

WILMA. Whoopee. Where is it?

ARABELLA. Here. (*She gives it to her.* WILMA *tears it open. She reads:*)

WILMA. "Dear Miss Thompson: Mr. Delafonte will be glad to see you anytime next week about your contemplated screen test. We suggest you call the office when you arrive in the city and we will set an exact time. Yours truly, Adele Murray." Well . . . Did you get yours?

ARABELLA. Yes.

WILMA. What did it say?

ARABELLA. The same.

WILMA. Exactly the same?

ARABELLA. Yes.

WILMA. Well, let's pack our bags. Hollywood, here we come.

ARABELLA. Wilma . . .

WILMA. Yes?

ARABELLA. I have to tell you something. . . . Well . . . I . . .

WILMA. What is it?

ARABELLA. Well . . . promise me you won't hate me, or stop being my friend. I never had a friend, Wilma, until you began being nice to me, and I couldn't stand it if you weren't my friend any longer. . . .

WILMA. Oh, my cow. Stop talking like that. I'll never stop being your friend. What do you want to tell me?

ARABELLA. Well . . . I don't want to go to see Mr. Delafonte, Wilma. . . .

WILMA. You don't?

ARABELLA. No. I don't want to be a movie star. I don't want to leave Harrison or my mother or father. . . . I just want to stay here the rest of my life and get married and settle down and have children.

WILMA. Arabella . . .

ARABELLA. I just pretended like I wanted to go to Hollywood because I knew you wanted me to, and I wanted you to like me. . . .

WILMA. Oh, Arabella . . .

ARABELLA. Don't hate me, Wilma. You see, I'd be afraid . . . I'd die if I had to go to see Mr. Delafonte. Why, I even get faint when I have to recite before the class. I'm not like you. You're not scared of anything.

WILMA. Why do you say that?

ARABELLA. Because you're not. I know.

WILMA. Oh, yes, I am. I'm scared of lots of things.

ARABELLA. What?

WILMA. Getting lost in a city. Being bitten by dogs. Old lady Leighton taking my daddy away. . . . (*A pause.*)

ARABELLA. Will you still be my friend?

WILMA. Sure. I'll always be your friend.

ARABELLA. I'm glad. Oh, I almost forgot. Your Aunt Gert said for you to come on home.

WILMA. I'll go in a little. I love to swing in my front yard. Aunt Gert has a swing in her front yard, but it's not the same. Mama and I used to come out here and swing together. Some nights when Daddy was out all night gambling, I used to wake up and hear her out here swinging away. Sometimes she'd let me come and sit beside her. We'd swing until three or four in the morning. (*A pause. She looks out into the yard.*) The pear tree looks sickly, doesn't it? The fig trees are doing nicely though. I was out in back and the weeds are near knee high, but fig trees just seem to thrive in the weeds. The freeze must have killed off the banana trees. . . . (*A pause.* WILMA *stops swinging—she walks around the yard.*) Maybe I won't leave either. Maybe I won't go to Hollywood after all.

ARABELLA. You won't?

WILMA. No. Maybe I shouldn't. That just comes to me now. You know sometimes my old house looks so lonesome it tears at my heart. I used to think it looked lonesome just whenever it had no tenants, but now it comes to me it has looked lonesome ever since Mama died and we moved away, and it will look lonesome until some of us move back here. Of course, Mama can't, and Daddy won't. So it's up to me.

ARABELLA. Are you gonna live here all by yourself?

WILMA. No. I talk big about living here by myself, but I'm too much of a coward to do that. But maybe I'll finish school and live with Aunt Gert and keep on renting the house until I meet some nice boy with good habits and steady ways, and marry him. Then we'll move here and have children and I bet this old house won't be lonely anymore. I'll get Mama's old croquet set and put it out under the pecan trees and play croquet with my children, or sit in this yard and swing and wave to people as they pass by.

ARABELLA. Oh, I wish you would. Mama says that's a normal life for a girl, marrying and having children. She says being an actress is all right, but the other's better.

WILMA. Maybe I've come to agree with your mama. Maybe I was going to Hollywood out of pure lonesomeness. I felt so alone with Mrs. Leighton getting my daddy and my mama having left the world. Daddy could have taken away my lonesomeness, but he didn't want to or couldn't. Aunt Gert says nobody is lonesome with a house full of children, so maybe that's what I just ought to stay here and have. . . .

ARABELLA. Have you decided on a husband yet?

WILMA. No.

ARABELLA. Mama says that's the bad feature of being a girl, you have to wait for the boy to ask you and just pray that the one you want wants you. Tommy Murray is nice, isn't he?

WILMA. I think so.

ARABELLA. Jay Godfrey told me once he wanted to ask you for a date, but he didn't dare because he was afraid you'd turn him down.

WILMA. Why did he think that?

ARABELLA. He said the way you talked he didn't think you would go out with anything less than a movie star.

WILMA. Maybe you'd tell him different. . . .

ARABELLA. All right. I think Jay Godfrey is very nice. Don't you?

WILMA. Yes, I think he's very nice and Tommy is nice. . . .

ARABELLA. Maybe we could double-date sometimes.

WILMA. That might be fun.

ARABELLA. Oh, Wilma. Don't go to Hollywood. Stay here in Harrison and let's be friends forever. . . .

WILMA. All right. I will.

ARABELLA. You will?

WILMA. Sure, why not? I'll stay here. I'll stay and marry and live in my house.

ARABELLA. Oh, Wilma. I'm so glad. I'm so very glad.

(WILMA *gets back in the swing. They swing vigorously back and forth. . . . A* MAN *comes in* R. C. *of the yard area.*)

MAN. I beg your pardon. Is this the Thompson house?

(*They stop swinging.*)

WILMA. Yes sir.

MAN. I understand it's for sale. I'd like to look around.

WILMA. No sir. It's not for sale. It's for rent. I'm Wilma Thompson. I own the house. My daddy rents it for me. . . .

MAN. Oh, well, we were told by Mr. Mavis . . .

WILMA. I'm sure. Mr. Mavis tries to sell everything around here. He's pulled that once before about our house, but this house is not for sale. It's for rent.

MAN. You're sure?

WILMA. I'm positive. We rent it for twenty-seven fifty a month. You pay lights, water and keep the yard clean. We are very particular over how the yard is kept. I'd be glad to show it to you. . . .

MAN. I'm sorry. I was interested in buying. There must have been a mistake.

WILMA. There must have been.

MAN. Where could I find your father, young lady?

WILMA. Why do you want to see him?

MAN. Well, I'd just like to get this straight. I understood from Mr. Mavis . . .

WILMA. Mr. Mavis has nothing to do with my house. My house is for rent, not for sale.

MAN. All right. (*The* MAN *leaves. He goes out* R. C. *of the yard area.*)

WILMA. The nerve of old man Mavis putting out around town that my house is for sale. Isn't that nervy, Arabella?

(ARABELLA *gets out of the swing.*)

ARABELLA. We'd better go. It'll be dark soon. The tree frogs are starting.

WILMA. It just makes me furious. Wouldn't it make you furious?

ARABELLA. Come on. Let's go.

WILMA. Wouldn't it make you furious?

ARABELLA. Yes.

WILMA. You don't sound like you mean it.

ARABELLA. Well . . .

WILMA. Well . . . what? . . .

ARABELLA. Nothing. . . . Let's go.

WILMA. Arabella, you know something you're not telling me.

ARABELLA. No, I don't. Honest, Wilma . . .

WILMA. You do. Look at me, Arabella . . .

ARABELLA. I don't know anything. I swear . . .

WILMA. You do. I thought you were my friend.

ARABELLA. I am. I am.

WILMA. Well, then why don't you tell me?

ARABELLA. Because I promised not to.

WILMA. Why?

ARABELLA. Well . . . I . . .

WILMA. What is it? Arabella, please tell me.

ARABELLA. Well . . . Will you never say I told you?

WILMA. I swear.

ARABELLA. Well, I didn't tell you before because in all the excitement in telling you I wasn't going to Hollywood and your saying you weren't going, I forgot about it . . . until that man came . . .

WILMA. What is it, Arabella? What is it?

ARABELLA. Well, I heard my daddy tell my mother that Mr. Lester had taken out a license to marry Mrs. Leighton.

WILMA. Oh, well. That doesn't surprise me too much. I've been looking for that to happen.

ARABELLA. But that isn't all, Wilma. . . .

WILMA. What else?

ARABELLA. Well . . .

WILMA. What else?

ARABELLA. Well . . .

WILMA. What else, Arabella? What else? . . .

ARABELLA. Well . . . My daddy heard that your daddy had put this house up for sale. . . .

WILMA. I don't believe you. . . .

ARABELLA. That's what he said, Wilma. . . . I . . . He said Mr. Lester came to him and wanted to know if he wanted to buy it. . . .

WILMA. Well. He won't do it. Not my house. He won't do it! (WILMA *has jumped out of the swing and runs out of the yard* U. C.)

ARABELLA. Wilma . . . Wilma . . . Please . . . don't say I said it. . . . Wilma . . .

(*She is standing alone and frightened as the lights fade. The lights are brought up in the area* L. *of* C. MINNA *is mixing some dough on the table.* MISS GERT *comes in.*)

GERT. She's not back yet?

MINNA. No. I knew when Arabella took that letter over there she wouldn't be here until good dark.

GERT. I just put in a call for Lester. . . . He is going to have to tell her about the marriage. It's his place. Don't you think so?

MINNA. I certainly do. I most certainly do.

(WILMA *comes running in* U. C. *of the kitchen area.*)

WILMA. Aunt Gert, do you know where I can find my daddy?

GERT. No, Wilma . . . I . . .

WILMA. Well, I've got to find him. I went over to the cotton gin but he'd left. I called out to his boardinghouse and he wasn't there. . . .

GERT. Well, I don't know, Wilma. . . .

WILMA. Is he gonna sell my house?

GERT. Wilma . . .

WILMA. Is he or isn't he?

GERT. I don't know anything about it. . . .

WILMA. Well, something's going on. Let me tell you that. I was sitting in the swing with Arabella when a man came up and said he wanted to buy it, and I said to rent and he said to buy, that Mr. Mavis had sent him over, and I told him he was mistaken and he left. Well, I was plenty mad at Mr. Mavis and told Arabella so, but she looked funny and I got suspicious and I finally got it out of her that Daddy was going to marry old lady Leighton and was putting my house up for sale. . . . (GERT *is crying.*) Aunt Gert. Isn't that my house?

GERT. Yes. I'd always thought so. . . .

WILMA. Then he can't do it. Don't let him do it. It's my house. It's all in this world that belongs to me. Let Mrs. Leighton take him if she wants to, but not my house. Please, please, please. (*She is crying.* MINNA *goes to her.*)

MINNA. Now, come on, honey. Come on, baby. . . .

WILMA. I wouldn't sell it, not even to get me to Hollywood. I thought this afternoon, before the letter from Mr. Delafonte came, I'd ask Aunt Gert to let me sell it, and go on off, but when I went over there and sat in my yard and rocked in my swing and thought of my mama and how lonesome the house looked since we moved away . . . I knew I couldn't . . . I knew I never would. . . . I'd never go to Hollywood before I'd sell that house, and he can't. . . . I won't let him. I won't let him.

MINNA. Now, honey . . . honey . . . Miss Gert, do you know anything about this?

GERT. (*Wiping her eyes.*) Minna, I don't. I heard at the card party that he was marrying Mrs. Leighton . . . but I heard nothing about Lester's selling the house. . . .

MINNA. Well, can he? . . .

GERT. I don't know. I just never thought my brother, my own brother . . . Oh, I just can't stand things like this. You see, it's all so mixed up. I don't think there was anything said in writing about Wilma's having the house, but it was clearly Alice's intention. She called me in the room before Lester and made him promise just before she died that he would always have the house for Wilma. . . .

MINNA. Well, why don't we find out? . . .

GERT. Well . . . I don't know how. . . . I left a message for Lester. I can't reach him.

MINNA. I'd call Mr. Bill if I were you. He's a lawyer.

GERT. But, Minna, my brother.

MINNA. I'd call me a lawyer, brother or no brother. If you don't, I will. I'm not gonna have what belongs to this child stolen from her by Mr. Lester or anybody else. . . .

GERT. All right. I will. I'll go talk to Bill. I'll find out what we can do legally.

(*She starts out* D. L. *of the area.* LESTER *comes in* U. C. *of the area.* MINNA *sees him coming.*)

MINNA. Miss Gert.

(GERT *turns and sees him just as he gets inside the area.*)

LESTER. Hello, Gert.

GERT. Hello, Lester.

LESTER. Hello, Wilma.

WILMA. Hello . . .

GERT. Wilma, I think you'd better leave. . . .

WILMA. Yes'm. . . . (*She starts out.*)

LESTER. Wait a minute, Gert. I've something to tell you all. I want Wilma to hear. . . .

GERT. I think we know already. Go on, Wilma.

WILMA. Yes'm.

(WILMA *leaves* D. L. *of the area.* MINNA *follows after her. A pause.*)

GERT. We've heard about the marriage, Lester.

LESTER. Oh, well. I'm sorry I couldn't be the one to tell you. We only decided this morning. There was a lot to do, a license and some business to attend to. I haven't told anyone. I don't know how the news got out.

GERT. You didn't really expect them to keep quiet about it at the courthouse?

LESTER. Oh. Well, of course I didn't think about that. (*A pause.*) Well, the other thing is . . . You see . . . I've decided to sell the house.

GERT. I know. Wilma just found out about that, too.

LESTER. Oh. Well, I'll explain the whole thing to you. You see, I felt . . . (GERT *starts to cry.*) Now what's the matter with you, Gert?

GERT. To think that my brother, my own brother, would do something like this.

LESTER. Like what? After all it's my house, Gert.

GERT. There's some dispute about that. The least I think you could have done, the very least, was come to tell your own child.

LESTER. Well, I'm here now to do that. I only put it up for sale at noon today. I've nothing to hide or be ashamed of. The house is in my name. Sibyl, Mrs. Leighton, doesn't like Harrison. You can't blame her. People have been rotten to her. We're moving to Houston. I'm selling this house to pay down on one in Houston. That'll belong to Wilma just the same, someday. Sibyl's agreed to that, and Wilma will really get a better house in time. And we always want her to feel like it's her home, come and visit us summers . . . and like I say when something happens to me or Sibyl the house will be hers. . . .

GERT. That's not the point, Lester. . . .

LESTER. What do you mean?

GERT. You know very well.

LESTER. I can't make a home for her over there, can I? She'll be grown soon and marrying and having her own house. I held on to this place as long as I could. . . . Well, I'm not going to feel guilty about it. . . .

GERT. I'm going to try to stop you, Lester. . . .

LESTER. Now look, Gert. For once try and be sensible. . . .

GERT. Legally I'm going to try and stop you. I'm going . . .

LESTER. Please, Gert . . .

GERT. . . . to call Bill and tell him the whole situation and see what we can do. If we have any rights I'll take it to every court I can. Brother or no brother. . . .

LESTER. Now look, don't carry on like this. Maybe I've handled it clumsily and if I have I'm sorry. I just didn't think. . . . I should have, I know . . . but I . . .

GERT. That's right. You didn't think. You never do. Well, this time you're going to have to. . . .

LESTER. Can't you look at it this way? Wilma is getting a better house and . . .

GERT. Maybe she doesn't want a better house. Maybe she just wants this one. But that isn't the point either. The sickening part is that you really didn't care what Wilma thought, or even stopped for a moment to consider if she had a thought. You've never cared about anyone or anything but yourself. Well, this time I won't let you without a fight. I'm going to a lawyer.

LESTER. Gert . . .

GERT. Now get out of my house. Because brother or no, I'm through with you.

LESTER. All right. If you feel that way.

(*He leaves* U. C. *of the area.* GERT *stands for a moment, thinking what to do next.* MINNA *comes in* D. L. *of the area.*)

MINNA. I was behind the door and I heard the whole thing.

GERT. Did Wilma hear?

MINNA. No, I sent her back to her room. Now you get right to a lawyer.

GERT. I intend to. He's gotten me mad now. I won't let him get by with it if I can help it. I think I'll walk over to Bill's. I don't like to talk about it over the telephone.

MINNA. Yes'm.

GERT. You tell Wilma to wait here for me.

MINNA. Yes'm. Want me to tell her where you've gone?

GERT. I don't see why not. I'll be back as soon as I finish.

MINNA. Yes'm. (GERT *leaves* U. C. *of the area.* MINNA *goes to the door and calls:*) Wilma. Wilma. You can come here now. (*She fills a plate with food and puts it on the table.* WILMA *comes in* D. L. *of the area.*) You better sit down and try to eat something.

WILMA. I can't eat a thing.

MINNA. Well, you can try.

WILMA. No. It would choke me. What happened?

MINNA. Your aunt told him not to sell the house, and he said he would, and so she's gone to see a lawyer.

WILMA. Does she think she can stop him?

MINNA. She's gonna try. I know she's got him scared. . . .

WILMA. But it's my house. You know that. He knows that. . . . Didn't she tell him?

MINNA. Sure she told him. But you know your daddy. Telling won't do any good, we have to prove it.

WILMA. What proof have we got?

MINNA. Miss Gert's word. I hope that's enough. . . .

WILMA. And if it isn't?

MINNA. Then you'll lose it. That's all. You'll lose it.

WILMA. I bet I lose it. I've got no luck.

MINNA. Why do you say that?

WILMA. What kind of luck is it takes your mama away, and then your daddy, and then tries to take your house. Sitting in that yard swinging I was the happiest girl in the world this afternoon. I'd decided not to go in the movies and to stay in Harrison and get married and have children and live in my house. . . .

MINNA. Well, losing a house won't stop you from staying in Harrison and getting married. . . .

WILMA. Oh, yes. I wouldn't trust it with my luck. With my kind of luck I wouldn't even get me a husband. . . . I'd wind up like Miss Martha working at the post office chasing Mr. Russell Walter until the end of time. No mother and no father and no house and no husband and no children. No, thank you. I'm just tired of worrying over the whole thing. I'll just go on into Houston and see Mr. Delafonte and get on out to Hollywood and make money and get rich and famous. (*She begins to cry.*)

MINNA. Now, honey. Honey . . .

WILMA. Minna, I don't want to be rich and famous. . . . I want to stay here. I want to stay in Harrison. . . .

MINNA. Now, honey. Try to be brave.

WILMA. I know what I'm gonna do. (*She jumps up.*) I'm going to see old lady Leighton. She's the one that can stop this. . . .

MINNA. Now, Wilma. You know your aunt don't want you around that woman.

WILMA. I can't help it. I'm going. . . .

MINNA. Wilma . . . you listen to me . . . (WILMA *runs out* U. C. *of the area.*) Wilma . . . Wilma . . . you come back here. . . .

(*But* WILMA *has gone.* MINNA *shakes her head in desperation. The lights fade. When the lights are brought up it is two hours later.* MINNA *is at the kitchen table reading the paper.* GERT *comes in* U. C. *of the area.*)

GERT. Well, we've won.

MINNA. What do you mean?

GERT. I mean just what I say. Lester is not going to sell the house.

MINNA. What happened?

GERT. I don't know what happened. I went over to see Bill and we talked it all through, and he said legally we really had no chance but he'd call up Lester and try to at least bluff him into thinking we had. And when he called Lester he said Lester wasn't home, and so I suggested his calling you know where.

MINNA. No. Where?

GERT. Mrs. Leighton's. And sure enough he was there, and then Bill told him why he was calling and Lester said well, it didn't matter as he'd decided not to sell the house after all.

MINNA. You don't mean it?

GERT. Oh, yes, I do. Where's Wilma?

MINNA. She's over there with them.

GERT. Over where with them?

MINNA. At Mrs. Leighton's.

GERT. Why, Minna . . .

MINNA. Now don't holler at me. I told her not to go, but she said she was going and then she ran out that door so fast I couldn't stop her.

(WILMA *comes running in* U. C. *of the area.*)

WILMA. Heard the news? House is mine again.

MINNA. Do you know what happened?

WILMA. Sure. Mrs. Leighton isn't so bad. Boy, I went running over there expecting the worst . . .

GERT. Wilma, what do you mean going to that woman's house? Wilma, I declare . . .

WILMA. Oh, she's not so bad. Anyway we've got her to thank for it.

MINNA. Well, what happened? Will somebody please tell me what happened?

WILMA. Well, you know I was sitting here and it came to me. It came to me just like that. See Mrs. Leighton. She's the one to stop it and it's got to be stopped. Well, I was so scared my knees were trembling the whole time going over there, but I made myself do it, walked in on her and she looked more nervous than I did.

GERT. Was your father there?

WILMA. No ma'm. He came later. Wasn't anybody there but me and Mrs. Leighton. I'm calling her Sibyl now. She asked me to. Did Arabella come yet?

MINNA. Arabella?

WILMA. I called and asked her to come and celebrate. I'm so excited. I just had to have company tonight. I know I won't be able to sleep anyway. I hope you don't mind, Aunt Gert. . . .

MINNA. If you don't tell me what happened . . .

WILMA. Well . . . Mrs. Leighton . . . I mean Sibyl . . . (ARA-BELLA *comes in* U. C. *of the area.* WILMA *sees her.*) Oh, come on in, Arabella.

ARABELLA. Hi. I almost didn't get to come. I told my mama it was life or death and so she gave in. But she made me swear we'd be in bed by ten. Did you hear about Mr. Delafonte?

WILMA. No? What?

ARABELLA. He's a crook. It was in the Houston papers tonight. He was operating a business under false pretenses. He had been charging twenty-five dollars for those screen tests and using a camera with no film in it.

WILMA. My goodness.

ARABELLA. It was in all the papers. On the second page. My father said he mustn't have been very much not to even get on the front page. He wasn't a Hollywood director at all. He didn't even know Lila Lee or Betty Compson.

WILMA. He didn't?

ARABELLA. No.

MINNA. Wilma, will you get back to your story before I lose my mind?

WILMA. Oh. Yes . . . I got my house back, Arabella.

ARABELLA. You did?

WILMA. Sure. That's why I called you over to spend the night. A kind of celebration.

ARABELLA. Well, that's wonderful.

MINNA. Wilma . . .

WILMA. All right. Where was I?

GERT. You were at Mrs. Leighton's.

WILMA. Oh, yes. Sibyl's. I'm calling her Sibyl now, Arabella. She asked me to.

MINNA. Well . . . what happened? Wilma, if you don't tell me . . .

WILMA. Well, I just told her the whole thing.

MINNA. What whole thing?

WILMA. Well, I told her about my mother meaning for the house to always be mine, and how I loved the house, and how I was lonely and the house was lonely and that I had hoped my daddy and I could go there and live someday but knew now we couldn't and that I had planned to go to Hollywood and be a movie star but that this afternoon my friend Arabella and I decided we didn't really want to do that, and that I knew then that what I wanted to do really was to live in Harrison and get married and live in my house and have children so that I wouldn't be lonely anymore and the house wouldn't. And then she started crying.

GERT. You don't mean it.

WILMA. Yes ma'm. And I felt real sorry for her and I said I didn't hold anything against her and then Daddy came in, and she said why didn't he tell her that was my house, and he said because it wasn't. And then she asked him about what Mother told you, and he said that was true but now I was going to have a better house, and she said I didn't want to have a better house, but my own house, and that she wouldn't marry him if he sold this house and she said they both had jobs in Houston and would manage somehow, but I had nothing, so then he said all right.

GERT. Well. Good for her.

MINNA. Sure enough, good for her.

WILMA. And then Mr. Bill called and Daddy told him the house was mine again and then she cried again and hugged me and asked me to kiss her and I did, and then Daddy cried and I kissed him, and then I cried. And they asked me to the wedding and I said I'd go and that I'd come visit them this summer in Houston. And then I came home.

MINNA. Well. Well, indeed.

GERT. My goodness. So that's how it happened. And you say Mrs. Leighton cried?

WILMA. Twice. We all did. Daddy and Mrs. Leighton and me. . . .

GERT. Well, I'm glad, Wilma, it's all worked out.

WILMA. And can I go visit them this summer in Houston?

GERT. If you like.

WILMA. And can I go to the wedding?

GERT. Yes, if you want to.

WILMA. I want to.

MINNA. Now you better have some supper.

WILMA. No. I couldn't eat, I'm still too excited.

MINNA. Miss Gert, she hasn't had a bite on her stomach.

GERT. Well, it won't kill her this one time, Minna.

WILMA. Aunt Gert, can Arabella and I go over to my yard for just a few minutes and swing? We'll be home by ten. . . .

GERT. No, Wilma, it's late.

WILMA. Please. Just to celebrate. I have it coming to me. We'll just stay for a few minutes.

GERT. Well . . .

WILMA. Please . . .

GERT. Will you be back here by ten, and not make me have to send Minna over there?

WILMA. Yes ma'm.

GERT. All right.

WILMA. Oh, thank you. (*She goes to her aunt and kisses her.*) You're the best aunt in the whole world. Come on, Arabella.

ARABELLA. All right.

(*They start* U. C. *of the area.* GERT *calls after them:*)

GERT. Now remember. Back by ten. Arabella has promised her mother. And you've promised me.

WILMA. (*Calling in distance.*) Yes ma'm.

(GERT *comes back into the room.*)

GERT. Well, I'm glad it's ending this way.

MINNA. Yes ma'm.

GERT. I never thought it would. Well, I said hard things to Lester. I'm sorry I had to, but I felt I had to.

MINNA. Of course you did.

GERT. Well, I'll go to my room. You go on when you're ready.

MINNA. All right. I'm ready now. The excitement has wore me out.

GERT. Me too. Leave the light on for the children. I'll keep awake until they come in.

MINNA. Yes'm.

GERT. Good night.

MINNA. Good night.

(GERT *goes out* D. L. *of the area.* MINNA *goes to get her hat. The lights fade. The lights are brought up in the* D. R. *area.* WILMA *and* ARABELLA *come in* U. C. *of the area and get in the swing.*)

WILMA. Don't you just love to swing?

ARABELLA. Uh huh.

WILMA. It's a lovely night, isn't it? Listen to that mockingbird. The crazy thing must think it's daytime.

ARABELLA. It's light enough to be day.

WILMA. It certainly is.

ARABELLA. Well, it was lucky we decided to give up Hollywood with Mr. Delafonte turning out to be a crook and all.

WILMA. Wasn't it lucky?

ARABELLA. Do you feel lonely now?

WILMA. No, I don't feel nearly so lonely. Now I've got my house and plan to get married. And my daddy and I are going to see each other, and I think Mrs. Leighton is going to make a nice friend. She's crazy about moving pictures.

ARABELLA. Funny how things work out.

WILMA. Very funny.

ARABELLA. Guess who called me on the telephone.

WILMA. Who?

ARABELLA. Tommy . . . Murray.

WILMA. You don't say.

ARABELLA. He asked me for a date next week. Picture show. He said Jay was going to call you.

WILMA. Did he?

ARABELLA. I asked him to tell Jay that you weren't only interested in going out with movie actors.

WILMA. What did he say?

ARABELLA. He said he thought Jay knew that. (*A pause.* WILMA *jumps out of the swing.*) Wilma. What's the matter with you? Wilma . . . (*She runs to her.*)

WILMA. I don't know. I felt funny there for a minute. A cloud passed over the moon and I felt lonely . . . and funny . . . and scared. . . .

ARABELLA. But you have your house now.

WILMA. I know . . . I . . . (*A pause. She points offstage* R.) I used to sleep in there. I had a white iron bed. I remember one night

Aunt Gert woke me up. It was just turning light out, she was crying. "I'm taking you home to live with me," she said. "Why?" I said. "Because your mama's gone to heaven," she said. (*A pause.*) I can't remember my mama's face anymore. I can hear her voice sometimes calling me far off: "Wilma, Wilma, come home." Far off. But I can't remember her face. I try and I try, but finally I have to go to my bureau drawer and take out her picture and look to remember. . . . Oh, Arabella. It isn't only the house I wanted. It's the life in the house. My mama and me and even my daddy coming in at four in the morning. . . .

ARABELLA. But there'll be life again in this house.

WILMA. How?

ARABELLA. You're gonna fill it with life again, Wilma. Like you said this afternoon.

WILMA. But I get afraid.

ARABELLA. Don't be. You will. I know you will.

WILMA. You think I can do anything. Be a movie star. . . . Go to Hollywood. (*A pause.*) The moon's from behind the cloud. (*A pause. In the distance we can hear the courthouse clock strike ten.*) Don't tell me it's ten o'clock already. I'll fill this house with life again. I'll meet a young man with steady ways and nice habits. . . . (*Far off* AUNT GERT *calls:* "Wilma. Wilma." WILMA *calls back:*) We're coming. You see that pecan tree out there?

ARABELLA. Uh huh.

WILMA. It was planted the year my mother was born. It's so big now, I can hardly reach around it. (AUNT GERT *calls again:* "Wilma. Wilma." WILMA *calls back:*) We're coming.

(*She and* ARABELLA *sit swinging.* WILMA *looks happy and is happy as the lights fade.*)

The Oil Well

The Oil Well has unusually close ties to Horton Foote's other plays. Once again, as in *The Old Beginning,* Harrison is changing, as reflected in the Thornton home's "strange mixture of styles." Here again is H. T. Mavis, eager now to convert the rural Southeast Texas countryside into a profitable source of crude oil. And here is talk of "Cousin Nadine" Thornton, who went on a vacation to New York City, where she found a husband. Her story had been telecast on NBC the previous year— 1952—as *The Travelers.* Except for the plays on a common theme (*The Roads to Home*) and the cycle *The Orphans' Home,* this play is the most tightly knit presentation of the Harrison mythology.

The Oil Well also has substantial links to another play not so specifically a part of the Harrison saga: *The Trip to Bountiful.* Both plays are about ties to the land. Loula Thornton, like Carrie Watts, takes more security from the land than she does from people. And Will, like Carrie, has hope and resilience that sustain him in the face of injustice and personal failure. In simplest terms, *Bountiful* and *The Oil Well* are Horton Foote's agrarian tales.

But this short play is more religious and political than *Bountiful*. Carrie Watts has had a loveless marriage, and Ludie, her son, has feared and turned from the past, Carrie's great source of strength. For this failure of imagination Ludie pays a heavy personal price, but his flight from their shared past also isolates him from his mother. So, Carrie's trip to Bountiful is a heroic, though lonely, search for the old connections that have sustained her when others, more human and contemporary, have failed. Bountiful, the land and the place, once again raises her up so that she can face the many forms of brokenness in her present life. To her mind, the land presents itself as an endless source of nourishment and strength. Her agrarian dream is undisturbed.

In *The Oil Well* the Thornton family has experienced the same agrarian ideal as Carrie Watts in *Bountiful*. Acts as simple as their daily noon meal or Will's reenactment of his father's concern for the weather suggest the orderliness and tradition of their lives. Mrs. Thornton gains "peace" from her "proper work." What is disturbing in *The Oil Well*, and what separates it from *Bountiful*, is the erosion of the agrarian vision within the mind of Will Thornton. Will is losing his pride in husbanding and his sense of the Harrison community. The "substance of his faith" has become oil, the new religion, and the only justification of his new values will be his acquisition of wealth. By replacing the love of the old rituals with the worship of money Will withdraws from his wife, loses his closeness to the land and his own past, and looks for the time when he'll be able to remove his children from the working world of Harrison. *Bountiful* is a psychological return to springs that never go dry; *The Oil Well* examines the degeneration of values and loss of intimacy that accompany the rise of the new religion: oil.

The Oil Well was first produced on the Goodyear Theatre on May 17, 1953, with Dorothy Gish and E. G. Marshall as Loula and Will Thornton.

The Oil Well

CAST

Mrs. Loula Thornton	Will Thornton
Thelma Doris Thornton	Second Man
Man	Roy Thornton
George Weems	Mamie Bledsoe

Place: A ranch near Harrison, Texas
Time: 1953

The living room and front porch (gallery) of an old-fashioned farmhouse. The house was built early in the nineteenth century and has been taken excellent care of. The living room, stage R., *is furnished in a strange mixture of styles. There are some antiques, left from better days, interspersed with Grand Rapids: a sofa, a table with a lamp on it, three straight chairs, one upholstered easy chair, a rocker placed by a window. On the walls are a calendar, family portraits and an oil painting of a woman in a boat combing her hair. There is a door* U. R. *of the living room leading off to the rest of the house. A door* L. C. *of the living room leads out to the porch. There are two windows looking out on the porch,* U. L. *and* D. L. *The porch or gallery, stage* L., *runs parallel to the living room. Steps are on the side of the porch facing the audience.*

MRS. LOULA THORNTON, *a woman in her sixties, is seated in a rocking chair by a window looking out over the gallery and front yard. She is dressed in a neat, well-starched Mother Hubbard. Her daughter,* THELMA DORIS, *comes up on the porch and to the front door* L. *of* C. *in living room.* THELMA DORIS *is in her early thirties. She has been working in town and has on a hat and gloves and carries a purse.* MRS. THORNTON *gets up and goes to her as she comes in the door.*

MRS. THORNTON. Thelma Doris, what on earth are you doing out here this time of day?

THELMA DORIS. I thought I'd better get out here and see just what is going on.

MRS. THORNTON. Why? What are you talking about?

THELMA DORIS. Roy came up to the courthouse about an hour ago. I had just come back from ten o'clock coffee and I was sitting there at my desk wondering what I could do to keep busy until lunchtime, and he said Papa had called him on the phone and was talking wild-like and said did he know where I was and he said he reckoned I was having my ten o'clock coffee and he told Roy to round me up and tell me to quit my job and for both of us to get out here as quick as we could.

MRS. THORNTON. I swanny. I knew it. I was sure of it.

THELMA DORIS. Well, what is it? Do you know why he called me?

MRS. THORNTON. Between you and me he's gone crazy, honey.

THELMA DORIS. Mama.

MRS. THORNTON. Gone completely crazy!

THELMA DORIS. Oh, no. Don't say that.

MRS. THORNTON. Oh, yes, he has. A man come out here late yesterday afternoon and offered him thirty-five dollars an acre for the farm, and then around eight o'clock last night, H. T. Mavis come out and offered him fifty dollars an acre and your papa as much as ordered him off the place.

THELMA DORIS. You don't mean it?

MRS. THORNTON. Oh, yes, I do mean it, honey. And then this morning he went out to the hands he had gotten to help him with the plowing, dismissed them all and come in here and put on his Sunday suit.

THELMA DORIS. His Sunday suit?

MRS. THORNTON. Yes ma'm. I said, "Will, what in the name of goodness are you doing with your Sunday suit on when it's Thursday?" And he said, "I'm not farming this year." I said, "And why not? How are we to eat? Much less keep up the payments at the bank." And he says, "My prophecy has come true. There's no need to farm." He says, "They're all after my land because it's swimming in oil." He says, "The land will be covered with derricks in another six months so why put in cotton because it would be just trampled under anyway by the trucks and the workmen?" (*A knock is heard at the back of the house.*) Did you hear somebody knocking at the back door?

THELMA DORIS. I think so. (*She hears the knocking again.*)

MRS. THORNTON. Yep. I knew I heard something. See who it is at the back door, Thelma Doris.

THELMA DORIS. Yes ma'm.

(*She gets up and goes out of the room through door* U. R. *A* MAN *has come into yard* L. *and gone up the porch to the front door. He knocks.* MRS. THORNTON *goes to the door and opens it.*)

MRS. THORNTON. Yes?

(*A* MAN *in his thirties is there. He is well dressed and prosperous looking.*)

MAN. How do you do?

MRS. THORNTON. How do you do? Were you the one knocking at my back door?

MAN. No ma'm. I just came up in the yard. There's another man at your back door. I saw him as I was coming up on the porch.

MRS. THORNTON. What's your business?

MAN. I'm looking for Will Thornton. Is this his place?

MRS. THORNTON. Yes, it is. But I couldn't tell you right off where he is. He ought to be out plowing, but he's not.

MAN. I see. Any idea where I might find him?

MRS. THORNTON. No sir, I haven't.

MAN. When do you expect him?

MRS. THORNTON. I couldn't tell you that either.

MAN. What time do you have your dinner?

MRS. THORNTON. Twelve o'clock, same as we've been having it for forty years.

MAN. Yes'm.

MRS. THORNTON. Now do you mind my asking you a question?

MAN. No ma'm.

MRS. THORNTON. What do you want to see Will Thornton about?

MAN. Are you Mrs. Thornton?

MRS. THORNTON. That's correct.

MAN. Well, let me congratulate you. The Southern States Oil and Sulphur Company wants to take a lease on your land.

MRS. THORNTON. I see.

MAN. Well, you don't look very pleased.

MRS. THORNTON. I'm not. I'm much more impressed with a good cotton crop.

MAN. Oh, well. I don't think you understand, Mrs. Thornton.

MRS. THORNTON. Yes, I do. I understand very well. . . .

MAN. Oh. Well, do you mind if I wait here on the gallery for your husband?

MRS. THORNTON. I'd thank you if you didn't. I'd prefer it if you'd leave my husband to farm in peace.

MAN. Look, Mrs. Thornton . . .

MRS. THORNTON. And I'd rather not discuss it any further.

(*She closes the door and goes inside the room. The* MAN *goes out* L., *shaking his head.* THELMA DORIS *comes in from the back through door* U. R.)

THELMA DORIS. Who were you talking to?

MRS. THORNTON. Some man that wants to see your papa on business. Who was at the back door?

THELMA DORIS. A man looking for Papa. He's an oilman.

MRS. THORNTON. Did he leave?

THELMA DORIS. No ma'm. He asked if he could wait until Papa came home.

MRS. THORNTON. Well, he's not going to. I'm going to get rid of him too. (*She gets up and starts for the door.*)

THELMA DORIS. Mama, wait! What if Papa is right?

MRS. THORNTON. What do you mean?

THELMA DORIS. What if we have oil here like he's always said?

MRS. THORNTON. Now look here, Thelma Doris. Don't you go encouraging your papa in this. I can see 1925, '33 and '38 all over again.

THELMA DORIS. But, Mama . . .

MRS. THORNTON. If there was oil here we would have known it by now. They discovered oil in this county in 1925. Since then oilmen have walked acrossed it, and ridden acrossed it, and tested and leased and sold and traded the whole of them twenty-eight years, and in all that time not one single soul has thought there was oil on this farm but your papa and two crooks, who didn't think so, but took advantage of your papa's faith.

THELMA DORIS. But what if they've been wrong all this time and Papa was right?

MRS. THORNTON. Then that's fine. But we've no business believing or acting like he's right until we see the oil.

THELMA DORIS. But, Mama . . .

MRS. THORNTON. No business at all. We still owe ten thousand dollars we borrowed on this place the last time he thought he was going to find oil. We're getting the loan down, but it's taken every ounce of your papa's and my strength and will to do it. If your papa don't put in a crop this year, we'll fall behind again. Now I'm too old to expect much out of life, but I do hope and expect and aim to die out of debt, so that this place can be free for you and Roy to do with as you please. So you'll favor me now if you'll go right back to town and stay on your job.

THELMA DORIS. I'm not going to quit my job. I just took the day off, that's all. Where's Papa now?

MRS. THORNTON. I don't know. But I'm hoping he'll come home with a little more sense than when he left, and I want you to promise me you'll stand behind me until he's out in that field plowing this afternoon.

THELMA DORIS. Yes ma'm.

MRS. THORNTON. Now I'm going out to get rid of that other gentleman, so your papa can get his mind on his proper work when he does come home.

THELMA DORIS. Yes ma'm.

(*She goes to window and looks out.* MRS. THORNTON *walks out of the room* U. R. *The lights fade. The lights are brought up on an area* D. R. *An old man is seated in a cane-bottom chair, smoking a cigar.* WILL THORNTON, *a tall, angular, nervous man in his middle sixties, comes striding up to him. He is dressed in a blue serge suit. The old man,* GEORGE WEEMS, *is in an old shirt and pants.*)

GEORGE. Morning, Will.

WILL. Howdy, Mr. George. . . .

GEORGE. What are you doing all dressed up? Going to a funeral?

WILL. Nope. Just come over to talk to you.

GEORGE. You need to dress up in a blue serge suit to come over and talk to me?

WILL. No sir. Put that on for my own benefit.

GEORGE. Start your plowing today?

WILL. No sir.

GEORGE. You better get started. This good weather won't last forever.

WILL. I am aware of that.

GEORGE. Have a chair?

WILL. No, thank you.

GEORGE. I've never seen better weather for plowing. Have you?

WILL. No sir. I don't believe I have, Mr. George.

GEORGE. Then why ain't you at it? I've been up since five and as soon as I take a nap I'm going back to it until sundown.

WILL. Mr. George. Have any men been over here trying to buy your land?

GEORGE. Yep. Matt Drew. H. T. Mavis. And two fellows come around to see about leasing today.

WILL. What did you say to them?

GEORGE. I said I wasn't interested.

WILL. We've got oil in our land, Mr. George.

GEORGE. Now, Will, I hate to dispute you . . .

WILL. I know we have. I've been saying it for twenty-eight years, and I know it's so. We're going to be rich men before we die. I couldn't sleep last night for thinking about it. It's the justification of my faith as I see it. I've held on to my land in spite of debt and fire and flood. Sometimes I'd be so tired I couldn't stand the thought of looking at another row of cotton, but every day when I went out to plow or to plant I'd say, don't give up. Hold on. There's oil here and you're gonna be rich.

GEORGE. That so?

WILL. You know that's so, Mr. George.

GEORGE. I've heard you say it often enough.

WILL. Well, it's so. And you're gonna live to see it's so. That's why I'm not planting this year, Mr. George, or plowing either.

I'm leasing my land for the first decent offer I get, and I'm gonna sit this spring and this summer out on my porch and watch the men come and put the wells up and I'm . . . (*He turns his head away. He's crying. His voice breaks.*) Excuse me, Mr. George. I just get overcome when I think about it. (*A pause.*) I was getting scared. I'm sixty-five and I was getting scared I wasn't going to live to see it. Then yesterday when Matt Drew and H. T. Mavis come around and offered to buy my farm, I knew. I knew clear as day it was going to happen. That my faith was going to be justified, and I was going to die a rich man.

GEORGE. What are you going to do with all that money when you get it?

WILL. I don't know, Mr. George. I don't dare to think about it. I started thinking last night and I had to stop. I got so excited my heart got to pounding and my breath caught short on me. If I hadn't made myself stop thinking about it, I swear I might have had a heart attack, and then I wouldn't live to be a rich man at all. (*A pause.*) There's so many things I want to do. Buy a new gas range for Loula, take Thelma Doris out of her job at the courthouse. Set my boy up in a business of his own. Get myself a television set, and a man to drive me around the country when I want to get up and go. (*A pause.*) What are you going to do?

GEORGE. Nothing.

WILL. Nothing. You mean you're gonna leave all that money in the bank? Just let it set there . . .

GEORGE. Nope. I'm not seeing my land tore up. I'm plowing, remember? And that's what you'll do if you've got any sense. There's no oil here, Will.

WILL. Don't say that.

GEORGE. There's no oil here. There's three or four fools with nothing better to do with their time and money than to go around looking and buying up what they can't use, but there's no oil here. . . .

WILL. There is. Oh, yes. There is. I've seen it in my dreams at night, gushing up out of the earth. Those dreams weren't for nothing. They was the substance of my faith, and you and Loula and all the doubters in the world ain't getting me to turn my back on my dreams and my birthright.

GEORGE. Go back and plant your crop, Will. Don't be a fool.

WILL. A fool? You're the fool. I'll be riding to California with my chauffeur while you're out here breaking your back riding a tractor. Don't you be a fool. I'm gonna be rich. I'm gonna be rich and it'll take more than you and your gloomy words to stop me.

(*He turns and strides out.* GEORGE *shakes his head sadly. The lights fade as the old man picks up his chair and goes out. The lights are brought up on the* THORNTON *living room.* THELMA DORIS *is there reading a magazine.* MRS. THORNTON *comes in* U.R.)

MRS. THORNTON. No sign of your papa yet?

THELMA DORIS. No.

MRS. THORNTON. It's twelve-thirty. I'll get things on the table.

THELMA DORIS. Want me to help?

MRS. THORNTON. No. Go ahead and look at your magazine.

(*She goes out the door* U. R. THELMA DORIS *gets up and goes out on the porch.* WILL *comes up to her from the yard* L.)

WILL. Hello, honey.

THELMA DORIS. Hello, Papa. (*She kisses him.*)

WILL. I guess Roy got my message to you.

THELMA DORIS. Yes sir.

WILL. Did you do like I sent word? Did you quit your job?

THELMA DORIS. Well, you see, Papa . . .

WILL. No point in your going on straining your eyes at that typewriter. We're going to be rich, honey. Your old papa's gonna make it. We're gonna be so rich we're gonna sit up nights and think what to do with all our money.

THELMA DORIS. Now you mustn't get too excited, Papa.

WILL. Don't say that to me, Thelma Doris. That's just how your mother talks. What do you think I'm made of? Tin? I am excited. Of course I'm excited. Aren't you?

THELMA DORIS. I was when I first heard. But then Mama says . . .

WILL. I know what your mama says. Plow. Plow. How can I think about plowing or anything . . . ?

THELMA DORIS. But, Papa, why don't you go on and get the plowing done and then if it happens, fine, and if it doesn't . . .

WILL. It's going to happen. What's the sense of plowing or planting when they're just gonna tear everything up to put down the wells? Where's your faith? I swear. What kind of a family do I have? My wife has no faith and my daughter . . .

THELMA DORIS. I have faith, Papa.

WILL. Then why are you talking to me about plowing?

THELMA DORIS. Well, it's for Mama's sake. (*A pause.*) I hate to bring up unpleasant things, but I remember last time and Mama does. And it scares her. You have to understand that. She went along with you last time, let you borrow on the farm, take all your savings . . .

(MRS. THORNTON *comes into the living room from door* U. R.)

WILL. All right. I made a mistake. I admitted that. I've said a million times it was wrong to do what I did. A man has to work with the companies and not try to have his own operation. And besides, I was taken in by crooks. . . . We never even got a well down . . . much less . . .

THELMA DORIS. I know. I know.

(MRS. THORNTON *comes out on the porch from the living room.*)

MRS. THORNTON. Dinner is on the table.

WILL. I ain't hungry.

MRS. THORNTON. Why?

WILL. Because I'm too excited to eat. George Weems said there was two men over to his place about leasing. I can't understand why they didn't come here too. I guess they'll come . . .

MRS. THORNTON. They've been here. Two men from the oil companies. I sent them away.

WILL. You didn't. Where did you send them to? What were their names?

MRS. THORNTON. I don't know who they were, or where they were going.

WILL. Why did you do that to me?

MRS. THORNTON. Because you promised me last time you wouldn't stop farming until we'd paid this debt off. You're going back on your promise, Will.

WILL. Now look . . .

MRS. THORNTON. Go out to the fields this afternoon. Start your plowing. Then I won't say a word to you about leasing or anything else.

WILL. Loula . . .

MRS. THORNTON. No. I won't listen to any arguments. I've listened to too many. I listened to you about buying land out in the Valley. And what did we get? A swamp. I listened about putting our well . . .

WILL. I was wrong then. This time . . .

MRS. THORNTON. I'm afraid, Will. I'm afraid. This way we can be left with nothing. No farm. No home. I'm sixty years old, Will, and I couldn't face that. . . . I . . . I . . .

WILL. All right. All right. You all go on and have your dinner.

MRS. THORNTON. Will . . .

WILL. I don't want to talk about it now.

MRS. THORNTON. Come on, Thelma Doris.

(WILL *goes off the porch and out* L. THELMA DORIS *and* MRS. THORN-
TON *go in the living room.* THELMA DORIS *starts for the* U. R. *door.*
She sees her mother sitting in rocking chair, looking out the window.)

THELMA DORIS. Come on, Mama . . .

MRS. THORNTON. I can't eat a bite myself now. I'm sick I'm so
worried.

THELMA DORIS. Now, Mama. Come on . . .

MRS. THORNTON. How can I eat? When he's acting this way . . .

THELMA DORIS. Mama . . .

MRS. THORNTON. Shh . . .

THELMA DORIS. What's the matter?

MRS. THORNTON. Yonder comes one of them oilmen. Your papa's
talking to him out in the yard.

THELMA DORIS. One of those that were here before?

MRS. THORNTON. No. A different one.

THELMA DORIS. Well, how do you know . . .?

MRS. THORNTON. I'd recognize them anywhere.

(WILL *comes in* L. *up on the porch and into living room.*)

WILL. Loula, I wish you'd come out here and talk to this fellow
with me.

MRS. THORNTON. I don't want to talk to anybody.

WILL. He says he's as sure there's oil on our land as he's ever been
in his life.

MRS. THORNTON. That's all right about that. I hope for your sake
it's true.

WILL. He wants to lease, I think.

MRS. THORNTON. And I'm not asking that you don't lease to him. Or to anybody you want to. But he could be wrong, Will, he could be wrong. (*A pause.*) Promise me you'll start the plowing.

WILL. All right. All right. Anything for peace. I'll get some hands this afternoon. (*He goes out on the porch. Another well-dressed young* MAN *is standing there, having come in* L.) Want me to bring a chair out?

MAN. No. We can sit here on the steps. If it's all right with you.

WILL. It's all right with me. (*A pause.*) What makes you think there's oil here?

MAN. Well, of course nobody can be dead sure. We both know that. But we've been making tests in this area and it looks as sure as anything can. (*A pause.*) I'm prepared to make you a real good offer for leasing.

WILL. How much?

MAN. Seven-fifty a month.

WILL. Yes sir. (*A pause.*)

MAN. You don't seem very impressed. That's a mighty good price I'm offering.

WILL. Yes sir. You forget. I got faith in this land. I know there's oil here. Your company guarantee to put down a well in six months?

MAN. Within three months.

WILL. Yes sir. (*A pause.*) I tell you what. I got two other men that came out to see me earlier. My wife sent them away. I figure it's only fair if I talk to them before coming to a decision.

MAN. All right. When do you think you'll know?

WILL. Sometime late this afternoon. I'd like not to waste any time.

MAN. All right. I'm not going to try to convince you. I don't have to. You won't get a better offer than mine. Here's my card. Call me at the hotel. I'll be there until six and back at eight.

WILL. Yes sir.

MAN. I follow the shell road until I hit the pavement to get to town?

WILL. That's right.

MAN. Good afternoon to you.

WILL. Good afternoon to you. (*The* MAN *goes off* L. WILL *goes back inside the house.* THELMA DORIS *and* MRS. THORNTON *have remained there during his scene with the oilman.*) He offered me a lease at seven hundred and fifty a month.

THELMA DORIS. Seven hundred and fifty. Why, Daddy, I never heard of anything like it.

WILL. That and a guarantee to have a well down in three months.

THELMA DORIS. Why, Daddy, I think that's wonderful. (*A pause.*)

WILL. Your mother don't think so.

MRS. THORNTON. I didn't say that. (*A pause.*)

WILL. Loula, I know I promised you about the plowing today, but I don't want to close with this man until I talk to those two other fellows. I'll go on in town and see if I can't find them. (*He starts for the door to porch. He pauses and turns back to* LOULA.) Please don't worry. I'll get that plowing done tomorrow no matter what happens. I swear . . .

(*She doesn't answer. He goes on out the front door, and down the steps and out* L.)

THELMA DORIS. Now, Mama. Don't look so unhappy. You have to admit this time it looks good.

MRS. THORNTON. The plowing's not done and tomorrow it could rain and the next day and the next . . .

THELMA DORIS. But doesn't it stand to reason, Mama . . .

MRS. THORNTON. Doesn't what stand to reason?

THELMA DORIS. That they wouldn't be paying seven hundred and fifty a month for a lease unless they were sure?

(MRS. THORNTON *gets up out of her chair.*)

MRS. THORNTON. I know what I'm going to do.

THELMA DORIS. What, Mama?

MRS. THORNTON. I'm gonna shame him. Thelma Doris, let's get in your car. I'm going out and hire me some hands and get this land plowed myself. Then he can lease sixty different ways for all I care.

THELMA DORIS. Mama, I don't see why . . .

MRS. THORNTON. Don't argue with me, Thelma Doris. My mind's made up.

THELMA DORIS. Yes ma'm.

(MRS. THORNTON *goes out the door* U. R. THELMA DORIS *follows. The lights fade. The lights are brought up. It is later the same afternoon. The* THORNTONS' *living room.* THELMA DORIS *is there reading a magazine.* ROY *comes in* L. *and goes up to the gallery to the living room. He is two or three years older than* THELMA DORIS. *He has a nice, pleasant face.* WILL *comes in* L. *He sits on the gallery steps.*)

ROY. Hello, Sister.

THELMA DORIS. Hello, Roy.

ROY. Supper ready?

THELMA DORIS. Yes, it is, but I'm waiting for Mama.

ROY. Where is she?

THELMA DORIS. She's still out in the field.

ROY. What's she doing out there?

THELMA DORIS. She insisted on hiring some hands to get it plowed this afternoon. Did you ride back with Papa?

ROY. Yep. He's out on the gallery. Said he wanted to sit out there by himself and think for a while. He's had an exciting day. Harrison is wild. He's had fifty million different schemes and propositions thrown at him. It sure looks like this is it.

THELMA DORIS. Does it, Roy? I hope so for Papa's sake.

ROY. It sure looks like it. He's walking around like he's in a trance. He started crying, driving out here. He said he just couldn't believe it was happening to him after all these years.

THELMA DORIS. Neither can I. Do you think we'll be real rich?

ROY. Real rich for us.

THELMA DORIS. Millionaires?

ROY. No. Not that much. But we could maybe make half a million.

THELMA DORIS. Is that so?

ROY. H. T. Mavis offered Papa a check for a hundred thousand dollars. Just for the mineral rights alone.

THELMA DORIS. He didn't?!

ROY. I heard him. He walked up to him in the drugstore and made the offer.

THELMA DORIS. What did Papa do?

ROY. You'd 'a' been proud of him. He was just as calm. Asked him not to rush him. He said let him think about it and talk it over with Mama. . . .

THELMA DORIS. What are you going to do if it happens and we're rich?

ROY. I don't know. I was talking to Papa about it driving out here. I'm gonna quit my job at the bank, I know that for sure. There's no future for me there.

THELMA DORIS. I guess not.

ROY. Papa's idea is for me to buy a business.

THELMA DORIS. What kind of business?

ROY. That's the trouble. I can't think of any I want. I guess I never thought it would happen so I never let myself think about having a business of my own. And now it's happened. . . .

THELMA DORIS. It hasn't happened yet, Roy. . . .

ROY. If you'd heard people in town this afternoon, you'd think it had happened. What'll you do?

THELMA DORIS. Quit my job in the courthouse.

ROY. Papa wants you to quit that now.

THELMA DORIS. I know, but Mama doesn't. And Mama's right. I'd like to travel. . . .

ROY. Where to?

THELMA DORIS. Cuba. I'm dying to go to Cuba.

ROY. What for?

THELMA DORIS. Well, I studied Spanish in high school for four years. I'd like to be able to use it some way before I die.

ROY. Can't you use it here? You can talk to the Mexicans.

THELMA DORIS. Oh, I'd feel self-conscious about talking Spanish here. People might think I'm putting on airs. Anyway, I want to get married and it looks like nobody is going to ask me here, so I guess I'll have to travel until I meet someone. (WILL *gets up and starts for the front door.*) That's how Cousin Nadine met her husband. Remember? She went to New York City on that trip and met him.

ROY. Oh, yes.

(WILL *comes in the door to living room.*)

WILL. Hello, Thelma Doris.

THELMA DORIS. Hello, Papa.

WILL. I guess Roy told you about all the excitement.

THELMA DORIS. Yes sir.

WILL. Some people are saying this might turn into one of the biggest fields in the state. It might even be like the old days. You're both too young to remember them like I do. When they first struck oil here, they rushed into the county from all parts of the country. The roustabouts and the roughnecks and the gamblers and the bootleggers and the camp followers. They threw up a town out of nothing in the middle of the prairie. Built it overnight. Every night and every day was like a Saturday. A town made out of boards and tin and tents. And the money came raining down. You couldn't hardly give land away here before that happened. Then all of a sudden a thousand dollars couldn't have bought a lot in the graveyard. And the money that was made was lost before you could turn around. Why, I knew a man, a dirt farmer, that couldn't even buy shoes for his children, got a check for three hundred thousand in one day. He cashed it, called all his children together and walked to every car agency in Harrison. He bought a car for himself and one for his wife and a car for each of his twelve kids. Fourteen cars before sundown. And every one different. A Ford and a Chevrolet and a Studebaker and a Stutz and a Rio and a Hudson and a Packard and a Lincoln and a Cadillac. Let each one pick out what they wanted. Had no garages to keep them in, so they used to park them all out the side of their house under the chinaberry trees. It was quite a sight to ride out there and see them. All them cars lined up under the chinaberry trees. (*A pause.*) Your mama out in the kitchen, Thelma Doris?

THELMA DORIS. No sir. She's still out in the field.

WILL. What's she doing out there?

THELMA DORIS. After you left, she got me to take her to hire some hands to get the plowing done.

WILL. Oh. (MRS. THORNTON *comes in the door* U. R.) Loula, I told you . . .

MRS. THORNTON. I know what you told me. But tomorrow it may rain and the next day and the next . . .

WILL. You didn't get up on the tractor?

MRS. THORNTON. No.

WILL. Where did you plow?

MRS. THORNTON. Over by the creek. We didn't get as much done as I wanted.

ROY. Your work may go to waste, Mama. If this develops into a real field . . .

MRS. THORNTON. And if it don't, then I know we'll eat next winter and pay what's due at the bank to keep this for us to plow and work again next year and the year after and the years after that until we're dead.

WILL. We've got some serious decisions to make, Loula. Once they're made and acted upon I'll . . .

MRS. THORNTON. What's the decisions?

WILL. Three different oil companies have offered me a lease. They are all substantially the same, it appears to me, but I don't feel qualified to act on any of them, and I don't think you will, so my recommendation is that if we decide to lease we call in a lawyer to advise us. . . .

MRS. THORNTON. What else is there to decide upon?

WILL. H. T. Mavis has offered me a check for a hundred thousand dollars for our mineral rights.

MRS. THORNTON. A hundred thousand dollars?

WILL. Yes ma'm.

MRS. THORNTON. My goodness! (*She goes and sits in a chair.*) Would he get the land too? And the house?

WILL. No ma'm. Just the mineral rights.

MRS. THORNTON. I see. (*A pause.*) Did you have a witness to the offer?

WILL. Yes ma'm. Roy and a half a dozen men in the drugstore heard him.

MRS. THORNTON. That's all there'd be to it? He'd give you a check and we'd turn over the mineral rights to him?

WILL. Yes ma'm.

MRS. THORNTON. I'd do it, Will.

WILL. Yes ma'm, but you'd 'a' had me sell this whole thing yesterday for fifty dollars an acre.

MRS. THORNTON. No, I wouldn't have. I just wanted you to get your mind off of oil and on your farming. I said I couldn't understand why you'd stop that when you were offered . . .

WILL. And I said I knew that if H. T. Mavis came around offering me fifty dollars an acre, something was up and I was wasting my time plowing. Because something bigger than plowing was about to happen. . . .

MRS. THORNTON. I know you did, and you were right. Now take this hundred thousand dollars so we can put up this tractor forever if we want to. . . .

WILL. And I say if H. T. Mavis is willing to write out a check for a hundred thousand dollars, something bigger yet is up. And I say if we have any faith at all, any faith or sense or gumption we won't get panicky now, but we will keep on playing in the game until we get everything that is coming to us.

MRS. THORNTON. What's coming to us?

WILL. Maybe as much as half a million.

MRS. THORNTON. Will . . .

WILL. Isn't that so, Roy? Didn't you hear men, well-educated men today saying as much as half a million might be coming to us?

ROY. Yes, I did, Mama. . . .

MRS. THORNTON. I'm not disputing that. I'm not disputing that's what could come to us. But what could come to us and what does come to us is not always the same thing.

WILL. Now, Loula . . .

MRS. THORNTON. Not the same thing at all. How many times have you stood out on that front gallery and looked out over those fields and seen the cotton waist high and covered with blossoms and said it could be a bale and a half an acre. And how many times have we waked in the night at the end of August and heard the rain and the thunder and the wind whipping and tearing that cotton until we're lucky to get three bales out of the whole thing. How many times have you or the children or me gotten what's coming to us? Now let's take this money . . .

WILL. But I have faith in my land. Mavis is taking a chance.

MRS. THORNTON. What kind of chance is he taking? He's rich. If he loses, he loses a hundred thousand dollars. But if we lose, we lose everything. I went out there today and did the work of a man, like I've been helping to do for forty years. But I knew today I was old. And you're old and the years are going fast and we don't even have our land clear. And what will happen to us in another ten years? Live off of Thelma Doris and Roy? I'm scared, Will. I'm scared. I've never stood up to you before, I've seen the years go and our having less and less, and didn't mind because there was still time to believe that next time something might happen to change it all, but there was never a next time. . . .

WILL. Loula . . . Loula . . .

MRS. THORNTON. And I'm scared there's never to be a next time. I'm scared, Will. I'm scared not to take that check.

WILL. All right. Then I'll sell him the land too. And the house. I'll sell the whole thing. I never want to see it again now. Not this house. Not these fields. . . . Is that how you want it?

MRS. THORNTON. That's how I want it. (A pause.)

WILL. Roy, go call Mavis and tell him to get his lawyers to draw up the papers. Tell him I want to sell everything. The house, the land. He can have it for a hundred and twenty-five thousand.

ROY. Yes sir. (He goes out the door U. R. THORNTON puts his head in his hands.)

MRS. THORNTON. I'm sorry, Will. I'm sorry. I hate to take a stand against you this way. You know that.

WILL. I know that. (*A pause.*) Well, it's done.

MRS. THORNTON. Are you hungry?

WILL. Not so much.

MRS. THORNTON. You had no dinner.

WILL. I know.

MRS. THORNTON. I'm hungry. Being outside all afternoon made me hungry. We'd all better try and eat. . . .

THELMA DORIS. I have supper all ready. All I have to do is get it on the table.

MRS. THORNTON. Will you get it, honey?

THELMA DORIS. Yes ma'm.

(*She goes out the door* U. R. MRS. THORNTON *goes to the window* U. L. *and looks out.* ROY *comes in the door* U. R.)

MRS. THORNTON. Did you get him?

ROY. Yes ma'm. (*A pause.*) He says the deal is off.

WILL. Off?

ROY. Yes sir. He says he just finished making a deal with George Weems.

WILL. George Weems?

ROY. Yes sir, and he says that took all his available cash. He said he couldn't afford to put out any more right now.

WILL. George Weems! I don't understand that. I was over to see Mr. George this morning, and he said he was having nothing to do with any of it because he didn't want his land tore up.

ROY. Mr. Mavis said he was sorry. That if you had been prepared to say yes right then, that it would have gone through. But that he thought by your attitude you weren't very interested. And so he went out to talk to George Weems and they made a deal right away.

WILL. All right, Roy. There's no changing it. (*A pause.*) I'm sorry, Loula.

MRS. THORNTON. That's all right, Will.

WILL. I don't understand that about my attitude, do you, Roy?

ROY. No, but that's what he said.

WILL. It's just that I thought I had better talk to you first, Loula. After all, for all I knew . . .

MRS. THORNTON. I know. (*She goes to the chair by the window, and looks out at the fields.*)

WILL. Of course I know someday we'll be glad he said no. I know we'll be laughing at H. T. Mavis and George Weems yet. I'm going to build you the finest house in Harrison, Loula, the first money we get. And then I'm going to buy a car and get us a chauffeur and have him drive us to California while they're getting the house ready for you.

MRS. THORNTON. That will be nice. (*She gets up.*) Let's go eat supper.

WILL. And tomorrow after I see a lawyer about which lease to take, then I'm coming right back here and finish up the plowing.

MRS. THORNTON. All right, Will.

(THELMA DORIS *comes in from the door* U. R.)

THELMA DORIS. Supper's on the table.

ROY. O.K.

THELMA DORIS. What did Mr. Mavis say?

ROY. He said no.

THELMA DORIS. He said no? I don't understand that, I thought . . .

ROY. I'll explain it to you later. Let's not talk about it anymore now. . . .

THELMA DORIS. But I thought . . .

ROY. I'll tell you later. Let's get our supper now.

THELMA DORIS. All right.

(*They turn to go out of the room.* MRS. THORNTON *and* WILL *follow.* LOULA THORNTON *gets halfway across the room. She begins to sway.*)

MRS. THORNTON. Will. Will. Help me.

(WILL *runs to her and takes her arm.*)

WILL. Loula, what is it?

MRS. THORNTON. Help me back to the chair. I'm just suddenly very tired. I guess I tried to do too much today. . . .

WILL. Rest. Rest . . . (*He gets her to a chair.*)

THELMA DORIS. Can I get you anything, Mother?

MRS. THORNTON. No. I just had a sinking spell there for a minute. As long as I sit here I'll be all right.

WILL. Maybe I should call a doctor?

MRS. THORNTON. No. No. I'm feeling fine now. You all go on with your supper.

ROY. Come on, Thelma Doris. I think Mama ought to be quiet.

THELMA DORIS. All right, but, Mama, I hope you learn a lesson from this. At your age you shouldn't be out in the fields all afternoon.

ROY. Come on . . . Thelma Doris.

(ROY *and* THELMA DORIS *go out the door* U. R.)

MRS. THORNTON. Please, you go too, Will.

WILL. No. I'm not hungry anyway. I told you that.

MRS. THORNTON. I was. I was so hungry. And now I've lost my appetite. (*She cries.*)

WILL. Loula, please . . .

MRS. THORNTON. I'm sorry. (*A pause. She dries her eyes.*) Help me up. I think I'd like to go out on the porch.

(WILL *helps her up. He takes her outside on the porch.*)

WILL. Want me to get a chair?

MRS. THORNTON. No. I'll sit on the steps.

(*He helps her down on the steps of the porch.*)

WILL. I swear, I wonder why Mr. George would want to tell me one thing and do another.

MRS. THORNTON. Maybe he didn't know at the time Mavis would offer him so much.

WILL. Maybe. I thought I felt a mosquito. It's early for mosquitoes.

MRS. THORNTON. Certainly is. Is it gonna be clear again tomorrow?

(WILL *gets up and looks at the sky.*)

WILL. Can't tell. There are a few clouds blowing in from the Gulf, it might shower a little during the night, but I think we can go on with the plowing tomorrow. (*A pause.*) How many times have I stood here like this, watching for signs of the weather? Wondering what the weather would do to us. How many times have I stood this way, watched my papa before me, his papa . . .

(*A woman's voice calls offstage from the yard.*)

MAMIE. Yoo-hoo. Cousin Loula. Yoo-hoo . . .

MRS. THORNTON. Yes?

MAMIE. It's Mamie Bledsoe.

MRS. THORNTON. Come in, Mamie.

(MAMIE BLEDSOE *comes in* L. *up to the steps. She is a stout woman in her early fifties. She is expensively dressed.*)

MAMIE. Oh, thank goodness you aren't in the middle of your supper. I was so afraid I was going to interrupt your supper. I've cut out supper, you know, until I get fifteen pounds off of me. Horace says I should cut out bridge parties. He says it's the refreshments that put weight on me. Not supper . . . which is natural to eat, according to Horace. I said maybe so, but I can't cut out bridge parties, and whoever heard of anyone going to a party and refusing the refreshments! Well, I just heard the news. Horace came in and said, "You heard about your Cousin Loula and your Cousin Will?" And I said, "No, what?" . . . He said, "They have oil interest in their land." I said, "Horace, you don't mean it." He said, "Yes, you must not have been out of the house today because that's all people have been talking about." And I said, "Well, I'm gonna ride right out there. She's Mama's fifth cousin and I want her to know just how happy I am." When's it gonna be?

WILL. What, Mamie?

MAMIE. The drilling?

WILL. I don't know exactly. I haven't signed a lease yet. I'm signing that tomorrow. Least I look to. I'm asking that a well be put down in two months.

MAMIE. Well, I don't want to miss that. I'll be here rooting for you. Cousin Will has always said there was oil here. Haven't you, Cousin Will?

WILL. Yes ma'm.

MAMIE. Aren't you just thrilled?

WILL. Yes ma'm.

(MRS. THORNTON *is crying.*)

MRS. THORNTON. Excuse me. (*She gets up and goes into the living room.*)

MAMIE. Why, what on earth is the matter with Cousin Loula?

WILL. She's a little upset, Mamie.

MAMIE. Overcome with happiness, I suppose.

WILL. No ma'm, with disappointment. You see, H. T. Mavis

offered us a hundred thousand dollars for our mineral rights. Loula wanted me to take it, but when I called him back he'd bought Mr. George Weems's interest out and figured he couldn't take on mine.

MAMIE. Well, now, I'm glad. A hundred thousand dollars . . . Why, that's nothing.

WILL. Yes ma'm.

(MRS. THORNTON *comes back out on the porch.*)

MRS. THORNTON. I'm sorry, Mamie. I tired myself out this afternoon.

MAMIE. I know, honey. Cousin Will was telling me all about it. Horace had told me about H. T. Mavis's offer and I had said to Horace earlier I hope they don't take it. I hope they don't. Horace said they'd be fools to.

MRS. THORNTON. Did Horace say that, Mamie?

MAMIE. He certainly did, honey. Those were his very words.

MRS. THORNTON. Well, that does make me feel better if Horace said that.

WILL. Me too. Horace is a mighty shrewd businessman.

MAMIE. Thank you, Cousin Will. I think he's smart. Of course, I wish he could get us some oil wells. But like I tell Horace, I guess that's in the hands of the Lord. We never had but one, you know. It came in dry. It'll be twenty years this March. I'll never forget what it was like out at the field that night waiting for it to come in. It was the most exciting night of my life, I can tell you that. Well, it couldn't happen to a nicer couple. Mama always did say that your luck was gonna change, sweet as you were. I know that time we had to take over one of your farms . . . Which farm was it Mama had to take over?

WILL. The one out on the prairie. . . .

MAMIE. And how come Mama had to take it over . . . I forget!?

WILL. She didn't take it over to be exact, Mamie. I had to sell it to her to raise some cash, to keep my other farms going. I had eight farms then, you know.

MAMIE. That's right.

WILL. I had lost heavily farming potatoes. They had thought you could plant potatoes here then. First year I did fine, but then we had one of those terrible wet years and they rotted in the ground. I lost heavily.

MAMIE. Well, was that how it was? Tom got that farm, you know, when our estate was divided up.

WILL. I know.

MAMIE. Well, anyway. I remember Mama saying then, "Will's luck is going to change someday. If there is any justice in this world . . ."

MRS. THORNTON. I hope so, Mamie. I hope so.

MAMIE. Hope? I know.

WILL. And I know.

MRS. THORNTON. Do you, Will? Do you?

WILL. Yes. I know so. (*He stands up and goes to the edge of the stage.*) I got my sign now. The sign and the plan. The answer to our years of barrenness. Our years of waiting. I got my sign now. The plan has been revealed. It's part of it that H. T. Mavis would tempt us and we would stand still and think what to do, and then the temptation be removed and taken away. My faith was shaken there for a while, Mamie, when that happened. But it's come back now. Strong and clear and firm. There's oil here. We will live to see it brought forth. We will live to use it and profit from it. Loula and myself and the children. (*He goes to his wife.*) I have faith, Loula. I have such faith.

(*He kisses her gently on the forehead as the lights fade. The lights are brought up. It is two months later. Several travel folders are on the table.* MRS. THORNTON *is in the living room. She is by the window*

*rocking and looking out over the fields. It is eight o'clock in the eve-
ning.* THELMA DORIS *and* ROY *come in* L. *and go up the steps to the
gallery and into the living room. They are carrying an empty picnic
basket.*)

ROY. Papa said thank you. It tasted good.

MRS. THORNTON. Did he eat anything?

ROY. He drank his coffee and ate part of a sandwich. There's
quite a crowd out there already from Harrison. Papa asked when
you were coming out.

MRS. THORNTON. What time do they expect to bring the well in?

ROY. They still can't say. Depends on how deep they have to go.
But they're certain to know one way or the other by tonight.

MRS. THORNTON. I hope so. I don't see how any of us can stand
the excitement much longer.

THELMA DORIS. I'm so nervous.

MRS. THORNTON. So am I.

THELMA DORIS. Everybody out there is tense and nervous.

ROY. Except Papa.

THELMA DORIS. That's true. Except Papa. He just stands there
like it was all over and done with and he had a million producing
wells. He talks to people and laughs and jokes. . . .

MRS. THORNTON. Who all's out there?

THELMA DORIS. From Harrison, there's Mr. Mavis and Mrs.
Mavis, of course. And the Williamses and Sedella Newton . . .

MRS. THORNTON. Has Mamie gotten there yet?

THELMA DORIS. Not yet.

MRS. THORNTON. I wonder what's happened to her? I phoned her
today but got no answer.

ROY. Oh, she'll be here. Don't you worry. She follows the bringing in of oil wells like some women do funerals.

THELMA DORIS. I saw her in town last week and she said she was going to New Orleans for a few days, but she'd take a plane home to be sure she made it in time. She asked me to wire her in case it looked like it might come in sooner than we expected.

(*The phone rings offstage.*)

ROY. I'll get it. (*He goes out* U. R. THELMA DORIS *cries.*)

MRS. THORNTON. Now what's the matter with you, Thelma Doris?

THELMA DORIS. It's got to be. It's just got to be. I'm so nervous, Mama. I haven't been able to keep a thing on my stomach for three days.

MRS. THORNTON. Maybe if you went back out there, it would keep you from worrying. I'll come in a little.

THELMA DORIS. I can't go out there. I'm all to pieces now. Being out there makes it ten times worse. Another day of this and I won't have a nerve left in my body. You just don't know what it's like, Mama. The noise and the confusion.

(ROY *comes back in from* U. R.)

ROY. Have you decided what kind of new car you're gonna buy?

MRS. THORNTON. What?

ROY. What kind of new car! (*Laughing.*) That was Don Thompson. He wanted to know if you and Dad would let him drive a car out tomorrow morning for you to look at.

MRS. THORNTON. My goodness! That's the fifth car agency to call today.

ROY. Well, you can look for him at nine o'clock. I think I'll get back out at the field. Are you coming, Thelma Doris?

THELMA DORIS. No. My stomach's upset.

ROY. So's mine, but I'm not going to sit in here. Do you want me to come for you as soon as it looks like they're going to mean business?

MRS. THORNTON. Please, Roy. (*He goes out to porch and off* L.) Why don't we look at your travel folders, Thelma Doris?

THELMA DORIS. Yes ma'm.

MRS. THORNTON. Have you got any on California?

(THELMA DORIS *goes to the table and picks up some travel folders.*)

THELMA DORIS. No ma'm. Just Cuba and Mexico.

MRS. THORNTON. Well, let me see the ones on Mexico. Long as everyone else is dreaming, I might as well too.

THELMA DORIS. The ones on Cuba are prettier.

MRS. THORNTON. I know, but I'm not planning to cross any water at my age. If I take a trip it will have to be done by car.

(THELMA DORIS *thumbs through some travel folders.* MAMIE *comes in* L. *She goes up the steps.*)

THELMA DORIS. Here's one on Mexico City.

MRS. THORNTON. Oh, yes. Let me see. (*She takes the folder and is thumbing through it when* MAMIE *is heard out on the porch calling* "Yoo hoo.") Come on in, Mamie.

(MAMIE *comes in the front door.*)

MAMIE. I got back. I told you I would, Thelma Doris.

THELMA DORIS. Yes ma'm.

MAMIE. What are you all doing, counting your money?

MRS. THORNTON. No ma'm. Looking at travel folders.

MAMIE. I took a plane to Houston so I'd get here in time. Then I hired me a taxi to bring me straight out. Cost me fourteen dollars and eleven cents. The taxi man says, "Why are you going to Harrison in such a hurry? Is there a death in your family?" I said, "No, there's no death. There's an oil well." "Yours?" he said. I said, "No, but in the family. A sweet dear cousin of mine. My fifth." And then I remembered it was twenty years ago tonight that our well came in. Dry. I've often said to Horace, "I can't understand it. I'm a good Christian woman, least I try to be, and why did our well have to come in dry?" Of course you know Horace. He can't understand at all how I feel. He says what do we need a well for? We have plenty. I said, "That's not the point, Horace. Gertrude Barsoty has plenty, too, and she never goes to church and is stuck up and never speaks to people and she has oil wells by the hundreds and all of them producing." I said to Horace, "I don't ask for much, but I do ask for one producing oil well before I die." (*A pause.*) Why aren't you all out at the field?

THELMA DORIS. I can't go. It makes me nervous.

MAMIE. Oh, I've never heard of such a thing. Cousin Loula, you and Thelma Doris come right out there with me. Why, everybody in town is there. They're all asking for you. It's just like election night.

MRS. THORNTON. I'll go if you will, Thelma Doris.

THELMA DORIS. Well, I . . .

MAMIE. Now come on. Why, you'll remember this night forever. I tell you right now I've been watching them bring in wells for twenty-eight years and I've never seen people look more confident. Never.

THELMA DORIS. Are you sure?

MAMIE. Never.

THELMA DORIS. Isn't that funny? I thought they looked worried. That's why I had to come in. You do think . . . ?

MAMIE. I know. I know. I don't think. I'm here to prophesy it's going to be a gusher. A great roaring gusher. You're gonna have your pictures in the paper, you're gonna have barrels of money to spend. And I'm gonna be proud to say that you're my fifth cousin. Now come on.

THELMA DORIS. All right. That perks me up. Come on, Mama.

MRS. THORNTON. Just a minute, let me get my hat.

THELMA DORIS. You don't need any hat. It's very mild out. Now come on.

MRS. THORNTON. All right.

(*They start out the front door as* WILL *comes into the living room from* L. *He seems very tired.*)

MAMIE. Why, Cousin Will.

WILL. Hello, Mamie.

THELMA DORIS. Come on, Mamie.

(*They go out to the porch and offstage* L. WILL *goes to his wife. He takes her in his arms.*)

WILL. Loula, I feel old. I feel so old. I'm scared. . . .

MRS. THORNTON. Now, Will. We've come this far. You've always had such faith.

WILL. I'm tired. I'm so tired.

MRS. THORNTON. I know. I know.

WILL. I want it so for the children and for you. You've earned your rest.

MRS. THORNTON. And you've earned your rest.

WILL. I never meant to squander our land this way. I always thought I'd add to it, and the farms went. One by one. . . . Other men prospered. But I couldn't seem to.

MRS. THORNTON. Now, Will. That's the past. We look ahead.

WILL. I have to sleep, Loula. I have to sleep. I haven't been able to sleep for a week. I didn't want you to know, but I've been tossing and tossing the whole night through.

MRS. THORNTON. I knew. They all thought you were so calm, but I knew. Now you come back to the bedroom and rest.

(*She leads him out* U. R. *as the lights fade. The lights are brought up. It is two hours later.* MRS. THORNTON *comes into the living room*

U. R. *She goes to the chair by the window.* ROY *comes into the yard* L., *up the porch steps and into the living room.*)

ROY. It's all over, Mama.

MRS. THORNTON. Is it? I've been sitting here by the window listening. Mamie said they might cheer. It certainly took them a
long time. Two hours ago . . .

ROY. All they got was salt water.

MRS. THORNTON. Oh, no, Roy. Oh, no.

ROY. Yes ma'm. Where's Papa?

MRS. THORNTON. He's sound asleep. I made him lie down to get
some rest and he fell asleep. (*A pause. She walks around the
room.*) Oh, poor Will. Poor Will. (THELMA DORIS *comes in from
outside* L. *She sees her mother. She starts to cry.*) Now, honey.
That's not going to do a bit of good. Not a bit of good in this
world.

THELMA DORIS. I know it's not. But it's not fair. It's not fair.

ROY. Old man George Weems walked over and said, "Tell Will
he was right. There's no oil here. But tell him he's lucky. He's
through with it. Now I reckon they won't rest until they come
digging around my place."

THELMA DORIS. Where's Papa?

MRS. THORNTON. He's asleep.

ROY. Who's going to tell him?

MRS. THORNTON. I will. What did H. T. Mavis say?

THELMA DORIS. Just shrugged his shoulders and walked away.

(WILL *comes in* U. R.)

WILL. Hello, children.

ROY. Hello, Papa.

(THELMA DORIS *starts to cry again.*)

WILL. What's the matter with Thelma Doris?

MRS. THORNTON. Nothing. It's just nerves. Will . . .

WILL. How long have I been asleep?

MRS. THORNTON. Almost two hours. Will . . .

WILL. Why are you all here? Why aren't you out at the field?

MRS. THORNTON. Will . . . I . . . you see . . .

WILL. That's all right. You don't have to tell me. I know. It came in dry.

THELMA DORIS. I'm sorry, Papa. I'm so sorry. (*She is crying again.*)

WILL. I knew. I knew three hours ago what it was gonna be. That's why I came on inside.

ROY. They can still go deeper. Mamie and a lot of people thought if they . . .

WILL. They went deep enough, I guess. There's no oil here, son. We can just forget all about that. I know when I'm licked. (*A pause.*) I think I better get on back to bed. Are you coming, Loula?

MRS. THORNTON. In a little, Will.

WILL. Good night, children.

THELMA DORIS. Good night, Papa.

(*He goes out.*)

ROY. It's not fair. It's not fair.

THELMA DORIS. It's broken his heart.

MRS. THORNTON. It'll mend. He'll be up in the morning working like he's done for forty years. I'm so glad we have our crop planted. . . .

(*A pause.* THELMA DORIS *goes over to the table and picks up the travel folders.*)

THELMA DORIS. I can forget about these, I guess.

ROY. We can forget about a lot of things.

THELMA DORIS. I guess.

ROY. I'm going to bed. I have to work tomorrow.

THELMA DORIS. So do I. Are you coming, Mama?

MRS. THORNTON. No. I'll sit for a while longer.

ROY. Good night.

MRS. THORNTON. Good night.

THELMA DORIS. Good night, Mama.

(*They go out.* MRS. THORNTON *turns off the light in the room except for a lamp on the table. She goes out on the porch. She stands for a moment looking out into the yard.* WILL *comes out* U. R. *She hears him and turns to him.*)

MRS. THORNTON. Couldn't you sleep?

WILL. (*Comes out front door onto porch.*) No ma'm.

MRS. THORNTON. Well, you'll be tired in a little while. That was a long nap you had. Come sit with me.

WILL. Yes ma'm. Want me to bring some chairs out?

MRS. THORNTON. No. I like to sit on the steps. (*She sits down. He sits beside her.*)

WILL. Children gone to bed?

MRS. THORNTON. Yes. They both have to work tomorrow.

WILL. So do I.

MRS. THORNTON. I know.

WILL. Things got kind of behind today and yesterday. But I'll catch up. (*A pause.*)

MRS. THORNTON. I was thinking about the first time I ever saw this house. I remember when you brought me out in the buggy to have Sunday dinner with your family. I was scared. My, I was scared. I don't think I've ever been so scared since.

WILL. I remember.

MRS. THORNTON. I remember when I came here as a bride.

WILL. I remember that too.

MRS. THORNTON. Forty years go fast.

WILL. Like nothing. Like nothing at all.

MRS. THORNTON. I hope you didn't mind too much, Will.

WILL. No sense in lying to you. It broke my heart at first. But it's been broken before and I guess it'll mend. It always has.

MRS. THORNTON. Of course it has. That's what I told the children.

WILL. And we've got lots to be grateful for. Our health . . . and our children. We certainly have fine children. . . . They never give us trouble. (A pause.) Loula . . .

MRS. THORNTON. Yes, Will?

WILL. Do you know what I was thinking in there?

MRS. THORNTON. What, Will?

WILL. Now I don't want you to get mad at me when I tell you, or to call me a fool . . .

MRS. THORNTON. I won't.

WILL. Now you promise?

MRS. THORNTON. I promise.

WILL. Well . . . I was thinking . . . maybe they were digging in the wrong place. That has happened, you know.

MRS. THORNTON. It has?

WILL. Lots of times. I've known out of a farm of a thousand acres for them only to find oil on ten. You've heard of that.

MRS. THORNTON. That's sure. I've heard of that.

WILL. And I heard H. T. Mavis say he was putting a well down on George Weems's place whether mine came in or not.

MRS. THORNTON. Is that so?

WILL. And H. T. Mavis is a lucky man.

MRS. THORNTON. Yes. He is. He certainly is.

WILL. And if he finds it there, it stands to reason they'll be back here. Because our place is next to Mr. George's. . . . Don't that stand to reason?

MRS. THORNTON. Yes, it does.

WILL. (*He is quite excited now.*) Of course, don't you worry. I'll go on raising my cotton. But it makes me feel so much better knowing there's still a chance. Don't it you?

MRS. THORNTON. Yes, it does.

WILL. Well, I'm glad you feel that way. I was afraid you might think I was foolish. A man has to have his hopes, don't he, Loula? I couldn't live without hoping. And if the time comes when there's a law against hoping, I want them to take me out and shoot me. That's how I feel about it. (*He stands up. He is more like the old* WILL *now as he walks* L. *in the yard.*) Yes sir. I see now how it will work out. For H. T. Mavis is a lucky man. And I'm lucky to be having a place next to the one he owns the mineral rights on. And you know something? It wouldn't surprise me if he weren't here the first thing in the morning to try and buy our rights. Thinking now he can get them for nothing. . . . But I'm gonna be too smart for him. Yes sir. I can see it all now. I was a fool to get discouraged. For a minute. I'll be building you that house in town yet. And we'll be on our way to California in no time. Come on. Walk over to the field with me. I wouldn't want people to think I was a poor sport.

MRS. THORNTON. All right, Will. I'll be glad to.

(*Suddenly he stops. His hurt and anguish seize him again. He almost screams with pain.*)

WILL. Loula. Loula . . .

MRS. THORNTON. What is it, Will? (*She runs to him.*)

WILL. Why does this come to a man? He's led on to believe, to expect . . . and then everything is knocked out of his hands. His hopes are dashed. There is failure again . . . I can't go through it anymore. I can't. It's better not to expect, not to hope. . . . Oh, Loula . . . Loula . . . My heart is broken.

(*She takes him in her arms.*)

MRS. THORNTON. I know, Will . . . I know. (*She is holding him, comforting him as she might a child.*) Cry. Get it all out. It's better to let it come out, then you'll be tired and able to sleep, and in the morning you'll be rested and can get on with the work to be done here. . . .

WILL. Yes'm. But I won't ever hope again, Loula. I can't. There's too much hurt when it doesn't happen. Do you hear that, Loula?

MRS. THORNTON. Yes, I hear you. You think that now. But you won't stop hoping. You can't. And I wouldn't want you any other way. Not any other way in this world.

WILL. Wouldn't you, Loula?

MRS. THORNTON. No. Now come on. . . . Let's go out to that field.

WILL. All right, Loula. All right.

(*She takes his arm. They go walking out of the yard L. as the lights fade.*)

The Death of
the Old Man

The Death of the Old Man and *The Tears of My Sister* first appeared on Gulf Playhouse in July and August of 1953. Foote had been approached by producer Fred Coe to write these two plays with a "camera eye"—that is, the television camera would itself be a character whose voice is heard but who is never seen. For both of the productions Arthur Penn, later to become famous for making *Bonnie and Clyde, Little Big Man* and other films, was the director. According to Foote, his working relationship with Coe and Penn was an exceptionally fruitful one. It obviously gave the writer an excellent opportunity to experiment with point of view and with the mobility of the television camera.

The Death of the Old Man has interesting connections with Foote's previous play, *The Oil Well,* and with *The Trip to Bountiful.* Like these two plays and much of Foote's other work, *The Death of the Old Man* takes place in a fallen world. Its Bountiful is the season of Rosa's birth, the "summer of the honeysuckle," which has long since been "rooted up." As Sealey puts it, "It's everybody for himself now, the women and the men, the brothers against the brothers." The acquisitiveness of *The Oil Well* has polluted Eden with sexual and fraternal discord.

But, as in all Horton Foote's work, the central issues in *The*

Death of the Old Man are personal, not just social. This play is about temptation and hope. The Old Man, Will Mayfield, like the Will (Thornton) of *The Oil Well*, is driven by his "hope"; it is his special word, he says. Thornton's faith was in oil; Mayfield's "faith and its substance" is in caring. He believes that affection will be returned, that love begets love, especially within families. When virtue isn't rewarded, this Will, like the other, is tempted by despair, until Rosa, Cousin Lyd and Sealey recover a sense of family feeling and gain the "peace and contentment" so precious to Foote's characters. Interestingly, though, where Will Thornton needed hope to face the future, Will Mayfield actually has to embrace his despair—to let go of a situation that has grown beyond his control—in order to gain his peace. In these plays Horton Foote is investigating both the power of faith and the tyranny of hope.

The real antagonist in *The Death of the Old Man* is the fear that "kindness has gone from the world, generosity has vanished." And the play's best reassurance in the face of this fear comes from the black man, Sealey. He has the qualities often found in literary representations of black servants who have been with their families for many years—loyalty, perseverance, empathy and intuition. But Sealey also has brought horrible truths to the family: the death of Rosa's boyfriend in World War I, the mother's fatal illness, the father's fall. In the process, like Minna Boyd in *A Young Lady of Property*, Sealey has become the interpreter of the emotional life of the whites; his world is never identical with theirs, but he is an ever-present guardian and teacher. While exemplifying the kindness and generosity so precious to Will Mayfield, Sealey also offers his "white family" the sense of continuity and tradition so precious to Horton Foote.

The Death of the Old Man is a parable about investing "in livin' things." But it is also an interesting experiment in point of view in which past blends with present to form a moving, impressionistic memory play.

The Death of the Old Man was first produced on Gulf Playhouse on July 17, 1953. Among the cast was Mildred Natwick in the role of Cousin Lyd.

The Death of the Old Man

CAST

Will Mayfield (*voice only*)   Rosa Mayfield
Miss Loula Jordan   Tom Mayfield
Sealey   Jack Mayfield
            Cousin Lyd

Place: Harrison, Texas
Time: Early summer, 1952

An old man, THE CAMERA, *opens his eyes slowly. He looks around the bedroom where he has been sleeping. It is the room in a rented house that he has slept in every day of his life for the last thirty years. The room is plain and bare. His bed is white iron. The wallpaper is ivory with small flowers on it. There is a dresser in the room with a washstand and a pitcher of white china. There are three straight chairs and a rocker. He is very sick and there are two people in the room watching over him. These people expect him to die, and he expects to die, and as he is very tired and very old he doesn't care very much one way or the other, except for his daughter* ROSA. *Sitting in the room waiting with him are* MISS LOULA JORDAN, *an old family friend, and a very old black man*, SEALEY. SEALEY *has worked for and with the old man or his family since the old man was born eighty years ago.*

The old man is named WILL MAYFIELD. *It is early in the morning at the beginning of summer.* MISS LOULA *is seated in the rocker fanning herself and thinking.* SEALEY *is dozing in a chair over in the corner of the room.*

THE OLD MAN (THE CAMERA). There's Miss Loula. Where's Rosa? Gettin' some sleep, I hope, I hope. I hope. I hope. My favorite word, hope. Made up my own motto once: "Hope and the world hopes with you, despair and you despair alone." Wish I could talk. I'd remind Rosa of that motto. (*The old black man opens his eyes and tiptoes across the room to take a look at* MR. WILL.) There's Sealey. Bless his heart. Well, he was present in the house the day I was born; I reckon it's fitting he be present the day I depart. (ROSA, *his daughter, comes into the room. She is in her early fifties. There is something virginal and fresh about her face in spite of her age. Virginal and fresh and a little old-fashioned. Her hair is piled high on her head, her dress is plain but very neat, and on her bosom is pinned a sprig of red verbena. Her eyes are red from crying.*) Hello, Rosa. (ROSA *goes over to* LOULA JORDAN. *She sits in a chair beside her. She begins to cry and* MISS LOULA *comforts her.*) I guess it's no good askin' you not to cry, Rosa.

ROSA. It was so sudden, Miss Loula. He had seemed so well and now he's so sick.

THE OLD MAN. Rosa, little Rosa. I'd stay on forever if I could. If it was in my power. (*A pause.* THE OLD MAN [THE CAMERA] *looks closely at* ROSA's *face.*) But it's not in my power, honey. And I'm tired, Rosa. I need a rest, I want to rest. (*A pause.*) I remember so well the summer you were born, Rosa. It was the summer of the honeysuckle. The honeysuckle had taken over our yard and the yards of the whole town. The smell of the flowers followed you everywhere. The town was filled with the smell of the honeysuckle. Strangers getting off the train would remark at the heavy odor. It was the summer of the honeysuckle and the chinaberry and the figs an' the dewberry. (ROSA *has wiped her eyes. She smiles at* MISS LOULA, *thanking her for her comfort, and tiptoes over to the window and looks out.*) That fall when you were four months old there was a storm. The worst I've ever seen. The wind came whippin' an' tearin' in from the Gulf. Trees a hundred years old were torn up by the roots, and the houses were brought down like nothing. You were four months old and Jack was two years and Tom, five. And I held you in my arms and I said to the Lord that if he would spare our house I would watch over you children and protect you and keep you from all harm. And I've tried, Rosa. I've tried. I can't do much about my promise now except to watch and wait and to hope in the kindness of my family and the world.

(ROSA *leaves the window and goes over to* SEALEY.)

ROSA. Sealey, you have been sitting here all night. Don't you think you ought to go now and try and get some sleep?

SEALEY. No ma'm. I don't intend to leave him. I was here when he come into the world and I intend to stay until he leave.

ROSA. But, Sealey, I'll call you if anything should happen.

SEALEY. Don't want to leave, Miss Rosa. Couldn't rest anyhow away from him.

ROSA. All right, Sealey. (*She goes back to* MISS LOULA.)

MISS LOULA. (*Whispering.*) What time are your brothers expected, Rosa?

ROSA. They should be here at any time. I'll be so relieved when they get here.

MISS LOULA. Poor Will. I guess he just wore out.

ROSA. Yes ma'm. I guess so. He walked to work yesterday in the heat. He complained of dizziness and tiredness at breakfast and I begged him not to walk to town, but you know Papa, always so conscientious about his work. . . .

MISS LOULA. I guess he had to be, Rosa.

ROSA. Yes ma'm. He had to be.

MISS LOULA. Well, he's the best man I know of. His home was open to his family always. He raised you and Tom and Jack and his brother's four children and a son of a third cousin. . . . It was a third cousin, wasn't it, Rosa?

ROSA. I believe so, Miss Loula.

MISS LOULA. (*Whispering.*) And as a consequence he is dying not owning his own home . . . leaving nothing to you.

ROSA. He always said, "I believe in investin' my money in livin' things. I believe in helpin' the poor an' the unfortunate. Not in storin' money up in banks." . . .

MISS LOULA. He did. He did. And he lived by what he believed. There was never less than twelve or fourteen at his table. It was always set, day or night. Set for kin and stranger, rich or poor. . . .

ROSA. Yes ma'm. He believed in investin' in livin' things.

MISS LOULA. Where are these livin' things now? Now that they have a chance to repay him for some of that kindness. Where are the nieces and the nephews and the cousins, or even his sons, Rosa? . . .

ROSA. Well, Miss Loula . . .

MISS LOULA. No. They should be here, Rosa. Your brothers should have been here last night. You would have come to them right away, not lettin' twelve hours pass. The brothers are late and the cousins and the nieces and the nephews send their regrets, other responsibilities. Well, I'm writing them all letters tellin' them exactly what I think. (*A pause. Again she whispers.*) Rosa, I hate to be frank. But what in the world is going to become of you? If . . .

(ROSA *turns her head away in pain.*)

ROSA. Don't ask me that, Miss Loula. I almost went crazy last night. Thinking . . . (MISS LOULA *puts her arm around* ROSA. *She comforts her.* ROSA *has covered her face with her hands, then slowly removes her hands from her face.*) I've lost my fear, Miss Loula. Last night I was terrified of hearing the question you've asked, but now that it's been asked I'm no longer afraid. I still can't answer the question, but I'm not afraid.

THE OLD MAN. But I'm afraid, Rosa. I'm afraid. I saw you try to go out into the world, once. I saw you try to work for Mr. Simon at his store, I saw you come home, sick, because of how he talked to you. I look to your brothers . . . now, because it was you insisted I prepare them for the world, rather than yourself. You, that baked cakes and made preserves to sell to help me pay for their education. I look to your brothers and your cousins, because we've shared with them and when they know fully how it is here, they'll share with you, return in full what has been given and then I can die. That is my faith and its substance.

(ROSA *goes over to her father. She stands looking down at him.*)

ROSA. Miss Loula. Sealey. Papa's eyes are open. His eyes are open. Come look. I'm gonna call the doctor and tell him.

(*She starts out of the room.* MISS LOULA *moves toward the bed. They look down at* THE OLD MAN *as the lights fade. The lights are brought up on the bedroom sometime later that day.* SEALEY *is in his chair nodding.*)

THE OLD MAN. Sealey. Sealey. Wake up. Wake up. I'm lonely. I can hear words, Sealey. Sealey, wake up, talk to this lonely old man.

(SEALEY *opens his eyes. He comes over to* MR. WILL's *bedside.*)

SEALEY. I know you can't talk, Mr. Will, so I knows I didn't hear you, but I swear in my sleep I almost thought I heard Mr. Will talkin' to me. I hear lots of things, Mr. Will, in the night, in my sleep. Things from long ago. (*In the distance can be heard a young woman's voice singing: "Good Night, Mr. Elephant," or "Hello, Central, Give Me Heaven," or "I'll Meet You Tonight in Dreamland."*) Like Miss Rosa singin' again like she did when she was a girl, or the day the boys went off to war after all of us worked so hard to get them through school, and we all was cryin' so for worry they wouldn' come back, an' the day they come home an' spent the summer an' went again off to the city to make their fortunes. They didn't make no fortune, did they, Mr. Will? They don't teach you how to do that in college, I guess. An' the world changes, Mr. Will. I know you'd agree with me there.

THE OLD MAN. "Hope, Sealey, and the world hopes with you. Despair . . ."

SEALEY. Oh, yes, it changes. When I was a boy I wouldn't believe how it could change if you'd tried to tell me. The young ladies are fillin' up the courthouse now, typin' and workin' like the men. Aeroplanes in the sky and so many wars I can't keep up with them, Mr. Will. It's everybody for himself now, the women and the men, the brothers against the brothers. I wonder what they would think of Miss Rosa takin' the one thing her mother had to leave her and selling it to give Mr. Jack money the time he went bankrupt to pay his debts and face the world again. Is he gonna remember that now, Mr. Will? I pray he does.

(*The door opens and* TOM *and* JACK *come in with* ROSA.)

ROSA. Sealey. Here are Mr. Tom and Mr. Jack.

(SEALEY *goes up to both of them. He takes their hands.*)

SEALEY. Oh, I'm so glad to see you both. And I know Miss Rosa's relieved.

ROSA. Yes, I'm very relieved, Sealey. Sealey, you take them over to see Papa. I have to go get dinner ready.

SEALEY. Yes ma'm. (*He goes over to* MR. WILL. *The boys follow him.*)

TOM. Hello, Papa.

JACK. Hello, Papa. (JACK *starts to cry and turns away.*)

TOM. Don't, Jack.

JACK. I'm sorry. (*He walks away from his father.*)

TOM. He can't understand what you say to him, can he, Sealey?

SEALEY. Doctor don't think so. Miss Rosa sent for him again when he open his eyes, but he say he can't hear.

TOM. I feel we've failed him, Sealey. He shouldn't have been workin' at his age. Well, Jack and I both have tried. I hope Papa realizes that. It's just that it costs so much to make even ends meet these days. Then when you put your children through college and you finally finish paying off your home, well, then you try to put by a few dollars for your own old age, and then prices have started going up so much . . . But I think Papa knows we meant to do our best, don't you, Sealey?

SEALEY. Yes sir. I'm sure.

(TOM *starts away over to* JACK. SEALEY *starts to follow.*)

THE OLD MAN. Don't leave me, Sealey. Don't leave me. I look in the faces of my boys and I don't know them. You forget the faces of your children seeing them maybe every seven years. We've grown apart, Sealey. They've put on the new faces. The faces of the people movin' into this town. The faces that the grandchildren of my friends are wearin'. . . . I want my boys, Sealey. I want my boys with their old faces. Or maybe I want a life, Sealey . . . a quiet easy life, easy money and easy land and easy crops. There's no ease in the faces of my boys. I'm afraid, Sealey, I'm afraid. I took my boys fishin' an' squirrel huntin' and swimmin' how many summer afternoons ago? I want back the boys I sent away, Sealey. Give me back my boys.

(*In the distance can be heard the voice of the young* ROSA: "Meet Me Tonight in Dreamland.")

SEALEY. I hear Miss Rosa. I hear her just like she was here in this room. An' it was a winter's night an' we were in the parlor an' supper was over an' her mama was playing an' she was singin'. I hear her jus' like . . .

TOM. Did you say somethin', Sealey?

SEALEY. I hear Miss Rosa.

JACK. Is she callin' us?

SEALEY. No sir. She's not callin'. She's singin'. She's singin' like she did when she was a girl and you was young men an' you was thinkin' about college an' the war was off somewhere there away off— (*He goes over to* JACK *and* TOM.)

THE OLD MAN. Don't leave me, Sealey. Don't leave—

SEALEY. I hear Miss Rosa. I hear . . .

TOM. (*Whispering.*) You realize, Jack, Papa doesn't even own this house.

JACK. (*Whispering.*) I know. It's hard to realize it all the years he's lived here. I told Myrtle Dee that this mornin'. "What was he thinkin' of," she said, "not to own his own house?" I would think he would do that much for Rosa.

TOM. Sarah said the same thing. I don't know myself what he was thinkin' of. Papa always made a pretty good salary.

JACK. Well, now, wait a minute. I was thinkin' about that on the train. It seemed like it was a pretty good salary thirty or forty years ago, but I bet Papa never got a raise and do you know what he actually made? Why, I bet he wasn't makin' more than two hundred a month when he took sick. Now you take what Mama's illness alone must have cost him, plus . . .

TOM. I know. I know. 'Course at one time he could have saved on his salary, made investments and had his money work for him now. But he was always strapped feedin' every stray cousin and niece and nephew that nobody else in this family of ours would take any kind of responsibility for, and where are they now when he's dying? Not a one of them showed up.

JACK. I guess they've got their own responsibilities, Tom—

TOM. Well, the seven he raised are going to take some responsibility, I can tell you that. My wife says that every one of them should be asked for a hundred dollars to see Rosa through for a while and I agree. Anything he might have saved to leave Rosa he spent on them.

JACK. Wait a minute, Tom, that would only come to nine hundred dollars if you and I contributed. That would be nice, but what is that going to solve? She doesn't even have this house to call her own. I didn't sleep last night worryin' what was to become of Rosa.

TOM. I know. What can she do? She hasn't been trained for anything. She can't type, she's so timid she tried to work in a store once, you remember, and she almost had a nervous breakdown.

JACK. But she's got to do somethin', Tom. I can't take care of her. Can you?

TOM. No. (*A pause.*) I promised once I would, though. And so did you. It was when the boy she was engaged to was killed in the

First World War and Mama took her on that trip to Kerrville to get over the shock, and one night we were talkin' to Papa and he said he doubted if Rosa would ever marry now, and you and I were sayin' how much she had done for us through the years and that we would never . . . (*He starts to cry.*) Oh, Jack. What's happened? We've all gotten so old and there's just trouble. Trouble. Trouble. All the time. My God, Jack.

JACK. Now come on, Tom. I refuse to feel guilty over it. I'd like to be like Papa and open my home to Rosa and the world, but the times have changed, Tom. People can't live that way anymore. (JACK *puts his hand on his shoulder.* TOM *composes himself.*)

THE OLD MAN. They can't. They can't. Then I've lost. My investment's wasted. Rosa. Rosa. I've led you gently by the hand through the years only to see your heart broken and broken and broken. . . . Let me out of this bed . . . let me out. . . . I'll work again. I'll fill the banks with money. I'll buy houses and land and protect us from the dark days because kindness has gone from the world, generosity has vanished.

(ROSA *comes into the room with an old woman. She is poor and work-worn but there is strength and love and kindness in her being.* ROSA *takes her over to* JACK *and* TOM.)

ROSA. Jack. Tom. You remember your Cousin Lyd.

(*They get up and shake hands.*)

COUSIN LYD. Hello, boys. It's been a long time. It's too bad we have to meet at such an occasion.

(ROSA *takes* COUSIN LYD *over to her father.*)

ROSA. Papa, look who's come. It's Cousin Lyd.

COUSIN LYD. Will. Will Mayfield. There are tears in your eyes. The best man I know of shouldn't be cryin'. Why, there should be such joy rememberin' all the good you've done in this world. (*She looks down at* THE OLD MAN.)

THE OLD MAN. I want to die now, Lyd. I want to die. I hate this world. I hate this world.

COUSIN LYD. All the very great good you've done in this world.
(*She is smiling down at him with love and tenderness as the lights fade.*)

The lights are brought up. It is late afternoon. The twilight can be seen outside the window.

SEALEY *is seated by the bed of* THE OLD MAN. MISS ROSA *comes into the room.*

ROSA. I can relieve you now, Sealey, if you'd like to go for a walk.

SEALEY. Yes ma'm. Maybe I will stretch my legs for a little bit. My old legs get kind of stiff sittin' around.

ROSA. Cousin Lyd has taken over in the kitchen. It seems like old times havin' Cousin Lyd around, doesn't it?

SEALEY. Yes ma'm. Miss Rosa, has you been singin' today?

ROSA. No, Sealey. I haven't sung in so long.

SEALEY. I been hearin' you singin' all day, Miss Rosa, like when you were a girl. I been hearin' your voice all through the house.

ROSA. Have you, Sealey?

(SEALEY *starts out of the room.*)

SEALEY. Miss Rosa . . .

ROSA. Yes, Sealey . . .

THE OLD MAN. Sealey, don't tell her. Don't tell her what you heard her brothers talkin' about. Don't tell her you heard them discussin' her like a bale of cotton or a sack of flour.

SEALEY. Miss Rosa, I have to tell you something. . . .

THE OLD MAN. Sealey. I beg you. I beg you. I beg you. . . .

SEALEY. The doctor say Mr. Will can't talk and he can't hear?

ROSA. Yes.

SEALEY. Well, I know he can't talk, but I know he can hear.

ROSA. How do you know that, Sealey?

SEALEY. Well, when you and Miss Lyd come to look at him and Miss Lyd seed tears in his eyes . . .

ROSA. Yes?

SEALEY. Well, I know where them tears come from. (*A pause.*)

THE OLD MAN. Sealey . . . Sealey . . .

ROSA. Why were they there, Sealey? . . .

(SEALEY *goes over and looks into* THE CAMERA.)

SEALEY. I swear he don't want me to tell you. I swear I can hear him like he talks to me. Maybe I just know what he thinks, like we've been knowin' what each other thinks since we were boys and never, never needed words between us. . . . (*He looks into* THE CAMERA.) Why can't I tell her, Mr. Will? Who is to tell her if I don't? For she has to know. She surely has to know.

THE OLD MAN. Then tell her, Sealey. Then tell her.

(*The young* ROSA *is heard singing far away.*)

SEALEY. Yes sir, I've always been the one to tell her the bad things. You never had the heart, nor her mama. It was always up to Sealey, and I could tell her. Not that it were easy. Not that I didn't love her better than my life, but I loved you too, and I knew what it did to you. I told her about the young man's dyin' way across the ocean over there. I told her her mama couldn't live to see the winter. I told her when you fell in the heat yester-day mornin' . . . and I have to tell her this, Mr. Will.

THE OLD MAN. (*In great pain and anguish.*) Then tell her. Then tell her.

(SEALEY *turns away. He is crying.*)

ROSA. Now, Sealey. Sealey. You've held up so long. You've been so brave. (*She follows* SEALEY.)

THE OLD MAN. The year you were born, Rosa, was the summer of the honeysuckle. The honeysuckle had taken over our yard and the yard of the whole town. It was the summer of the . . . They've rooted up the honeysuckle, child. They've planted the yards with strange flowers. . . .

(SEALEY *has dried his eyes.*)

SEALEY. Miss Rosa, what's to become of us? I heard Mr. Jack and Mr. Tom here in this room and they ain't goin' to see to you, Miss Rosa, like they always promised. Oh, no. They're findin' their excuses. They're gonna desert you, Miss Rosa. And me. I'm an old man and it wouldn't matter to me except it would please me to know I was at least bein' thought about. . . .

ROSA. I'm thinkin' of you, Sealey. Where I go, you go.

SEALEY. Where is that gonna be?

ROSA. I don't know. But I'm not afraid, Sealey. And I don't want you to be.

THE OLD MAN. You might well be afraid, honey. The doors aren't open any longer to the maiden sister and the maiden aunt. You might well be. The cousins and the brothers have shut their doors.

SEALEY. I am afraid, Miss Rosa. Afraid for you. And he's afraid, Miss Rosa. . . . He knows he's gonna die and he's afraid for you.

ROSA. Papa. (*She goes over to* THE CAMERA.) Papa. Are you afraid? Don't be, Papa. Don't be. We've had a lovely life, Papa. We've had so much gentleness and kindness. And the past. Think of the sweetness of the past. The winter evenings and the summer evenings, the talking and the singing and the love and the joy. . . . And don't hold hard feelings against Jack or . . . They have their responsibilities. Sealey and I will make a living. I can bake cakes and preserve for the people. (*She looks into his eyes.*) And I'd do it again, Papa. I'd throw open this home to the world, Papa, and feed it and love it if the world wanted to come in. . . .

(*In the distance can be heard the voice of the young* ROSA.)

SEALEY. I can hear Miss Rosa singing. I can hear Miss Rosa . . . singing . . .

ROSA. And I can still sing, Sealey. I can still sing.

(*There is a knock on the door and* ROSA *goes to answer it.* COUSIN LYD *comes into the room. She and* ROSA *walk over to the bed.*)

COUSIN LYD. How's the patient?

ROSA. Better I think, Cousin Lyd.

COUSIN LYD. 'Course he's better. (*She smiles down at* WILL. *She and* ROSA *start for the chairs.*) It's nice to be cookin' for a family again. I'm alone so much of the time I don't cook much anymore. There's no fun in cooking for yourself. (*A pause.* COUSIN LYD *looks at* ROSA.) Rosa, I've been wanting to talk to you.

ROSA. Yes ma'm.

COUSIN LYD. It's something I was gonna wait for a while to talk about, but I got to thinkin' in the kitchen that you might be worryin'. . . .

ROSA. Yes ma'm.

COUSIN LYD. It's about my store. You know I have to do everything myself. Pump the gasoline, get the bait to sell to the fishermen, but it gives me independence and I wouldn't live any other way. I could never have started my store without your papa, Rosa, he loaned me the money and gave me a life. Wouldn't even take a note. I paid him back the money, but I couldn't ever pay him back for the faith and the courage. Here's what I've been trying to say, Rosa. We're two women alone. Why don't you come and live with me?

ROSA. Why, Cousin Lyd . . .

COUSIN LYD. It's not much I'm offerin'. But it is a home, and a job and a livin'. And there's a place for Sealey. . . .

ROSA. Cousin Lyd, that's very generous of you. . . .

COUSIN LYD. Someday the store will be yours anyway, Rosa. I'd planned it that way. I've put in my will that it's to come to you.

ROSA. Have you, Cousin Lyd?

COUSIN LYD. And you might as well start now learning how to take care of it. And you'd be doing me a favor, a real favor. It's lonesome down there and I'd like some of my own around me. . . .

ROSA. Thank you, Cousin Lyd. I'd be happy to accept.

THE OLD MAN. And I thank you, Lyd. I thank you. I eternally thank you.

(JACK *and* TOM *come into the room.*)

JACK. Hello, Rosa. Hello, Cousin Lyd.

(TOM *nods his head in greeting.*)

TOM. (*Whispering to* ROSA.) How's Papa?

ROSA. No change. The doctor was here earlier.

THE OLD MAN. There is a change now, Rosa. A great, great change.

JACK. We've been walkin' around Harrison.

TOM. It's a lot different than when we lived here.

JACK. It sure is. Regular little city. Awful prosperous looking.

TOM. Of course we haven't seen it in seven years, you know, Jack. I guess Rosa wouldn't notice how it had changed.

JACK. Imagine property is worth quite a bit here now. Too bad Papa didn't buy when it was cheap.

(TOM *gets up and calls* ROSA *to one side of the room.*)

TOM. (*Whispering.*) Rosa. We have to have a talk, you and me and Jack, very soon. I know you're worrying what's to become of you if anything happens to Papa. . . . Now we thought we'd get together a little money . . .

ROSA. Thank you, Tom. But that won't be necessary. I'm going to live with Cousin Lyd. . . . Sealey and I will work with her in the store.

TOM. Oh. When did this come about?

ROSA. She just asked me.

TOM. Oh. I know Jack will be glad to hear. He was worried. . . . (*He goes over to* JACK.) Rosa is going to work with Cousin Lyd.

JACK. (*Forgetting* COUSIN LYD *is in the room.*) But Cousin Lyd lives at the end of nowhere, Rosa. She sells gasoline . . .

COUSIN LYD. And fish bait and fish when I have the strength to go out and catch it. And notions and Cokes and cigarettes and there's very little profit in any of it. But it's fed me for forty years and it'll feed Rosa when I'm gone. Anyway, it's all I have to give.

ROSA. And I accept it. I'm happy to accept it.

TOM. Oh, sure. It's certainly very nice of Cousin Lyd. You'll probably be very happy out there. You always liked quietness, Rosa.

ROSA. Yes. (*A pause.*)

TOM. Rosa, Jack and I are both pretty tired. We thought we might lie down for a while before supper.

ROSA. Why, certainly, go along.

(*They start out of the room.*)

JACK. If there's any change in Papa, you'll call us right away?

ROSA. Certainly.

(*They go out.*)

COUSIN LYD. I have a piano at my house, Rosa. I'll play and maybe you'll sing in the evenings.

ROSA. That will be nice.

COUSIN LYD. I'll go finish gettin' supper ready.

ROSA. Yes ma'm. (COUSIN LYD *starts out.*) And thank you, Cousin Lyd. Thank you again.

COUSIN LYD. That's all right, Rosa. (*She goes.*)

ROSA. Well, we have a home now, Sealey. A home and a life. . . .

SEALEY. Yes'm. I'll like it down on the Gulf. It's so cool at night. We can work in the store and fish and in the evenings, Miss Lyd can play and you can sing. Just like in the old days. . . .

ROSA. Yes . . .

THE OLD MAN. And I can die now, Rosa. I can die. In peace and contentment. Because I know what's gonna happen to you. Maybe it isn't what I dreamed for you in that long ago time, but then that's the way with dreams. And it doesn't matter. I don't know why you're being taken away down at the edge of nowhere selling bait and gasoline, but it doesn't matter as long as you're happy and I can see in your face you're happy . . . and so I'm happy. Thank you, Lyd. . . . Thank you again. . . . Good-bye . . . little Rosa . . . Sealey. . . . (*The voice of the young* ROSA *is heard singing softly and happily in the distance.*) Good-bye. Good-bye. . . . Good-bye. . . .

(*His eyes close as he whispers good-bye and he dies as the lights fade.*)

The Tears of My Sister

The Tears of My Sister is the second of the two "camera eye" plays Horton Foote wrote for producer Fred Coe and director Arthur Penn. As in the previous play, *The Death of the Old Man*, so in *The Tears of My Sister* the main character is represented by the camera. Cecilia's thoughts are heard by the audience, but she is never seen.

In this second play Foote also took the experiment a step further by employing a young, inexperienced narrator. Consequently, *The Tears of My Sister* is one of the earliest dramatic presentations of another motif in the playwright's work: the tension between the innocence of the young and the fallen world of their elders. Writing in the same vein as *The Tears of My Sister*, Foote would soon make his first adaptation for film, the screenplay of novelist Clinton Seeley's *Storm Fear* (1956), the story of a young boy's downward path to adult deception and violence. Six years after that first adaptation would come, of course, Foote's Academy Award–winning screenplay for Harper Lee's *To Kill a Mockingbird*, in which Scout, the young heroine, makes a similar journey.

But *The Tears of My Sister* is more than an exercise in point of view. It is also one of Horton Foote's darkest representations of the lives of women early in this century—and to some extent even to this day. In one of Foote's most telling passages, Cecilia casually explains, in her mother's words, the loneliness felt by females who can't be true to their feelings in the face of male fantasies about women:

> Mama says men understand not a thing about the sorrows of women. She says it just scares them. She says all men want women to be regular doll babies all the time. Happy and good-natured and with no troubles.

In *The Tears of My Sister,* despite all the protests of the Monroe women, marriage is shown as little more than a shortcut to financial security. Without love, Foote asserts, the institution is little more than the business deal that follows the tears of the title.

Once again it is tempting to see these characters as versions of later Foote creations. Though certainly less verbal and open than Laura, Cecilia demonstrates a worshipful interest in and fear for her older, more attractive sister that is similar to Laura Vaughn's reverence for her sister, Elizabeth, in *Courtship,* from *The Orphans' Home Cycle.* Bessie, Cecilia's sister, is a young Carrie Watts (*The Trip to Bountiful*) about to marry a man she doesn't love, or a Helen Crews (*The Midnight Caller*) facing her ex-lover at the window in the middle of the night. Stacey Davis is no less a literary brother of Will Kidder in *Lily Dale,* from *The Orphans' Home Cycle;* like Will, Stacey is an intense and nervous man of money and work. In *The Tears of My Sister,* as in most of these plays, Horton Foote creatively works and reworks his dramatic ground for themes and variations.

Readers familiar with only Foote's screenplays may be surprised to find in a teleplay of the 1950s such a remarkably dark study of women without men. Here the death of the father has "broken" Bessie and Mrs. Monroe. Even Cecilia, the young narrator, is allowed only a few more moments of ignorance before reality descends on her. Most chilling of all are Mrs. Monroe's reassurances that tears before marriage are natural and Miss Sarah's memory of the blood on Patience Anne Weems's shoes, peeking out below her gay red dress. That frightening image summarizes this inverted world where money has more value than love, and women are worshiped rather than understood.

The Tears of My Sister was first produced on Gulf Playhouse on August 14, 1953. Kim Stanley was the voice of Cecilia Monroe, as she was later the voice of the adult Scout in the film To Kill a Mockingbird.

The Tears of My Sister

CAST

Cecilia Monroe (*voice only*)   Bessie Monroe
Mr. Williford   Mrs. Monroe
Miss Sarah Lewis   Stacey Davis
Syd Carr (*voice only*)

Place: Harrison, Texas
Time: Late summer, 1923

The girl, CECILIA (THE CAMERA), *is seated on the front porch of an old Victorian house that has served as a boardinghouse-hotel for many years.*

The porch and the house have recently been painted white. The girl, THE CAMERA, *looks up and down the length of the porch. Green wicker rocking and straight chairs line the porch. There are pots of fern and verbena and geraniums. The porch is surrounded by a railing, and a lattice with roses and coral vines and Virginia creeper growing on it shields it from the direct rays of the sun.*

There is a sign on the wall . . . "Room and Board." It is the late afternoon of a day at the end of summer in the year 1923.

The girl, THE CAMERA, *examines the face of* MR. WILLIFORD, *who is asleep in his chair and snoring ever so gently.* MR. WILLIFORD *is an elderly gentleman very formally attired. His cane rests by his chair.*

CECILIA (THE CAMERA). My gracious! Mr. Williford is snorin' again. There ought to be a law against Mr. Williford's snorin'. His snorin' woke me up five times last night. First time I thought it was thunder and as I'm mortally afraid of hurricanes, I was about to call out to Mama in her room and then I said to myself, "You silly goose, that's just Mr. Williford snorin'." (*A pause.* MR.

WILLIFORD *brushes a fly away from his face.*) Of course, there's good in everything. I wouldn't have heard Bessie cryin' if Mr. Williford hadn't woke me up. . . . Bessie can cry quieter than anybody I ever knew of. Now, me. When I cry, I bawl, but not Bessie. She cries so quiet.

(*An old woman comes hobbling out of the boardinghouse. It is* MISS SARAH LEWIS. *She is also dressed very formally and very coolly. She has bright, alert eyes and a very sharp tongue. She is humming a hymn to herself.*)

CECILIA. Isn't that pitiful? Miss Sarah Lewis thinks she's in church all the time. One minute she thinks she's the choir and the next minute she thinks she's the preacher.

(MISS SARAH *goes to a chair beside* MR. WILLIFORD. *She starts talking to herself.*)

CECILIA. I reckon she thinks she's the preacher now. Oh, well, one thing about livin' in a boardin'house, there is always somethin' interestin' to occupy your thoughts and your attention.

(CECILIA's *sister,* BESSIE, *comes out the door of the boardinghouse. She is older than* CECILIA, *gentle and lovely looking. She stands by the door for a moment framed by the fading sunlight. She carries a ukulele in her hand. She strums the ukulele gently for a moment and then walks over to the edge of the porch and picks a rose off the vine. She smells the rose and then picks another. She is humming a sentimental song to herself.*)

CECILIA. I swear, I think my sister Bessie is the prettiest thing on the face of this earth. Mama agrees with me. But Bessie just laughs when you tell her that.

(BESSIE *smells the other rose and smiles to herself. She looks as if she knew some wonderful secret.*)

CECILIA. I swanny. My sister Bessie laughs at the drop of a hat. She laughed when she failed the sixth grade, she laughed when Mama couldn't afford to buy her a new dress for the dance last winter. Of course, she cried when our cat got poisoned and when Papa died two years ago. Why, she cried then like her heart would break and would never mend in this world. (*A pause.* BESSIE *walks up and down the porch strumming the uke.*) Of course, I cried then and Mama did, goodness knows. But not like Bessie. Bessie cried for six months. She still cries when you mention Papa's name. I don't know why she was cryin' last night though. Nobody mentioned Papa's name to her in the middle of the night, certainly. It's all very mysterious to me anyway. Mama has forbidden me to talk to her about Bessie's cryin' in the night this way or anything until suppertime. Mama says I talk too much. (*She looks at* MR. WILLIFORD *and then at* MISS SARAH.) I wish I could talk to someone about it. There's so much I don't understand. Mama says she puts it all down to happiness. I wish I could go along with that. (BESSIE *puts the uke down. She smells the roses.*) Bessie ought to be happy. Certainly she's engaged to a lovely man and he's so rich you just can't imagine it. So maybe Bessie is cryin' for happiness. I don't know. Now you take me. I've got plenty to cry about if I put my mind to it. I'll be lucky, Mama says, to get any kind of a husband. Much less a rich one. Oh, well.

(BESSIE *has come over to* CECILIA. *She hands her one of the roses.*)

BESSIE. Here's a rose for you, Sissie.

CECILIA. Thank you, Bessie.

(BESSIE *stands smiling at* CECILIA. *She is pinning the rose in her own hair.*)

BESSIE. Does it look all right in my hair this way, Sissie?

CECILIA. Uh huh.

(BESSIE *walks over to* MR. WILLIFORD. *She shakes him gently.*)

CECILIA. Now look at that. Bessie can get by with anything. Wakin' up Mr. Williford or anything. Why, if I tried wakin' him up I bet he'd hit me.

BESSIE. Mr. Williford. You've been asleep for over an hour. You won't rest good tonight if you go on sleepin'.

(MR. WILLIFORD *opens his eyes.*)

MR. WILLIFORD. Oh, hello, Bessie. It's a lovely afternoon, isn't it?

BESSIE. Yes sir.

MR. WILLIFORD. When you get my age, Bessie, there's nothin' left to do but sleep.

BESSIE. Well, you can't sleep all the time. You have to talk to me sometimes.

MR. WILLIFORD. I'm always glad to talk to you, Bessie. I was sayin' to Miss Sarah Lewis the other mornin', you've brought a great deal of happiness to us old folks here at the hotel. Why, I said, "Miss Sarah, what did lonely old people like us do before Bessie moved here?" Didn't I remark that to you, Miss Sarah?

MISS SARAH. Yes sir. And what did I tell you?

MR. WILLIFORD. Miss Sarah said she was prayin' for some happiness to come into our lives and the minute you walked into our house she knew her prayers had been answered.

MISS SARAH. Were, too. She's pretty. But she's not vain. She's sweet, but she's sincere. And she spreads happiness all around her. The man to get Bessie will be a fortunate man. In the words of Proverbs: "Who can find a virtuous woman? for her price is far above rubies. She perceiveth that her merchandise is good. Her candle goeth not out by night."

(BESSIE *turns her head away. She is crying.*)

CECILIA. Look yonder. Bessie is turnin' her head away. I bet Bessie is cryin'. You'd have to look in her eyes to know it. She cries so quiet. Why are you cryin', Bessie? I want to know. It worries me, Bessie. You're my sister and I love you. Why are you cryin'?

MR. WILLIFORD. Miss Bessie, would you favor us with a song?

(BESSIE *wipes her eyes. They don't notice what she is doing.*)

BESSIE. Yes sir.

MR. WILLIFORD. A nice happy one, Bessie.

BESSIE. Yes sir.

(BESSIE *takes up her ukulele. She plays and sings "The Sheik of Araby." She has a sweet, gentle, natural voice.* MR. WILLIFORD *turns to* MISS SARAH *and whispers something in her ear.*)

CECILIA. Mr. Williford doesn't think Bessie ought to marry Stacey. I heard him tellin' Miss Sarah that last week. They didn't know I was listenin'. He said he thought it was a crime she was marryin' a man twenty years older'n she was. He didn't care how rich he was or how poor we were. Well, like Mama says, that's a slanderous thing for Mr. Williford to say. He isn't twenty years older than Bessie. He's only sixteen years older.

(BESSIE *has finished her song. She rests the ukulele in her lap.*)

MR. WILLIFORD. Stacey comin' to see you tonight, Bessie?

BESSIE. Yes sir.

MR. WILLIFORD. When's the weddin'?

BESSIE. Early next month. Soon as the cotton crop is in.

(*She picks up the ukulele again. She begins "The Sheik of Araby" once more, this time only humming the tune as she plays the melody on the ukulele softly and almost wistfully.*)

CECILIA. Well, what's wrong with that, Mr. Williford? Stacey says he couldn' enjoy his honeymoon until after the cotton crop is in. Mama says she can understand that attitude thoroughly. Mama says they're gonna have a lovely honeymoon. They'll go to New Orleans and stay for two weeks at a hotel and be waited on the whole time by bellboys. I'd like to stay in a hotel for two weeks in New Orleans and be waited on by bellboys.

MISS SARAH. Stacey's rich. His papa was rich and his grandpapa was rich and Stacey's richer. (*She turns directly to* BESSIE.) How old are you, honey?

BESSIE. Eighteen.

MISS SARAH. How old is Stacey?

BESSIE. I don't know exactly. Somewhere in his thirties.

CECILIA. Now why do you say a thing like that, Bessie? I don't understand you sometimes. Of course, you know exactly and I know exactly and Miss Sarah knows exactly. Stacey is thirty-four. I heard Miss Sarah ask him the last time he came to call. And like Mama says, What's everybody gettin' so excited about a man bein' thirty-four? Especially if he's rich.

(MRS. MONROE, BESSIE *and* CECILIA's *mother, comes out the screen door. She is in her early forties. She is a pretty woman, but her face has a worried, harried look.*)

MISS SARAH. Mrs. Monroe. How old is Stacey?

MRS. MONROE. He's thirty-four, Miss Sarah. You know that as well as I do.

MISS SARAH. No, honey. I didn't know. . . .

MRS. MONROE. I don't know why you don't know, Miss Sarah. You've asked me every day for the last ten. He's thirty-four. Bessie is eighteen. (BESSIE *gets up out of her chair and walks toward the edge of the porch.*) Bessie . . .

BESSIE. Yes'm.

MRS. MONROE. Where are you going?

BESSIE. For a walk.

MRS. MONROE. Be back in fifteen minutes. Supper's in fifteen minutes.

BESSIE. Yes'm.

(MRS. MONROE *comes over close to* CECILIA. *She sits in a rocking chair.* MR. WILLIFORD *closes his eyes.* MISS SARAH *rocks and hums a hymn to herself.*)

CECILIA. My mama's pretty too, I think. Bessie looks like Mama. Mama says she's broken the last two years. She says havin' to be father and mother to us has broken her. It makes me nervous when she talks like that so I always get her to change the subject. Mama says when Bessie is married she's movin' us back to Houston.

(MRS. MONROE *looks over at* CECILIA.)

MRS. MONROE. I tell you, Cecilia, when Bessie is married I'm takin' the next train to Houston with you. Harrison isn't the same town at all that I remember as a girl. The people are all vicious and spiteful. Did you hear Miss Sarah just then? She knows how old Stacey is and she knows how old Bessie is. (MRS. MONROE *leans her head back in her chair and rocks violently.*)

CECILIA. Mama, Bessie was cryin' last night. I wish you'd listen to me about it because it scares me to wake up and hear my sister cryin'. I've heard her cryin' for many a night and it scares me, Mama. The tears of my sister scare me.

(MRS. MONROE *pauses in her rocking.*)

MRS. MONROE. The idea of every day askin' me how old Stacey is. The old cat. The more I think about it, the madder I get.

CECILIA. Mama, I wish I knew how to tell you so you'd listen to me. I heard Bessie cryin' last night. It isn't like Bessie to cry. It scares me, Mama. It scares me so.

(*A pause. We hear* BESSIE *plunking the ukulele away off in the distance.*)

MRS. MONROE. Have you heard Bessie cryin' anymore at night? Well, don't tell me if you have, because I don't want to hear about it. It's natural for a young girl about to be married to cry at night. She's cryin' out of happiness. A normal girl always has her spell of cryin' before she's married.

CECILIA. You see? That's what she always says. And when I ask her why it's normal, she gets mad. Oh, there's so much I don't understand and when I ask Bessie she just shrugs her shoulders and laughs, and when I ask Mama she just gets mad. Who's to tell me? Oh, there's so much I want to know about. Who's to tell you? Miss Sarah? Mr. Williford? Who's to tell you? Well, I'm not gonna addle my brains with worryin' about it. Life is certainly mysterious. I must say I get one good surprise every day. But this is the first time I've ever heard of people cryin' out of happiness.

(MRS. MONROE *is resting her head back against the rim of the chair.*)

MRS. MONROE. You'll cry someday, honey. You'll cry in the night that way when you're fixin' to get married. You'll cry out of happiness. (MRS. MONROE *rocks gently back and forth.* MISS SARAH *sings her hymn.* MR. WILLIFORD *is snoring again.*) Yes ma'm. You'll cry in the night someday, honey. Then you'll understand why your sister is crying. You'll understand she's cryin' out of sheer happiness.

(BESSIE *has come back on the porch. She sits by her mama. She plays the ukulele softly.*)

MRS. MONROE. Bessie, your sister worries about your cryin' at night. I tell her someday she'll be cryin' in the night. Cryin' out of happiness. Won't she, Bessie?

(BESSIE *doesn't answer. She continues strumming the ukulele. The mother goes back to her rocking. There is music as the lights fade.*)

The lights come up on the front porch of the boardinghouse. It is after supper around nine the same night. MR. WILLIFORD *is there snoring.* MISS SARAH *is seated in her same chair near him. She is again humming to herself. In the distance can be heard music from a Mexican dance. The music is very far away. At the far end of the porch near* CECILIA (THE CAMERA) *is* STACEY DAVIS. *He is thirty-four but looks much older. He is very conservatively dressed and has a driven, worried look about his face. He opens his pocket watch and looks nervously at it. This is a gesture that he repeats all the time he is on the porch.* MRS. MONROE *is seated near* STACEY. *She looks out into the yard anxiously. After a moment she gets up out of her chair and goes to the edge of the porch looking out into the yard.*

CECILIA. Things are humming around here for a change. Stacey called just as we were at supper and said he wanted to marry Bessie right away. Mama told Bessie and she asked to be excused from the table. She told Mama she was going for a walk and would be back a little before eight. She hasn't come back yet.

MRS. MONROE. Excuse me, Stacey. I just think I'll walk to the edge of the walk and see if I can see her comin' down the street.

STACEY. Yes ma'm. (*She starts off the porch.* STACEY *gets up out of the chair nervously. He calls to her.*) Mrs. Monroe.

(MRS. MONROE *pauses anxiously. She goes back to* STACEY.)

MRS. MONROE. Yes, Stacey?

STACEY. I want to get married to Bessie next week. I'm gonna forget all about the cotton crop. I want to definitely get married to Bessie next week.

MRS. MONROE. All right, Stacey. I told you it was fine with me. I'm sure it's fine with Bessie.

STACEY. Did she say it was fine?

MRS. MONROE. I don't really remember what her exact words were.

STACEY. Yes ma'm.

CECILIA. Well, she didn't say it was fine, Mama. She just asked to be excused from the table.

(MRS. MONROE *starts away again. She looks over at* MISS SARAH *and* MR. WILLIFORD. *She comes back to* STACEY. *She whispers in his ear.*)

MRS. MONROE. And if you're worried about those silly rumors concernin' Bessie and Syd Carr, I can tell you right now it's just all mean gossip. Bessie has had a few dates with Syd Carr to go to the picture show and to ride in the afternoons when you were busy out at the farms or at the gin, but she was always home by nine-thirty on her night dates. You said yourself you didn't mind her having a date now and then when you were busy. (*She starts away. She turns back to* STACEY.) But as for Syd Carr goin' to the next county to get a license to marry my daughter, why it's the most ridiculous thing I've ever heard of and the whole story was made up by someone to make trouble.

STACEY. Yes ma'm.

MRS. MONROE. So please don't worry about it, Stacey. Because I'm not worried one bit. Bessie has met a friend and has forgotten the time, that's all that happened.

STACEY. Yes ma'm. (*She starts away again.*) But did you tell her I called and asked you if we could get married next week?

MRS. MONROE. Yes sir. I've told you a hundred times, Stacey, so stop worryin'. I'm not worried. I refuse to worry.

(*This time she goes off the gallery.* STACEY *sits in his chair opening and closing his watch.*)

CECILIA. Mama is worried, though. I can always tell when Mama's worried. Well, I'm a little worried myself. Bessie is usually the promptest thing I know of. She's always down here dressed and waitin' for Stacey fifteen minutes before he comes to call. And here it is nine and there's no sign of her.

MISS SARAH. What time is it, Stacey?

STACEY. Five after nine, Miss Sarah.

MISS SARAH. Any word from Bessie?

STACEY. No ma'm. Her mama just walked to the corner to see if she can see her comin'.

CECILIA. Maybe I ought to tell Stacey about Bessie's cryin'. Maybe he could explain that to me so I could understand. Maybe . . . Oh, I don't know that Stacey would understand at all. Mama says men understand not a thing about the sorrows of women. She says it just scares them. She says all men want women to be regular doll babies all the time. Happy and good-natured and with no troubles.

STACEY. Cecilia, I'm gonna ride around town in my car and see if I can find Bessie. I'm worried.

CECILIA. All right, Stacey.

(*He walks off the porch.*)

MISS SARAH. And he has a right to be worried. I knew a girl once, Patience Anne Weems. Walked off from home one night on her wedding eve and has never been heard of since. That was seventy-two years ago. (*She shakes* MR. WILLIFORD.) Mr. Williford. Bessie was due back at eight o'clock and it's nine o'clock now and she hasn't returned.

MR. WILLIFORD. Is that so?

MISS SARAH. I was rememberin' Patience Anne Weems. You know they've never heard of her. She walked off on the eve of her weddin' . . .

MR. WILLIFORD. Well, this isn't the eve of Bessie's weddin'. She is not to be married for another week.

MISS SARAH. Well, it's almost the eve of her weddin'. You remember hearin' about Patience Anne Weems! Her mama went up to her room to kiss her good night and she was gone.

MR. WILLIFORD. I remember. She came back though. Or some people think it was her. Her sister said it wasn't, but the old colored man that worked for them said it was. He said that Patience Anne had a mole on her right wrist and that this old woman that came back and claimed to be Patience Anne Weems had a mole on her right wrist. But you never could convince her sister. She went to her grave thinkin' her sister walked into the river and was drowned.

CECILIA. Oh, my goodness. I wish they wouldn't talk about things like that. I hope Bessie doesn't go walkin' into any river this time of night. . . . I hope Mama has sense enough to go down there and see. I'd go myself but I'm scared of the river in the daytime much less the night. I'm scared of snakes and the river is just alive with snakes.

(MRS. MONROE *comes back on the porch.*)

MISS SARAH. Any sign of Bessie?

MRS. MONROE. No.

MISS SARAH. I was tellin' Mr. Williford. The whole thing puts me in mind of Patience Anne Weems.

MRS. MONROE. Well, it doesn't put me in mind of Patience Anne Weems at all.

MISS SARAH. Does me. Patience Anne Weems walked off one night and was never heard of since. . . .

MRS. MONROE. I'd like to change the subject if you don't mind.

MISS SARAH. Don't mind at all.

MRS. MONROE. Where's Stacy?

MISS SARAH. Went off in his car to find Bessie. (MRS. MONROE *sits down beside* CECILIA. *In the distance can be heard the music from the Mexican dance.*) The Mexicans are havin' a dance. I love to hear their music. They are the prettiest waltzers in this world. Patience Anne Weems loved to waltz. I was just a little girl but my mama and daddy used to take me to all the dances and let me sit and watch. I can see Patience Anne Weems plain as day, waltzin' and waltzin'. I thought she was the prettiest thing I ever saw. I can see her. I can see her . . . waltzin' and waltzin' . . .

CECILIA. And I hear Bessie cryin'. I hear my sister cryin'. . . . Mama. I'm afraid. I'm afraid. I'm afraid.

MISS SARAH. One night she waltzed until there was blood on her shoes. She wore a red dress and she waltzed and she waltzed and she waltzed! She was the Queen of the Ball . . . the Queen . . .

CECILIA. Mama. I'm afraid. Don't sit there. I'm afraid. I hear my sister and she's cryin' . . . and it's not for happiness, Mama. It's not happiness . . .

(BESSIE *appears on the porch.* MRS. MONROE *goes to her.*)

MRS. MONROE. Bessie. (*She takes her in her arms.*) Honey, where have you been? I was worried. I was so worried.

BESSIE. Mama. Mama. (*She starts to cry. She cries openly and her mother holds her tight.*) Mama, I can't marry Stacey. I can't. I can't! I can't!

MRS. MONROE. Oh, yes you can, honey. We'll have a long talk about it. We'll have a long talk about it.

BESSIE. Mama, I can't marry Stacey. Don't ask me to. I can't! I can't! (*She runs off the porch out into the night.* MRS. MONROE *goes to the edge of the porch calling gently, but firmly.*)

MRS. MONROE. Bessie, come on back now. Come on back. Let's go to my room and talk about it. Bessie. Bessie.

(*She is standing there calling as we dissolve to: A small bedroom in the boardinghouse. It is the room of* BESSIE *and* CECILIA. *We can see a small white iron bed, a dresser and two straight chairs. There is a window at the front of the room and moonlight pours into the window. Voices can be heard mumbling in the next room.*)

CECILIA. Oh, I can't sleep. Mama and Bessie are in Mama's room. They've been talkin' for nearly two hours. (BESSIE *comes out of her mother's room. She looks at* CECILIA's *bed, decides she's asleep and walks across the room to her own bed.* MR. WILLIFORD *can be heard snoring down the hall.*) Now Mr. Williford has started his snorin' again. (THE CAMERA, CECILIA, *sits up in bed and looks over at her sister in her bed.* BESSIE *has her eyes closed.*) Now Bessie's in bed and not cryin' an' that puzzles me, because the way she was cryin' in Mama's room there for a while I thought she'd be cryin' all night. (*We hear crying in the mother's room.*) Now Mama's cryin'. She cries soft like Bessie, but I can hear her and somebody ought to go in to her. (*She gets up out of bed and goes over to* BESSIE's *bed.*) Bessie? Bessie? Are you asleep? Mama's cryin', Bessie. Wake up. Mama's cryin'. And I'm cryin', Bessie, because I'm scared. I'm scared. I'm scared. I'm scared in this old boardinghouse with Mr. Williford snorin' every night and Papa dead and you cryin' and Mama cryin'. . . . (*In the distance and very far away*

we hear a young man's voice calling: "Bessie. Bessie. Bessie.")
What's Syd Carr doin' callin' my sister's name this time of night?

(*The young man's voice is heard again:* "Bessie. Bessie. Bessie." BES-
SIE *runs out of bed. She takes a dressing gown and puts it around her.
She runs to the window. She stands at the window whispering rather
than calling to the young man outside.*)

BESSIE. I'm marryin' Stacey, honey. I'm marryin' him because my
mama and my sister need me and I have to think of my mama
and my sister. . . . And someday you'll be glad and I'll be glad.
Mama says so. And I hope so, honey. I hope so. I hope so.

(MRS. MONROE *comes into the room. . . . She goes to the window and
pulls* BESSIE *back. She screams out the window.*)

MRS. MONROE. Stop callin' my daughter's name. She's not goin'
away with you. I've told you and she's told you. Now get out
of this yard and leave us alone before I call the police. (MRS.
MONROE *leaves the window and turns to* BESSIE. BESSIE *is crying
again. The music from the Mexican dance can be heard.*) All right,
honey, all right. (MRS. MONROE *is crying now too.*) Cry. Get it all
out. It hurts now, but someday you're gonna be glad. We have to
be practical in this world, honey. We have to be practical. Try
not to cry, honey. It upsets your sister to hear you cry. She's too
young to understand.

(BESSIE *dries her eyes. She stays snuggled in her mother's arms. The
music of the dance can be heard.*)

CECILIA. Maybe. But I love my sister, Mama, and I'm sorry for
my sister and I'm sorry for you. (*Her sister and her mother, of
course, don't hear her. They stand listening to the night and the music,
their arms around each other.*) And maybe I don't know why, but
I'm cryin' too, Mama. Cryin' for my sister and cryin' for you.

(*There is silence. We watch the figures of the two women for a moment and there is music as the lights fade.*)

John Turner Davis

Many who have seen Horton Foote's plays have praised the accuracy of his Texas places. This praise is justified, for the authenticity of speech and setting in Foote's work is one of its greatest strengths. But the record of his evolution as an artist shows that he grew in these plays of the 1950s as literal facts and details were made increasingly resonant and expressive. Ironically, his places were best served by his willingness to compromise specific truths in pursuit of more universal and artistic themes.

In *John Turner Davis*, for example, the dryness of the Texas landscape begins to suggest the loneliness and isolation of the characters, and the rain they long for becomes a figure of the love, mercy and grace that makes their lives valuable and worthy. Once again, as in *A Young Lady of Property*, a pecan tree appears as a sign of continuity. An owl's appearance in that tree validates the wisdom of John Turner's commitment to a new family order. Like Beckett's characters in *Waiting for Godot*, these characters wait, seemingly the creatures of careless luck. But the road that ties Hazel to Thurman to John Turner Davis isn't just lucky. The tradition that it represents finally connects the young orphan to others; it's more a matter of grace than mere luck.

Though John Turner Davis, like many of the characters in Foote's later work, is largely unaware of it, his struggle for place and identity begins when he starts shedding illusions about himself and his past. In his dialogue with the Whytes he comes to realize that his aunt and uncle tried to abandon him and to admit that he made up the Sandusters. "Epiphany" is probably too strong a word to describe his transformation, but John Turner, like Horace Robedaux in *The Orphans' Home Cycle* and like Mac Sledge in *Tender Mercies*, slowly comes to face his predicament. As Foote has said of all the major characters in the collection of plays entitled *Harrison, Texas*, John Turner Davis must "do battle with [his] ignorances, fantasies, and insecurities to accept finally, happily or unhappily, the life around [him]."

This emphasis on the individual's essential responsibility for his or her own life overrides what might at first appear a play about social problems. Like *The Dancers* (first produced on television only a few months after *John Turner Davis*) and like *The One-Armed Man* of the 1980s, *John Turner Davis* recognizes class injustices. Early in this play Inez and Hazel are full of righteous pity toward the itinerants. The ladies take a few minutes from their discussion of cut glass to feel sorry for the "poor little thing" John Turner Davis. But it is also true, as Thurman Whyte complains, that he and Hazel are lonely in their childlessness. What could have been a simple "problem play" is absorbed into a play about the essential injustice of the human condition. All, poor and rich alike, have their crosses to bear, and the solutions to social problems which society provides—here, the boys' home where John Turner Davis can learn "a trade"—may take second place to the human solution a family can offer.

Orphans, physical and emotional ones like John Turner Davis, appear often in Horton Foote's Texas landscape. Among them are Mamie Borden's daughter in the early play *Only the Heart* (1943) and Horace Robedaux in *Roots in a Parched Ground* (1977) and the cycle of plays that accompany that story. Eventually the condition becomes epidemic as all Foote's major characters are haunted by a sense of rootlessness and disconnection that, the playwright feels, is part of the modern sensibility. Foote's orphaned men and women crave ties to others, a place to make their own, a sense of identity that brings the peace and contentment we all long for.

John Turner Davis was first produced on Philco Television Playhouse on November 5, 1953, under the direction of Arthur Penn. Fred Coe was producer.

John Turner Davis

CAST

John Turner Davis	Sheriff
Paul	People at the River Camp:
Hazel Whyte	Miss Sarah
Inez	Old Man
Thurman Whyte	Man
Miss Fanny Dee	Woman

Place: Harrison, Texas
Time: 1933

The lights are brought up on the far D. R. *area.* JOHN TURNER
DAVIS, *a boy of twelve, is sitting on the ground taking a rock out
of his shoe. He is dressed in faded, torn overalls and his shoes are
old and worn. He wears no stockings. Offstage* R., PAUL, *a
black man, can be heard calling to his horse.*

PAUL. Hoa. Hoa. (*And then to* JOHN TURNER DAVIS.) Hey, boy.

JOHN TURNER. (*Calling offstage to* PAUL.) Yep?

PAUL. (*Offstage.*) Where are you goin'?

JOHN TURNER. Into Harrison.

PAUL. (*Offstage.*) You want a ride?

JOHN TURNER. Thank you. As soon as I get my shoe tied. (*He
begins to tie his shoe.* PAUL *comes in* D. R.)

PAUL. There are two houses out on this river road. I may have to
stop and deliver ice to one of them, but I'll git you to Harrison
quicker'n you kin walk it. You didn't look like you was in too
much of a hurry, anyways.

JOHN TURNER. I'm in a hurry. I just didn' know the way, so I
couldn' go too fast.

PAUL. Where you comin' from?

JOHN TURNER. The river.

PAUL. Been fishin'?

JOHN TURNER. Nope.

PAUL. I hope you ain't been swimmin'. That river's not safe to swim in. There's whirlpools in that river an' suck holes an' alligators. . . .

JOHN TURNER. I know all about that. I ain't been swimmin'.

PAUL. What were you doin' down there?

JOHN TURNER. I been livin' down there.

PAUL. Oh. Well, let's go.

(*They go out* R. *as the lights fade. The lights are brought up* L. *on the gallery and yard of a house. The gallery is cool and comfortable look-ing, two steps off the ground. At either end there are vines growing and on the gallery are one rocking chair and two straight chairs. A woman in her early forties,* HAZEL, *is there dusting the chairs. She is a plain woman but with a great deal of kindness in her face. After a moment she goes to the steps and looks to either side of the stage.* INEZ, *a woman about her age, calls from offstage* L.)

INEZ. Hazel! What are you doin' standin' out in that sun? (INEZ *comes up to the front gallery steps. She has a parasol over her head.*) You're gonna have a sunstroke, honey.

HAZEL. I just came outside. I'm lookin' to see if the iceman is in sight.

INEZ. Well, I wouldn't put a foot off that porch without somethin' over my head. I let Horace take the car to work this mornin', so I had to walk to town for my mail, and I swear to you I had to stop and rest four times makin' it back home—parasol and all. Oh, I think this sun is gonna burn us all up.

HAZEL. I know.

INEZ. It's just ruinin' the cotton.

HAZEL. I know. Can you sit down for a minute?

INEZ. Just for a minute. I've got to go home and get my dinner on the table.

HAZEL. I'm sorry I can't offer you anything cool to drink, but I'm all out of ice.

INEZ. That's all right. (*A pause.*) I don't see why you live out on this old river road, Hazel. If I could find me a house in Harrison big enough for my family, I'd move so fast!

HAZEL. Well, some people like town and some people don't.

INEZ. But how do you stand it? I'd think you'd get so lonesome. . . .

HAZEL. No ma'm. I was born here, you remember. The river road is home to me. When our house burned and my daddy had to move us into town, I just didn't feel right. I told Thurman when we were courtin' that I wanted one thing understood if I married him; that I didn't want diamonds and I didn't want cars but that the first money we got ahead, I wanted him to build me a house on the river road. (*She looks around the porch.*) It's cooler out here too, you know. At least it is on my front gallery. I'm so grateful for my front gallery. I know I said to Thurman when we were plannin' the house, I didn't care what else I had as long as I had me a cool front gallery, and I must say I have it.

INEZ. It is cool. But lonely. I never sit on my front gallery because there is nothin' to see. What's the use of a gallery if nobody passes by to speak to?

HAZEL. Well, I like it. (*A pause.*) It's gonna change our luck livin' out here. I told Thurman that. I said I haven't had any luck and my papa didn't have, nor no one in my entire family, since our house burned and we moved away from the river road. Move me back there and watch my luck change! . . .

INEZ. Has it changed your luck?

HAZEL. No ma'm, but it will. It will change our luck. I prophesy that Thurman's business is gonna improve and I prophesy that

. . . Well, you just wait and see. All kinds of things are gonna happen to us out here.

INEZ. Do you think there's oil out here?

HAZEL. I don't know about that. But all kinds of things are gonna happen to us out here. You just wait and see. . . . Inez, I got some new cut glass yesterday. Do you want to see it?

INEZ. All right, but I hate to go into your house.

HAZEL. Why?

INEZ. Because it's always so spotless. My kids have just made a shambles out of my house. But what can you do? I've just given up tryin' to have anything nice anymore.

HAZEL. Oh, yonder comes Paul. (*She calls* L.) Paul! Paul! Ice! Fifty pounds!

(PAUL *comes in* L., *carrying the ice. He is followed by* JOHN TURNER DAVIS.)

PAUL. I was about ready to pass you by, Mis' Whyte. I said to myself, I said, surely Mis' Whyte don't need no ice today.

HAZEL. Oh, yes, I do! It goes so in this heat.

PAUL. Heat's burnin' up the cotton. It better rain 'fore the week is out, or there's gonna be no cotton in this county again this year.

INEZ. Oh, don't say that, Paul!

PAUL. I don't have to say it. Just look around you! Cotton is burnin' up, everywhere you look.

INEZ. Whose little boy is that, Paul?

PAUL. I don't know'm. I met him walkin' into town along the river road. He says he belongs to some of them people camped out along the river bank.

INEZ. What's your name, little boy?

JOHN TURNER. John Turner Davis.

(PAUL *disappears around the side of the porch.*)

HAZEL. What's your mama and daddy thinkin' about, lettin' you walk aroun' in this heat with no hat on your head?

JOHN TURNER. I don' have no mama an' daddy.

HAZEL. You don't?

JOHN TURNER. No ma'm. I belong to my Uncle Delbert an' my Aunt Velma. They went off in the truck to try an' find some cotton to chop, day before yesterday. They left me with the Sandusters. They said they'd be back las' night. They didn't show up, an' when I woke up this mornin' the Sandusters was all gone. I didn' know what to do, an' a man down there told me to git into Harrison an' tell the sheriff an' let him git word to my aunt an' uncle.

(PAUL *comes back into the yard.*)

INEZ. Paul, you leave him with me. . . . I'll take him to my house. He'll have a sunstroke ridin' aroun' in this sun.

JOHN TURNER. Oh, no ma'm, I wouldn' have no stroke. I picked cotton in worse sun than this, an' no hat on my haid.

PAUL. Well, come on, boy, if you're comin' with me. My ice is meltin' out in that wagon. You want ice tomorrow, Mis' Whyte?

HAZEL. Tomorrow? This afternoon! I'd like more ice, I know, this afternoon.

PAUL. Yes'm. Come on, boy! (*He goes out of the yard* L. JOHN TURNER *follows after him.*)

INEZ. Poor little thing! I bet he hasn't had a good meal in a month. They live on fish and meal and fatback down at that river camp.

HAZEL. I know; I've seen the way they live down there. Did you ever see the way they have to live?

INEZ. Yes, it's pitiful, isn't it?

HAZEL. Yes, it is. I guess they just follow the cotton crop from place to place.

INEZ. I guess.

HAZEL. Makes you grateful, doesn't it?

INEZ. Yes, it does. . . . Well, let me see your cut glass.

HAZEL. Oh, yes. I'd forgotten all about that.

(*They go inside the house. The lights fade. The lights are brought up* D. R. *This area has now become a section of* THURMAN WHYTE's *store.* MISS FANNY DEE *is sitting on a stool, fanning herself slowly and deliberately.* THURMAN WHYTE *stands beside her. He is a heavyset man in his late forties.*)

MISS FANNY. Business is terrible all over town, Thurman. You can just shoot a cannonball down the streets. All the merchants are standin' at the doors of their stores with their faces down to here! (*She points down to her knees.*) I've never known it so quiet.

THURMAN. Well, they can say what they want to me about the oil and the rice and whatever else they think they've got in this country—when the cotton crop fails, the merchants starve to death.

MISS FANNY. I know.

THURMAN. Well, it can't get any worse; that's for sure.

MISS FANNY. That's for sure!

THURMAN. I laugh and kid Hazel. You know, she always said when we moved back out to the river road our luck was gonna change. Well, we've been there three years now and I've had a crop failure facin' me every year. But she still says our luck is gonna change. And she believes it.

MISS FANNY. I know. (*She wipes her brow in desperation.*) Isn't it hot?

THURMAN. Yes ma'm. But I'll tell you, Miss Fanny, like I tell my wife; talkin' about it never helped.

MISS FANNY. I wasn't talkin' about it. I was just remarkin'. How is Hazel standin' the heat?

THURMAN. Pretty well, it gets quite cool at nights over at our place. (PAUL *comes in* R.) What can I do for you, Paul?

PAUL. I've come to collect for the ice.

THURMAN. All right, Paul.

(PAUL *hands him a bill, and he reaches into his pocket and takes out some money.*)

PAUL. Thank you. . . . Did Mis' Hazel tell you about that little boy that was with me when I took the ice to your house this mornin'?

THURMAN. The one that came from the river?

PAUL. That's right.

THURMAN. Yep. She was tellin' me about it at dinner.

PAUL. I was just talkin' to the sheriff. He tells me he thinks his people has just run off and left him. He said he'd been down to the river askin' the people down there about it, and they all said they thought his folks had run off and left him.

THURMAN. Is that so? Too bad!

PAUL. It sure is. He was a nice little boy.

THURMAN. Hazel said so.

PAUL. Well, 'bye, y'all.

(PAUL *goes out* R. THURMAN *stands there for a minute thinking.*)

THURMAN. Isn't that awful? What gets into people to run off and leave a little boy like that? I don't understand it. Seems like people that don't want or care anything about children have a plenty. And you take a couple like me and Hazel, just eatin' our hearts out for a child—and we have none.

MISS FANNY. I know. There's not much justice in that.

THURMAN. Miss Fanny, I think I'm gonna take a walk to the drugstore.

MISS FANNY. Nobody else is doin' any business, I can tell you that. You can just save yourself a trip.

THURMAN. I'm not goin' to see if anybody else is doin' business, Miss Fanny. I'm goin' to get myself a Coca-Cola. I'll be back in fifteen minutes, in case I'm needed.

MISS FANNY. Which drugstore are you gonna be in?

THURMAN. Thornton's. And, Miss Fanny, will you call Hazel and remind her tonight is my poker night? I won't be home for supper.

MISS FANNY. Yes sir.

(*He goes out* R. *The lights fade. The lights are brought up on the gallery and yard.* HAZEL *is sitting there rocking and fanning herself. It is nearly sundown.* JOHN TURNER DAVIS *comes into the yard from* L.)

JOHN TURNER. Howdy do, ma'm.

(HAZEL *looks up and sees the boy standing there.*)

HAZEL. Yes?

JOHN TURNER. I'm tryin' to find my way back to the river. I got lost. How far is it back to the river?

HAZEL. About a mile. And you're headin' in the wrong direction to find the river. You have to go back that way!

JOHN TURNER. Yes ma'm.

HAZEL. Aren't you the boy that was here this mornin' with the iceman?

JOHN TURNER. Yes ma'm. . . . I guess I'd better git started before dark comes on. I'm liable never to find that old river in the dark. (*He starts out of the yard.*)

HAZEL. Excuse me, boy. What's your name again?

JOHN TURNER. John Turner Davis. (*A pause. He comes up the steps to the porch. He looks around at the porch.*) It's cool on your porch.

HAZEL. Yes, it is. The vines keep it cool. There's a breeze from the Gulf startin', that helps. . . . (*It begins to rain.*) That's rain.

JOHN TURNER. Yes ma'm. (*The rain is falling very hard now.*) That's a good thing. Might give the folks some cotton to pick. I sure hope it's not too late for the cotton crop. We could all stand a good cotton crop. Rich and poor alike. . . .

HAZEL. Did the sheriff get hold of your aunt and uncle for you?

JOHN TURNER. No ma'm, not yet.

HAZEL. That's too bad.

JOHN TURNER. Yes ma'm. But I'm not discouraged.

HAZEL. Won't you sit down until the rain is over?

JOHN TURNER. Yes ma'm. I guess I better wait here until the rain stops, if you don' mind.

HAZEL. Why, no, I'd be so glad to have you. (*He sits down on a chair.*) I love the sound of rain. When I was a little girl, John Turner, I used to always dress up and play lady on the days that it rained. I'd get dresses down that belonged to my mama and my grandma and my great-aunts. I lived in a big old house out here on the river road, with lots of rooms in it—and my mama was a saver. She would save dresses and shoes and petticoats and—I don't know what all.

JOHN TURNER. I never lived in a house longer than a month at a time. I'd like to live in a house someday. (*A pause.*) The sheriff says he don' hold out any hopes of findin' my aunt and uncle. He tried to discourage me about it. He wanted to send me to a home. So I thought to myself: this jail is no place for me. An' I left. Sheriff says he'd bet his last dollar they've run off an' left me. Well, he's wrong.

HAZEL. Why, I'm sure he's wrong.

JOHN TURNER. Anyway, I ain' no orphan, you know. I got a mama an' papa somewhere. I don' know where, but somewhere. I asked Uncle Delbert an' Aunt Velma where, but they never would tell me. I asked them if they were ever gonna tell me. An' they said they would, someday. But that day never came. I don' reckon I'd know my mama an' my papa if I passed them right on the street. 'Course, I don' know if they'd want me now, if I did find them.

HAZEL. Why, of course your mama and papa would want you.

JOHN TURNER. Then why did they give me away in the first place? Aunt Velma says it was because they felt sorry for her. An' that may be. But I still don' think they must have cared much about me. I've seen the poorest kind of people, with enough kids to make you dizzy thinkin' about it, but try to take one of them kids an' they'd fight you until they killed you or you killed them. Aunt Velma fought to keep me once. Uncle Delbert had to go off an' leave us because he had no money to buy gas for the truck, an' he had to hitch himself a ride to get himself a job to make a little money, an' a sheriff come along and says they couldn't raise me right an' he was gonna take me and put me in a home; an' then my aunt took a gun an' said if they touched me she'd kill him or he'd have to kill her; an' he knew she meant it too. He backed right away. (A pause.) That's why I know they haven't left me now. I don't care what that sheriff or fifty sheriffs say—or what the fool people down at the river say. Aunt Velma an' Uncle Delbert are comin' back here to get me.

HAZEL. I'm sure they will, son.

JOHN TURNER. You got a husband?

HAZEL. Yes.

JOHN TURNER. Where's your husband?

HAZEL. He isn't here. He's off playin' poker.

JOHN TURNER. Oh. (A pause.) Where are your children?

HAZEL. We don't have any.

JOHN TURNER. Yes ma'm. (*A pause.*)

HAZEL. The rain's over.

JOHN TURNER. Yes ma'm. But that wasn't no rain; that was a shower. That's worse than havin' the dry spell. That'll just rot what's left of the cotton.

HAZEL. I guess . . . (*He whistles a tune softly to himself.*) That's a pretty little song. What's the name of that song, son?

JOHN TURNER. I don' know, ma'm. It's just a song Uncle Delbert always was whistlin'. They call a song like that a reel song, you know. (*He laughs to himself.*) There's an old lady livin' down at the river bottom an' she thinks it's a mortal sin to sing or to whistle one of them songs. She thinks the only thing fit to sing is a hymn. If anyone starts to sing one of them reel songs around her, she'll pick up a rock and chuck it at you. She hit Uncle Delbert once—right in the back of the head. He cussed until Aunt Velma told him she was gonna hit him in the head with another rock, if he didn't stop. (*A hoot owl is heard in the distance.*) Listen to that old hoot owl! Don' ever kill a hoot owl! That's the wuss kind of luck there is. That's wuss than crossin' ten black cats.

HAZEL. John Turner . . .

JOHN TURNER. Yes ma'm.

HAZEL. When was the last time you ate today?

JOHN TURNER. Noontime. Sheriff fed me.

HAZEL. Aren't you hungry?

JOHN TURNER. Well, I'm pretty hungry. . . .

HAZEL. Why don't you let me fix you a sandwich, and get you a glass of buttermilk?

JOHN TURNER. Well, that would be mighty nice—but I wouldn' care to put you to any trouble.

HAZEL. Wouldn't be puttin' me to a bit of trouble.

JOHN TURNER. Yes ma'm.

HAZEL. You wait here. I'll bring it out to you.

JOHN TURNER. Yes ma'm.

(*She goes.* JOHN TURNER *sits on the steps, whistling his song to himself as the lights fade. The lights are brought up again on the yard and gallery of the* WHYTE *house. The stage is empty. Offstage* L. *we hear* PAUL *call:*)

PAUL. Ice. Ice!

(JOHN TURNER *comes running out the door of the house. He stands on the gallery looking out into the yard.* HAZEL *calls from in the house:*)

HAZEL. John Turner, tell Paul I want fifty pounds this morning.

JOHN TURNER. (*Calling back.*) Yes ma'm. (PAUL *comes into the yard from* L.) Mis' Hazel says she wants fifty pounds, please.

(PAUL *comes up to him on the gallery.*)

PAUL. Ain't you the little boy that I brung into town yestidy?

JOHN TURNER. That's right.

PAUL. What's happened to you?

JOHN TURNER. Nothin'. I just had me a bath an' got my hair slicked down with some of Mr. Thurman's hair oil. I'm livin' here with Mis' Hazel an' Mr. Thurman until my aunt an' uncle come an' git me.

PAUL. How're they gonna find you, sittin' here on Mis' Whyte's front gallery—when they left you at the river?

JOHN TURNER. Well, I worried about that some. But Mis' Hazel figured that out. She called the sheriff an' got him to go down to the river and tell everybody down there where I could be found, when my aunt an' uncle come for me. I been sittin' here lookin' for them up an' down the road. I got it all figured out. They're comin' today. Today is the fourth day. Once before they went off an' stayed four days. Their ole truck broke down, an' it took

Uncle Delbert that long to earn the money to git it fixed up. You can hear that ole truck a mile away—chokin' an' sputterin'. . . . I'm gonna hear it, an' then I'm gonna jump off this porch an' run down the road to meet them.

PAUL. Well, I hope you're right. (HAZEL *comes out of the house onto the gallery.*) Mornin', Miss Hazel.

HAZEL. Mornin', Paul.

PAUL. I'll get your ice right away.

HAZEL. Thank you. And just go in the back porch. I've made plenty of room for it in the icebox.

PAUL. Yes ma'm. (*He goes out of the yard* L.)

HAZEL. Well, John Turner, what have you been doin'? Countin' your money?

JOHN TURNER. (*Laughs.*) No ma'm. I've been sittin' here waitin' for my folks to come up the road. Won't they be surprised when I tell them what's happened to me! You do think the sheriff went down to the river an' told them people?

HAZEL. Yes, I do.

JOHN TURNER. Yes ma'm. I just would hate for anything to happen wrong. I woke up last night an' I thought: what if they come in during the night an' saw I wasn' there an' went off again? It gave me the cold creeps thinkin' about that. I almost got up out of bed an' went on down there. Then I was afraid you an' Mr. Thurman would worry about me. I just don't know what to do. (*He jumps up.*) Is that a truck?

HAZEL. I didn't hear anything.

JOHN TURNER. I guess it wasn' nothin'. I been hearin' trucks all mornin'.

HAZEL. Now you're gonna wear yourself out, waitin' this way. You've been sittin' here three hours. They may come today and they may not, but sittin' here and waitin' like this won't help a bit.

JOHN TURNER. Yes ma'm. But I know they're comin' today. Today is the fourth day, an' you see before . . .

HAZEL. And if they come, they're gonna find you. The sheriff has taken care of that. Now why don't we walk downtown and get some new clothes for you, and get your hair cut? . . .

JOHN TURNER. Thank you, ma'm. But I just as soon stay here, if it's all the same with you.

HAZEL. It's fine with me, if that's what you want to do.

(PAUL *comes back into the yard.*)

PAUL. Want to ride up the road on the wagon with me for a piece?

JOHN TURNER. No, thank you. I'm gonna sit right here an' wait.

PAUL. Well, good luck.

(*He goes on out* L. JOHN TURNER *sits on the steps looking up and down as the lights fade. The lights are brought up* D. R. *This area has now become a section of the* SHERIFF's *office. The* SHERIFF *is seated there reading a paper.* THURMAN *comes in* R.)

THURMAN. Sheriff . . .

SHERIFF. Hello, Thurman.

THURMAN. Sheriff, have you heard any word about that little boy's folks?

SHERIFF. No. Now I told you, Thurman, I'd call you.

THURMAN. I know, but—Hazel is wartin' me to death about it.

SHERIFF. I'm sorry, Thurman. There's nothin' more I can do. I've gotten in touch with all the officers from here to Lou'siana and down to the Valley. Now I think they've run off from the boy. . . .

THURMAN. Yes sir. But you understand he doesn't think that. Hazel says . . .

SHERIFF. And I can't help about what he thinks. I told him right here yestidy—but he wouldn't listen to me, and left.

THURMAN. Yes sir. But if you're right, what's to become of him?

SHERIFF. Well, there are homes for boys we can get him into. I know a good one out in West Texas. They turn out fine boys out there.

THURMAN. Yes sir.

SHERIFF. Would you like me to talk to him again?

THURMAN. No sir, I'll talk to him. Or Hazel will. You understand, he's a nice boy.

SHERIFF. I understand that. But this happens all the time, you know, especially when times git hard and people have trouble makin' ends meet. They just go off and leave their kids. . . .

THURMAN. I see. Then you don't hold out any hope at all?

SHERIFF. I'd say one in a thousand.

THURMAN. Then there still is hope?

SHERIFF. I said one in a thousand. Now if you can call that hope, you're welcome to it.

THURMAN. Yes sir. Hazel says he's been sittin' on the gallery all day just lookin' up and down the road—waitin' . . .

SHERIFF. Well, I'd be glad to talk to him again.

THURMAN. No. We'll talk to him.

(THURMAN *goes out* R. *as the lights fade. The lights are brought up on the* WHYTE *gallery and yard. It is twilight.* JOHN TURNER *is still sitting on the steps.* HAZEL *comes out the front door. She sits beside him.*)

HAZEL. It's quiet out here, isn't it?

JOHN TURNER. Yes ma'm.

HAZEL. My neighbor down the road can't stand it out here because of the quiet. But I like it that way.

JOHN TURNER. Yes ma'm. (*A pause.*)

HAZEL. Soon be time for Mr. Thurman to be home.

JOHN TURNER. What time is it?

HAZEL. About six. He's always home by six-fifteen, unless he stays in town for something.

JOHN TURNER. Yes ma'm. . . . Ole sun is about to set. When I used to be ridin' the highways with my aunt an' uncle, we'd race the sunset sometimes. We always would camp out at night, an' Uncle Delbert liked to settle down before dark. He said he could tell more about the ground we was gonna sleep on if he looked it over before the sun was down. . . . Aunt Velma says she looks forward, someday, to stay in one place, sun rise an' sun set, winter an' summer for the rest of time. . . . Uncle Delbert said he didn' know when that day was gonna be. Because she was like him, an' if you tried to tie the two of them to one place for more than two weeks they both was champin' at the bit. . . . Aunt Velma said, well, she was gettin' less an' less like that as time went by. . . . Well, I hate to admit it, but it looks like they're not comin' today. I guess they're gonna set a new record. I guess they're gonna stay away this time for five days. I know they're worryin' about me. I'm glad they don' know the Sandusters have gone off an' left me all alone. They'd plum die. . . . I'm gonna get up at six o'clock tomorrow mornin'. I'm gonna dress, an' I'm gonna be sittin' here. . . . I know what they've been doin': sittin' by the side of some old road. You see, that old truck broke down, an' it took money to haul it into town and get it fixed, an' Uncle Delbert he had to go someplace, maybe walk ten or twelve miles to git the work to earn the money to git the truck fixed or . . . (A pause.) Oh, I'm just whistlin' in the dark. It's got me worried. I don' know what could have happened to 'em.

(THURMAN comes into the yard from L. with a package.)

THURMAN. Hey!

HAZEL. Hello, honey. (They kiss.)

THURMAN. How are you, John Turner?

JOHN TURNER. Pretty fair.

THURMAN. I brought you some clothes.

JOHN TURNER. Yes sir. Thank you. But you shouldn' have bothered.

THURMAN. It was no bother. Why don't you go in and try them on and see how they fit?

JOHN TURNER. Yes sir. Thank you. (*He takes package and goes into the house.*)

THURMAN. I think I got him the right size. I got him a set of clothes for Sunday and a set for every day.

HAZEL. That was nice. I tried to get him downtown. I wanted to get his hair cut, but he wouldn't budge off this porch. He's been sittin' right here lookin' up and down that road since seven this mornin'. Did you talk to the sheriff?

THURMAN. Yes. He says there's one chance in a thousand they'd turn up.

HAZEL. But did you tell him that the boy's convinced they're coming back?

THURMAN. I told him.

HAZEL. What did he say about that?

THURMAN. He said he'd bet anything he had that they didn't turn up. He says he'd be glad to come over here and talk to the boy again. He says the boy has to understand they won't come back.

HAZEL. Is he gonna come talk to him?

THURMAN. No, I said you or me could tell him.

HAZEL. But he just said . . .

(JOHN TURNER *comes out dressed in new overalls. He seems a little awkward and shy.*)

THURMAN. Come on out here, boy, and let us have a look at you. (*He comes up to them.*) Well, that's a pretty good fit, if I do say so myself. Do they feel comfortable?

JOHN TURNER. Yes sir.

THURMAN. Turn all the way around. (*The boy does so.*) How does it look to you, Hazel?

HAZEL. It looks just fine. Are they good and sturdy?

THURMAN. Yes, the best thing I had in the store. Do you like them, boy?

JOHN TURNER. Yes, I do.

(HAZEL *starts for the house.*)

HAZEL. I think I better get supper started. (*She starts through the door.* JOHN TURNER *calls to her:*)

JOHN TURNER. Mis' Hazel. I'm gettin' worried. I'm gettin' awful worried. I don' know what could have happened to my folks. If you all don' mind, I think I'd feel better if I slipped down to the river, an' just spoke to somebody down there myself. You see, I know the sheriff talked to people down there, but I'd feel better if I spoke to them myself. People can be funny an' they may not remember . . .

HAZEL. John Turner, I'm sure . . .

JOHN TURNER. I just gotta go down there. I didn't sleep all last night for fear they would drive up at night an' look around an' not see me an' turn around an' leave again.

HAZEL. Why would they do that?

JOHN TURNER. I don' know, but I gotta go down there. I gotta talk to people myself.

HAZEL. Well, all right.

JOHN TURNER. An' I gotta wait on, down there. I gotta be there when they come. It was nice of you to have me here, but I can't enjoy myself now for worryin' about them missin' me some way. (*A pause.*) I'm sorry I put you to all the trouble about the clothes, but I'll take 'em off now. . . .

HAZEL. You can have the clothes, boy. We meant for you to have them.

JOHN TURNER. Yes ma'm. But I'd feel better if I didn't take 'em. My aunt an' uncle might not like it. I'll just git in my own clothes, if you don' mind. . . .

THURMAN. John Turner!

JOHN TURNER. Yes sir?

THURMAN. Sit here beside me!

JOHN TURNER. Yes sir.

THURMAN. Well, I don't know how to tell you this, boy—but I've had another long talk with the sheriff—and he tells me . . .

JOHN TURNER. Yes sir.

THURMAN. . . . that he doesn't look for your aunt and uncle back.

JOHN TURNER. Yes sir.

THURMAN. Now I know how you must feel; you're not gonna be satisfied with his opinion or anyone else's . . .

JOHN TURNER. No sir.

THURMAN. . . . so why don't you let me take you to the river, and we can talk to the folks down there, and you can satisfy your-self about whether they've come or not, and whether they'll be told the proper things when they do come, and then I can bring you on back here to wait.

JOHN TURNER. No sir.

THURMAN. But, boy . . .

JOHN TURNER. No sir. Because I know what'll happen—if it ain' already happened. It come to me just in there, while I was puttin' my clothes on, an' it's scarin' me nearly out of my mind. They're gonna come back, an' hear about me, an' drive by in the night, an' see what a nice place you have, an' figure you all will take good care of me, maybe, an' then ride off again without me.

HAZEL. Why would they do a thing like that, John Turner?

JOHN TURNER. I don' know why. I don' know why. . . . Because they're afraid they can't git enough to feed me. They're afraid . . . (*A pause.*) I'm sorry now I ever come into town. I wouldn' have come at all, but I got hungry. An' I made it all up about the Sandusters. There's no Sandusters down there. I told you a lie, an' the sheriff a lie. My aunt and uncle slipped off from me, like they done three times before when times was hard an' they didn' have no money to buy food. But always before, their consciences got to hurtin' them so they'd turn aroun' an' come back for me. I kep' thinkin' they would this time. I kep' thinkin' . . .

HAZEL. Did they tell you that's what they were gonna do?

JOHN TURNER. Yes ma'm. They always git to talkin' that way when times are hard an' they don' have much to eat. They say they're gonna put me in a home, where I can git good food an' clothes; an' then I get scared an' slip away in the brush until they git over feelin' that way; an' most times they git over it by mornin', an' this is one of the times they didn'. I heard the truck leavin' from out in the brush, an' I run after them, hollerin' for them not to leave me, but they wouldn' stop. I heard Aunt Velma cryin', but they wouldn' stop, an' I couldn' catch them. (*He is crying now.* HAZEL *holds him close to her.*)

HAZEL. John Turner. John Turner. They'll come tomorrow. You said yourself they always come back. They'll come tomorrow. Maybe even tonight. Maybe tonight while we're havin' our supper there'll be a knock on the door and we'll go to the door and they'll be standin' there. . . .

JOHN TURNER. No ma'm. I just can't take the chance. I'm scared. I've gotta go on back down there. I should've thought of this last night.

HAZEL. John Turner . . .

JOHN TURNER. I thank you both for all your kindness, but I gotta go.

HAZEL. John Turner . . .

THURMAN. Hazel, the boy knows what he has to do.

JOHN TURNER. I'll go in an' take off the clothes now.

THURMAN. You don't have to do that, boy. We want you to have them. It would make us feel bad if you didn't take them.

JOHN TURNER. Yes sir.

THURMAN. Please take them!

JOHN TURNER. All right. Thank you. (*A pause. They look uncomfortably at each other.*) I guess I better git started if I'm goin'.

HAZEL. Can't you just have supper first?

JOHN TURNER. No ma'm. I'll just go on now.

THURMAN. Let me drive you in my car.

JOHN TURNER. I'd rather walk, if you don' mind.

THURMAN. All right.

(JOHN TURNER *goes to* HAZEL; *he holds out his hand.*)

JOHN TURNER. I sure do thank you for your kindness.

HAZEL. That's all right.

(*He turns to* THURMAN.)

JOHN TURNER. And thank you for your kindness.

THURMAN. That's all right, boy.

(JOHN TURNER *turns and goes down the steps.* THURMAN *and* HAZEL *stand watching him go offstage* L. *After a moment,* HAZEL *stands waving in the distance. She calls:*)

HAZEL. Good-bye, John Turner! Good-bye! (*He doesn't hear her. She and* THURMAN *sit down on the steps together.*) Was it hot in town?

THURMAN. Yes, it was.

HAZEL. Cool out here!

THURMAN. Yes, it is. (THURMAN *stands up and looks off into the distance.*) He's out of sight now. He's clean out of sight now.

HAZEL. Are you ready for your supper?

THURMAN. No, I'll wait a little while. (*He sits down again. They look out into the yard.*)

HAZEL. Really, we have a lot to be thankful for, Thurman, when you come to think of it. We own our own home, and we have our car, and your business isn't makin' us rich, but we get along. . . .

THURMAN. I know.

HAZEL. And we have a happy marriage, and we should be thankful for that. . . .

THURMAN. I'm thankful for it. I wouldn't trade places with any man in this world.

HAZEL. I wouldn't, either. (*He takes her hand.*) I pray, for his sake, they're there. I pray—I pray—I pray.

THURMAN. I know.

(*They sit in silence as the lights fade. The lights are brought up again on the front gallery. The stage is empty. It is later that night.* HAZEL *comes out of the house. She has on her dressing gown. She looks up and down the yard. After a moment,* THURMAN *comes out of the house; he has his robe on.*)

THURMAN. What are you doin' up, Hazel?

HAZEL. I just couldn't sleep.

THURMAN. I couldn't either.

HAZEL. I thought you were asleep.

THURMAN. No. I've been tryin' to fall asleep, but I couldn't. I heard you get out of bed, and I almost called to you—and then I heard you come out here. (*He looks up at the sky.*) If I know anything about clouds it's gonna rain hard before this night is through.

HAZEL. It wouldn't surprise me at all. I've known all along we were gonna make a cotton crop.

(*The hoot owl is heard.*)

THURMAN. Listen to that old owl! Looks like we've got a permanent visitor.

HAZEL. I know. He appears about sundown and stays the night.

THURMAN. You mean he wakes up then. He's probably been here all day too, sleepin' up in that old pecan tree.

HAZEL. I hadn't thought of that. (*A pause.*) I heard it was bad luck to kill one of those. Did you ever hear that?

THURMAN. Yes, I have.

HAZEL. John Turner told me that last night.

THURMAN. I guess he's been at the river long ago.

HAZEL. Oh, long ago! I hope he feels more easy in his mind now.

THURMAN. I hope. . . . It looks like rain and it smells like rain.

HAZEL. Yes, it does.

(*They sit in silence for a moment, then* THURMAN *gets up.*)

THURMAN. Hazel, I can't sleep until I find out what's happened to that boy. I'm goin' on down there and see how he's made out.

HAZEL. I wish you would. I'd certainly feel better.

THURMAN. I'll get my clothes on. Do you want to come?

HAZEL. No, I'll stay here.

THURMAN. All right.

(*He goes into the house. The lights fade. The lights are brought up* D. R. *A camp by the river. Four or five ragged and hungry people are sitting by a fire, staring at the flames. An old woman,* MISS SARAH, *is there quietly singing a hymn to herself. An* OLD MAN *is near her, chewing a twig.*)

OLD MAN. How many hymns do you know, Miss Sarah?

MISS SARAH. More'n I could count, or you could count, or any known man could count.

OLD MAN. I reckon.

(*She goes back to singing.* THURMAN *comes up to the group from* R. *He goes over to the* OLD MAN.)

THURMAN. Excuse me.

OLD MAN. Shh! Miss Sarah is singin' us a hymn.

THURMAN. I'm sorry. (*He looks around the group for someone else to talk to. He goes over to a* MAN *at the edge of the group.*) Excuse me.

MAN. Uh huh!

THURMAN. I'm tryin' to locate a little boy, John Turner Davis is his name. He was livin' here with his aunt and uncle, and they went off and left him. . . .

MAN. They come back, though.

THURMAN. When?

MAN. Last night about sundown. They asked about him, and we told them what the sheriff said, and they got in their truck and went off, and they come back in about an hour and put up a tent. When I got up at daybreak they had gone off again. Then about two hours ago the boy come here lookin' for them. I told him they'd come and gone. He didn't say nothin'. He just turned around and went off. My wife says she thought he was cryin', but it was gettin' dark by then and I couldn't see.

THURMAN. You don't know which way he went?

MAN. No sir. (*He turns to* WOMAN *by him.*) Do you know which way that little boy went?

WOMAN. He went back up the road. A man stopped him and asked him why he was cryin', an' he said, "For no reason"—and just kept a-goin'. Then I went after him and hollered and said wouldn' he like to share our supper with us. But he said he wasn't hongry—and kept on.

THURMAN. He went down that road?

WOMAN. Yes sir.

THURMAN. Thank you. (*He goes* R. *The old woman continues singing. The lights fade. They are brought up on the* WHYTE *yard and gallery.* HAZEL *is still there. She looks anxiously out into the yard.* THURMAN *comes in from* D. L.) I got there too late.

HAZEL. Too late?

THURMAN. Yes, he'd gone. He was right. His folks came yesterday about sundown, and they were told where he was, and they must have come by here and thought we were gonna keep him, and they went off again without him; and when he got to the river he was told that, and they say when he heard that he just went off back down the road. I went up and down every road leadin' to the river, drivin' my car slow as I could, callin' his name. . . . But he wouldn't answer if he heard me. (*A pause.*) Did you ever ask him to stay on here?

HAZEL. No, I didn't think we had the right to.

THURMAN. I guess we didn't. . . . Oh, honey, we don't have no luck. We don't have no luck at all.

HAZEL. Don't say that!

THURMAN. We don't.

HAZEL. You said yourself we had a lot to be grateful for. . . .

THURMAN. I know, but I wanted to keep that little boy, Hazel— the worst kind of way.

HAZEL. I know, but we couldn't have kept him. Thurman, it wouldn't have been right as long as there was a chance his folks were comin' for him.

THURMAN. I know. . . . I'm gonna call the sheriff. Maybe he can find him. He just can't go wanderin' around the country by himself—a twelve-year-old boy!

HAZEL. I know. (*He goes inside the house.* HAZEL *covers her face with her hands.* JOHN TURNER *comes in* D. L. *and up to the steps. She hears him and looks up.*) John Turner? Is that you?

JOHN TURNER. Yes ma'm. I was comin' by here, an' I seen you on the steps.

HAZEL. I'm so glad you came. Let me call Thurman. (*She calls into the house:*) Thurman! Thurman! We've got company! We were worried about you, John Turner.

JOHN TURNER. Were you?

HAZEL. Yes, we were. You see, Thurman went down to the river to find out how you were gettin' along, and couldn't find no sign of you anywhere—and then he went up and down all the roads in his car callin' to you. . . .

JOHN TURNER. Yes ma'm.

(THURMAN *comes out the front door.*)

HAZEL. Look who's here, Thurman!

THURMAN. Where did you come from, boy?

JOHN TURNER. I was just walkin' down the road, an' I said to my-self, "Is that Mis' Hazel sittin' on them steps?" an' I come up to see, an' it was. (*It begins to rain.*) There's rain. That ought to be good for the cotton.

THURMAN. I prophesied rain. Didn't I prophesy rain, Hazel?

HAZEL. Yes, you did. Are you hungry, John Turner? (*She goes into the house.*)

JOHN TURNER. That's a hard rain. That's a growin' rain. That rain will make enough cotton to keep everybody busy. I'm glad about that.

THURMAN. So am I.

JOHN TURNER. Seems like every time I come here we get a rain of some kind. Last time it was a shower.

THURMAN. I know.

JOHN TURNER. Well, my aunt an' uncle have gone off for good, I guess. Now I got no mama an' papa an' no aunt or uncle. I got 'em, I guess, but I don' know where they are. So might as well not have 'em for all the good they doin' me. . . . I thank you for comin' after me. I heard you callin' me, but I was cryin' so hard at the time, I was ashamed to answer. I'm over my cryin' now. I'll set here awhile, if you all don' mind, until the rain is through. Then I'll go on into town an' see the sheriff—see if he can figure out what's gonna become of me. I thought, there for a while, I'd run around on my own, but that's a lonesome kind of life, I decided after about four hours in that dark woods. Everybody tells me there's a home that boys can go to, where they can give you an education and teach you a trade. . . . The sheriff said yestidy I'd be better off there. I couldn' see it, of course, at the time.

THURMAN. John Turner, we don't want you to go to any place. John Turner, we don't have a boy; and we're lonesome, and if you'd like to stay here, we'd sure like for you to stay here.

JOHN TURNER. Yes sir. I wouldn't care to put you out any. . . .

THURMAN. You wouldn't be puttin us out. You'd be doin' us the biggest kind of favor.

(HAZEL *comes out with the sandwich.*)

JOHN TURNER. Yes sir.

HAZEL. Here you are!

JOHN TURNER. Thank you. (*He eats the sandwich.*) All my life I wanted to live in a house. I reckon I could get used to livin' in a house, same as anyone.

THURMAN. 'Course you could. (*He turns to* HAZEL.) I asked John Turner to stay on here with us, Hazel.

HAZEL. Oh, I'm so glad. Will you stay, John Turner?

JOHN TURNER. Yes ma'm. If you want me. (*The rain has stopped.*) Doggone if that isn't just another old shower! That's hard on the cotton.

THURMAN. Yes, it is. Well, I was wrong; I thought sure this would be a real rain.

HAZEL. It's gonna rain.

JOHN TURNER. How do you know?

HAZEL. Because—I know. I know.

THURMAN. And she might be right, John Turner. She might be right. You see, livin' on this road has always been lucky for her, and she says the luck is to be passed on to me, and now I guess to you.

JOHN TURNER. I certainly hope so. I could use some luck.

(*The rain has started again, harder than before.*)

THURMAN. You see?

JOHN TURNER. Yes sir.

THURMAN. Are you tired, boy?

JOHN TURNER. Yes sir. I'm tired, but I'm not sleepy.

THURMAN. Neither am I. I'm happy, but I'm not sleepy.

HAZEL. Well, why don't we just sit here then and listen to the rain?

(*The three of them sit quietly, listening to the sound of the rain as the lights fade.*)

The Midnight Caller

If for no other reason, *The Midnight Caller* would be important because it was the first play by Horton Foote in which Robert Duvall acted, though he was not in the original television production in December of 1953. Rather he was first cast, as Harvey Weems, in a later production of the play directed by Sanford Meisner at the Neighborhood Playhouse. Foote was impressed with Duvall's work in that production, but the two artists never worked directly together on *The Midnight Caller*. However, several years later, when the film *To Kill a Mockingbird* was being cast, Foote's wife, Lillian, remembered Duvall's work in the play and suggested that the young actor be considered for the part of Boo Radley. Duvall was cast in the part—his first film role—and the creative relationship between the actor and the playwright began with the filming of that celebrated novel. *

---

* More than twenty years later both Foote and Duvall were honored with Academy Awards for their contributions to another collaborative effort, the film *Tender Mercies*—Foote for his screenplay, Duvall for his portrayal of the central character, Mac Sledge.

But *The Midnight Caller* is far more than a footnote to the lives of two great artists. It summarizes much of Foote's writing for live television, and it is the last of his early plays to consider the theme of attachment. Because the play contains characters who more fully explain their motives and actions than do the men and women in Foote's later work, *The Midnight Caller* also clearly displays Foote's understanding of love and its limits.

The play reprises many of the situations, characters and themes of the plays Foote wrote for television during the 1950s. *The Midnight Caller* is set in a family home that has become a boardinghouse; the dislocation is felt here as strongly, though not as obviously, as in *John Turner Davis* or *The Traveling Lady*. Once again the crisis is precipitated by parents who want to control their children, and, as in other works of the period by Foote, going away from such control is a healthy impulse. Harvey Weems is another Foote character for whom good looks and prosperity are no assurance of happiness; drinking and failed love are crosses for all classes and races. Obsession with financial security can destroy love, as in *The Tears of My Sister*, but wealth is no guarantee of happiness either.

The Midnight Caller is also an excellent example of Horton Foote's use of humor. The chorus of women who surround Helen are driven by the quirkiness and compulsiveness that is typical of many of Harrison's most enduring, and funny, personalities. Rowena's romanticism over clothes and the harvest moon, Alma Jean's hard-won indifference and Cutie's habitual crying serve as a backdrop for Helen's pilgrimage from sad to secure love. These comic figures are never condescended to, are never the butt of Foote's humor, because the pain and struggle of their experience form the subtext of the play. Loneliness, aging, love that's no match for illusions are the villains here, not silly people. Even Alma Jean's call for separation of the sexes and a return to "my peace and my quiet" is a thin camouflage for her own struggle with isolation. What makes these characters humorous is also what gives them their humanity—their sometimes rigid, sometimes futile, but often courageous struggle to find identity and meaning in their lives. As Miss Rowena tells the other two: "I could think of a million other lives I'd rather lead, if I let myself, but this is my life so I try and make the best of it."

While *The Midnight Caller* is typical of Foote's plays of the fifties in many ways, it is also unique in this period as a study of self-destructive attachments. Like characters in his other plays set in Harrison, these are haunted by the melancholic loneliness that seems to inhabit Horton Foote's Southeast Texas coast. But unlike the previous characters, for whom loving connections are sufficient, Helen Crews learns that even love isn't a panacea. The loneliness that makes love a necessity for healing can also, as in the case of Harvey Weems, lead to a neurotic dependency, a debilitating "tie that binds." So, like Will Mayfield (*The Death of the Old Man*) before her, Helen is freed by learning "to quit"; she gives up the hopeless struggle with Harvey's alcoholism. Helen's decision to leave for Houston with Ralph Johnston is predicated on this crucial qualification to all the previous plays:

> How can you save someone that doesn't want to be saved? Because he [Harvey] doesn't want to be saved. Not from drink, not from loneliness, not from death. And you have to want to be. And that's what I've learned from these four years.

Compared with one important female character from Foote's later work—Rosa Lee in the film *Tender Mercies*—Helen is more self-assured and articulate. She explains things better and is more convinced that her decisions will shape her life. But she shares with Mac Sledge's wife an intuition that with or without love a person's life is his or her own. Even her love for Harvey Weems cannot save him from his own self-destructiveness; Rosa Lee's supportive love for the alcoholic Mac can help him to recover— but only because something in Mac himself "want[s] to be saved." Foote's courageous people cooperate in their own healing as his victims cooperate in their own destruction.

The Midnight Caller was first produced on Philco Television Playhouse on December 13, 1953. Vincent J. Donehue was director; Fred Coe, producer.

The Midnight Caller

CAST

Alma Jean Jordan   Mrs. Crawford
Cutie Spencer   Mr. Ralph Johnston
Miss Rowena Douglas   Helen Crews
Harvey Weems

Place: Harrison, Texas
Time: 1952

The living room, part of the front yard and part of a small bed-room of MRS. CRAWFORD's *boardinghouse in Harrison, Texas. The living room occupies most of the stage area. It is mainly de-fined by the use of furniture but there is a very low wall down* L. *to suggest a bay window, a screen* L. C., *an open arch* D. R. *to indicate the front door, and stairs* U. R. *leading to bedrooms. There is an entrance above stairs,* U. R., *leading to the dining room. The living room is furnished with a small sofa with a low table in front,* R. *of* C., *a small chair up* C., *a hassock, a low table and a rocking chair near the suggested bay window. Directly upstage is a raised platform large enough to have a small bed and a table with a lamp. This becomes the bedroom of* HELEN CREWS. *This area is only lit when used in the action. The section of the yard visible is immediately in front of the front door of the house, extending across downstage to the corner of the bay window.*

ALMA JEAN *is seated on small armchair, working a crossword puzzle.* CUTIE *enters through arch* D. R.

CUTIE. Hey, Alma Jean.

ALMA JEAN. Hey, Cutie. You're late.

CUTIE. I know, I had a hard day. I had so much work to do and I decided to stay until I got everything finished up.

ALMA JEAN. You're a fool. I'm here to tell you that you're the biggest fool in the whole state of Texas. Mr. H. T. Mavis works you until it's a shame. Do you think he appreciates it? No indeed. Why, you got fifteen dollars less bonus than I did last Christmas.

CUTIE. I like the work.

ALMA JEAN. You're a fool. Well, I don't know. Maybe we're all fools. What kind of a life is this, living in this one-horse town, pounding typewriters all day?

(MISS ROWENA DOUGLAS *comes into the room, upstage* L. MISS ROWENA *is in her sixties. She has a pleasant, sweet face. She dresses a bit eccentrically, and rather dramatically. Right now she has on a very feminine tea gown.*)

MISS ROWENA. Dear ones, forgive me for comin' to supper this way, but I have to dress for tonight and I just thought I'd take my bath before supper and put on somethin' rather informal. Dear Mrs. Crawford tells me this is my last opportunity to dress so informally with the gentleman comin' tomorrow to live in our midst. It'll be excitin', won't it, girls, havin' a real live man amongst us? A mature, distinguished man from all I've heard.

ALMA JEAN. They're all the same if you ask me. Personally, I think Mrs. Crawford is makin' a mistake not holdin' out a while longer until she can have a girl here. I won't feel comfortable with a man in the house. I can tell you that.

MISS ROWENA. You won't feel comfortable? Why not, honey?

ALMA JEAN. I just won't. I have to work with them all day at the courthouse. I don't want to have to live in the same house with them.

MISS ROWENA. Now, Alma Jean, don't be bitter. It doesn't become you. . . .

ALMA JEAN. I'm not bitter. I just don't like a man runnin' around the house I live in. If I had, I would have gotten married a long time ago.

CUTIE. Did Mrs. Crawford tell you she'd rented the other room too?

MISS ROWENA. Another man, honey?

CUTIE. No ma'm. Helen Crews and her mama have had a falling-out over Harvey Weems and she's movin' in here.

MISS ROWENA. Well, I declare.

ALMA JEAN. (*Stopping her work on the puzzle.*) Cutie Spencer, you don't mean what you're sayin'?

CUTIE. Oh, yes, I mean it. Of course I mean it.

ALMA JEAN. Has Mrs. Crawford lost her poor mind? You don't mean to tell me she's invited Helen Crews to live here.

CUTIE. I didn't say she invited her. I reckon Helen came and asked her for a room. . . .

ALMA JEAN. That settles it. I'm movin' out. I'll live in a tourist court before I'll put up with that.

CUTIE. Now what is the matter with you, Alma Jean?

ALMA JEAN. (*Rising.*) What's the matter with me? I don't want my reputation destroyed utterly. I cherish my reputation. I have watched all my life that no one can hold up one spot of blemish against my reputation.

CUTIE. And how in the world is this going to affect your reputation? . . .

ALMA JEAN. Helen Crews's name is on the tongue of everybody in Harrison and you know that as well as I do. Her own mama has ordered her out of her house. . . .

CUTIE. Well, what if she has?

ALMA JEAN. What if she has? . . .

CUTIE. I think her mama is half crazy. And she's mean as she can be. All I can see that Helen Crews did was fall in love with the wrong man.

ALMA JEAN. Oh, is that so?

CUTIE. Yes ma'm, that's so. And you know as well as I do that if they had gotten married like they planned, the whole thing would be forgotten. . . .

ALMA JEAN. Not by me. I can tell you that. Never by me.

CUTIE. How can you be so hard, Alma Jean? How in the world can you be so hard? . . .

ALMA JEAN. I am not hard.

CUTIE. You certainly are.

ALMA JEAN. I am not and I won't have you say I am.

CUTIE. Well, I think you're being very hard. . . .

ALMA JEAN. Well. And I don't intend to stay here and be insulted. (*She marches out of the room. She goes up the stairs, upstage* R. *The crossword puzzle is left on table.*)

CUTIE. Oh, my goodness.

MISS ROWENA. You'll have to beg her pardon, Cutie, the poor girl can't help behavin' like that.

CUTIE. I will not beg her pardon. I spend half my life begging her pardon. I will not . . .

MISS ROWENA. Yes, you will, honey. Yes, you will. (MISS ROWENA *crosses to rocking chair, down* L.)

CUTIE. I know. I guess I will. (*She goes to the stairs. She starts to call. Then she thinks better of it.*) Well, I'll wait for a while. Harvey did love Helen Crews, Miss Rowena, I don't care what anybody says.

MISS ROWENA. (*Sitting in chair.*) I believe it.

CUTIE. Why, I was goin' with Skeet Williams at the time. And they were best friends from boyhood. And Skeet told me that Harvey Weems told him many a time that he loved Helen. And look what she did for him. (CUTIE *crosses to hassock. She sits.*)

MISS ROWENA. I know it.

CUTIE. Why, Harvey used to slip out of his mama's house every night of his life before he started goin' with Helen and get dead dog drunk and ride all over Harrison County until he'd just pass out.

MISS ROWENA. I believe it.

CUTIE. He told Skeet all about it. He said after he met Helen he'd call her up any time of the day or night and she'd get in the car with him and ride until his nerves were calmed. He said one night they rode to the Gulf and he asked Helen to marry him and she said she would if he swore never to touch another drop of whiskey and right then and there he took his whiskey bottle and threw it in the Gulf and it just floated away and for the longest kind of time he never took another drink.

MISS ROWENA. I believe it. I believe it. And probably never would have had another drink if they had gotten married. And I bet they would have been married if his mama had stayed out of it and her mama had stayed out of it.

CUTIE. Well, they didn't. And they'll never get married now. I knew that when he left town with his mama and stayed away those six months. And now he's back and drinking and Helen won't see him. And I don't reckon I blame her.

MISS ROWENA. Isn't it a shame? Harvey Weems was the handsomest boy I think I ever laid eyes on, don't you, Cutie?

CUTIE. Yes ma'm. I think without a doubt he was.

MISS ROWENA. And rich. Had everything in this world, it seems like, to make him happy. . . .

(ALMA JEAN *comes into the room from stairs.*)

ALMA JEAN. If you care to apologize, Cutie, I'll come back in the living room.

CUTIE. All right. I'll apologize, Alma Jean.

ALMA JEAN. O.K. I accept the apology. (*She crosses into room.*) But I'm not hard and I'm not bitter and I don't appreciate you and Miss Rowena saying so.

CUTIE. Well, you may not be hard and bitter, but you're too sensitive for your own good and that's the living truth.

ALMA JEAN. I'm not sensitive.

CUTIE. You are.

ALMA JEAN. I'm not.

CUTIE. O.K. Let's change the subject. You're not. (CUTIE *crosses to sofa.*)

ALMA JEAN. Do you think I'm sensitive, Miss Rowena? (*She goes over to* MISS ROWENA.)

MISS ROWENA. Do you want the truth, honey?

ALMA JEAN. Yes.

MISS ROWENA. All right. I do. I'm not blamin' you for it, but I do. You can't be sensitive and endure our life, honey. You'll be torn to pieces if you continue to be. . . .

ALMA JEAN. What's wrong with our life? I like my life.

MISS ROWENA. Do you, Alma Jean?

ALMA JEAN. Yes I do. Don't you?

MISS ROWENA. No. I don't like mine. I could think of a million other lives I'd rather lead, if I let myself, but this is my life so I try and make the best of it. (ALMA JEAN *looks at her like she thinks she's crazy.* MISS ROWENA *goes to the window and looks out.*) I love the fall. I love the smell of the wood smoke. I love the coolness in the air and I love the look of the skies at night. The stars seem so much brighter and closer.

ALMA JEAN. I think the fall is real dull unless you like football and I can't stand football. Everybody tryin' to hurt everybody else.

MISS ROWENA. I always feel a little lonely in the fall though. Everything seems to me a little lonely; the stars and the sky and the trees. Wonder why that is?

CUTIE. Hadn't thought about it.

MISS ROWENA. I said good-bye to Robert Henry in the fall and to Chester Taylor. . . . I never said good-bye to Lee Edwards. My mama insisted I stay in my room and she said good-bye to him. (*A pause.*) I love Friday nights though. Winter, spring, fall. . . . Life always seems so carefree and frivolous on a Friday night. Don't you love Friday nights, Cutie?

CUTIE. Yes ma'm. I do.

MISS ROWENA. Ever since I was a little girl I've looked forward to Friday nights. It was always the night I felt free of responsibilities.

ALMA JEAN. I'd like them better if I had Saturdays off like you do.

MISS ROWENA. Well, that's why teachin' school is the loveliest job there is. You're always sure of bein' free on Saturday and Sunday. (*A pause.* MISS ROWENA *continues standing at the window.*)

ALMA JEAN. Miss Rowena, what are you doin'?

MISS ROWENA. Watchin' the lightnin' bugs. They'll be gone before we know it. Now that summer's over.

(MRS. CRAWFORD *comes into the room from the dining room entrance up* R., *followed by a man.* MRS. CRAWFORD *is an energetic woman of fifty or fifty-five. The man is the new boarder,* RALPH JOHNSTON. *He is in his middle thirties, nice looking, neatly but inexpensively dressed.*)

MRS. CRAWFORD. Girls, I would like you to meet our new guest. He arrived a day early. . . .

(*The three women rise.*)

MISS ROWENA. Oh, heavens, Mrs. Crawford, I'm so embarrassed, look at me.

MRS. CRAWFORD. You look all right to me.

MISS ROWENA. But I'm not dressed to meet a gentleman.

MRS. CRAWFORD. You look fine to me. Now Mr. Johnston is just gonna be treated like homefolks like everybody else. . . . (MRS. CRAWFORD *points to* MISS ROWENA.) This is Miss Rowena Douglas actin' so coy over here, Mr. Johnston.

MISS ROWENA. Mr. Johnston.

MR. JOHNSTON. How do you do.

MRS. CRAWFORD. And Miss Cutie Spencer.

CUTIE. Hey there.

MRS. CRAWFORD. And Miss Alma Jean Jordan.

MR. JOHNSTON. How do you do.

MRS. CRAWFORD. Like I told you girls, Mr. Johnston moved here from Teague. He's to be with the gas company.

MISS ROWENA. How lovely. I hope you'll be happy here, Mr. Johnston.

MR. JOHNSTON. Thank you. (*He goes to a chair.*)

MISS ROWENA. I bet you don't know what I'm doin' here at the window screen, Mr. Johnston.

MR. JOHNSTON. No ma'm.

MISS ROWENA. Tell him, Alma Jean.

ALMA JEAN. Watchin' lightnin' bugs.

MISS ROWENA. What do you think of that, Mr. Johnston? I'd like a penny for every hour I've spent at the window or the screen door watchin' lightnin' bugs. It's a custom I've brought with me from my childhood. I was a lonely child, Mr. Johnston, because of my frail health, and to amuse myself at the twilight I used to sit at the window or the screen door by the hour and watch and count the lightnin' bugs.

MR. JOHNSTON. Is that so?

(*A woman's voice calls from outside* D. R.: "Mrs. Crawford." MRS. CRAWFORD *gets up from her seat.*)

MRS. CRAWFORD. Come on in, Helen. (HELEN CREWS *comes in the front door, down* R. *She is a mature-looking girl in her late twenties. She has a strong face, with a great deal of sensitivity about it. She is carrying a suitcase.*) Put your suitcase by the stairs, Helen, and come say hello to everybody. (HELEN *puts her suitcase by the stairs and comes into the room.*) I believe you know everybody, Helen, except Mr. Johnston. This is Miss Crews, Mr. Johnston. She's coming to live here too.

MR. JOHNSTON. How do you do, Miss Crews.

HELEN. How do you do.

MISS ROWENA. Welcome, Helen.

HELEN. Thank you.

CUTIE. Hello, Helen.

HELEN. Hello, Cutie. Alma Jean.

ALMA JEAN. How do you do. (*She gets up and walks up the stairs.*)

MRS. CRAWFORD. Come on, Helen. I'll show you to your room.

HELEN. Thank you.

(*They go out, up the stairs.* HELEN *takes her suitcase.* MISS ROWENA *is looking out the window.*)

MISS ROWENA. There's goin' to be a full moon before the night's over, Mr. Johnston. A harvest moon. I think the harvest moon is the most romantic of all. The saddest and the most romantic. Spring's way behind and the summer's in the process of being forgotten and the winter won't be long in comin'. (*A pause. She laughs.*) But I guess just the old people think of things like that. The young people don't. They laugh and chatter all day in school just the same, winter, spring or fall.

(MRS. CRAWFORD *and* HELEN *come back in from stairs.*)

MRS. CRAWFORD. Let's all go in and eat. Where's Alma Jean?

CUTIE. You all go ahead. I'll call her. (*They all go into the dining room.* CUTIE *goes to the door and calls:*) Alma Jean. Supper. (*She stands at the stairs waiting.* ALMA JEAN *comes in.*) Alma Jean, I think that was the rudest thing I ever saw. I wouldn't treat another human being that way no matter what in the world . . .

ALMA JEAN. You tend to your own business. I'll act just as I please. I'm not payin' my good money here to get lessons in manners, Miss Cutie Spencer. You be polite to those you want to be polite to and I'll be polite to those I want to be polite to.

(MRS. CRAWFORD *comes in from the dining room.*)

MRS. CRAWFORD. Come on, girls. Supper's on the table.

CUTIE. Yes ma'm.

(*They both start for the dining room. The lights dim, and come up on* HELEN CREWS's *room on upstage platform. It is later that night.* HELEN *has been busy putting her things away. There is a knock on her door.*)

HELEN. Yes? (*A man's voice calls out:* "It's Ralph Johnston.") Just a minute. (*She quickly puts a few scattered personal things away and then opens the door.*)

MR. JOHNSTON. Been unpacking?

HELEN. Yes, I have.

MR. JOHNSTON. So have I. All through?

HELEN. Just about.

MR. JOHNSTON. Would you care to ride downtown with me and have a drink?

HELEN. Oh, no, thank you. I'm very tired.

MR. JOHNSTON. Oh. Well, I suppose it is kind of late.

HELEN. Another time.

MR. JOHNSTON. Sure. Do you work in Harrison too?

HELEN. Yes, I do. I'm a stenographer.

MR. JOHNSTON. Oh. Were you born around here?

HELEN. Yes, I was born here in Harrison.

MR. JOHNSTON. Oh. Well, good night.

HELEN. Good night. (*He goes. She closes the door. She switches out the light from behind the door. She falls across the bed crying. She sobs for a moment. There is a knock again at the door, very gentle this time and hesitant. She quickly dries her eyes. She calls:*) Yes?

MR. JOHNSTON. (*Calling.*) It's Ralph Johnston again. Is everything all right?

HELEN. Yes. Everything is all right. Thank you.

MR. JOHNSTON. O.K.

(*He goes on. She hears him go down the stairs. She turns the lights back on. She starts to unpack again, when she starts again to cry, this time silently. She sinks into a chair, covering her face with her hands. The lights dim and come up on the living room of the* CRAWFORD *house.* CUTIE *comes in, finds a magazine and starts to read.* MISS ROWENA *comes in the front door.*)

CUTIE. How was the bridge party?

MISS ROWENA. Fine. There were just two tables. What did you do?

CUTIE. Went to the picture show.

(MISS ROWENA *sits in the cane rocking chair.*)

MISS ROWENA. Everybody else in bed?

CUTIE. Looks like it. I don't really know. I just got here myself, lights were all out upstairs. I asked Alma Jean to go to the picture show with me, but she said she wasn't speakin' to me and shut her door in my face.

MISS ROWENA. Well, I know you'd like to get married and I want you to get married, but I hope for all our sakes that Mr. Johnston takes a shine to Alma Jean and marries her. I think we'd all be so much better off. Don't you?

CUTIE. (*Giggles.*) Yes ma'm. (*A pause.*) I'm never going to get married, Miss Rowena.

MISS ROWENA. Now don't say that. Why would you say that? A nice pretty girl like you.

CUTIE. I say it because I know it. I'll never be asked now. Oh, I'm not bitter about it, mind you. It would have been nice, but I know it'll never happen. I'll be workin' for Mr. Mavis and livin' at Mrs. Crawford's until I'm ready to go wherever lady stenographers go to.

MISS ROWENA. Don't talk foolish. (*A pause.*) I'll see you get married yet. I'll see you get married and Helen and maybe even Alma Jean. (*She looks at the window.*) Look, Cutie, yonder it comes over the tops of the trees. Yonder comes the harvest moon.

(CUTIE *comes to look out the window.* ALMA JEAN *and* RALPH JOHNSTON *come in the front door* D. R.)

ALMA JEAN. Hello, Miss Rowena. Hello, Cutie.

MISS ROWENA. Hello.

CUTIE. Heh.

ALMA JEAN. I've been showin' Mr. Johnston the sights of Harrison. I was sittin' here all alone and feelin' awfully sorry for myself when Mr. Johnston asked me to ride to the drugstore for a drink.

MISS ROWENA. Won't you sit down, Mr. Johnston?

MR. JOHNSTON. Thank you, ma'm, but I think I'll go on upstairs. I'm real tired. (*He starts for the stairs.*) Thank you, Alma Jean, for coming with me.

ALMA JEAN. That's all right. I enjoyed myself.

MR. JOHNSTON. Good night, you all.

(*The ladies all bid him good night and he goes up the stairs.* ALMA JEAN *looks to see if he's gone. She goes over to the others.*)

ALMA JEAN. I found out a lot about him. His wife and he just got a divorce. I think he's very lonely. He asked me all about you all. I told him a thing or two.

CUTIE. I bet you did.

ALMA JEAN. Now what do you mean by that remark?

CUTIE. Nothin'. Now don't be sensitive, Alma Jean.

ALMA JEAN. He said he thought he heard Helen cryin' in her room. He asked me if she had any troubles. I said plenty. I put him straight about her right away. He seemed very surprised.

MISS ROWENA. Oh, I saw poor Harvey Weems walkin' around the square drunk as I was comin' home. It was the first time I'd seen him since he came back from his trip. It gave me such a funny feelin'.

ALMA JEAN. Well, I hope he don't come around here hollerin' for her. I'm puttin' my foot down if he does.

(HELEN *comes down the stairs.*)

HELEN. Oh, I didn't know anyone was in here. I couldn't sleep.

CUTIE. Pull up a chair and join the sorority. We were just discussin' our new male roomer.

HELEN. Thank you. (*She sits on the sofa.* MISS ROWENA *gives another little gasp of excitement.*)

MISS ROWENA. Just look at the moon, girls. Just look at that full moon. (*She looks up at the sky.*)

"I see the moon
And the moon sees me,
God bless the moon
And God bless me."

(*She looks at the other women.*) Look at the moon, girls. Look at the harvest moon.

(*The four women look at the moon. The lights fade. They are brought up again. It is two weeks later on a Friday night.* MISS ROWENA, CUTIE *and* ALMA JEAN *are in the living room.* MISS ROWENA *is in the rocker.* CUTIE *is on the couch.* ALMA JEAN *walks around the room.*)

ALMA JEAN. Well, Miss Crews and Mr. Johnston are out together again. I don't understand it. He knows perfectly well what kind she is. Well, that's a man for you. I'm not surprised his wife divorced him. (*A pause.*) Well, I'm a nervous wreck. I don't know about you all. I told Mrs. Crawford today that if something wasn't done about the situation I was definitely goin' to have to look for another place. (*A pause.*) Look there. There it starts. There goes a car drivin' slow. They're expectin' a show.

CUTIE. Alma Jean. I swanny you have the biggest imagination.

ALMA JEAN. It's not my imagination. It's all over town that four nights last week Harvey Weems came over here at twelve o'clock and stood out in the front yard and cried and called Helen's name. Of course that didn't bother her. She has no shame. She walks down the streets of the town just like nothin' has happened.

MISS ROWENA. Honey, she is mortified by it. She told Mrs. Crawford so when Mrs. Crawford spoke to her about it.

ALMA JEAN. Then why doesn't she do something about it?

CUTIE. Alma Jean. What can she do?

ALMA JEAN. She can tell him to stop.

MISS ROWENA. But I'm sure she has, honey. He only comes around when he's drunk. She can't help that. What else can she do but have him arrested and you know none of us want to see poor Harvey arrested.

ALMA JEAN. All right. Take up for her. But if it happens again either I go or she goes and I told Mrs. Crawford that. And if she stays Mrs. Crawford will only be able to get riffraff in my place. No self-respectin' person will move in here with her under the same roof. And I told Mrs. Crawford that.

CUTIE. Let's change the subject.

ALMA JEAN. Why?

CUTIE. Because I'm tired of talkin' about it. There are other things in the world to talk about.

ALMA JEAN. Not as far as I'm concerned. This is the burning issue as far as I'm concerned. (*She goes to the door* U. R. *and calls:*) Mrs. Crawford. Mrs. Crawford. Come out here, if you please. There's another car goin' by slow. It's the third one in the last half-hour and don't tell me it's my imagination. This house is becomin' a place of curiosity just like her mama's house used to be. Pretty soon they'll be chargin' admission to hear her midnight caller cryin' in the front yard and callin' her name. (*A pause.*) What has she got? Will you tell me what has she got? I understand the appeal of Gene Tierney or Rita Hayworth. But Helen Crews? She's a perfectly plain girl.

CUTIE. Helen was always quite popular with boys, Alma Jean.

ALMA JEAN. With what boys? Drunks and divorcees? Yonder comes the fourth. The fourth car in half an hour. (*She runs to the stairs calling.*) Mrs. Crawford. Mrs. Crawford. (MRS. CRAWFORD *calls back:* "I'm coming. I'm coming.") I feel like a freak in a sideshow.

MISS ROWENA. Well, honey, those cars are not comin' to see you.

ALMA JEAN. Yes. But they're comin' to see the house I live in.

(MRS. CRAWFORD *comes down the stairs.*)

MRS. CRAWFORD. Now what is it? I was in bed asleep.

ALMA JEAN. In bed asleep. Well, I wish I could sleep. I haven't closed my eyes for a week. The fourth car just passed by here driving slow and gaping.

MRS. CRAWFORD. How do you know?

ALMA JEAN. How do I know? I know. Because I heard people uptown today sayin' they were gonna be out tonight for the show. Because everybody in town knows how he comes into our yard and carries on. Because her own mama told me today it was the same at her house, every time he started drinking. Only in those days Miss Helen used to go out to him and get in a car and drive off with him at twelve or one or two o'clock in the mornin'. That's the kind of girl she is. That's the way she and her mother had their fights. That poor mother. . . . She knows what kind of a girl Helen Crews is. . . .

(HELEN *has come in the front door.*)

HELEN. You don't know what you're talkin' about, Alma Jean. You don't know at all what you're talkin' about. (ALMA JEAN *starts up the stairs.*) Did you hear what I said, Alma Jean? You don't know what you're talkin' about.

ALMA JEAN. There's nothin' I have to say to you.

HELEN. There's plenty I have to say to you.

ALMA JEAN. Well, I don't intend to listen to it. (*She starts for the stairs.* HELEN *grabs her by the arm.*)

HELEN. You will listen to it. You will listen to every word of it. Just what did my mother say to you? (*A pause.* ALMA JEAN *doesn't answer. She turns and looks at* HELEN *defiantly.*) Did my mother say that she never wanted me to go with any boys? Or my sister? Did she tell you that my sister ran off to get married and my mother has never spoken to her since? Did she tell you that? Did my mother tell you that I never left the house in my life on a date without a fight? Without such a fight that the whole evening was ruined for me? Did she tell you that?

ALMA JEAN. I don't know anything about that. . . . I . . .

HELEN. Of course you don't. Well, there's lots you don't know. Did she tell you that I loved Harvey and that Harvey loved me and that we were going to be married? . . .

ALMA JEAN. Well, if you love him so much how can you go runnin' off every night with the first man that asks you for a date?

HELEN. I said I loved him. And I did love him. I loved him for four years. I stood by him for four years. And don't forget that I stood by him in spite of his mama and my mama, and I fought to win him. And I almost won but I didn't win after four years, so I quit. Because I had to quit. Because I've seen too many people spend their lives fighting fights they can't win.

MISS ROWENA. Girls! Let's don't get on with this, we're all excited. Here comes Mr. Johnston. Now let's just change the subject.

MRS. CRAWFORD. Alma Jean is just a little high-strung, Helen. She doesn't mean a thing she says. She really has the best heart in the world. She just hasn't had much rest lately because of Harvey's visits. . . .

MISS ROWENA. Shh. Now let's all just change the subject. Let's all talk of pleasant things. Here comes Mr. Johnston. (RALPH JOHNSTON *comes in the front door.*) Hello, Mr. Johnston. Come, pull up a chair.

MR. JOHNSTON. Thank you. (*He sits in the small armchair. There is an uncomfortable silence.*) I wish I could find a garage a little closer for my car at nights, Mrs. Crawford. It's a little inconvenient walkin' two blocks in rainy weather.

MRS. CRAWFORD. Well, I'll inquire around and see if I can't locate a place for you. (*There is another uncomfortable pause.*)

MISS ROWENA. Look at the leaves fallin'. The leaves are fallin' so fast. Pretty soon the pecan trees will have no leaves at all. How's the pecan crop gonna be, Mrs. Crawford?

MRS. CRAWFORD. I think it's gonna be all right. First norther they'll come falling onto the ground. Then I'm gonna rout you all out of bed to help me pick them up before they get stolen away. I think it's awful the way people will come into your yard and help themselves to your pecans. Don't you?

ROWENA. I do. I think it's perfectly awful.

(CUTIE *suddenly starts to cry.*)

CUTIE. Excuse me. I'm sorry. (*She goes running up the stairs.*)

MISS ROWENA. Poor Cutie. I think it's awful the way she has to work. That job is makin' her nervous. Don't you think so, Mrs. Crawford?

MRS. CRAWFORD. I guess so.

(*There is another uncomfortable silence.* ALMA JEAN *goes up the stairs.*)

MISS ROWENA. My goodness, everybody is so high-strung tonight.

MRS. CRAWFORD. Well, I think we'd all better get some sleep.

MISS ROWENA. I think so. (*She starts out.*)

MRS. CRAWFORD. Good night.

MISS ROWENA. 'Night.

(*They go up the stairs.* RALPH JOHNSTON *goes over to* HELEN. *He tries to take her in his arms and to kiss her. She moves nervously away from him.*)

HELEN. I'm sorry, Ralph. I'm sorry. . . . I guess I'm nervous tonight like everybody else because of my midnight caller. (*A pause.*) I think I'd just better give up the ghost and move away. It'll make it easier certainly for Harvey to do whatever he has to do, and my mother and his mother and me.

RALPH. Helen . . .

HELEN. Harvey can't go, or wouldn't if he could. And what do I do? How can I stop a gentleman who's had too much to drink from coming to my front yard at night and callin' my name? Ask him? I have. Beg him? I have. (*She looks up at the sky.*) The leaves are fallin'. Falling all over town. The streets will soon be covered and the yards. (*A pause.*) Oh, it all began so long ago that I don't remember the beginning and so how can I possibly know the end? And I don't know who to blame. My mother? For wantin' to keep me and my sister locked up with her forever? How can I blame her? We're all she had. My father died when we were just babies. We were literally all she had. (*A pause.*) My mother never liked Harrison. She wasn't born here, she was born fourteen miles out in the country on a farm. Maybe she should have stayed there. Maybe it would have all been different. . . . She was very rich at one time. My father lost everything speculating on the cotton market. Maybe my father's to blame. Or Harvey's mother. . . . Or Harvey. Or me. I've spent many an hour trying to figure that one out and I can't figure that one out. (*A pause.*) Of course, I don't regret it. You understand that? I don't regret it at all. He was lonely and I was lonely and he needed me very much at the time and I needed him. Of all the people in the world then, you would suspect of being lonely, Harvey Weems was the last. And yet for all his good looks and his money, he was the loneliest person alive. He was lonelier than I was and that was very lonely. I remember the day I discovered that. I came into the drugstore and he was sitting at the counter and we spoke, and though I'd known him all my life, I looked at him this day as he spoke and I knew then how lonely he was in spite of his looks and his money. And I guess he knew I knew. And I guess he wanted to be saved from his loneliness and I wanted to be saved from mine, because two days later he called and asked me for a date. And those nights, then, he came to my window and called to me it wasn't for lack of respect like people think. It was because Mama would answer the phone without my knowin' and not tell me he had called. She hated him from the first in spite of his money and his good looks and his family name, just like his mama hated me from the first. And their hate licked us, because what was the need to end our loneliness turned into a battle between four people and then the town. (*We hear a man's voice down the street calling* HELEN'*s name.*) Yonder he goes. Like some lost ghost calling my name. He's so drunk, he's forgotten where I live. (*A pause. She cries out.*) I tried to save him. I wanted to save him like I never wanted to do anything in my life. But I couldn't win. I reckon I didn't know enough. But if I had known enough, how could I have won? How can you save someone that doesn't want to be saved? Because he doesn't want to be saved. Not from drink, not from loneliness, not from death. And you have to want to be. And that's what I've learned from these four years. (HARVEY WEEMS *has come into the yard from the* R. *He stands very quietly, singing softly to himself. He is very drunk. There is a kind of dignity in his drunkenness.* HELEN *sees him. She goes quickly to him, out the front door, calling softly as she goes.*) Harvey. (*He doesn't answer if he hears or sees her. He stands there immobile, singing quietly to himself.*) Harvey . . . (HARVEY *doesn't look up. He stands with his head down singing.*)

HARVEY. "Blessed be the tie that binds . . . In Christian brother-hood . . ." (HARVEY *starts to cry. It is a quiet kind of crying, pathetic and moving.* HELEN *goes to him. She touches his arm in warmth and compassion.*)

HELEN. Don't cry, Harvey. Please don't cry. I can't stand to see you cry. You go home now. (HARVEY *looks at her for the first time.*)

HARVEY. Helen . . .

HELEN. Harvey, please go home. I worry about you when you're out alone this way.

HARVEY. Come with me, Helen. I'll get my car and we'll ride and ride and ride . . .

HELEN. We've been all through that, Harvey. I can't go with you.

HARVEY. Please, Helen.

HELEN. I can't. (HARVEY *looks at her as if he heard her for the first time.*)

HARVEY. You can't ride with me, Helen?

HELEN. No.

HARVEY. Who's to ride with me, Helen?

HELEN. I don't know.

HARVEY. (*He is crying again now.*) I'm lonely. I'm so lonely.

HELEN. Please, Harvey. (HARVEY *controls himself. He looks at her.*)

HARVEY. Are you mad at me because I'm drinking?

HELEN. I'm not mad at you.

HARVEY. But you don't love me anymore? (*Pause. She doesn't answer.*) Do you love me anymore?

HELEN. No, Harvey.

HARVEY. Why, Helen?

HELEN. I just don't, Harvey. You go home now. (*He stands as if he hadn't heard her. He quietly begins his song again.*)

HARVEY. "Blessed be the tie that binds . . ."

(MRS. CRAWFORD *and* MISS ROWENA *come into the living room from stairs.* CUTIE *and* ALMA JEAN *are behind them. They look out the window and the front door.* MRS. CRAWFORD *goes out to* HELEN *in yard.*)

MRS. CRAWFORD. Helen, please get him to go home.

HELEN. I'm tryin', Mrs. Crawford, I'm tryin'. . . .

ALMA JEAN. (*At window.*) Look yonder. Yonder goes a car. Drivin' slow. (*She screams.*) Move on. There are decent people livin' here.

MISS ROWENA. Shh, Alma Jean.

ALMA JEAN. Puttin' on a sideshow at twelve-thirty in the morning. Somebody call the sheriff.

MISS ROWENA. Shh, Alma Jean.

ALMA JEAN. He's crazy. You ought to lock up crazy people.

(HELEN *has* HARVEY *by the arm again.*)

HELEN. Please, go home, Harvey.

HARVEY. You want me to go home?

HELEN. Yes.

HARVEY. Then I'll go home. (*He starts out. He pauses.*) Good night, Helen. Pleasant dreams, Helen.

HELEN. Good night, Harvey.

(*He starts slowly out of the yard. He goes out* R. HELEN *stands watching him go.* MRS. CRAWFORD *goes back into the house.* MISS ROWENA *comes outside. She stands close to* HELEN.)

MISS ROWENA. He's drunk. He's so drunk. Where's it gonna end, Helen? Where's it gonna end? I taught Harvey, you know. I was teachin' music appreciation in those days. I remember I had the fifth grade and I taught Harvey to sing "When Day Is Done." He sang it beautifully too. Sang it before the whole school assembly, as I remember. Oh, he's so drunk, Helen. Where's it gonna end? Where's it all gonna end?

HELEN. I don't know, Miss Rowena. I don't know.

(MISS ROWENA *goes back into the house.* MRS. CRAWFORD *turns to* CUTIE *and* ALMA JEAN.)

MRS. CRAWFORD. All right, girls. Let's all get some sleep now.

(*She takes them by the arm and they all go up the stairs.* HELEN *is still standing there.* RALPH JOHNSTON *comes over to her.*)

HELEN. (*Turns to* RALPH *and embraces him.*) Help me, Ralph. Help me. Help me. Help me.

(*He holds her in his arms for a moment. She sobs. He is holding her closely, passionately. The lights fade. The lights are brought up on the living room of the* CRAWFORD *boardinghouse.* MISS ROWENA *is there.* CUTIE *comes hurrying in. It is late the next afternoon.*)

CUTIE. Miss Rowena. Miss Rowena . . .

MISS ROWENA. What is it, honey?

CUTIE. Alma Jean is in her room packing.

MISS ROWENA. What?

CUTIE. She's in her room packin'. She vows her mind's made up. She vows she's leavin' us.

MISS ROWENA. Oh, now, she mustn't be hasty. I'll go talk to her right away.

(MRS. CRAWFORD *comes in from the dining room.*)

CUTIE. Mrs. Crawford. Do you know that Alma Jean is upstairs in her room packing to leave?

MRS. CRAWFORD. Why, no.

CUTIE. She is. I talked to her for half an hour tryin' to change her mind. She says that nothin' can change her mind after last night. . . .

MRS. CRAWFORD. That silly girl.

CUTIE. She says she can't go on livin' here. She says that Harvey Weems comin' here every night is makin' her very nervous. She said she made nothin' but mistakes today at her work. She says . . . (*She cries.*) It's makin' me nervous, too. I'm sorry. I don't like givin' way to my feelin's this way but something has to be done. It's makin' me extremely nervous, Mrs. Crawford. I made mistakes all day today, and I couldn't eat lunch and I have a splittin' headache. . . .

MISS ROWENA. I know. I know just how you feel, Cutie. You needn't apologize. This can't go on, they'll have to lock the poor boy up. . . .

MRS. CRAWFORD. They have. I just talked to the sheriff. They locked him up late this afternoon.

MISS ROWENA. They have?

MRS. CRAWFORD. Yes ma'm. It was at the request of his mother. (*A pause.*) After he left here last night, he tried to harm himself.

CUTIE. Oh, no.

MISS ROWENA. Harvey Weems?

MRS. CRAWFORD. Yes ma'm. He tried to hang himself.

MISS ROWENA. Harvey Weems? The handsome Harvey Weems? Oh, I'm sorry. I'm so sorry. I'm so sorry. (*A pause.*) I taught him in school, you know. It doesn't seem like more than yesterday I was teachin' him in school. I had him in music appreciation and I taught him to sing "When Day Is Done." He had a sweet voice. A lovely, sweet voice. And now they've locked him up.

(ALMA JEAN *comes down the stairs into the room.*)

ALMA JEAN. Mrs. Crawford, I suppose you've been informed by Cutie of my decision. I've given you plenty of warning, you'll have to admit. I told you over and over that I was reachin' the breakin' point. . . . (*She looks at the women.*) What's the matter? What's happened?

CUTIE. They've locked up Harvey Weems. He tried to harm himself.

ALMA JEAN. Oh, I'm very sorry to hear that. When did that happen?

CUTIE. After he left here last night.

MRS. CRAWFORD. The sheriff just called me. I had left a message for him to call. I felt I had to put in a complaint after what had been goin' on here at night. I didn't want to, you understand, but I felt I had to. . . .

CUTIE. Of course you did.

MRS. CRAWFORD. Well, anyway, I did. And he said it was all right now, because they had locked him up.

ALMA JEAN. Is that so?

CUTIE. So now you can unpack, Alma Jean.

ALMA JEAN. Oh, no, thank you. I'm goin' anyway. This house has changed with that divorced man here and that woman. I don't care to stay any longer in this house.

MRS. CRAWFORD. Well, suit yourself about that, Alma Jean, but they're leavin' too.

ALMA JEAN. Leavin'? Where are they goin'?

MRS. CRAWFORD. They're goin' to Houston. They're gonna be married.

ALMA JEAN. Oh.

MRS. CRAWFORD. Helen called me from work to tell me. They're leavin' tonight.

MISS ROWENA. That's lovely. Isn't that lovely?

(CUTIE *starts to cry.*)

CUTIE. What's the matter with me? I cry over the least thing these days. I cry when I hear Harvey Weems is locked up and I cry when I hear Helen Crews is gettin' married.

ALMA JEAN. Well, in that case, I'll stay. I'll unpack my things.

(HELEN *and* MR. JOHNSTON *come in from outside.* ALMA JEAN *leaves the room.* MISS ROWENA *goes up to them.*)

MISS ROWENA. We heard the news, honey. We just heard the news and we're rejoicin' for you.

HELEN. Thank you.

MISS ROWENA. I think you have the loveliest and the sweetest bride in Harrison, Mr. Johnston.

MR. JOHNSTON. Thank you, ma'm.

MISS ROWENA. And to think it happened here, Mrs. Crawford! Romance bloomed and blossomed here in this very house.

MRS. CRAWFORD. I know.

CUTIE. Congratulations to you both. (*Again she starts to cry.*) Excuse me. (*She goes up the stairs.*)

MISS ROWENA. Poor Cutie has been very emotional lately. . . .

MRS. CRAWFORD. Helen, will you all be here for supper?

HELEN. No, thank you, Mrs. Crawford. We have our packin' to do and we don't want to get in to Houston too late. I'll leave our address with you before we leave in case anyone wants to get in touch with us.

MRS. CRAWFORD. All right, Helen.

HELEN. We'll say good-bye before we leave.

MRS. CRAWFORD. All right, Helen. (HELEN *and* MR. JOHNSTON *start towards the stairs.*) Helen . . . (HELEN *stops.*)

HELEN. Yes?

MRS. CRAWFORD. Helen . . . did you hear . . . ?

HELEN. About Harvey?

MRS. CRAWFORD. Yes.

HELEN. Yes ma'm. I did. I had to go and talk to him before he'd go. (*She cries.*) Oh, it was awful, Mrs. Crawford. It was just awful.

MRS. CRAWFORD. I'm sorry, Helen, to have brought it up. I just thought if you didn't know . . .

HELEN. I know. (*She turns to* RALPH.) Come on, honey. (*They go up the stairs.*)

MRS. CRAWFORD. I'll get supper on the table.

MISS ROWENA. Yes ma'm.

(CUTIE *comes back in the room. She picks up the crossword puzzle. The lights dim and come up on* HELEN'S *bedroom.* RALPH *knocks.*)

HELEN. Come in.

(RALPH *enters the room.*)

RALPH. All ready?

HELEN. Yes, I am. Are you?

RALPH. Uh huh.

HELEN. Ralph.

RALPH. Uh huh?

HELEN. Maybe I should wait a few days . . .

RALPH. What for, Helen?

HELEN. Maybe there's somethin' I can do. . . .

RALPH. There's nothin' more you can do. You were told that.

HELEN. I know.

RALPH. You waited four years, Helen.

HELEN. I know.

RALPH. Come on, Helen. You're to be my wife now. Come on.

HELEN. All right, honey.

(*He kisses her and holds her close. Then he picks up the suitcase once more and they go out, closing the door. The lights dim and come up on the living room.* MRS. CRAWFORD *sits on the couch, reading.* CUTIE *sits on the hassock.* MISS ROWENA *is in her rocking chair.*)

MISS ROWENA. Wonder what's playin' at the picture show? (*No one hears her.*) I said I wonder what's playin' at the picture show?

CUTIE. A Western at one and a gangster at another.

MISS ROWENA. Oh.

(HELEN *and* RALPH *come into the room from upstairs.*)

HELEN. We're all ready.

(MRS. CRAWFORD *gets up.*)

MRS. CRAWFORD. Well, we're gonna miss you two.

HELEN. Thank you. Good-bye, Miss Rowena. Good-bye, Cutie. (MISS ROWENA *and* CUTIE *and* MRS. CRAWFORD *hover about them. They wish them good-bye, congratulations, etc.* RALPH *and* HELEN *start out.*) Tell Alma Jean good-bye for us.

MRS. CRAWFORD. I will.

(*They leave, going out front door.* MISS ROWENA *looks out the window after them. She waves good-bye once more.*)

MISS ROWENA. There they go. There they go. (*She turns back from the window.* MRS. CRAWFORD *goes to the stairs and calls:*)

MRS. CRAWFORD. Alma Jean. You can come down now. They're gone. (MRS. CRAWFORD *goes to sofa, sits.*)

CUTIE. It suddenly seems so quiet and so still. It's no quieter than usual, I suppose, but it seems that way. I reckon we were all so on edge half waiting to hear Harvey every night, that we were gettin' sensitive to the least noise. I know I was.

(ALMA JEAN *comes down the stairs.*)

ALMA JEAN. Thank goodness things are back to normal for a change. (*A pause.*) Oh, well, I hope you've learned, Mrs. Crawford. Men and women don't mix. There's bound to be trouble when men move into the same house with women. I've been livin' in boardin'houses for seventeen years and I never saw it to fail, once a man moves in trouble begins. I could have had him, you know. If I'd wanted him. He asked me out that first night, you remember. But I let him know that I had my mind on other things. Besides, I didn't think he was one bit attractive, did you?

MISS ROWENA. Yes I did, honey. I must admit I thought he was very attractive. (CUTIE *starts to cry again. She gets up and goes out the front door.*) Poor thing. She's been cryin' at the least provocation. (*She goes to the rocking chair by the window.*)

ALMA JEAN. Well, they can call me an old maid if they want to. But I like my peace and my quiet.

MRS. CRAWFORD. I guess we all do, Alma Jean.

(ALMA JEAN *goes over to the crossword puzzle at the table. She picks it up.*)

ALMA JEAN. I've seen the girls that get married. I wouldn't trade places with a one of them. Not one. I can go where I please, do what I please, spend my money like I please. (*She takes the crossword puzzle and goes to a chair.*) Every friend I have that's married envies me. (MRS. CRAWFORD *is dozing on the sofa.*) It would take more than Mr. Ralph Johnston to make me give up my independence. I went with a boy once in high school. I almost married him too. Then my mother took me aside and gave me a good talkin'-to. She let me know how hard she had to work. She said she had to work harder takin' care of children and a house than five women at the courthouse. The next night when my friend came to call I wasn't home. (*She sees* MRS. CRAWFORD *is asleep and not listening. She puts the crossword puzzle down. She goes over to* MISS ROWENA.) I bet everybody sleeps good tonight.

MISS ROWENA. I think a good norther would help us all. It's too hot for this time of the year. We are way in November.

ALMA JEAN. I know it. Well, that's the trouble with this part of the country. You either freeze to death or you're burnin' up. Never any moderation.

(CUTIE *comes in the front door.*)

MISS ROWENA. Lights are goin' on all over town. I love to see the lights go on.

CUTIE. Yes ma'm.

ALMA JEAN. Anybody care to have a little game of honeymoon bridge?

MISS ROWENA. I don't believe so, thank you.

ALMA JEAN. Cutie?

CUTIE. No, thank you.

ALMA JEAN. I tried workin' the crossword puzzle tonight. Did you?

CUTIE. Uh huh.

ALMA JEAN. That was the hardest crossword puzzle. I see no reason in makin' them so hard you can't work them. Do you?

CUTIE. Nope.

(ALMA JEAN *looks over at* MISS ROWENA.)

ALMA JEAN. What are you doin', Miss Rowena? Countin' lightnin' bugs? . . .

MISS ROWENA. No ma'm. Just thinkin'.

ALMA JEAN. What were you thinkin' about?

MISS ROWENA. Thinkin' about how it was quiet and not quiet. Thinkin' about how one person ends up in the crazy house and thinkin' how another goes off to get married. And others sit on front galleries and rock their lives away. Thinkin' about all the things I've seen an' heard sittin' on the front galleries of Harrison. Thinkin' about how I'll never sit on this gallery again without hearin' Harvey Weems as he walked drunk through the streets of the town callin' the name of Helen Crews. . . . Thinkin' about . . .

(*Away off and very far in the distance we hear* HARVEY *calling* "Helen. Helen.")

CUTIE. You hear him?

ALMA JEAN. He's callin' from the jail.

MISS ROWENA. So he is.

(*We hear the call again.*)

CUTIE. You hear him?

(*We hear again:* "Helen. Helen.")

MISS ROWENA. She's gone, Harvey. Gone to Houston. Gone . . .

(*She has whispered this so he can't possibly have heard her, but the town is silent once more except for the rocking of* MISS ROWENA's *chair . . . as the lights fade.*)

The Dancers

A passing knowledge of Horton Foote's work demonstrates that he is interested in children (*Storm Fear, To Kill a Mockingbird, Tender Mercies*) and the aging (*The Trip to Bountiful, The Death of the Old Man*). *The Dancers* and the later play *Blind Date* show that he is also interested in adolescents. And here, as in the later play, Foote's sympathies are with the young people and the natural process of growing up. The elders, Inez and Elizabeth, try to control the dating of the young people, making arrangements for cars and flowers and insisting that Horace and Emily go out together. Worse yet, Elizabeth disapproves of Emily's boyfriend and apparently is trying to use Horace to drive a wedge between the young sweethearts. The plot of the story—that is, the fact that things work out happily—suggests that Herman, Inez's husband, has the appropriate view of how to handle adolescents' difficulties when he tells his wife to "leave the boy alone. He'll be all right."

Under the surface of this simple story lies another, more political one of class awareness and power struggles. The differences between the wealthy and the less well-off are implied in Inez's offhand remark that the Davis family can't afford an expensive, fashionable dress for Mary Catherine, the girl Horace wants to take to the dance. A more subtle form of control is suggested by the assumption that anybody would want to go out with Emily because she is "the prettiest and most popular girl in Harrison." Behind the comic intrigue of Inez and Elizabeth lies a game of social intrigue and one-upmanship that runs as deep as oil wells in the landscape of Harrison.

But, as these plays make clear, Horton Foote is not a political writer in the usual sense. There is always in his writing, as in that of William Faulkner and Reynolds Price (two Southern writers whose work he admires), an understanding of the social realities, "sweet" or not, that the characters must accept, adjust to, grow or die in. Foote's best characters are those who face themselves and their life situations, which are never ideal or even just, with realism and courage.

The beauty in the relationship between Horace and Mary Catherine begins when they are able to admit to each other their lack of confidence. But the gaining of confidence, a theme which is later reiterated between Horace Robedaux and Elizabeth Vaughn in *Courtship,* is less important than are the openness and mutuality between the youngsters. Once Horace and Mary Catherine discover their shared anxiety, they find the courage to set out for the dance. For these adolescents, intimacy breeds the confidence to grow.

Dance is an integral part of Horton Foote's theater. Throughout the 1940s his work was influenced by a number of gifted dancers and choreographers, including Pearl Primus, Valerie Bettis and Martha Graham. During that decade he even experimented with plays based on the principles of dance. Later, when Foote returned to dramatic realism (with *The Chase* in 1952), dancing remained a significant, if less visible, element of his work. In the dance a more physical and emotional side of human experience is released; intimacy becomes possible. But the movements of the dance are also governed by the rules of the form. Dance balances feeling with order, desire with tradition. In *The Dancers,* as in other plays by Foote, the dance is a precious, fleeting time when private desires and public needs, sensual spirits and fraternal affections are brought into harmony. It's as close as his characters get to a transcendent moment.

The Dancers was first produced on Philco Television Playhouse on March 7, 1954, under the direction of Vincent J. Donehue. The role of Emily Crawford was played by Joanne Woodward; Horace was played by James Broderick. Fred Coe was producer.

The Dancers

CAST

A Waitress	Horace
Inez Stanley	Mary Catherine Davis
Elizabeth Crews	Velma Morrison
Emily Crews	Tom Davis
Herman Stanley	Mrs. Davis

Place: Harrison, Texas
Time: Early summer, 1952

The stage is divided into four acting areas. D. L. *is the living room of* INEZ *and* HERMAN STANLEY. D. R. *is part of a small-town drugstore.* U. R. *is the living room of* ELIZABETH CREWS. U. L. *is the yard and living room of* MARY CATHERINE DAVIS. *Since the action should flow continuously from one area to the other only the barest amount of furnishings should be used to suggest what each area represents. The lights are brought up on the drugstore,* D. R. *A* WAITRESS *is there.* INEZ STANLEY *comes into the drugstore. She stands for a moment thinking. The* WAITRESS *goes over to her.*

WAITRESS. Can I help you?

INEZ. Yes, you can if I can think of what I came in here for. Just gone completely out of my mind. I've been running around all day. You see, I'm expecting company tonight. My brother Horace. He's coming on a visit. (ELIZABETH CREWS *and her daughter* EMILY *come into the drugstore.* EMILY *is about seventeen and very pretty. This afternoon, however, it is evident that she is unhappy.*) Hey . . .

ELIZABETH. We've just been by your house.

INEZ. You have? Hello, Emily.

EMILY. Hello.

ELIZABETH. We made some divinity and took it over for Horace.

INEZ. Well, that's so sweet of you.

ELIZABETH. What time is he coming in?

INEZ. Six-thirty.

ELIZABETH. Are you meeting him?

INEZ. No—Herman. I've got to cook supper. Can I buy you all a drink?

ELIZABETH. No, we have to get Emily over to the beauty parlor.

INEZ. What are you wearing tonight, Emily?

ELIZABETH. She's wearing that sweet little net I got her the end of last summer. She's never worn it to a dance here.

INEZ. I don't think I've ever seen it. I'll bet it looks beautiful on her. I'm gonna make Horace bring you by the house so I can see you before the dance.

WAITRESS. Excuse me. . . .

INEZ. Yes?

WAITRESS. Have you thought of what you wanted yet? I thought I could be getting it for you.

INEZ. That's sweet, honey . . . but I haven't thought of what I wanted yet. (*To* ELIZABETH *and* EMILY.) I feel so foolish, I came in here for something, and I can't remember what.

WAITRESS. Cosmetics?

INEZ. No . . . you go on. I'll think and call you.

WAITRESS. All right. (*She goes.*)

INEZ. Emily, I think it's so sweet of you to go to the dance with Horace. I know he's going to be thrilled when I tell him.

ELIZABETH. Well, you're thrilled too, aren't you, Emily?

EMILY. Yes ma'm.

ELIZABETH. I told Emily she'd thank me someday for not permitting her to sit home and miss all the fun.

EMILY. Mama, it's five to four. My appointment is at four o'clock.

ELIZABETH. Well, you go on in the car.

EMILY. How are you gonna get home?

ELIZABETH. I'll get home. Don't worry about me.

EMILY. O.K. (*She starts out.*)

INEZ. 'Bye, Emily.

EMILY. 'Bye. (*She goes on out.*)

ELIZABETH. Does Horace have a car for tonight?

INEZ. Oh, yes. He's taking Herman's.

ELIZABETH. I just wondered. I wanted to offer ours if he didn't have one.

INEZ. That's very sweet—but we're giving him our car every night for the two weeks of his visit. Oh—I know what I'm after. Flowers. I have to order Emily's corsage for Horace. I came in here to use the telephone to call you to find out what color Emily's dress was going to be.

ELIZABETH. Blue.

INEZ. My favorite color. Walk me over to the florist.

ELIZABETH. All right.

(*They go out as the lights fade. The lights are brought up* D. L. *on the living room of* INEZ STANLEY. HERMAN STANLEY *and his brother-in-law,* HORACE, *come in.* HERMAN *is carrying* HORACE'S *suitcase.* HERMAN *is in his middle thirties.* HORACE *is eighteen, thin, sensitive, but a likable boy.*)

HERMAN. Inez. Inez. We're here. (*He puts the bag down in the living room.* INEZ *comes running in from* R.)

INEZ. You're early.

HERMAN. The bus was five minutes ahead of time.

INEZ. Is that so? Why, I never heard of that. (*She kisses her brother.*) Hello, honey.

HORACE. Hello, Sis.

INEZ. You look fine.

HORACE. Thank you.

INEZ. You haven't put on a bit of weight though.

HORACE. Haven't I?

INEZ. Not a bit. I'm just going to stuff food down you and put some weight on you while you're here. How's your appetite?

HORACE. Oh, it's real good. I eat all the time.

INEZ. Then why don't you put on some weight?

HORACE. I don't know. I guess I'm just the skinny type.

INEZ. How are the folks?

HORACE. Fine.

INEZ. Mother over her cold?

HORACE. Yes, she is.

INEZ. Dad's fine?

HORACE. Just fine.

INEZ. Oh, Herman, did you ask him?

HERMAN. Ask him what?

INEZ. Ask him what? About his tux.

HERMAN. No, I didn't. . . .

INEZ. Honestly, Herman. Here we have him a date with the prettiest and most popular girl in Harrison and Herman says ask him what. You did bring it, didn't you, Bubber?

HORACE. Bring what?

INEZ. Your tux.

HORACE. Oh, sure.

INEZ. Well, guess who I've got you a date with. Aren't you curious?

HORACE. Uh huh.

INEZ. Well, guess. . . . (*A pause. He thinks.*)

HORACE. I don't know.

INEZ. Well, just try guessing. . . .

HORACE. Well . . . uh . . . uh . . . (*He is a little embarrassed. He stands trying to think. No names come to him.*) I don't know.

INEZ. Emily Crews. Now isn't she a pretty girl?

HORACE. Yes. She is.

INEZ. And the most popular girl in this town. You know her mother is a very close friend of mine and she called me day before yesterday and she said, "I hear Horace is coming to town," and I said yes you were, and she said that the boy Emily is going with is in summer school and couldn't get away this weekend, and Emily said she wouldn't go to the dance at all but her mother said that she had insisted and wondered if you'd take her. . . .

HORACE. Her mother said. Does Emily want me to take her?

INEZ. That isn't the point, Bubber. The point is that her mother doesn't approve of the boy Emily is in love with and she likes you. . . .

HORACE. Who likes me?

INEZ. Emily's mother. And she thinks you would make a very nice couple.

HORACE. Oh. (*A pause.*) But what does Emily think?

INEZ. Emily doesn't know what to think, honey. I'm trying to explain that to you. She's in love.

HORACE. Where am I supposed to take her to?

INEZ. The dance.

HORACE. But, Inez, I don't dance well enough. . . . I don't like to go to dances . . . yet . . .

INEZ. Oh, Horace. Mother wrote me you were learning.

HORACE. Well . . . I am learning. But I don't dance well enough yet.

INEZ. Horace, you just make me sick. The trouble with you is that you have no confidence in yourself. I bet you can dance.

HORACE. No, I can't. . . .

INEZ. Now let's see. (INEZ *goes to the radio and turns it on. She comes back to him.*) Now come on. Show me what you've learned. . . .

HORACE. Aw, Sis . . .

HERMAN. Inez. Why don't you let the boy alone?

INEZ. Now you keep out of this, Herman Stanley. He's my brother and he's a stick. He's missing all the fun in life and I'm not going to have him a stick. I've sat up nights thinking of social engagements to keep him busy every minute of these next two weeks— I've got three dances scheduled for him. So he cannot not dance. Now come on, dance with me. . . . (*He takes her by the arm awkwardly. He begins to lead her around the room.*) Now that's fine. That's just fine. Isn't that fine, Herman?

HERMAN. Uh huh.

INEZ. You see all you need is confidence. And I want you to promise me you'll talk plenty when you're with the girl, not just sit there in silence and only answer when you're asked a question. . . . Now promise me.

HORACE. I promise.

INEZ. Fine. Why, I think he dances real well. Don't you, Herman?

HERMAN. Yes, I do. Just fine, Inez.

INEZ. Just a lovely dancer, all he needs is confidence. He is very light on his feet. And he has a fine sense of rhythm—why, brother, you're a born dancer—

(HORACE *is smiling over the compliments, half wanting to believe what they say, but then not so sure. He is dancing with her around the room as the lights fade. They are brought up on the area* U. R. EMILY CREWS *is in her living room. She has on her dressing gown. She is crying. Her mother,* ELIZABETH, *comes in from* U. R.)

ELIZABETH. Emily.

EMILY. Yes ma'm.

ELIZABETH. Do you know what time it is?

EMILY. Yes ma'm.

ELIZABETH. Then why in the world aren't you dressed?

EMILY. Because I don't feel good.

ELIZABETH. Emily . . .

EMILY. I don't feel good. . . . (*She begins to cry.*) Oh, Mother. I don't want to go to the dance tonight. Please, ma'm, don't make me. I'll do anything in this world for you if you promise me . . .

ELIZABETH. Emily. This is all settled. You are going to that dance. Do you understand me? You are going to that dance. That sweet, nice brother of Inez Stanley's will be here any minute. . . .

EMILY. Sweet, nice brother. He's a goon. That's what he is. A regular goon. A bore and a goon. . . .

ELIZABETH. Emily . . .

EMILY. That's all he is. Just sits and doesn't talk. Can't dance. I'm not going to any dance or anyplace else with him and that's final. (*She runs out* R.)

ELIZABETH. Emily . . . Emily . . . You get ready this minute. . . . (*The doorbell rings. Yelling.*) Emily . . . Emily . . . Horace is here. I want you down those stairs in five minutes . . .

dressed. (*She goes out* L. *and comes back in followed by* HORACE, *all dressed up. He has a corsage box in his hand.*) Hello, Horace.

HORACE. Good evening.

ELIZABETH. Sit down, won't you, Horace? Emily is a little late getting dressed. You know how girls are.

HORACE. Yes ma'm. (*He sits down. He seems a little awkward and shy.*)

ELIZABETH. Can I get you something to drink, Horace?

HORACE. No ma'm.

(*A pause.* ELIZABETH *is obviously very nervous about whether* EMILY *will behave or not.*)

ELIZABETH. Are you sure I can't get you a Coca-Cola or something?

HORACE. No. Thank you.

ELIZABETH. How's your family?

HORACE. Just fine, thank you.

ELIZABETH. I bet your sister was glad to see you.

HORACE. Yes, she was.

ELIZABETH. How's your family? Oh, I guess I asked you that, didn't I?

HORACE. Yes, you did.

(ELIZABETH *keeps glancing off* R., *praying that* EMILY *will put in an appearance.*)

ELIZABETH. I understand you've become quite an accomplished dancer. . . .

HORACE. Oh . . . well . . . I . . .

ELIZABETH. Inez tells me you do all the new steps.

HORACE. Well—I . . .

ELIZABETH. Excuse me. Let me see what is keeping that girl. (*She goes running off* R. HORACE *gets up. He seems very nervous. He begins to practice his dancing. He seems more unsure of himself and awkward. . . . We can hear* ELIZABETH *offstage knocking on* EMILY'S *door. At first* HORACE *isn't conscious of the knocking or the ensuing conversation and goes on practicing his dancing. When he first becomes conscious of what's to follow he tries to pay no attention. Then gradually he moves over to the far* L. *side of the stage. The first thing we hear is* ELIZABETH'S *genteel tapping at* EMILY'S *door. Then she begins to call, softly at first, then louder and louder.*) Emily. Emily. Emily Crews. Emily Carter Crews. . . . (*The pounding offstage is getting louder and louder.*) Emily. I can hear you in there. Now open that door.

EMILY. (*Screaming back.*) I won't. I told you I won't.

ELIZABETH. Emily Carter Crews. You open that door immediately.

EMILY. I won't.

ELIZABETH. I'm calling your father from downtown if you don't open that door right this very minute.

EMILY. I don't care. I won't come out.

ELIZABETH. Then I'll call him. (*She comes running in from* R. HORACE *quickly gets back to his chair and sits.*) Excuse me, Horace. (*She crosses through the room and goes out* U. R. HORACE *seems very ill at ease. He looks at the box of flowers. He is very warm. He begins to fan himself.* ELIZABETH *comes back in the room from* U. R. *She is very nervous, but she tries to hide her nervousness in an overly social manner.* ELIZABETH *has decided to tell a fib.*) Horace, I am so sorry to have to ruin your evening, but my little girl isn't feeling well. She has a headache and a slight temperature and I've just called the doctor and he says he thinks it's very advisable that she stay in this evening. She's upstairs insisting she go, but I do feel under the circumstances I had just better keep her in. I hope you understand.

HORACE. Oh, yes ma'm. I do understand.

ELIZABETH. How long do you plan to visit us, Horace?

HORACE. Two weeks.

ELIZABETH. That's nice. (*They start walking offstage* L.) Please call Emily tomorrow and ask her out again. She'll just be heartbroken if you don't.

HORACE. Yes ma'm. Good night.

ELIZABETH. Good night, Horace. (HORACE *goes out.* ELIZABETH *calls out after him.*) Can you see, Horace? (*In the distance we hear* HORACE *answer.*)

HORACE. Yes ma'm.

ELIZABETH. Now you be sure and call us tomorrow. You hear? (*She stands waiting for a moment. Then she walks back across stage to* U. R., *screaming at the top of her voice.*) Emily Carter Crews. You have mortified me. You have mortified me to death. I have, for your information, called your father and he is interrupting his work and is coming home this very minute and he says to tell you that you are not to be allowed to leave this house again for two solid weeks. Is that perfectly clear?

(*She is screaming as she goes out* U. R. *The lights are brought down. They are brought up immediately* D. R. *on the drugstore. It is half an hour later.* HORACE *comes in. He seats himself at the counter. He still has the box of flowers. The drugstore is deserted. A* WAITRESS *is up near the front with her arms on the counter. She keeps glancing at a clock.* HORACE *is examining a menu. . . .*)

HORACE. Can I have a chicken salad sandwich?

WAITRESS. We're all out of that.

HORACE. Oh. (*He goes back to reading the menu.*)

WAITRESS. If it's all the same to you, I'd rather not make a sandwich. I'm closing my doors in ten minutes.

HORACE. Oh. Well, what would you like to make?

WAITRESS. Any kind of ice cream or soft drinks. (*She looks up at the ice cream menu.*) Coffee is all gone.

HORACE. How about a chocolate ice cream soda?

WAITRESS. O.K. Coming up. (*She starts to mix the soda. She talks as she works.*) Going to the dance?

HORACE. No.

WAITRESS. The way you're all dressed up I thought for sure you were going.

HORACE. No. I was, but I changed my mind.

(MARY CATHERINE DAVIS *comes in the drugstore from* D. R. *Somehow she has gotten in her young head the idea that she is a plain girl and in defiance for the pain of that fact she does everything she can to make herself look plainer.*)

WAITRESS. Hello, Mary Catherine. Been to the movies?

MARY CATHERINE. Yes, I have.

(*The* WAITRESS *puts the drink down in front of* HORACE. *He begins to drink.*)

WAITRESS. What'll you have, Mary Catherine?

MARY CATHERINE. Vanilla ice cream.

WAITRESS. O.K. (*She gets the ice cream. She talks as she does so.*) There weren't many at the picture show tonight, I bet. I can always tell by whether we have a crowd in here or not after the first show. I guess everybody is at the dance.

MARY CATHERINE. I could have gone, but I didn't want to. I didn't want to miss the picture show. Emily Crews didn't go. Leo couldn't get home from summer school and she said she was refusing to go. Her mother made a date for her with some bore from out of town without consulting her and she was furious about it. I talked to her this afternoon. She said she didn't know yet how she would get out of it, but she would. She said she had some rights. Her mother doesn't approve of Leo and that's a shame because they are practically engaged.

WAITRESS. I think Emily is a very cute girl, don't you?

MARY CATHERINE. Oh, yes. I think she's darling.

(HORACE *has finished his drink and is embarrassed by their talk. He is trying to get the* WAITRESS's *attention but doesn't quite know how. He finally calls to the* WAITRESS.)

HORACE. Miss . . .

WAITRESS. Yes?

HORACE. How much do I owe you?

WAITRESS. Twenty cents.

HORACE. Thank you. (*He reaches in his pocket for the money.*)

WAITRESS. Emily has beautiful clothes, doesn't she?

MARY CATHERINE. Oh, yes. She does.

WAITRESS. Her folks are rich?

MARY CATHERINE. She has the prettiest things. But she's not a bit stuck up. . . .

(HORACE *holds the money out to the* WAITRESS.)

HORACE. Here you are.

WAITRESS. Thank you. (*She takes the money and rings it up on the cash register.* HORACE *goes on out. The* WAITRESS *shakes her head as he goes.*) There's a goofy nut if I ever saw one. He's got flowers under his arm. He's wearing a tux and yet he's not going to the dance. Who is he?

MARY CATHERINE. I don't know. I never saw him before.

(*The* WAITRESS *walks to the edge of the area and looks out. She comes back shaking her head. She sits on the stool beside* MARY CATHERINE.)

WAITRESS. (*While laughing and shaking her head.*) I ought to call the sheriff and have him locked up. Do you know what he's doing?

MARY CATHERINE. No. What?

WAITRESS. Standing on the corner. Dancing back and forth. He's holding his arm up like he's got a girl and everything. Wouldn't

it kill you? (MARY CATHERINE *goes to the front and looks out.*)
See him?

MARY CATHERINE. No. He's stopped.

WAITRESS. What's he doing?

MARY CATHERINE. Just standing there. Looking kind of lost.
(MARY CATHERINE *comes back to the counter. She starts eating her ice
cream again.*)

WAITRESS. Well—it takes all kinds.

MARY CATHERINE. I guess so.

(*She goes back to eating her ice cream. The lights are brought down.
The lights are brought up on the area* D. L. *The living room of the*
STANLEYS. INEZ *is there reading a book.* HERMAN *comes in.*)

HERMAN. Hi, hon.

INEZ. Hello. . . .

HERMAN. What's the matter with you? You look down in the
dumps.

INEZ. No. I'm just disgusted.

HERMAN. What are you disgusted about?

INEZ. Horace. I had everything planned so beautifully for him
and then that silly Emily has to go and hurt his feelings.

HERMAN. Well, honey, that was pretty raw, the trick she pulled.

INEZ. I know. But he's a fool to let that get him down. He should
have just gone to the dance by himself and proved her wrong. . . .
Why, like I told him. Show her up. Rush a different girl every
night. Be charming. Make yourself popular. But it's like trying to
talk to a stone wall. He refused to go out anymore. He says he's
going home tomorrow.

HERMAN. Where is he now?

INEZ. Gone to the movies.

HERMAN. Well, honey. I hate to say it, but in a way it serves you right. I've told you a thousand times if I've told you once. Leave the boy alone. He'll be all right. Only don't push him. You and your mother have pushed the boy and pushed him and pushed him.

INEZ. And I'm going to keep on pushing him. I let him off tonight because his feelings were hurt, but tomorrow I'm going to have a long talk with him.

HERMAN. Inez. Leave the boy alone.

INEZ. I won't leave him alone. He is my brother and I'm going to see that he learns to have a good time.

HERMAN. Inez . . .

INEZ. Now you just let me handle this, Herman. He's starting to college next year and it's a most important time in his life. He had no fun in high school. . . .

HERMAN. Now he must have had some fun. . . .

INEZ. Not like other people. And he's not going through four years of college like a hermit with his nose stuck in some old book. . . . (*She jumps up.*) I'll never forgive Elizabeth for letting Emily behave this way. And I told her so. I said, "Elizabeth Crews, I am very upset." . . .

(*She is angrily walking up and down as the lights fade. They are brought up D. R. on the drugstore area. The WAITRESS is there alone. MARY CATHERINE comes in from D. R.*)

WAITRESS. Did you go to the movies again tonight?

MARY CATHERINE. Uh huh. Lila, do you remember when I was telling you about Emily's date and how she wouldn't go out with him because he was such a bore?

WAITRESS. Uh . . .

MARY CATHERINE. Oh. I just feel awful. That was the boy sitting in here. . . .

WAITRESS. Last night? . . .

MARY CATHERINE. Yes. I went riding with Emily and some of the girls this afternoon and we passed by his sister's house and there sat the boy.

WAITRESS. Shh . . . shh . . . (*She has seen* HORACE *come into the area from* D. R. *He comes to the counter. He seems very silent. He picks up a menu.*) Back again tonight?

HORACE. Uh huh.

WAITRESS. What'll you have?

HORACE. A cup of coffee. . . .

WAITRESS. All out. We don't serve coffee after eight unless we happen to have some left over from suppertime. . . .

HORACE. Thanks. (*He gets up.*)

WAITRESS. Nothing else?

HORACE. No, thanks.

(*He goes over to the magazine rack. He picks up a magazine and starts looking through it.* EMILY CREWS *comes in from* D. R. *She doesn't see* HORACE. *She goes right over to* MARY CATHERINE.)

EMILY. Leora and I were riding around the square and we saw you sitting here. . . .

(MARY CATHERINE *points to* HORACE. EMILY *turns around and sees him. She looks a little embarrassed. He happens to glance up, and sees her.*)

HORACE. Hello, Emily.

EMILY. Hello, Horace. . . . Do you know Mary Catherine Davis?

HORACE. No. How do you do.

EMILY. I feel awfully bad about last night, Horace. My mother says that you know I wasn't really sick. I just wanted to tell you that it had nothing to do with you, Horace. It was a battle be-

tween me and my mother. Mary Catherine can tell you. I promised the boy I go with not to go out with any other boys. . . .

HORACE. Oh, that's all right. I understand.

EMILY. You see, we've gone steady for two years. All the other
boys in town understand it and their feelings are not a bit hurt if I
turn them down. Are they, Mary Catherine?

MARY CATHERINE. No.

EMILY. Mary Catherine is my best friend and she can tell you I'm
not stuck up. And I would have gone anyway, except I was so
mad at my mother. . . .

MARY CATHERINE. Emily is not stuck up a bit. Emily used to date
all the boys before she began going with Leo steadily. She even
had a date with Gus Meredith. All the other girls wouldn't go
with him because they thought he was so fat and unattractive,
but Emily said she wouldn't hurt his feelings for the world and she
went with him. Didn't you, Emily?

EMILY. Uh huh. How long are you going to be here, Horace?

HORACE. Well, I haven't decided, Emily.

EMILY. Well, I hope you're not still hurt with me.

HORACE. No, I'm not, Emily.

EMILY. Well, I'm glad for that. Mary Catherine, can you come
with us?

MARY CATHERINE. No, I can't, Emily. Velma came in after the
first show started and I promised to wait here for her and we'd
walk home together.

EMILY. Come on. We can ride around and watch for her.

MARY CATHERINE. No. I don't dare. You know how sensitive
Velma is. If she looked in here and saw I wasn't sitting at this
counter she'd go right home and not speak to me again for two or
three months.

EMILY. Velma's too sensitive. You shouldn't indulge her in it.

MARY CATHERINE. I'm willing to grant you that. But you all are going off to college next year and Velma and I are the only ones that are going to be left here and I can't afford to get her mad at me.

EMILY. O.K. I'll watch out for you and if we're still riding around when Velma gets out, we'll pick you up.

MARY CATHERINE. Fine. . . .

EMILY. 'Bye. . . .

MARY CATHERINE. 'Bye. . . .

EMILY. 'Bye, Horace.

HORACE. Good-bye, Emily.

(*She goes out* D. R.)

MARY CATHERINE. She's a lovely girl. She was my closest friend until this year. Now we're still good friends, but we're not as close as we were. We had a long talk about it last week. I told her I understood. She and Eloise Dayton just naturally have a little more in common now. They're both going steady and they're going to the same college. (*A pause.*) They're going to Sophie Newcomb. Are you going to college?

HORACE. Uh huh.

MARY CATHERINE. You are? What college?

HORACE. The University. . . .

MARY CATHERINE. Oh, I know lots of people there. (*A pause.*) I had a long talk with Emily about my not getting to go. She said she thought it was wonderful that I wasn't showing any bitterness about it. (*A pause.*) I'm getting a job next week so I can save up enough money to go into Houston to business school. I'll probably work in Houston someday. If I don't get too lonely. Velma Morrison's oldest sister went into Houston and got herself a job but she almost died from loneliness. She's back here now working at the courthouse. Oh, well . . . I don't think I'll get lonely. I think a change of scenery would be good for me.

(VELMA MORRISON *comes in* D. R. *She is about the same age as* MARY CATHERINE. *She is filled with excitement.*)

VELMA. Mary Catherine, you're going to be furious with me. But Stanley Sewell came in right after you left and he said he'd never forgive me if I didn't go riding with him. I said I had to ask you first, as I had asked you to wait particularly for me and that I knew you were very sensitive.

MARY CATHERINE. I'm very sensitive. You're very sensitive. . . . I have never in my life stopped speaking to you over anything.

(*A car horn is heard offstage.*)

VELMA. Will you forgive me if I go?

MARY CATHERINE. Oh, sure.

(VELMA *goes running out.*)

VELMA. Thank you. (*She disappears out the door.*)

MARY CATHERINE. I'm not nearly as close to Velma as I am to Emily. I think Emily's beautiful, don't you?

HORACE. Yes. She's very pretty.

MARY CATHERINE. Well, Lila's going to kill us if we don't stop holding her up. Which way do you go?

HORACE. Home.

MARY CATHERINE. I go that way too. We can walk together.

HORACE. O.K.

(*They go out of the area.*)

MARY CATHERINE. Good night, Lila.

WAITRESS. Good night.

(*They continue walking out as the lights fade. The lights are brought up on the living room of the* CREWS's *house.* ELIZABETH CREWS *is there, crying.* EMILY *comes in.*)

EMILY. Mother, what is it? Has something happened to Daddy?

ELIZABETH. No. He's in bed asleep.

EMILY. Then what is it?

ELIZABETH. Inez blessed me out and stopped speaking to me over last night. She says we've ruined the boy's whole vacation. You've broken his heart, given him all kinds of complexes and he's going home tomorrow. . . .

EMILY. But I saw him at the drugstore tonight and I had a long talk with him and he said he understood. . . .

ELIZABETH. But Inez doesn't understand. She says she'll never forgive either of us again. (*She starts to cry.*)

EMILY. Oh, Mother. I'm sorry. . . .

ELIZABETH. Emily, if you'll do me one favor . . . I promise you I'll never ask another thing of you again as long as I live. And I will never nag you about going out with Leo again as long as I live. . . .

EMILY. What is the favor, Mother?

ELIZABETH. Let that boy take you to the dance day after to-morrow. . . .

EMILY. Now, Mother . . .

ELIZABETH. Emily. I get down on my knees to you. Do me this one favor. . . . (*A pause.*) Emily . . . Emily . . . (*She is crying again.*)

EMILY. Now, Mother, please. Don't cry. I'll think about it. I'll call Leo and see what he says. But please don't cry like this. . . . Mother . . . Mother . . .

(*She is trying to console her as the lights fade. The lights are brought up on* U. L. *It is* MARY CATHERINE's *yard and living room. Music can be heard in the distance.* HORACE *and* MARY CATHERINE *come walking in* D. L. *and go up the* C. *of the stage until they reach the upstage area.*)

MARY CATHERINE. Well, this is where I live.

HORACE. In that house there?

MARY CATHERINE. Uh huh. (*A pause.*)

HORACE. Where is that music coming from?

MARY CATHERINE. The Flats. . . .

HORACE. What's the Flats?

MARY CATHERINE. I don't know what it is. That's just what they call it. It's nothing but a bunch of barbecue restaurants and beer joints down there and they call it the Flats. There used to be a creek running down there that they called Willow Creek but it's all dry now. My father says when he was a boy, every time the river flooded, Willow Creek would fill up. The river doesn't overflow anymore since they took the raft out of it. I like to come out here at night and listen to the music. Do you like to dance? . . .

HORACE. Well . . . I . . .

MARY CATHERINE. I love to dance.

HORACE. Well . . . I don't dance too well.

MARY CATHERINE. There's nothing to it but confidence.

HORACE. That's what my sister says. . . .

MARY CATHERINE. I didn't learn for the longest kind of time for lack of confidence and then Emily gave me a long lecture about it and I got confidence and went ahead and learned. Would you like to come in for a while?

HORACE. Well . . . if it's all right with you. . . .

MARY CATHERINE. I'd be glad to have you.

HORACE. Thank you.

(*They go into the area.* MARY CATHERINE's *father,* TOM DAVIS, *is seated there in his undershirt. He works in a garage.*)

MARY CATHERINE. Hello, Daddy.

TOM. Hello, baby.

MARY CATHERINE. Daddy, this is Horace.

TOM. Hello, son.

HORACE. Howdy do, sir. (*They shake hands.*)

MARY CATHERINE. Horace is Mrs. Inez Stanley's brother. He's here on a visit.

TOM. That's nice. Where's your home, son?

HORACE. Flatonia.

TOM. Oh, I see. Well, are you young people going to visit for a while?

MARY CATHERINE. Yes sir.

TOM. Well, I'll leave you then. Good night.

MARY CATHERINE. Good night, Daddy.

HORACE. Good night, sir. (*He goes out* U. L.) What does your father do?

MARY CATHERINE. He works in a garage. He's a mechanic. What does your father do?

HORACE. He's a judge.

MARY CATHERINE. My father worries so because he can't afford to send me to college. My mother told him that was all foolishness. That I'd rather go to business school anyway.

HORACE. Had you rather go to business school?

MARY CATHERINE. I don't know. (*A pause.*) Not really. But I'd never tell him that. When I was in the seventh grade I thought I would die if I couldn't get there, but then when I was in the ninth, Mother talked to me one day and told me Daddy wasn't sleeping at nights for fear I'd be disappointed if he couldn't send me, so I told him the next night I decided I'd rather go to business school. He seemed relieved. (*A pause.*)

HORACE. Mary Catherine. I . . . uh . . . heard you say a while ago that you didn't dance because you lacked confidence and uh . . . then I heard you say you talked it over with Emily and she told you what was wrong and you got the confidence and you went ahead. . . .

MARY CATHERINE. That's right. . . .

HORACE. Well . . . It may sound silly and all to you . . . seeing I'm about to start my first year at college . . . but I'd like to ask you a question. . . .

MARY CATHERINE. What is it, Horace?

HORACE. How do you get confidence?

MARY CATHERINE. Well, you just get it. Someone points it out to you that you lack it and then you get it. . . .

HORACE. Oh, is that how it's done?

MARY CATHERINE. That's how I did it.

HORACE. You see I lack confidence. And I . . . sure would like to get it. . . .

MARY CATHERINE. In what way do you lack confidence, Horace? . . .

HORACE. Oh, in all kinds of ways. (*A pause.*) I'm not much of a mixer. . . .

MARY CATHERINE. I think you're just mixing fine tonight.

HORACE. I know. That's what's giving me a little encouragement. You're the first girl I've ever really been able to talk to. I mean this way. . . .

MARY CATHERINE. Am I, Horace? . . .

HORACE. Yes.

MARY CATHERINE. Well, I feel in some ways that's quite a compliment.

HORACE. Well, you should feel that way. (*A pause.*) Mary Catherine . . .

MARY CATHERINE. Yes, Horace?

HORACE. I had about decided to go back home tomorrow or the next day, but I understand there's another dance at the end of the week. . . .

MARY CATHERINE. Uh huh. Day after tomorrow.

HORACE. Well . . . I . . . don't know if you have a date or not . . . but if you don't have . . . I feel if I could take you . . . I would gain the confidence to go . . . I mean . . .

MARY CATHERINE. Well, Horace . . . You see . . .

HORACE. I know I'd gain the confidence. My sister is a swell dancer and she'll let me practice with her every living minute until it's time for the dance. Of course I don't know if I could learn to jitterbug by then or rumba or do anything fancy, you understand, but I know I could learn the fox-trot and I can waltz a little now. . . .

MARY CATHERINE. I'm sure you could.

HORACE. Well, will you go with me?

MARY CATHERINE. Yes, Horace. I'd love to. . . .

HORACE. Oh, thank you, Mary Catherine. I'll just practice night and day. I can't tell you how grateful Inez is going to be to you. . . . Mary Catherine, if we played the radio softly could we dance now?

MARY CATHERINE. Why certainly, Horace.

HORACE. You understand I'll make mistakes. . . .

MARY CATHERINE. I understand. . . . (*She turns the radio on very softly.*)

HORACE. All right.

MARY CATHERINE. Yes. . . . (*He approaches her very cautiously and takes her in his arms. He begins awkwardly to dance.* MARY CATHERINE *is very pleased and happy.*) Why, you're doing fine, Horace. Just fine.

HORACE. Thank you, Mary Catherine. Thank you.

(*They continue dancing.* HORACE *is very pleased with himself although he is still dancing quite awkwardly. The lights fade. The lights are brought up on the area* D. L. *It is early next morning.* INEZ *is there reading.* HORACE *comes in whistling. He seems brimming over with happiness.*)

INEZ. What are you so happy about?

HORACE. I'm just happy.

INEZ. Wait until you hear my news and you'll be happier.

HORACE. Is that so?

INEZ. Miss Emily has seen the light.

HORACE. What?

INEZ. She has succumbed.

HORACE. What do you mean?

INEZ. She has crawled on her knees.

HORACE. She's crawled on her knees? I don't get it. . . .

INEZ. She has eaten dirt.

HORACE. Sister, what's this all about?

INEZ. Last night around ten o'clock she called in the meekest kind of voice possible and said, "Inez, I've called up to apologize to you. I have apologized to Horace in the drugstore." Did she?

HORACE. Uh huh.

INEZ. "And now I want to apologize to you and to tell you how sorry I am I behaved so badly." . . .

HORACE. Well. Isn't that nice of her, Inez?

INEZ. Wait a minute. You haven't heard the whole thing. And then Her Highness added, "Tell Horace if he would like to invite me to the dance to call me and I'd be glad to accept." And furthermore, Elizabeth called this morning and said they were leaving for Houston to buy her the most expensive evening dress in sight. Just to impress you with.

HORACE. Oh . . . (*He sits down on a chair.*)

INEZ. Brother. What is the matter with you? Now are you gonna start worrying about this dancin' business all over again? You are the biggest fool sometimes. We've got today and tomorrow to practice.

HORACE. Inez . . .

INEZ. Yes?

HORACE. I already have a date with someone tomorrow. . . .

INEZ. You do?

HORACE. Yes. I met a girl last night at the drugstore and I asked her.

INEZ. What girl did you ask?

HORACE. Mary Catherine Davis. . . .

INEZ. Well, you've got to get right out of it. You've got to call her up and explain just what happened.

HORACE. But, Inez . . .

INEZ. You've got to do it, Horace. They told me they are spending all kinds of money for that dress. I practically had to threaten Elizabeth with never speaking to her again to bring this all about. Why, she will never forgive me now if I turn around and tell her you can't go. . . . Horace. Don't look that way. I can't help it. For my sake, for your sister's sake, you've got to get out of this date with Mary Catherine Davis . . . tell her . . . tell her . . . anything. . . .

HORACE. O.K. (*A pause. He starts out.*) What can I say?

INEZ. I don't know, Horace. (*A pause.*) Say . . . well, just tell her the truth. That's the best thing. Tell her that Emily's mother is your sister's best friend and that Emily's mother has taken her into Houston to buy her a very expensive dress. . . .

HORACE. What if Mary Catherine has bought a dress? . . .

INEZ. Well, she can't have bought an expensive dress. . . .

HORACE. Why not?

INEZ. Because her people can't afford it. Honey, you'll be the envy of every young man in Harrison, bringing Emily Crews to the dance. . . . Why, everybody will wonder just what it is you have. . . .

HORACE. I'm not going to do it.

INEZ. Horace . . .

HORACE. I don't want to take Emily, I want to take Mary Catherine and that's just what I'm going to do.

INEZ. Horace . . .

HORACE. My mind is made up. Once and for all. . . .

INEZ. Then what am I gonna do? (*She starts to cry.*) Who's gonna speak to Elizabeth? She'll bless me out putting her to all this trouble. Making her spend all this money and time . . . (*She is crying loudly now.*) Horace. You just can't do this to me. You just simply can't. . . .

HORACE. I can't help it. I'm not taking Emily Crews—

INEZ. Horace . . .

HORACE. I am not taking Emily Crews.

(*He is firm. She is crying as the lights fade. The lights are brought up on U. L. area.* MARY CATHERINE's *father is seated there. He is in his undershirt. In the distance dance music can be heard.* MRS. DAVIS *comes in from* L.)

MRS. DAVIS. Don't you think you'd better put your shirt on, Tom? Mary Catherine's date will be here any minute.

TOM. What time is it?

MRS. DAVIS. Nine o'clock.

TOM. The dance has already started. I can hear the music from here.

MRS. DAVIS. I know. But you know young people, they'd die before they'd be the first to a dance. Put your shirt on, Tom.

TOM. O.K.

MRS. DAVIS. As soon as her date arrives we'll go.

TOM. O.K.

(MARY CATHERINE *comes in from* L. *She has on an evening dress and she looks very pretty.*)

MRS. DAVIS. Why, Mary Catherine. You look lovely. Doesn't she look lovely, Tom?

TOM. Yes, she does.

MRS. DAVIS. Turn around, honey, and let me see you from the back. (*She does so.*) Just as pretty as you can be, Mary Catherine.

MARY CATHERINE. Thank you. (HORACE *comes in* D. L. *in his tux with a corsage box. He walks up the* C. *of the stage to the* U. L. *area.*) That's Horace. (*She goes to the corner of the area.*) Hello, Horace.

HORACE. Hello, Mary Catherine.

MARY CATHERINE. You've met my mother and father.

HORACE. Yes, I have. I met your father the other night and your mother yesterday afternoon.

MRS. DAVIS. Hello, Horace.

TOM. Hello, son.

MRS. DAVIS. Well, we were just going. You all have a good time tonight.

HORACE. Thank you.

MRS. DAVIS. Come on, Tom.

TOM. All right. Good night and have a nice time.

MARY CATHERINE. Thank you, Daddy. (*They go out* L. HORACE *hands her the corsage box. She takes it and opens it.*) Oh, thank you, Horace. Thank you so much. (*She takes the flowers out.*) They're just lovely. Will you pin them on for me?

HORACE. I'll try. (*He takes the corsage and the pin. He begins to pin it on.*) Will about here be all right?

MARY CATHERINE. Just fine. (*He pins the corsage on.*) Emily told me about the mix-up between your sister and her mother. I appreciate your going ahead and taking me anyway. If you had wanted to get out of it I would have understood. Emily and I are very good friends . . . and . . .

HORACE. I didn't want to get out of it, Mary Catherine. I wanted to take you.

MARY CATHERINE. I'm glad you didn't want to get out of it. Emily offered to let me wear her new dress. But I had already bought one of my own.

HORACE. It's very pretty, Mary Catherine.

MARY CATHERINE. Thank you. (*A pause.*) Well, the dance has started. I can hear the music. Can't you?

HORACE. Yes.

MARY CATHERINE. Well, we'd better get going. . . .

HORACE. All right. (*They start out.*) Mary Catherine. I hope you don't think this is silly, but could we practice just once more? . . .

MARY CATHERINE. Certainly we could. . . .

(*They start to dance.* HORACE *has improved although he is no Fred Astaire. They are dancing around and suddenly* HORACE *breaks away.*)

HORACE. Mary Catherine. I'm not good enough yet. I can't go. I'm sorry. Please, let's just stay here.

MARY CATHERINE. No, Horace. We have to go.

HORACE. Please, Mary Catherine . . .

MARY CATHERINE. I know just how you feel, Horace, but we have to go. (*A pause.*) I haven't told you the whole truth, Horace. This is my first dance too. . . .

HORACE. It is?

MARY CATHERINE. Yes. I've been afraid to go. Afraid I wouldn't be popular. The last two dances I was asked to go and I said no.

HORACE. Then why did you accept when I asked you?

MARY CATHERINE. I don't know. I asked myself that afterwards. I guess because you gave me a kind of confidence. (*A pause. They dance again.*) You gave me confidence and I gave you confidence. What's the sense of getting confidence, Horace, if you're not going to use it?

(*A pause. They continue dancing.*)

HORACE. That's a pretty piece.

MARY CATHERINE. Yes, it is.

(*A pause. They dance again.* HORACE *stops.*)

HORACE. I'm ready to go if you are, Mary Catherine.

MARY CATHERINE. I'm ready. (*They start out.*) Scared?

HORACE. A little.

MARY CATHERINE. So am I. But let's go.

HORACE. O.K.

(*They continue out the area down the* C. *of the stage and off* D. R. *as the music from the dance is heard . . . and the lights fade.*)

The Man Who
Climbed
the Pecan Trees

During the twenty-eight years between *The Dancers* and this play Horton Foote's life and career changed a great deal. He wrote a few more scripts for television between 1954 and 1964, but became a much-sought-after screenwriter after winning an Academy Award in 1962 for his adaptation of Harper Lee's novel *To Kill a Mockingbird*. He wrote intermittently for film in the ten years after *Mockingbird*, completing two noteworthy screenplays—*Baby, the Rain Must Fall* (1964; from his own play *The Traveling Lady*) and *Tomorrow* (1972; from a short story by William Faulkner), a major work of American independent filmmaking. Throughout this period (1965 to the late seventies), when almost none of his work was being staged, Foote steadfastly continued to write plays. Eventually, in the late 1970s, with the beginning of *The Orphans' Home Cycle*, as well as new adaptations for PBS and finally the screenplay for *Tender Mercies*, his work for the theater once again began to be produced. *The Man Who Climbed the Pecan Trees*, his first one-act play in almost three decades, was a result of this revival.

As his creative life went through many changes, Horton Foote's fictional world was transformed as well. Helen Crews of *The Midnight Caller* and the young couple of *The Dancers* were among the most resourceful of Horton Foote's characters, but the Campbells of this later play have little courage to face themselves and to accept responsibility for their lives. Mrs. Campbell is trapped by her innocent need to find everything "all right" and to "look on the bright side." Her children, especially Brother, are so obsessed with money that the loss of seventy-five thousand dollars is the source of endless shame. And Stanley and Bertie Dee, once seemingly perfect childhood sweethearts, have become two bitter adult children living out their fathers' fantasies. Even Stanley's impulse to start over is tainted by his need to retreat from reality and once again become his mother's boy.

The Man Who Climbed the Pecan Trees is Foote's darkest short play to that time, because, written after the disorder of the sixties, it reflects the breakdown of the traditional social contracts that the playwright observed during that troubled decade. Threats of violence are commonplace, and, as the apparent affair between Bertie Dee and Wesley Cox suggests, familial bonds of trust are fractured. Sexual license (as in the story of the Jacksons) and a radical narcissism (as in Stanley's complaint that he has been cheated out of his childhood and youth) have left the family and normal social intercourse in shambles.

In this play the Campbells have lost the sense of order and proportion that comes from living with a sense of the past. Mrs. Campbell speaks for the new style in Harrison: "Don't look back now, don't look back. And if you do only think of the pleasant things." The past in *The Man Who Climbed the Pecan Trees* is a sentimental fantasy kingdom composed of the "pleasant things" Mrs. Campbell insists on. With the loss of an authentic and nurturing sense of history, friendship, community and the family order become threatened.

This brokenness is the source of Stanley's bizarre actions with the pecan trees of the play's title. In Horton Foote's work children often express their need for roots by planting small trees. Once they feel secure in their world, they show an adventurous spirit by climbing large ones. This is one way Scout and Jem in *To Kill a Mockingbird* and Margaret Rose in *The Traveling Lady* demonstrate their natural desire to explore and play. But

Stanley's life is not like theirs; he is out of step with the natural rhythms of life. His frantic and senseless trips to the pecan trees reveal how unhappily disconnected he is from the venerable past the trees represent. Without essential ties to others, Stanley loses the courage to act; at the end of the play he is left clinging pathetically to his mother, in terror that he'll fall.

As the previous plays make clear, healthy attachments are the salvation of Foote's orphaned, lonely characters. In most of the plays of the 1950s sustaining connections give the Harrisonians a place from which to explore their lives more adventurously and creatively. Attachments are just as crucial in the plays of the eighties, but the sense of dislocation is so profound in *The Man Who Climbed the Pecan Trees* that roots must become the subject of the play, not wings. Re-acquiring a sense of tradition, a home to live in, is the deepest need in this play, as it will be in Foote's *Orphans' Home Cycle* later.

The Man Who Climbed the Pecan Trees was first produced by The Loft Studio, Los Angeles, in 1982, on a program with *Blind Date*. Directed by William Traylor, the production featured Peggy Feury as Mrs. Campbell and Albert Horton Foote, the playwright's son, as Stanley. The play's first New York production was at the Ensemble Studio Theatre in July 1988, under the direction of Curt Dempster.

The Man Who Climbed the Pecan Trees

CAST

Mrs. Campbell	Stanley
Brother	Bertie Dee
Davis	

Place: Harrison, Texas
Time: September 1938

The living room of the CAMPBELL *house.* MRS. CAMPBELL, *52, is there with her oldest son,* BROTHER, *35.*

MRS. CAMPBELL. Murray St. John just called and said Davis and Stanley had driven him to Iago and were on their way here.

BROTHER. Why did they take Murray St. John to Iago?

MRS. CAMPBELL. I don't know. I didn't ask him. (*She looks out the window.*) The lights are on at Stanley's house. Bertie Dee is still awake. I would call over and tell her Stanley is with Davis, but I never know what kind of mood I'll find her in.

BROTHER. How long has Stanley been acting so strangely?

MRS. CAMPBELL. Well, he's been drinking heavily for a while. He comes over usually after supper to have a visit with me and the last few months I couldn't help but notice he was very full every time he came over. A number of times he would just go to sleep sitting right on that chair, and then after he would visit or sleep for a while, he would get up and say he had to go down to the office and do some work. I don't sleep too well since Daddy died and I would lie in bed after, listening for his car to come home. I would be nervous, you know, because of his drinking, afraid he'd get in a wreck. Anyway it would be later and later and later when

I'd finally hear his car drive into his garage. Sometimes not until four in the morning and finally I called Davis and I said, "Davis, come over here, I have to have a talk with you. Stanley is not getting home until four in the morning." "I know that," he said, "and we have certainly to face something. He is behaving peculiarly." "In what way?" I asked. "He is drinking," he said. "I am aware of that," I said, "although I pretend not to notice even when he goes off to sleep right in front of me." "Well," he said, "when he gets drunk late at night he goes down to the courthouse square and climbs the pecan trees. Someone saw him doing that one night, and now word has gotten around town," Davis said, "and people stay up all night just to watch him." "Does Bertie Dee know about this?" I asked. "Yes," he said. "And how does she take it?" "She told me," he said, "that she hoped he would fall and break his neck." And he said, "I said, 'Bertie Dee, you don't mean that.' 'Yes, I do,' she said." (*She cries.*) I'm so glad Daddy didn't live to see how this marriage has turned out. She's very bitter and hard, you know. She does nothing at all to keep him from drinking. "Please ask him not to drink," I said to her the other day. "I don't care what he does," she said. "Think of your son," I said. "He shouldn't see his daddy drink all the time." "You ask him not to drink," she said, "since it worries you so much." (*He gets up.*) Where are you going?

BROTHER. I'm going back to Houston.

MRS. CAMPBELL. Why? I thought you had come to spend the night.

BROTHER. I did. But I'm too nervous. All these troubles get me wild. I come down here to get away from my own troubles and all I hear are Stanley's troubles. Anyway I shouldn't come here.

MRS. CAMPBELL. Why, it's your home.

BROTHER. I lost seventy-five thousand dollars.

MRS. CAMPBELL. You didn't do it on purpose.

BROTHER. How could I have been such a fool? How could I have let Phil Beaufort deceive me so?

MRS. CAMPBELL. We were all deceived. I was. Davis. Stanley. Sarah . . .

BROTHER. But I was the original sap. I got you all involved. Why out of all the people in Harrison, Texas, did he pick me out to get involved in his scheme?

MRS. CAMPBELL. Don't look back.

BROTHER. Seventy-five thousand dollars!

MRS. CAMPBELL. I never look back. I have two wonderful daughters. One dead. Three wonderful sons . . .

BROTHER. I am a failure. A stupid failure!

MRS. CAMPBELL. You were president of the oil company for two years.

BROTHER. A fraudulent oil company.

MRS. CAMPBELL. Shh, I hear a car. Let's talk of happy, pleasant things in front of Stanley. (*A pause.*) I miss Daddy. Those were happy times, when Daddy was alive and we were all living at home. "Who's your favorite?" Mrs. Harper asked me once. "I have none," I said. "Don't hand me that," she said. "You have a favorite. Everybody does." "I don't know about everybody," I said, "but I have five children and I love each one just as much as the others. Daddy and I live for our children," I said. "Our deepest wish is to see them all well and happy." (*She cries.*)

BROTHER. Now, Mama. Please don't cry. You have been so brave.

MRS. CAMPBELL. I know. I don't mean to cry. I know everything is going to turn out all right. Baby Sister and Daddy are in heaven, so they are at peace. Davis is married and has a sweet, hardworking wife, a little sarcastic, but I don't let that upset me and he has two lovely sons. Stanley has this drinking problem. But if we're patient and understanding he'll overcome that, and you will soon land on your feet again. And you may not be president of an oil company, but you will be very successful. I am sure of that. And though your first marriage wasn't a success, your second marriage is a happy one. So let's all count our blessings. Let's don't just look on the gloomy side. Let's . . .

(DAVIS, *26, and* STANLEY, *30, enter.*)

DAVIS. I asked Murray St. John to call you. Did he?

MRS. CAMPBELL. Yes. Why were you and Stanley in Iago with Murray St. John?

DAVIS. He was on the courthouse square when I got there. He needed a ride home.

MRS. CAMPBELL. Stanley, your brother is here. Say hello to your brother.

STANLEY. How is Phil Beaufort?

BROTHER. How would I know? I haven't seen him since the bankruptcy proceedings.

MRS. CAMPBELL. Now let's don't bring up unpleasant things. I want us all to count our blessings. I was doing that with Brother just before you came in.

STANLEY. Guess what Davis and I did.

DAVIS. Not Davis! You did. I had nothing to do with it.

MRS. CAMPBELL. What did you do? If it's something terrible I don't want to hear about it.

STANLEY. I called the Houston operator and I said, "I want the number in Houston of Philip Beaufort," and she found it for me, and I called him up.

MRS. CAMPBELL. When?

STANLEY. Just now. Davis took me by the office and I called him.

BROTHER. Oh, Jesus!

MRS. CAMPBELL. And what did he say?

STANLEY. He said, "What in the hell do you mean waking me up at this time of the night? Are you drunk?" "Drunk enough," I said, "to ask you a few questions. Why did you involve my brother in a fraudulent scheme that took all my mother's reserves? You have known us all your life. Why did you do this to us, Phil Beaufort? You are a monster," I said. "I am drunk enough to tell you that. We are all aware in this family the kind of monster you are. You married a sweet girl, named Marjorie Halliday, from Harrison, took her to Houston, bullied and mistreated her, and when her father tried to interfere you stabbed and killed him and hired a slick lawyer to get you off, saying it was self-defense."

MRS. CAMPBELL. And what did he say?

STANLEY. He hung up on me. I'm going to call him back.

DAVIS. No you're not!

STANLEY. The hell I'm not! I'm going to call him every day. I will never let him forget what he has done. Seventy-five thousand dollars! (STANLEY *sings:*) "In the gloamin', Oh, my darlin' . . ." (*A pause.*) Where is Marjorie Halliday?

MRS. CAMPBELL. She's in Houston. Dora Vaughn does social work and she says Marjorie and her children applied for relief. She says she has broken. She has married again. (*A pause.*)

BROTHER. I have failed you all.

DAVIS. Oh, come on, Brother.

BROTHER. I can never get over my feeling of shame.

STANLEY. (*Singing.*) "In the gloamin', Oh, my darlin' . . ." (*He gets up.*) I am going back downtown. I have to write my editorial.

DAVIS. No, Stanley. You have done all your work for the week. You told me that.

STANLEY. Except for one editorial, I forgot.

DAVIS. Do it tomorrow.

STANLEY. No, tonight. (*He passes out.*)

MRS. CAMPBELL. Was he up in the pecan trees when you got down there?

DAVIS. Yes.

MRS. CAMPBELL. Was he hard to get down?

DAVIS. And it's embarrassing, let me tell you. I feel like a fool standing there and begging him to come down out of the tree.

MRS. CAMPBELL. Oh, I hated to call you and ask you to go down there, but I didn't know who else to turn to. The night watchman called me and said he was drunk on the square and we'd better come for him. "I'll call Davis," I said. "I hate like sin to do it, but I will."

BROTHER. (To DAVIS.) Did he call Phil Beaufort?

DAVIS. Yes.

BROTHER. Oh, Jesus!

DAVIS. I'm going home. I have to get up early in the morning.

BROTHER. Don't you think we'd better take him home first?

DAVIS. Bertie Dee won't let him in the house when he's drunk.

MRS. CAMPBELL. Let him sleep on the couch. He'll be all right there. (DAVIS goes.) He stays here almost every night now. He just goes to sleep there on the couch. I said to Philip Beaufort once, you know, "How could you have done this to us? My sons trusted you. You've taken everything we have in a worthless scheme." "I did not think it was worthless," he said. "I lost too. I am bankrupt." "You will never prosper," I said. But he has. He has prospered. I understand he has a fine new house, a lovely car and is back in the oil business.

BROTHER. Yes, he is. I am leaving Houston, because everywhere I turn I see signs of his prosperity. It's making me sick. I am moving to Galveston, or Dallas, so I won't be constantly reminded of his prosperity.

(STANLEY wakes up.)

STANLEY. Mama, I apologize.

MRS. CAMPBELL. Shh, now. That's all right.

STANLEY. I have not behaved like a gentleman and I apologize. Where is Brother?

MRS. CAMPBELL. Here he is.

STANLEY. Brother, please accept my apology.

BROTHER. You owe me no apology. I owe you one.

STANLEY. Why?

BROTHER. You know.

STANLEY. Forget it.

MRS. CAMPBELL. I am moved to tears by the sweetness of you both. You were always extremely loyal brothers growing up. Daddy used to say, "We should be very thankful our boys are so loyal to each other. They never think of themselves first, but only of each other. You never see one without the other."

STANLEY. (*Singing.*) "In the gloamin', Oh my darlin' . . ." (*A pause.*) I want to start all over. I want you and me and Davis to move back in here and start all over.

MRS. CAMPBELL. What about the girls?

STANLEY. What about them?

MRS. CAMPBELL. Don't you want them here too, with you starting all over?

STANLEY. Baby Sister is dead. Sarah is married to Wesley Cox and you know about Wesley Cox and Bertie Dee.

MRS. CAMPBELL. Oh, my God! Don't start that, Stanley!

STANLEY. I called him up too. I said, "Wesley Cox, I know all about you and Bertie Dee."

MRS. CAMPBELL. Oh, my God!

STANLEY. Let's start all over. Sarah, Baby Sister, Davis, Brother and me. How do you do that?

BROTHER. What?

STANLEY. Start all over.

BROTHER. I don't know.

STANLEY. (*Singing.*) "In the gloamin', Oh, my darlin' . . ."

(BERTIE DEE, *30, enters.*)

MRS. CAMPBELL. Hello, Bertie Dee. Stanley just got here. Davis brought him. He was very tired so I told him to spend the night on the couch here. I was going to call you and tell you. I knew you hadn't gone to bed because your light was still on. Davis just left. He has to get up at five-thirty every morning. Brother, Stanley and I were just having a little talk about old times. Brother, say hello to Bertie Dee.

BROTHER. Hello, Bertie Dee. How's Son?

BERTIE DEE. Son is all right.

BROTHER. I guess he's grown quite a bit since I saw him last.

BERTIE DEE. I don't remember when you saw him last.

BROTHER. It's been at least three months. Is he asleep?

BERTIE DEE. Yes.

BROTHER. It seems every time I come to visit Mama, he's asleep.

BERTIE DEE. Stanley . . . (*He doesn't answer.*) Stanley . . .

MRS. CAMPBELL. I think he's asleep, Bertie Dee. He was very tired. Davis said he was working late meeting a deadline for the paper.

BERTIE DEE. Stanley, don't play possum with me. (*She goes over to him. She shakes him.*) Open your eyes! I said don't play possum with me. You don't fool me.

MRS. CAMPBELL. Stanley, are you asleep? See, I think he is asleep.

BERTIE DEE. He is not. He's pretending.

BROTHER. How is your father, Bertie Dee?

BERTIE DEE. What?

BROTHER. How is your father?

BERTIE DEE. He's all right.

MRS. CAMPBELL. Daddy and Mr. Graham were the closest of friends. They had coffee every morning together and every afternoon. They would go to Outlar's Drugstore in the morning for their coffee and to Rugeley's in the afternoon, so as not to hurt anyone's feelings. Their fondest wish was to see Bertie Dee and Stanley married. That was a happy day for the both of them, for all of us, let me tell you. Everyone said, "Aren't they young to be married?" I was married to Daddy at sixteen. We had many happy years together. If you remember, it was Mr. Graham who came here to tell me Daddy had died. He was crying like his heart would break, he was crying so he could hardly speak the words. He grieved so, Mr. Graham said, he lost ten pounds.

BROTHER. Bertie Dee, how is your mother?

BERTIE DEE. What?

BROTHER. How is your mother?

BERTIE DEE. She's all right.

MRS. CAMPBELL. She is a homebody just like me. Neither of us care for society.

BERTIE DEE. I'm not leaving here, Stanley, until you talk to me.

MRS. CAMPBELL. What do you want to talk about, Bertie Dee? Can't it wait until morning?

BERTIE DEE. No!

BROTHER. Maybe we should go into the other room, Mama, so they can have a private conversation.

BERTIE DEE. No. You both stay here. I want you to be witnesses to this conversation. (*She goes to* STANLEY. *She shakes him.*) Stanley! Open your eyes! (*He does so.*)

STANLEY. Well? . . .

BERTIE DEE. Are you crazy? I think he is. I think he should be locked up in the asylum in Austin.

MRS. CAMPBELL. Now don't say that, Bertie Dee.

BERTIE DEE. I do. Do you know what he just did? He called Wesley Cox in Port Arthur, waked him out of a sound sleep to accuse him of having an affair with me.

MRS. CAMPBELL. Oh, my God!

BERTIE DEE. He's crazy! He's insane!

STANLEY. Wesley Cox, Robert Ferguson, Willy Davis, I've called them all. I've called them all and told them no wool was being pulled over my eyes.

BERTIE DEE. He's insane, he's crazy, stark raving mad! Your son, your precious son, is crazy, insane!

MRS. CAMPBELL. He didn't know what he was doing or saying in the condition he's in. I'll get him to call them all up in the morning and explain the condition he was in. I'll call Wesley Cox now myself, to explain. Wesley Cox is very understanding. He's a fine boy, like one of my own sons. Now you go home and get your rest, and Stanley will get his rest, and in the morning I'll have a good long talk with Stanley. And Davis will and Brother will and I am sure we can once and for all get him to see how foolishly he is behaving. (*A pause.*) We all have our troubles. Mrs. Lehigh was here this afternoon to tell me about the Jacksons. She said she thought it would make me feel better to learn that we were not the only ones taken advantage of by a crook. It seems that Mrs. Stone Taylor was having an affair with Mr. Haus and she and Mr. Stone Taylor were closest friends of the Jacksons. Of course, many people thought that Mr. Jackson and Mrs. Stone Taylor had had an affair earlier. Anyway, Mr. Haus and Mrs. Stone Taylor got the Jacksons to invest four hundred thousand dollars of the money Mrs. Jackson had inherited from her father and they made Mr. Jackson vice-president of some corporation Mr. Haus was president of . . . and . . .

(BERTIE DEE *cries.*)

BERTIE DEE. I'm going crazy. I'm the one that's going crazy. I'm the one that will end up in the Austin insane asylum.

MRS. CAMPBELL. Now, now . . . it's going to be all right. Your father was Daddy's first friend here, you know. His first friend and his best friend. When he came here to start the paper he came home that first week and he said, "I've met the nicest fellow, name of Graham. And guess what?" he said. "He has the prettiest little girl, nine years old." And he looked over at Stanley, who was lying on the couch just as he is now, and he said, "I think she's just about right for Stanley." And Stanley blushed so we all had a good laugh.

BERTIE DEE. What's my life like? Married to a man drunk all the time?

MRS. CAMPBELL. Not all the time, honey. I'm very sensitive to his being in that condition and sometimes he comes over here and I smell nothing on his breath. I tell him if he only knew how wise and intelligent he is when sober . . .

BERTIE DEE. Getting drunk, climbing pecan trees . . .

STANLEY. I want to start all over again. I want me and Davis and Brother all living here again, so we can start all over. . . .

(BERTIE DEE *gets up.*)

BERTIE DEE. I'm going home. (*She leaves.* STANLEY *gets up.*)

STANLEY. I'm going home too.

MRS. CAMPBELL. Are you sure she'll let you in, Stanley?

STANLEY. I'm sure. (*He leaves.*)

(MRS. CAMPBELL *goes to the window.*)

MRS. CAMPBELL. I hope she'll let him in, but I doubt it.

BROTHER. She did have an affair with Wesley Cox.

MRS. CAMPBELL. Change the subject please. I don't care to hear that. I knew it. She won't let him in.

BROTHER. Where will he go?

MRS. CAMPBELL. He'll come back here. (*She walks away from the window.*) I don't want him to think I was spying on him. That would embarrass him if he thought we were watching. When he comes back in here, we'll just pretend like we didn't know what had happened.

BROTHER. What happened to the Jacksons?

MRS. CAMPBELL. The Jacksons? Oh, yes. Well, that Mr. Haus took them and their four hundred thousand dollars, just like Phil Beaufort took our seventy-five thousand dollars. They are very bitter and very upset, Mrs. Lehigh says. "I wish they could take it in the Christian way you have," she said. "How did you take your loss so calmly?" she asked. "Because," I said, "I know that money isn't everything. I have my health. I have four wonderful living children, a beloved husband and a daughter that are dead and lots of wonderful memories." Peek out the window and see if Stanley is still in the yard.

(BROTHER *looks out the window.*)

BROTHER. No.

(STANLEY *comes back in.*)

MRS. CAMPBELL. Hello, Son. Glad you came back. (STANLEY *doesn't answer. He goes to the window and looks out.*) Do you all remember when Daddy built this house? We came here with nothing from Lake Charles and we rented a sweet little frame house across from the Cochrans, and I was certainly very happy there, but one day Daddy came in and he said, "Guess what? I am going to build you a two-story brick house on a nice lot and it will have everything in it you ever wanted, rooms for all the children and a big living room with a piano so they can bring their friends and sing and dance." "Won't it be very expensive, Daddy?" I said. "Yes," he said, "but I want to do it." And he did. And I thought it would take all our money and it did. But when Daddy died, I found that he had seventy-five thousand in insurance money and we were rich. . . .

BROTHER. Rich, until Phil Beaufort convinced me to ask you for it to invest in his worthless schemes.

MRS. CAMPBELL. Don't look back now, don't look back. And if you do only think of the pleasant things. . . . When Stanley married Bertie Dee, Daddy said, "I want them living right next door to us. I am going to the bank and arrange a loan so they can build their house." And he did.

STANLEY. (*Singing.*) "In the gloamin', Oh, my darlin' . . ."

MRS. CAMPBELL. "Because we have been so happy in our house I want them to have a house of their own to be happy in," Daddy said.

STANLEY. You know what I just saw?

BROTHER. What?

STANLEY. I just saw my brother-in-law, Wesley Cox, go into my house. What do you think of that?

BROTHER. I don't think anything of it, because you couldn't have seen him. Wesley Cox is ninety miles away in Port Arthur.

STANLEY. Who did I see go in there if it wasn't Wesley Cox?

BROTHER. No one went in there, Stanley.

STANLEY. They go in there all the time. Ask Mama. She'll tell you. Don't they go in there all the time, Mama?

MRS. CAMPBELL. I don't think so, Son.

STANLEY. You may not think so, but I know so. Do you have a gun in this house, Mama?

MRS. CAMPBELL. Now you know I don't keep guns here. I hate guns. I used to say to your daddy, "I want my boys to be real boys. I want them to play football, baseball, go out for track, but I don't want them near guns." We have had such tragedy from guns. That oldest Beck boy went out hunting with the Peebles boy, who was his best friend, and the Peebles boy's gun went off by mistake and shot and killed the Beck boy, and . . .

(BERTIE DEE *comes in.*)

BERTIE DEE. Do you have an aspirin?

MRS. CAMPBELL. Yes, I do. Upstairs in my bathroom. Do you have a headache?

BERTIE DEE. Yes. (*She starts out.*)

MRS. CAMPBELL. I'll get them for you. (*She goes.*)

STANLEY. Who was it I saw go into my house? (BERTIE DEE *doesn't answer. She looks at* BROTHER *and sighs.*) Was it Wesley Cox? Was it Robert Ferguson? Was it Willy Davis? They are all having affairs with her, you know. Everybody in town is switching. Rebecca and Jack Harris, Virginia and Douglas, Laurie Borden and anybody she can grab, Rosanna and Doc, Jenny and Brother Polk. I could have affairs, you know. All I want. Plenty of women want me. I would name them all for you if I wasn't such a gentleman. Who was that went into our house? Who was that went into our house? Who was that went into our house?

BROTHER. Tell him, for God sakes, Bertie Dee, that nobody went into your house.

BERTIE DEE. It don't do any good to tell him anything. I'm talked out. Worn out. Beat! (*She turns on him savagely.*) Look, mister, if you can believe this tired old body can do anything except get to work in the morning and home at night, you'll believe anything.

STANLEY. I see you at the dances. Dancing with all the men. I see how you hold them. . . . I see . . .

BERTIE DEE. What dances? We haven't been to a dance in ten years except the Christmas dance. I go nowhere now, because I'm worn out slaving at the paper, because you're so drunk you can't attend to it.

STANLEY. (*Singing.*) "In the gloamin', Oh, my darlin' . . ."

(MRS. CAMPBELL *comes in with a box of aspirin. She goes to* BERTIE DEE.)

BERTIE DEE. Thank you. Come on home, Stanley. I'm dead for sleep and I can't get to sleep with you peeking through the windows. You woke Son up just now. You almost scared him to death. "What is Daddy doing outside looking in the window?" he asked. "Is he drunk again?" "Yes, unfortunately," I said. Come on with me, Stanley. I'll put you to bed.

STANLEY. I don't want to go to bed.

BROTHER. You have to go to bed, Stanley. You can't sit up all night talking. We all have to be up early in the morning.

STANLEY. Then go on to bed if you want to. I don't need you to stay with me. Fortunately, I have friends that will be happy to see me anytime . . . night or day. . . .

BERTIE DEE. Name me one.

STANLEY. What did you say?

BERTIE DEE. I said name me one. You don't have a friend left in this town that doesn't run the other way when they see you coming. And you know it.

STANLEY. Oh, sure.

BERTIE DEE. Sure!

MRS. CAMPBELL. Well, why don't we just change the subject. Do you know what tomorrow is?

STANLEY. Valentine's Day.

BERTIE DEE. (*Shaking her head in disbelief.*) He's really gone. Valentine's Day!

STANLEY. Christmas?

BERTIE DEE. Oh, shut up, Stanley. You're just making a fool of yourself.

MRS. CAMPBELL. It's Daddy's and my wedding anniversary. If he was with us we would have been married forty years. I want us all to go out to the cemetery tomorrow and put flowers on his and Baby Sister's graves, so they will know we haven't forgotten them.

STANLEY. Who was the best man at my wedding? Was it Davis or Brother?

MRS. CAMPBELL. Stanley, how can you forget something like that? Mr. Graham gave Bertie Dee away and Daddy was your best man. Brother and Davis were ushers. Sarah was a bridesmaid and Baby Sister was the flower girl. Daddy wasn't here for Sarah's wedding and Brother gave her away, because he was the oldest.

STANLEY. Michael Dalton . . .

MRS. CAMPBELL. What about Michael Dalton?

STANLEY. I could walk into his house right now, even if he and his wife and children were sound asleep in bed, and he would welcome me.

BERTIE DEE. The hell he would! Just try it and see!

STANLEY. Les Hines.

BERTIE DEE. Les Hines. He thinks you're crazy. Every time I meet him uptown he says, "Where is Stanley? Up in the pecan trees?"

STANLEY. Vernon May.

BERTIE DEE. He's dead.

STANLEY. Who is?

BERTIE DEE. Vernon May.

STANLEY. When did he die?

BERTIE DEE. Five years ago.

STANLEY. What happened?

BERTIE DEE. I don't know what happened. He just died.

STANLEY. Well, if he were alive I could go see him anytime . . . day or night.

BERTIE DEE. Well, I can't answer for Vernon May because he's dead, but I know what his wife thinks. She told me day before yesterday that if it were her husband getting drunk and climbing pecan trees in the courthouse square she would have him put away.

MRS. CAMPBELL. He's always been crazy about climbing trees. Ever since he was a little boy. Do you all remember that? Whenever his daddy and I couldn't find him, he would be high up in some tree.

BERTIE DEE. Well, a lot of boys like to climb trees, but name me one grown man, besides this fool, that climbs them on the courthouse square at all hours of the night.

BROTHER. Mama, when was the last time you heard from Baby Sister's children?

MRS. CAMPBELL. At Christmas. I wrote and asked them if they could come here for a visit this summer, but her husband hasn't answered my letter. He's very peculiar, you know. He didn't want Baby Sister to have anything to do with her family. I'm surprised he let us bring her back here to be buried beside Daddy. That would have finished me off, let me tell you, if he had refused to let her be brought back here. I've had many a cross, but that would have just finished me off. (*She reaches for a picture off a table.*) Look at Daddy in his Shriner's cap. I remember the day he had that taken. Oh, it was a happy day for him when you both joined the Masons. "My cup runneth over," he said. "My two oldest boys are both Masons." He wanted you both so to become first-degree Masons, but that wasn't to be. Like I told him, "Let's look on the bright side. They are at least Masons and someday you will inspire them to become first-degree Masons. You have inspired them in so many ways to marry young, to go into business, to build nice, comfortable houses for their families. . . ."

BERTIE DEE. Stanley, are you coming home?

STANLEY. No.

BERTIE DEE. Then don't ever come home.

MRS. CAMPBELL. Now, Bertie Dee.

BERTIE DEE. I mean it! Don't ever come home, because from now on day or night I won't let you in.

STANLEY. I'll kick the goddamn door down. Whore . . . I know why you won't let me in, so you can whore with every man in town. That's why I have no friends. You've taken them all with your whorish ways. You think you can keep me out? I'll kick the goddamn door in and I'll have a gun with me when I do and I'll shoot you and the bastard I catch you in bed with. I don't care if it's Wesley Cox or Davis or Brother.

BROTHER. Leave me out of this.

MRS. CAMPBELL. Bertie Dee, I wish you and Stanley could go and talk to the preacher.

BERTIE DEE. Let your crazy son go talk to the preacher. I don't need to. (*She gets up.*) But you better keep him over here from now on, because if he tries to get in my house again I'm calling the law and I'm going to have him arrested. (*She goes.*)

BROTHER. Whose name is their house in?

MRS. CAMPBELL. It is in both their names. Daddy and Mr. Graham built it for them as a wedding present. Remember? He laughed and told Mr. Graham, "I'm going to be selfish and put them right next door to me." He had a dream of one day having you all live in houses next to each other, that way he said we could all go through life together. "And when they have children," he said, "we'll build their houses next to our houses." Well, it didn't work out that way. Daddy died and you, Brother, moved into Houston to go into the oil business with Phil Beaufort. Sarah and Wesley Cox preferred Port Arthur.

STANLEY. (*Singing.*) "In the gloamin', Oh, my darlin', When the lights are soft and low . . ."

MRS. CAMPBELL. I want you to promise me one thing in front of your brother. That you will never climb those pecan trees in the courthouse square again no matter how drunk you get. You can fall and break your neck when you're in that condition. Can't he, Brother?

BROTHER. He sure can. I would hate to try and climb them sober. Much less drunk.

MRS. CAMPBELL. Will you promise me that?

STANLEY. (*Singing.*) "In the gloamin', Oh, my darlin', When the lights are soft and low . . ."

MRS. CAMPBELL. He was always the climber in the family, you know. He climbed every tree in our yard. He went down to the river and climbed the live oaks and the pin oaks. Whenever I wanted to find Stanley I would always look for him somewhere up in the trees. "What are you doing up there?" I once asked him. "Trying to get to heaven," he said. He was joking, of course. "Don't fall," I said, "and hurt yourself or you might land in the other place." I was joking, of course. That's one thing about us, I'll have to say, we've always had a sense of humor. We've always had time for a good joke. We've never minded a little fun.

STANLEY. (*Singing.*) "In the gloamin', Oh, my darlin' . . ."

MRS. CAMPBELL. The main thing is that none of us get discouraged. We have our troubles, certainly. Everybody does. But if we try to look on the bright side as much as possible . . .

STANLEY. Do you remember when the old courthouse was there and they had long slides out of the upstairs windows to be used in case of fire and when we were boys we used to go into the courthouse yard and slide down those slides by the hour? And then when we got tired of that we played football on the lawn. (*A pause.*) Why do I get so drunk, Mama?

MRS. CAMPBELL. Oh, I don't know that, honey. I wish I did.

STANLEY. I did go to see the preacher, but he wasn't home. His wife was there and she asked me what I wanted to see him about and I said, "First, my drinking," and she said, "He'll pray for you about that, but don't get your hopes up as his own brother is a drunkard and he prays for him twice a day and he still drinks same as before." And then I told her about Bertie Dee and she said it didn't surprise her one bit, no one was faithful to their wives and husbands anymore. She says the things that go on at the dances over at the opera house was enough to turn your hair green if you were a Christian woman. She said she knew of ten women all friends of Bertie Dee's all having affairs with married men, and that the wives and the husbands of the men and women involved didn't mind as they were all having affairs themselves. "Well," I said, "some of them are going to mind one of these days and then there is going to be a killing like when Ted Bowen found out about his wife and the Garland boy, and shot him down right in front of the Palace Theater." And Jordan Buchanan would have killed Luke Goddard when he found out he was having an affair with his wife if someone hadn't tipped Luke off and gotten him out of town before Jordan could get to him.

(BROTHER is asleep. He snores slightly.)

MRS. CAMPBELL. Look at Brother. He's gone to sleep on us. We'd better all go to bed now.

STANLEY. Has Bertie Dee gone to bed?

MRS. CAMPBELL. Yes, don't you remember? She left a while ago.

STANLEY. Has she turned the light out?

MRS. CAMPBELL. Yes, she has.

STANLEY. We were married at eighteen. We were married in the Baptist Church to please Bertie Dee's father. The church was packed. She was crying like her heart would break. It was really embarrassing. I said to Daddy, "Why is she crying?" "She's scared, probably," he said. "Scared of what?" I said. "You know," he said. But she wasn't scared of that. We went to Galveston on our honeymoon and she met another couple on their honeymoon and she danced every dance with him . . . holding him real close the way she liked to dance with everybody but me. And I could have danced every dance with his wife, only I didn't feel like dancing and she didn't feel like dancing. . . . (A pause.) I have been cheated. Married at eighteen and cheated.

MRS. CAMPBELL. I was married at sixteen. Tomorrow is our anniversary.

STANLEY. Daddy was my best man.

MRS. CAMPBELL. Yes, he was.

STANLEY. Help me, Mama . . .

MRS. CAMPBELL. I want to help you, Son. Any way I can. Brother does, Davis does.

STANLEY. Help me, Mama. I'm going to fall out of one of those trees one night and kill myself.

MRS. CAMPBELL. I know that. That's what has me half-crazy.

STANLEY. Bertie Dee and Wesley Cox are having an affair.

MRS. CAMPBELL. Oh, I hope not, Son. I surely hope not.

STANLEY. Bertie Dee cried the day Wesley Cox married Sarah, let me tell you. I walked into her bedroom and she was crying and I said, "Why are you crying?" "Because the thought of a wedding makes me sad," she said. "I cried at my own. I had no childhood, no youth, no nothing . . . there should be a law against marriage at eighteen," she said. (*A pause.*) When I was a boy I climbed the water tower once. I could see the whole town from up there. It was a clear day and I could see everything for miles. The river, the courthouse, the gin, the pumping plant, the houses in town, the farms . . . Help me, Mama . . . or someday I'm gonna fall and kill myself. (*He sings:*) "In the gloamin', Oh, my darlin' . . ." (*A pause.*) Am I falling now, Mama?

MRS. CAMPBELL. No, honey. You're right here beside your mama. I'm not going to let you fall.

STANLEY. Where are we, Mama?

MRS. CAMPBELL. In the dining room of our house. The house Daddy built for us all.

STANLEY. Is Bertie Dee here?

MRS. CAMPBELL. No, sweetheart. She's in your house.

STANLEY. Hold me, Mama. Don't let me fall.

(*She holds him.*)

MRS. CAMPBELL. I'm holding you, honey. I'm holding you.

(*He gives a cry of pain and terror.*)

STANLEY. Did I fall, Mama?

MRS. CAMPBELL. No, darling. You're right here. Beside me. Right here . . .

STANLEY. (*Singing.*) "In the gloamin', Oh, my darlin' . . ."

(*As the lights fade.*)

A Nightingale

(from *The Roads to Home*)

The Roads to Home is a trilogy of one-act plays first presented in March of 1982. Just as the plays in *The Orphans' Home*
form a cycle, these plays, which share some characters and
themes, should be read and considered as a group. Though they
are for the most part about Harrison people, the *Roads to Home*
trilogy takes place away from home, in Houston and Austin.

Written soon after *The Orphans' Home Cycle* and referring
to the Vaughn family, particularly Laura, *The Roads to Home* is a
companion piece to that work. The stories of Horace Robedaux
are about the need for a home, for finding attachment and a
sense of belonging. *The Roads to Home,* on the other hand, is a
trilogy about the loss of place, but not just the loss of the physical
environment of Harrison. Like *The Man Who Climbed the Pecan
Trees, The Roads to Home* is a dark play about emotional displacement and loss of identity.

A Nightingale, the first play of the trilogy, describes Harrison
as a place where the traditional principles of order are breaking
down. The Baptist preacher has run off with another man, and

Annie's father has been murdered by his best friend in an argument over money. Houston is no better. Annie's fantasy duet with Laura Vaughn and Mabel's trips to the restroom of the Milby Hotel to hear the gossip from Harrison are, like Mrs. Campbell's views on the past in *The Man Who Climbed the Pecan Trees*, pathetic imitations of genuine intimacy and rootedness. Annie's "dear old Harrison" is no longer available either to those who stayed home or to the displaced Harrisonians in Houston.

This displacement is the real antagonist in *A Nightingale*. Like *The Displaced Person*, the teleplay Foote adapted from a Flannery O'Connor short story in 1977, *A Nightingale* is about the pressures on uprooted people, in this case the Yankee Gayles. According to Annie, her mother never was happy in Harrison; she hated the rain, the medical care, the saloons. The initial dislocation comes from the way the Gayles are ostracized. As a Yankee, Annie Gayle can never join the U.D.C., for example. But the disease of rootlessness seems to feed on itself after a while. Appropriately, the Gayles' house in Harrison burns down, and even in Houston Annie fears she'll be poisoned in her own home. Everyone in *A Nightingale* wishes he or she were someplace else. Mrs. Gayle wishes she were back in Rhode Island, the Harrisonians wish they were in a town without Yankees, and the people of Houston wish they were back in a place like Harrison.

A Nightingale is also interesting as an examination of the dark side of the religious impulses so valuable in *Tender Mercies*, which was written at nearly the same time. Here, Vonnie and Mabel try to teach Annie the Lord's Prayer rather than minister to her real needs, and then they pity Annie for not knowing the prayer. Though there is a genuine hunger in the play for a system of beliefs and values that would give direction and meaning to the characters' lives, for many, like Vonnie and Mabel, easy literalism and the public display of religion are more important than a genuine sense of compassion. Prayer and true belief certainly have a place in Foote's work; in *Tender Mercies*, for example, Rosa Lee's religion gives her remarkable strength and purpose. But the characters in *A Nightingale* have little of the empathy that comes from recognizing that everyone has his or her own good reasons. And so Annie's response to the other women serves as a sad reminder to those who would put on religion: "I don't need prayer. Thank you. I need to be mature and self-reliant, a doctor told me. I need tenderness and mercy."

In A Nightingale, as in The Man Who Climbed the Pecan Trees, innocence is not enough. Vonnie's sentimentality, evidenced by her love of movies with a "sweet love story," and the pious religion she shares with Mabel will not save the hapless Annie.

The trilogy The Roads to Home was first presented by the Manhattan Punch Line Theatre, Inc., in association with Indian Falls Productions, at the Manhattan Punch Line Theatre in New York City on March 25, 1982. The play was directed by Calvin Skaggs and featured Rochelle Oliver as Vonnie Hayhurst, Carol Goodheart as Mabel Votaugh and Hallie Foote, the playwright's daughter, as Annie Gayle Long.

A Nightingale

Mabel Votaugh
Vonnie Hayhurst
Annie Gayle Long
Mr. Long

Place: Houston, Texas
Time: Early April, 1924

The kitchen of MABEL *and* JACK VOTAUGH *around seven in the morning.* MABEL, *42, is at the window looking outside. After a moment, she comes back into the room and goes to the stove and pours herself a cup of coffee. She stands drinking the coffee, thinking, when a neighbor,* VONNIE HAYHURST, *40, comes in.*

VONNIE. Morning, Mabel. (MABEL *hasn't heard her enter and is so startled by the greeting that she almost drops the coffee cup.*) Oh, I'm sorry I scared you. I thought you heard me come in.

MABEL. No. Heavens. I was lost in thought. I didn't hear any-thing. I was half expecting company and . . .

VONNIE. Oh, well then, if you're expecting company I'll go and come back another time.

MABEL. No. No. Don't go.

VONNIE. I'm not sensitive. I don't want to be in the way if you're expecting company. It's just that I saw Jack leave a while ago for work, and I thought I'd come over to let you know I'm back from my trip before I started my housework.

MABEL. I'm glad you did. I've missed you while you were away.

VONNIE. Who is your company?

MABEL. Oh, God. (*She sighs.*) You know that sad little girl from Harrison that used to come over here all the time?

VONNIE. Oh, yes.

MABEL. Well, she's the one.

VONNIE. Oh. She lives on the other side of Houston now, doesn't she?

MABEL. She does.

VONNIE. How does she come all the way over here?

MABEL. By streetcar.

VONNIE. It must take her forever.

MABEL. I suppose. She tells me she rides the streetcars day and night.

VONNIE. I thought she had stopped coming over here?

MABEL. She had. Then right after you left on your vacation she started coming over here again. She comes every day now. And she sits and she sits and she sits and she sits. Sometimes, she doesn't say a word. Sometimes, she talks just as normal as you and me and sometimes she just babbles, going a mile a minute. I don't know what her husband is thinking of, letting her roam around like this.

VONNIE. She has a husband?

MABEL. Oh, yes. Didn't you know that?

VONNIE. I guess I did, but I've just forgotten.

MABEL. And two sweet little children. And a mother and a brother. The brother is up north in school someplace. Some rich fancy school. They all come from the North originally, you know. I wrote my sister the other day and I asked her if she knew where the mother is. She is a sensible woman, even though she's had this miserable sad life, and I'm sure she doesn't know . . .

VONNIE. (*Interrupting.*) Why was her life so sad?

MABEL. Whose?

VONNIE. The mother's.

MABEL. Oh, well. She was a Yankee, you see, and when they first moved to Harrison when she was a bride, they were very coolly received. Then they lost four children out of six, and she and her husband never were congenial, even though he made money every which way he turned. He had a store, he made money. He owned farms, he made money. He had a ranch, he made money. He was president of the bank. And then we had a series of crop failures and his best friend was a planter named Sledge; and Mr. Sledge had seven years of crop failures and he kept borrowing from the bank to keep going and one day Mr. Gayle, that was her father's name, without any warning, Mr. Sledge said, foreclosed on him and took all of his land and his plantation house. And that same afternoon Mr. Sledge came into town as Mr. Gayle came out of the bank with Annie, and Mr. Sledge, they say, called his name, and Mr. Gayle walked over to him. He shot him, killing him, right in front of Annie. There was a trial, but Mr. Sledge pleaded temporary insanity and got free. We all felt sorry for Mrs. Gayle and her daughter and son, but they were left all kinds of money, and they traveled around a lot, up north mostly. Annie went to college someplace up there, and the next thing I heard she had married Mr. Long and was living in Houston. When Mama and Sissy came to visit me, we went calling on her. She didn't live far from me then. She said her mother traveled back and forth between Rhode Island and Houston. She showed us a picture of her husband and she said he was in business in Houston. The business of spending her money, Mama said later she'd heard. And she already had the two children. They were only a year apart and were still babies, but she had three in help, so she didn't seem burdened. The week after Mama and Sissy left she returned my call and then it started. She used to come every day. Sometimes before Jack left for work and she'd stay all day until Jack came home at night. Just talking about old times in Harrison, you know, and all the people we knew back then, until Jack said I had to call her mother or her husband or somebody and tell them to keep her home, since he thought she was crazy. I said I didn't think she was crazy as much as upset, and I couldn't call them. But he did. He talked to the husband and he said he wasn't nice about it at all. But anyway, she stopped her visits and the next we knew they had bought a palace of a house on the other side of Houston by the bayou, and we didn't hear another word from her until ten days ago when she appeared one morning, and said she had been riding the streetcar. I guess it was deceitful of me, but I didn't tell Jack about her coming back, but she stayed on last night until he came home, and he pitched a fit when he saw her. He marched right to the phone to call her husband, but he wasn't home, and he called again this morning before he left for work and he still wasn't home. But Jack said he would get hold of him if he had to call out there every five minutes, and I guess he did because she certainly hasn't come this morning. She is usually here by seven at the latest. How was your trip?

VONNIE. Oh, it was lovely. I hadn't seen my sister and her children for a year, and you know how children grow in a year. I just wouldn't have recognized the children at all. Sweet little things, you know. And the parties. Morning, noon and night. Coffee, teas and luncheons, bridge, dinner, picture show parties. I said, "Sister, you all are wearing me out; I will have to go back to Houston for a rest." And I've gained, too. All that rich food. Sister just begged me to stay another month. "No, I better not," I told her. "I don't want my husband to get too used to my not being around." That's how Celia Edwards lost her husband, you know.

MABEL. Who is Celia Edwards?

VONNIE. Oh, that's right. I guess she had moved before you got here. She lived at the end of the block. She went away one summer to visit her family. She stayed for two months, and when she came home, she found her husband had taken up with someone else and wanted a divorce.

MABEL. Did she give it to him?

VONNIE. Yes she did.

(ANNIE GAYLE *comes in.* MABEL *glances at* VONNIE.)

MABEL. Good morning, Annie. Have you met my next-door neighbor, Mrs. Hayhurst?

(ANNIE *looks at her.*)

VONNIE. Good morning.

ANNIE. Is she from Harrison?

VONNIE. No, honey. I'm from Louisiana. Monroe, Louisiana. I have never seen Harrison. Heard a lot about it though. It must be a lovely town from all I've heard. My husband works for the railroad just like Mabel's and we get passes and some Sunday I'm going to take a train ride into Harrison.

(ANNIE *shapes a gun with her finger.*)

ANNIE. (*Pointing at no one.*) Pow. Pow. Pow. (*Then she is silent and withdrawn.* MABEL *and* VONNIE *exchange glances.*)

MABEL. How are your children? (ANNIE *doesn't answer.*) She has two lovely children. A beautiful girl and a handsome little boy. The little girl is named Esther and the boy Davis. Was Davis named after your husband? (*Again no answer from* ANNIE.) Let's see now. Esther is six and Davis four and a half. (ANNIE *begins to vocalize, practicing scales, quietly at first. Then louder and louder.* VONNIE *and* MABEL *exchange glances and shake their heads in sadness.* ANNIE *stops vocalizing. She stands up, curtsies and then goes to the center of the room and sings, very simply and beautifully and with deep feeling, "My Old Kentucky Home."*) She has such a sweet voice doesn't she? She sings just like a nightingale.

VONNIE. I don't know. I've never heard a nightingale sing. Have you?

MABEL. No. That's just an expression, you know.

VONNIE. I know that, but it just occurred to me I had never heard a nightingale. I had a cousin that sang some. They called her the Mockingbird of the South.

MABEL. Jenny Lind was known as the Swedish Nightingale.

VONNIE. Oh, yes. So she was.

ANNIE. Do either of you ladies sing alto?

VONNIE. No, heavens. I can't carry a tune.

ANNIE. Laura Vaughn sings alto. She lives in Dallas. I wrote her five times that I was coming to Dallas soon on a visit, so we could sing duets once again like we did when we were girls back in dear old Harrison.

MABEL. And they did too. They sang beautiful duets together. Like two nightingales.

(ANNIE *sits down.*)

ANNIE. Do you remember that time back in dear old Harrison, when Randy Lewis and Marjorie Hancock and Elizabeth Vaughn gave a concert for charity. Elizabeth played the piano and Randy sang and Marjorie recited. "Your turn will come next," my mama said. But we were gone by the next year. Gone from dear old Harrison. I hope sincerely to go back there one day to give that recital if Laura Vaughn will return too and sing a duet with me. I am practicing night and day for that event.

MABEL. Would you like a cup of coffee, Vonnie?

VONNIE. No, thank you.

MABEL. Annie?

(ANNIE *doesn't answer. Again she shapes her hand as a gun and goes* "Pow. Pow. Pow.")

VONNIE. (*Ignoring her.*) It's been a lovely spring, hasn't it?

MABEL. Too much rain though. Sissy says the cotton farmers in Harrison are about to lose their minds. Wet years, you know, are death on the cotton. My papa used to always say, "I don't care how dry it gets, we'll always make some kind of a crop, but when it starts in raining you can just forget cotton and everything else."

VONNIE. Annie, what church are you affiliated with?

ANNIE. None.

VONNIE. None?

ANNIE. None.

VONNIE. (*To* MABEL.) What church is her family affiliated with?

MABEL. I don't know. They weren't churchgoers as I remember. What church were your sweet mother and father associated with, honey? (ANNIE *doesn't answer.*) I think they were Presbyterians or Episcopalians. They certainly weren't Catholics, I know that.

ANNIE. My husband, Mr. Long, is a Catholic. He's studying for the priesthood.

MABEL. No, you have that wrong, Annie. He's a married man. Married to you, sweetheart, a married man can't be a priest.

ANNIE. He's a priest and he says Mass every morning before breakfast. (*A pause.*) Harrison is not such a nice town after all, you know. My mama never did care for it. She always said when I was growing up and saying how much I loved dear old Harrison and all my friends—Laura Vaughn, Cootsie Reynolds, Essie Hawkins and Callie Anne Knolt—"No, this is not such a nice town. The streets are too muddy when it rains, like a boghole, it rains all the time." Day and night. Rain. Rain. Rain. Rain. "Watch out," she used to say. "We are all going to get web feet from the rain." Web feet. Quack. Quack. Quack. "I am sorry I ever left Rhode Island," she said. "I regret the day. We would never have lost the children if we had stayed in Rhode Island. They have proper doctors there, and the swamps are drained and the rivers don't flood every other year, bringing typhoid and malaria, diphtheria and yellow fever." "Go on back to Rhode Island," Papa said. "No one is stopping you." "Oh, you would like that," she said. "A saloon every time you turn around, this is not a nice town." And it was not a nice town. Mama was right. It was certainly not a nice town. "What's Mae Reeves and her husband doing driving out to the country every night not getting home until one or two in the morning? What's going on?" "He's embezzled the funds of his bank," Papa told her. "He's been riding out in the country to try and talk to people to keep their money on deposit and if he can't persuade them the bank will go under, for there is no money left in that bank now to withdraw. He gambled away some of it, loaned the rest foolishly to friends and now can't collect it. He's a bad banker, a corrupt untrustworthy banker. They've closed the bank, and he's sent to the penitentiary. I've bought their house and we're moving in." "I will not move in there," Mama said. "I will not move into that tragic house. I will not." (*She stops talking as abruptly as she began. She begins to laugh softly. Then she opens her purse and takes out pictures of her children. She hands them to* VONNIE *and* MABEL.) Don't I have a sweet little brother and sister?

MABEL. That's not your brother and sister, honey. They're your children, Esther and Davis. (*To* VONNIE.) Aren't they lovely? (*To* ANNIE.) Where's your brother now? Still up north?

ANNIE. Harrison isn't such a nice town. Mama said she was glad that house Papa made us move into burned down and we could move back to our other house. That was a fine enough house for her, Mama said.

MABEL. Oh, I remember that fire. It was terrible. We were awakened in the middle of the night. Mama sent her cook over to wake us up and we all sat on her front gallery and watched the flames. . . .

ANNIE. Harrison is not such a nice town. Did you hear about the Baptist preacher? He ran off with Sis Gallagher's husband. Left her ashamed and mortified to face the town with two small children to raise.

MABEL. That's all forgotten, darling. Sis Gallagher's husband has come back to her now. It was sad. She had to leave Harrison. He stayed away for two years. Our dear Baptist church almost never recovered from that scandal.

ANNIE. Mr. Sledge murdered Papa, you know. He was his best friend and he murdered him. We were walking out of the bank . . .

MABEL. Now, honey. It's no use going over all that. Is it? Nothing can be done about that now.

ANNIE. I saw him, you know. I said, "Papa, he has a gun." "I'm not scared of him," Papa said. "He is a coward." And then he called out, "Sledge, you're a coward, you come one more step near me and I'll thrash you." "Papa, please," I said, "he has a gun. Papa . . ." (*She pauses.*) I went to him lying on the pavement. Miss Rosa Gilbert came up to me and she said to pray like you've never prayed before. "I don't know how to pray," I said. "Get down on your knees," she said, "and Jesus will tell you what to say." "He's bleeding," I said. "Call a doctor." "Pray," she said. She held me and she began to pray out loud and Papa was bleeding and people came running from everywhere then. Dr. White, Dr. Burton and Dr. Ellroy. And they stood looking at him and Miss Rosa was praying and Dr. Ellroy said, "You can stop your praying now, Rosa, he's dead." And he was. He was dead. And someone called Mrs. Vaughn and she went to tell Mama, and when Mrs. Vaughn walked into our house Mama said, "Is there something wrong with Mr. Gayle?" "He's been shot," Mrs. Vaughn said. "He was killed." (*A pause.*) Do you know my husband, Mr. Long? Papa never knew him. I had only been out with two gentlemen before Papa died. I met Mr. Long in Houston once when we had to come back to look after Papa's business interests. I love Houston. I love riding the streetcars. I get up early in the morning, get on a streetcar, and ride out to visit one of my friends from Harrison. Inez Pate and her sister Mrs. Knott. Don't tell anybody back in Harrison, but they are terribly poor. Proud but poor. Inez cried and told me all her troubles last week. I wrote Mama and said to send them a hundred dollars at once. Mr. Long says I'm extravagant. He says he is not rich like my poor dead papa, and that my extravagance will ruin him. "I hope not, Mr. Long," I said. "I hope not." Did you all know that Laura Vaughn married Cole Dawson? They live in Dallas. He works for

Sears Roebuck. Quite a comedown, some catty people say, for a
daughter of Henry Vaughn. I write Laura three times a day—so
far she hasn't answered my letters. I hope she is happy. I surely
hope she is happy. I want more than anything in this world to
visit her and sing duets. (*She turns to* VONNIE.) What church are
you affiliated with?

VONNIE. Baptist. (*She laughs and winks.*) Born one. Expect to
die one.

ANNIE. Did you know that preacher that ran off with Sis Gallagher's husband?

VONNIE. No, fortunately.

ANNIE. Did you, Miss Mabel?

MABEL. Oh, yes. I knew him. Never liked him. I knew from the
moment I saw him something was wrong. I told my son to keep
away from him. And I told my husband, I said, "Jack, something
is wrong with that man." "That's your imagination, Mabel," he
said. "You're always imagining things." I do have a vivid imagination, you know. But even I couldn't imagine exactly what was
wrong with him.

VONNIE. What kind of a preacher was he?

MABEL. I don't remember that. At the time I wasn't going to
church a great deal. My feelings had been hurt. I had been faithfully playing the piano at the church services for more years than
I can remember and there was a faction in the church headed by
old Brother Payne who wanted to have a pipe organ installed,
and the reason they wanted it was because a woman with dyed
hair named Lorena Jackson, very rich, had just moved into town
and she played the pipe organ. So old Brother Payne and the
Paynites voted in the pipe organ, and Lorena Jackson as the
organist, saying, of course, that I could still play the piano, but
not the organ. "I can learn the organ," I said, but they said it
would take too long and since I know when I'm not wanted I
said, "Well, you can just get Lorena Jackson to play the piano

too, because I'll not put my foot back in that church," and I didn't for several years. But then Mama and Sister said I was setting a very poor example for my son, so I agreed to go back, although I still won't shake Brother Payne's or any of the Paynites' hands. He's a snake, you know. He's always getting up and making long prayers about unifying the congregation. Oh, it's all very well, I said to myself, for you to talk about unifying. You have your pipe organ, which the church can't afford, and Lorena Jackson with her dyed hair as the organist, while I sit here with my feelings hurt.

ANNIE. Miss Rosa Gilbert is a Methodist. She lives in Houston now. She used to come and see me all the time. She wanted me to come to her Sunday School class in the Methodist church.

VONNIE. Which Methodist church?

ANNIE. The one here in Houston.

VONNIE. I know that, honey. But which one? There are a number of Methodist churches in the city of Houston.

MABEL. First Methodist, I believe, Vonnie.

ANNIE. But she's not allowed to come to the house anymore because my husband, Mr. Long, caught her praying in the living room. She was on her knees praying for my poor dead papa, and Mama and my brother up north in military school and my sweet children Renee and Nathan.

MABEL. Honey, you mustn't get the names of your children confused. Your little girl is named Esther, remember? And your little boy is named Davis.

ANNIE. Then who are Renee and Nathan?

MABEL. I think they were the names of two of your mama's children that died.

ANNIE. Maybe. Anyway, Mr. Long caught her praying and since he is a Catholic it made him furious.

MABEL. Catholics pray, honey.

VONNIE. Not like regular Christians. They have a funny way of praying.

MABEL. Anyway, I don't think Mr. Long is a Catholic.

VONNIE. What is he?

MABEL. I don't know, but he doesn't look like a Catholic to me.

ANNIE. He's a Catholic. A Catholic priest, and he said if there was any praying done at our house, he would do it. I said, "Teach me to pray, Mr. Long. I want to know how to pray." I think if I'd been able to pray like Miss Rosa asked me to when my papa was shot, he'd be living instead of dead.

MABEL. You mustn't burden yourself with that, honey.

ANNIE. Do you ladies pray?

VONNIE. I do.

MABEL. Oh, yes.

ANNIE. Teach me to pray.

VONNIE. You can't teach something like that, honey. That's between you and God. Ask God to teach you. He will.

ANNIE. I have. But he hasn't.

MABEL. Do you know the Lord's Prayer?

ANNIE. No ma'm.

VONNIE. Well, then we'll teach that to you, honey.

ANNIE. Why?

MABEL. Because when you know that and someone says you should pray, you can just repeat that. Now—"Our Father which art in heaven. Hallowed be thy name . . ."

ANNIE. Pow. Pow. Pow. Pow.

VONNIE. Now stop that. That's the devil trying to keep you from your Christian duty.

ANNIE. Pow. Pow. Pow. Pow.

MABEL. That old dyed red-haired organist, Lorena Jackson, used to go over to the Baptist Church and practice day and night. I said to Jack, "She's just doing that to humiliate me." "I don't think she's studying about you at all," he said. "Oh, yes," I said. "It's a vicious plot of the Paynites to humiliate me." "Ride by there sometimes," he said, "and see whose car is parked in front." "Whose?" I asked him. "Mr. Lopez," he said. "Mr. Lopez? What's he doing there?" "Figure it out for yourself," he said. "Why, that's scandalous," I said. "The deacons should know about it." "Who is going to tell them?" he said. "I am not. Are you?"

VONNIE. What happened?

MABEL. Nothing, as usual. The last I heard she was still practicing and he was still over there, listening, he says.

VONNIE. Is this lady organist a married woman?

MABEL. Oh, yes. And Mr. Lopez a married man. He's a deacon in the church besides.

VONNIE. A woman from a lovely family in Monroe is having an affair.

MABEL. Is she married?

VONNIE. Oh, yes.

MABEL. Is the man she's having an affair with married?

VONNIE. No. He's quite a bit younger than she is. He jerks soda in her husband's drugstore, and he has off the nights the husband works, and she goes for long walks out in the country, even though it's dark as pitch, and then he rides out in his car to where she's walking and she gets in his car and they ride off together. I have a cousin that sits in his car uptown and every time he sees that soda jerk's car driving out of town, he follows him in his car. I said, "Cousin, you are going to get shot one of these days." The preacher preached a very strong sermon condemning adultery. She was there, and they said the preacher was looking right at her the whole time.

(*There is a knock at the door.* MABEL *goes. She opens it.* MR. LONG, *35, is there.*)

LONG. Miss Mabel. Good morning.

MABEL. Good morning, Mr. Long. Won't you come in? (*He enters.*) This is my neighbor, Mrs. Hayhurst.

VONNIE. How do you do, Mr. Long.

LONG. Mrs. Hayhurst.

MABEL. We've been having such a nice visit with Annie. . . .

LONG. Your husband left a message with my secretary at work. I just got it or I would have been here before. My secretary said he called me at home last night and this morning and couldn't reach me. I don't know why. I was home both times.

VONNIE. Maybe he had the wrong number.

LONG. Maybe he did. Lehigh 8170?

MABEL. I don't remember but I'll write it down so he'll be sure and have it right the next time.

LONG. And I'm listed in the phone book.

MABEL. Where is Mrs. Gayle now? Still up north?

LONG. No. She's back south again.

MABEL. (*To* VONNIE.) Mrs. Gayle's Annie's mother.

VONNIE. Oh, yes.

MABEL. We were all friends back in Harrison. Is Mrs. Gayle here in Houston?

LONG. No, not at present.

MABEL. Well, tell her hello for me when you see her.

LONG. I will. (*He turns to his wife.*) Annie, are you ready? (*She doesn't move.*) Let's say good-bye to the ladies now, Annie.

ANNIE. Can I ride the streetcar home?

LONG. Sure.

VONNIE. What church are you affiliated with, Mr. Long?

LONG. None at present.

MABEL. Someone remarked that you were a Catholic.

LONG. They were mistaken. Let's say good-bye now, Annie. I have some important appointments today at the office.

(ANNIE *is silent and doesn't move.*)

VONNIE. What line of work are you in, Mr. Long?

LONG. Produce.

ANNIE. My daddy owns a bank.

LONG. Did own a bank, Annie. He's dead now. Remember? Annie sometimes gets a little confused. It was the birth of the second child that seemed to upset her.

ANNIE. Pow. Pow. Pow. Pow.

MABEL. Have you been to Harrison lately, Mr. Long?

LONG. No.

MABEL. How long since you've been there?

LONG. A year last fall. I went duck hunting with some friends. They have a hunting lodge on the coast.

VONNIE. I was telling your sweet little wife I've never seen Harrison. But my husband works for the railroad, like Mabel's, and we get passes, of course, and some Sunday we're going to take a ride on the train into Harrison and look it over, so we'll know what you all are talking about. I'm from Monroe, Louisiana. I didn't think I could live any other place in the world. I've just come back from there. I had a month's visit. It was just like I'd never been away. Have you ever been to Monroe?

LONG. No.

VONNIE. You've been to Louisiana, of course.

LONG. Yes ma'm. I've been to Louisiana a number of times.

VONNIE. Someday you'll have to see Monroe. I just love it. We have quite a few Catholics there, you know. But, of course, there are a lot of Catholics all over Louisiana.

(LONG *looks at his watch.*)

LONG. Now we have to go, Annie.

ANNIE. Pow. Pow. Pow.

LONG. Would you ladies be good enough to leave me alone with my wife for a few minutes?

MABEL. Certainly.

(*She and* VONNIE *leave. He waits for a minute to be sure they're gone. He lowers his voice when he speaks so as not to be heard outside the room.*)

LONG. Annie. I'm asking you to be reasonable now. (*A pause.*) Look at me please, Annie, and pay attention to me. I can't stay away from my job any longer. I'll lose my job if I do. You don't want that to happen. Do you? (*A pause.*) What am I going to do with you, Annie? You promised me faithfully you wouldn't go off from home anymore. I can't stay home and watch you. I have work to do.

ANNIE. Are you a preacher or a priest?

LONG. Annie, when you talk foolish like that I'm not going to answer you at all. You're just doing that to upset me, Annie. Come on now.

ANNIE. Don't touch me, or I'll scream. Where is my mama?

LONG. Now you know where she is.

ANNIE. Get me my mama.

LONG. She's not in Houston.

ANNIE. Where is she?

LONG. Now you know where she is. I told you five times this

morning. I'm not going to repeat it again. (*He grabs her.*) Annie, come on. I cannot keep this up. Come on. (*She pulls away.*) Do you want to be locked up? Is that what you want? Do you want to be sent away to the asylum in Austin, because that's what we are surely going to have to do if you don't get hold of yourself.

ANNIE. I know two lovely boys in Austin.

LONG. I'm not talking about the University, Annie, I'm talking about the asylum.

ANNIE. That's what I'm talking about. There are two boys from Harrison there. Dave Dushon and Greene Hamilton. Greene is older than Dave. Dave is my brother's age. Greene is, I believe, a year or two older than I am. That would make him—let's see . . . how old am I?

LONG. Annie, we are wasting time. I can't afford to stay away from work. I will lose my job.

ANNIE. How old am I?

LONG. You know very well how old you are. You just say these things to upset me. Well, I hope you're happy, because I am upset. I am very upset.

ANNIE. I'm sorry. I don't mean to upset you. I never mean to upset you. (*She cries.*) I am very nervous. I am frightened. I don't sleep well at nights. I am tired from lack of sleep. I am very tired.

LONG. I know. I know. (*A pause.*) But let's go home now and I'm sure you will be able to sleep.

ANNIE. I'm afraid to go home.

LONG. Now what are you afraid of?

ANNIE. I'm afraid of being killed like Papa.

LONG. Who would want to kill you?

ANNIE. You know.

LONG. No, I don't. I have no idea who could want to do that.

ANNIE. They want to poison me. I don't dare eat a thing prepared in that house for fear of being poisoned.

LONG. Now no one is trying to poison you. Now, Annie, we went over all that last night and I finally convinced you to eat your food and nothing happened, did it?

ANNIE. No.

LONG. Don't you trust me?

ANNIE. Yes.

LONG. Do you like seeing me unhappy?

ANNIE. No. I don't like seeing anybody unhappy. That's why I like riding the streetcars. Everybody is so happy on the streetcars. They just laugh and have such a good time. Are you unhappy?

LONG. Yes.

ANNIE. Why?

LONG. Because you don't keep your promises to me. You don't stay home and rest so you can get well.

ANNIE. If I stay home will that make you happy?

LONG. Yes, it most certainly will.

ANNIE. Why?

LONG. Because I want to see you well.

ANNIE. Why?

LONG. Because you're my wife and I love you. Will you come with me now?

ANNIE. Yes, I will. Are you going to ride home with me on the streetcar?

LONG. No. I'll put you on your streetcar, but I'll have to take another. I have to go down to work, remember. (*Calling.*) Miss Mabel. (MABEL *and* VONNIE *come in.*) We're going. Thank you.

MABEL. That's quite all right. Can't I offer you a cup of coffee before you go?

LONG. No, thank you. I have to be getting back to work.

VONNIE. What do you do, Mr. Long?

LONG. I'm in produce.

VONNIE. Oh, yes. You told us.

MABEL. Annie, I've written something down for you.

ANNIE. What is it?

MABEL. It's the Lord's Prayer. Now you memorize it and when you feel yourself getting nervous you just say it.

VONNIE. I have three things I say in times of stress—the Lord's Prayer, the Ninety-First Psalm and the Twenty-Third Psalm.

ANNIE. I don't need prayer. Thank you. I need to be mature and self-reliant, a doctor told me. I need tenderness and mercy. (*A pause.*) My husband never knew my father. The other day on the streetcar, out by Montrose someplace, a man came up to me, a perfect stranger, and he said, "Mr. Sledge didn't kill your father, your husband killed your father." "Mr. Long?" I said. "Yes," he said. "He did not," I told him. "He didn't even know my father." "He killed him," he said. "No," I said. "You are sadly mistaken. Mr. Sledge, my father's best friend, killed him. He killed him in cold blood, in front of my very eyes." (*A pause.*) You go on back to work please, Mr. Long, and let me visit with these ladies a little longer.

LONG. You can't stay here, Annie. Mr. Jack doesn't want you here. He's very upset by your coming over here.

ANNIE. I know that. But I promise to leave before he gets here. I'll take the streetcar and go home and he'll never know I've been here.

LONG. Now you don't want to stay in a place where you're not welcome, Annie. Besides, these ladies, I'm sure, have work to do.

ANNIE. Can I go to Dallas tomorrow to see Laura Vaughn?

LONG. No . . .

ANNIE. Can I . . . ? (*But she doesn't finish her sentence. She turns to the two women.*) Will you come to see me, ladies?

MABEL. Yes, we will. And you come back to see us some-times. . . .

ANNIE. Thank you.

(LONG *and* ANNIE *leave.*)

MABEL. That's so sad, isn't it?

VONNIE. Oh, yes. Imagine her not knowing the Lord's Prayer.

MABEL. I'm sure she knows it, but she's just forgotten that she does. What are you doing today?

VONNIE. I thought I might take the streetcar and go downtown and see a matinee. There is a picture at the Kirby I think I'd like to see.

MABEL. What's the name of it?

VONNIE. I forget, but it's a sweet love story, someone told me. I saw the sweetest picture, by the way, when I was in Monroe. I told Sister I just had to take an afternoon off from the parties and go and see a picture. So Sister said, "All right, I'll give you a picture show party," and I said, "No, I'm going to be frank, I've had a number of lovely picture show parties since I've been here, and although I appreciate all the attention you show me by giv-ing me picture show parties, I didn't enjoy the parties at all, be-cause the ladies always talk all the time the picture is going on, and just when something interesting is about to happen, one of your friends will say, 'How do you like Houston?' or 'Do you play a lot of bridge in Houston?' or 'How do you like living in a big city?'" And then they all start giving their opinion about bridge, or Houston or cities, until like I told Sister we might as well just stayed at somebody's house and talked. So Sister was understand-ing, and asked if I minded if she went along, and I said no, if she promised not to say a word and not to read the titles out loud, which is a bad habit Sister has, and she said she wouldn't.

MABEL. What was the name of the picture you saw?

VONNIE. You know, I was trying to think of it last night to tell Eddie, and I couldn't remember it to save my life. Milton Sills and Alice Joyce were in it. They were in love with each other and then he had an accident and went blind. Sister was so overcome when he went blind I thought she would have to get up and leave. She said it was the saddest picture she had ever seen in her whole life, and I can't say I completely agree with her on that, but it was certainly sad.

MABEL. I think I'll go downtown, too, and do some shopping. Then I may stop by the Milby Hotel. There are usually some ladies from Harrison in there to use the restrooms. I always enjoy talking to them. I get the news of my friends that way.

VONNIE. Do you think they will put Annie away?

MABEL. I don't know. I just don't know. Mama says it's loneliness. Mama says as rich as they are, they ought to hire some nice refined widow from Harrison to come and stay with them to keep her company and help with the children.

VONNIE. Who stays with the children now, I wonder.

MABEL. Oh, I don't know. They have all kinds of help, but no one she can be congenial with. And she needs a nice white lady that wouldn't be expected to do any housework, but could just talk to her about all the things she likes to talk about—you know, things that happened when she was living back in Harrison. Now she and I weren't especially congenial back in Harrison. I knew her, of course, but we'd never think of visiting, because of the difference in our ages, but I tell you as upsetting as she is sometimes, I used to look forward to her visits, because we know all the same people back there.

VONNIE. My sister is coming here to see me next month.

MABEL. Is she? I look forward to meeting her.

VONNIE. I said, "Don't expect me to entertain you the way you all entertain me." I said, "People just don't live that way in Houston, you know."

MABEL. I'm certainly giving a luncheon for her.

VONNIE. I felt sure you would. I told her, "I know my friend Mabel will give you a luncheon," and I'll have a picture show party for her, of course, and let her talk all the way through it if she wants to, and Eddie said he'd take us to supper at the San Jacinto Inn. Have you ever been there?

MABEL. No, heavens. Jack won't go anyplace.

VONNIE. Thank you for having Eddie over for supper while I was gone. He said you had such a good meal.

MABEL. Oh, we enjoyed having him.

VONNIE. I tried to have Jack for supper the last time you went to Harrison, but he wouldn't come.

MABEL. No, he won't go anyplace. It was the same in Harrison. He wouldn't even go to church. Work, eat and sleep. That's all he knows. Mama said, when we were still living in Harrison, "Sometimes I think you spend too much time over here at my house. I think you should stay home and visit with your husband." "Well, why, Mama?" I said. "He never talks. We just have Quaker meetings." Oh, you know, Vonnie, he's a good man, but he's so quiet.

VONNIE. Eddie is certainly a talker. I used to wonder when I was in Monroe what he'd do when he came home at night without someone to talk to. He called me up once on the phone, and I knew it was because he was lonesome and didn't have anyone to talk to. I said, "Do you want me to come home, I will if you want me to?" "No," he said. "Stay and get your visit out."

MABEL. He was home every night, too. I could tell the minute he got there, because he always turned the lights on, all over the house.

VONNIE. Bless his heart. I said, "Eddie, go over and visit with

Mabel and Jack, if you're lonesome." "Oh, they don't want to fool with me," he said. "They've had me for a lovely dinner already."

(ANNIE *comes back in.*)

ANNIE. Excuse me.

MABEL. Why, Annie. I thought you were on your way home.

ANNIE. Yes ma'm. I started home. Mr. Long put me on the streetcar for home, and he took the streetcar for downtown. I had just gotten past the first stop when I looked around and saw I didn't have my children, so I said to the conductor, "Stop this streetcar at once." "Madam," he said, "I can't stop it until the next corner." "At once," I said. "I have lost my children. I am in distress." "Oh, I am so sorry," he said, and he stopped the streetcar and I got off and I went running back to the stop on the opposite side of the street to wait for the next car going to your house, but then I got frantic and I thought what will my two little children think of their mother going off and leaving them, so I ran back here every step of the way.

MABEL. Annie, your children are not here.

ANNIE. Don't tell me that.

MABEL. No, honey. They must be back at your house.

ANNIE. No, I brought them here with me this morning. Don't you remember?

VONNIE. No, dear. You didn't bring them here. I was here too, with Mabel when you came, and there were no children with you. You had pictures of them, you remember. Which you showed us.

ANNIE. A little boy and a little girl.

VONNIE. Their pictures. But no children. None.

MABEL. Now you stay here with Vonnie and I'll go call your house, and I bet you I'm going to find out your children are there waiting for you. (*She goes.*)

ANNIE. Isn't she sweet? She is the sweetest friend.

VONNIE. Where does your husband come from, honey?

ANNIE. Mr. Long?

VONNIE. Yes.

ANNIE. I don't know where he comes from. He never told me that.

VONNIE. Weren't you curious?

ANNIE. No.

VONNIE. Where do his mother and father live?

ANNIE. I don't know.

VONNIE. Didn't you ever ask?

ANNIE. No.

VONNIE. Have you met them?

ANNIE. Who?

VONNIE. Mr. Long's mother and father.

ANNIE. No. I wanted to be in the U.D.C. auxiliary, you know, very badly. Every girl in town that I knew was, you know. Laura and Cootsie and Velma and Pauline. Miss Mabel's mother runs the U.D.C., and I said to my mama, "I want to be in the U.D.C. auxiliary too, with all my sweet friends." "You can't," she said. "Why?" I said. "Because we were on the wrong side." "When were we on the wrong side?" I asked her. "During the War," she said. "What War?" "The Civil War." "What in the world does the U.D.C. auxiliary have to do with that?" I said. "Everything," she said. "All of those girls in the auxiliary had fathers and grandfathers who fought for the Confederacy. That's why it's called the U.D.C. It stands for the United Daughters of the Confederacy."

(MABEL *comes in.*)

MABEL. They are there. I knew they were. They send their love to you. Vonnie, she has two precious children.

VONNIE. Yes, I know. I saw their pictures. Remember?

MABEL. The pictures don't do them justice. You have never seen two such beautiful children in your whole life.

VONNIE. Who do they look like, Annie or Mr. Long?

MABEL. A combination of both. No mistaking who the parents are. They are just precious.

ANNIE. I've got to go home now.

MABEL. Do you, honey? We've enjoyed your visit.

ANNIE. Thank you. I've been nervous. I wake up nervous, but I've got to go home now and see to my children. I have to fix supper for my children and Mr. Long. I haven't a thing in the house to eat. Anyway, I'll stop at the Piggly Wiggly now and stock up.

VONNIE. I like Westheimer's myself.

ANNIE. I'm trying to remember that prayer.

MABEL. Just take this paper with you. See, I've written it all out for you. You take it with you on the streetcar and anytime you need to remember it, take it out of your purse and read it over a number of times, and before you know it, you will have memorized it.

ANNIE. Thank you. If I don't get hold of myself they are going to send me away, you know.

VONNIE. Who?

ANNIE. Mr. Long, for one.

VONNIE. Where will they send you?

ANNIE. Up to Austin in the asylum. Mr. Long is beside himself, he told Mama. Greene Hamilton and Dave Dushon are there, Mama says, and they are very happy there. They are both from lovely families. (*A pause.*) My children weren't home, were they?

MABEL. Now, Annie . . .

ANNIE. That's all right. I remember now, quite clearly. Mama took them to give me a rest, she said, because the responsibility is too much for me she feels at present. And I suppose it is. Anyway, I think sometimes I will never in this world see them again.

MABEL. Now you know your mother is going to let you see them again.

ANNIE. I suppose. Papa would, but they killed him. Mr. Sledge. (*She gets up. She leaves.*)

VONNIE. Poor thing. Are her children at her house?

MABEL. No. A woman working there told me her mother took them yesterday.

(ANNIE *comes back in.*)

ANNIE. Are you ladies going to have lunch in town today?

VONNIE. Yes, I think I will.

MABEL. I think so too.

ANNIE. And that's what I think I will do. Then I think I'll go to a matinee at the picture show.

VONNIE. There's a sweet picture at the Kirby. They say . . .

ANNIE. (*Singing.*) "The sun shines bright on my old Kentucky home . . ." (*A pause. She looks at the ladies.*) I'm going to Kentucky, you know. To the Derby—Mr. Long and Laura Vaughn and her husband and myself are all going up by rail. I look forward to it so. Laura Vaughn is my very best friend. (*She continues singing.*) "So weep no more, my lady, weep no more today . . ."

(*As the lights fade.*)

The Dearest of Friends

(from *The Roads to Home*)

The *Roads to Home* trilogy dramatizes the loss of a sense of place. But it is not just "dear old Harrison" that has been lost. It is the deeper loss of the feeling of attachment, of belonging, that haunts the action of *The Roads to Home*. The first of the plays, *A Nightingale*, describes how one broken life, that of Annie Gayle Long, is part of a general breakdown of community in Harrison and Houston. Harrison doesn't welcome its displaced citizens, friend murders friend, and well-intentioned church people gossip and fight imaginary personal battles rather than minister to others. Meanwhile, the characters are sentimentally drawn to a pathetically saccharine image of the old Harrison.

The Dearest of Friends is about the same people and the same loss of traditional order as *A Nightingale*, but the focus of the second play is narrower. Rather than reexamine the larger context, *The Dearest of Friends* looks at intimate family relationships. The main character of *A Nightingale*, Annie, has now been committed to an asylum in Austin, and so the second play shifts to the two couples—Mabel and Jack, Vonnie and Eddie—in the aftermath of a traumatic train ride to Harrison.

The central irony of *The Dearest of Friends* is that the marriage of Vonnie and Eddie becomes threatened while they are traveling to Harrison in search of a new Eden. In the minds of Mabel and Vonnie, Harrison is a place where the old virtues and order are still possible. But on the train Eddie meets Rachel Gibson, with whom he subsequently has an affair which puts his marriage in jeopardy. The tradition and continuity that the family represents in Horton Foote's work is crumbling before their sleepy eyes.

This sense of being cut loose from patterns of meaning and purpose is what makes the play simultaneously so comic and sad. The prayers of the righteous and the social pressure of the industrious are equally ineffective. Mr. Lewis, the Harrison banker, has a nervous breakdown when the town leaders confront him with his affair, and Vonnie waits, and waits, though silence is the only answer to her prayers. In *A Nightingale* the shift in values, the loss of direction, remained outside the house, only leading Annie, the outsider, to take her endless, aimless rides on the streetcars. Now, in the second play, the dearest of friends themselves experience the shifting patterns of human relations and their own futile attempts to respond to a changing scene. Eddie, like most Foote characters, tries his best. "I'm very confused," he says. "I've tried to live right all my life, to be good and do the right thing." As their space becomes filled with too many Coke bottles and too much cigarette smoke, what is good and right becomes unclear. Confusion becomes the most formidable antagonist.

The Dearest of Friends

CAST

Mabel Votaugh   Vonnie Hayhurst
Jack Votaugh   Eddie Hayhurst

Place: Houston, Texas
Time: Early fall, 1924

The living room of JACK *and* MABEL VOTAUGH's *apartment.*
JACK *is in an easy chair with his eyes closed.* MABEL *comes in.*
She gets a crossword puzzle and begins to work on it.

MABEL. Jack, what is a seven-letter word beginning with *k* that
means . . . ? (JACK *begins snoring slightly. She looks over at him,*
realizing he is asleep. She sighs, goes back to work on the puzzle. After
a beat she goes to the window and looks out. Then she gets a deck of
cards and begins a game of solitaire. VONNIE *enters.* MABEL *gestures*
to her to be quiet and VONNIE *tiptoes across the room to* MABEL.
MABEL, *pointing and whispering.*) Jack is asleep.

VONNIE. I can see that.

MABEL. (*Whispering.*) Do you want to play some honeymoon
bridge?

VONNIE. (*Whispering.*) All right.

(MABEL *shuffles and deals the cards and they begin to play. They play*
in silence for a beat. JACK *opens his eyes.*)

JACK. Mabel.

MABEL. Yes.

JACK. What time is it?

MABEL. Eight o'clock. Vonnie is here.

JACK. Is Eddie with her?

MABEL. No.

JACK. Where is he?

MABEL. I don't know. (*To* VONNIE.) Where is he?

VONNIE. Still at work.

JACK. At eight o'clock at night? Isn't he still on the day run?

VONNIE. Yes, but he's been working two shifts lately.

JACK. Since when?

VONNIE. Since day before yesterday.

JACK. What's today?

MABEL. It's Thursday.

JACK. Thursday the what?

MABEL. The twelfth.

JACK. And tomorrow is the thirteenth then?

MABEL. Yes.

JACK. Friday the thirteenth.

MABEL. Yes. Thank God I'm not superstitious.

(*He closes his eyes.* VONNIE *begins crying.*)

JACK. Who is that crying?

MABEL. Vonnie.

JACK. Why is she crying?

MABEL. I don't know, Jack. Mercy—

JACK. Aren't you going to ask her? She may be sick.

MABEL. Are you sick, Vonnie honey?

(VONNIE *shakes her head "no" and then cries even louder.* JACK *sits up in his chair and stares at her.* MABEL *is sincerely distressed for her friend. She looks at* JACK *helplessly, as if to say, What can I do?* JACK *begins to vigorously pantomime that she do something.* MABEL *pantomimes back that she feels inadequate and helpless.* VONNIE *gets up and runs out of the room.*)

JACK. What's wrong with her? (MABEL *doesn't answer him.*) Do you know?

MABEL. Yes.

JACK. Well, what is it?

MABEL. I can't tell you.

JACK. Why?

MABEL. Because I promised I wouldn't. Vonnie swore me to secrecy.

JACK. Is she going to come over here every night of our lives, start to cry and then run home?

MABEL. She's only done that four times.

JACK. Five.

MABEL. Four.

JACK. Five. Anyway, I know what's wrong.

MABEL. What?

JACK. I can't say.

MABEL. Why?

JACK. I promised I wouldn't. (*He closes his eyes again.*) Anyway, we won't be bothered by that Gayle girl anymore.

MABEL. Why do you say that?

JACK. I know it. I ran into her husband coming home from work today. Her mother had her committed. They sent her to Austin. He said you get the best care in a state institution.

MABEL. Do you believe that?

JACK. That's what he said. He said the last few weeks had been quite a trial.

MABEL. In what way?

JACK. He didn't say.

MABEL. Who has the children?

JACK. Her mother.

MABEL. Where are they?

JACK. In Houston someplace.

MABEL. Poor little things. (JACK *closes his eyes.*) Jack. Jack. (*He opens his eyes.*)

JACK. Yes.

MABEL. What do you know that you can't tell me? (*He doesn't answer. He closes his eyes.*) Jack. Jack. What is it you know that you can't tell me?

(*He begins to snore. She sighs. She takes up the crossword puzzle again. Then she puts it aside and starts another game of solitaire.* VONNIE *comes back in. She has stopped crying. She sits at the table.*)

JACK. Who is that?

MABEL. Vonnie.

JACK. Did she come back?

MABEL. Yes.

JACK. When?

MABEL. Just now. (*He opens his eyes and looks at* VONNIE *and then closes them again.* MABEL *to* VONNIE.) Shall we continue our game?

VONNIE. Yes, and I promise not to give way to my feelings again. I'm so ashamed.

MABEL. Well, don't worry about it. Over here you are among friends.

VONNIE. Dear friends. Dear, dear friends. I think friends are the most precious things on earth.

MABEL. And I agree.

VONNIE. Here I am, far, far away from Monroe, Louisiana.

JACK. How far is it to Monroe, Louisiana, from Houston?

MABEL. I thought you were asleep.

JACK. I was, but I woke up.

MABEL. Well, go on back to sleep.

JACK. How far is it from Monroe, Louisiana, to here, Vonnie?

VONNIE. I don't know exactly. Maybe three hundred and fifty miles. (JACK goes back to sleep. The women play cards. JACK begins to snore. VONNIE, whispering.) Does Jack suspect anything?

MABEL. I don't know.

VONNIE. Does he ask any questions?

MABEL. Once in a while.

VONNIE. Like what?

MABEL. Like, "Why is Vonnie so emotional?"

VONNIE. I guess I am very emotional.

MABEL. Yes, you are.

VONNIE. I cry at the least thing.

MABEL. I know. I don't blame you.

VONNIE. I know you don't. You are such a dear, dear friend.

MABEL. I try to be.

VONNIE. I pray Jack never has to know.

MABEL. Well, I'll never tell him. You won't have to worry about that.

VONNIE. I'd die of mortification if he ever found out. (They play cards.) Is he asleep?

MABEL. Yes.

VONNIE. Sound asleep?

MABEL. Yes.

VONNIE. Do you think he'll wake up if we talk?

MABEL. Not if we keep our voices down low.

VONNIE. I didn't sleep at all again last night.

MABEL. You are going to ruin your health if you don't start sleeping. Have you eaten today?

VONNIE. No.

MABEL. Let me fix you a sandwich. You have to eat.

VONNIE. No. I'd choke on it. Even the sight of food makes me nauseous.

MABEL. Oh, Vonnie. Vonnie. Vonnie.

VONNIE. I blame myself really.

MABEL. Oh, my God. Don't say that. How can you possibly blame yourself?

VONNIE. I do. I do. I just do. I am being punished for something.

MABEL. What on earth for?

VONNIE. I don't know. I just am.

MABEL. That's a lot of nonsense and you know it.

VONNIE. If we only hadn't taken that trip to Harrison, but I'd heard so much about it from you and Annie Gayle.

MABEL. Jack ran into her husband today. They said they had to put her away.

VONNIE. Oh, where?

MABEL. She's in Austin.

VONNIE. Have you ever been to Austin?

MABEL. Four times. Three times to the U.D.C. convention when Mama was state president. I was living in Harrison then and I represented our J. E. B. Stuart chapter. And once to a Baptist convention . . .

VONNIE. Is it a nice town?

MABEL. I think so. The state capitol is there.

VONNIE. I know that. I learned that in school.

MABEL. And Texas University.

VONNIE. Oh, yes.

MABEL. And the asylum where poor sweet Annie is. Her new home. God bless her.

VONNIE. I wonder if she can receive letters?

MABEL. I'm sure.

VONNIE. I'd like to write to her. I wonder what her address would be?

MABEL. I don't know. I'll get Jack to ask Mr. Long the next time he sees him. Maybe one day I'll get Jack to get a pass from the railroad and I'll go to Austin to visit her.

VONNIE. You better watch out riding on trains with your husband. You never know who your husband will meet.

MABEL. My husband won't meet anyone because he's a stick. I can't get him out of the house except to go to work. He'll never go to Austin with me. He'll never go anyplace.

VONNIE. I wish Eddie had never gone to Harrison with me that Sunday. . . .

MABEL. Now please, it's done. Don't dwell on it. You'll get all upset again.

VONNIE. Oh, I know. But I can't help wondering what my life would be like if we'd stayed home and gone to church. But I was bound and determined he'd take me on the train to see Harrison, because I'd heard so much about it. And take me he did, so I've got no one to blame but myself. I had packed us a lovely lunch to have on the train, and we had just gotten into Sugarland when he said he was hungry and so we had our lunch and he said he was going up to the smoker for a cigar and I decided to have a little nap and when I woke up I saw him talking to this lady two seats ahead of us, and I got up to go to the restroom and when I came back he was in our seat and I said, "Who was that lady you were talking to?" and he said, "Oh, just some lady who says she is from Harrison." He said he didn't catch her name, and I said, "Do you think she knows Mabel and Jack?" and he said he didn't ask and he said he was going to take a nap and I started to go over and introduce myself and ask if she knew you all, but just as I was going I noticed she was taking a nap too, so I decided to read a magazine instead. And when we got to the station at Harrison, she got off the train right away and by the time *we* got off she was nowhere in sight. We had a lovely day too. We went to the Nation Hotel for dinner like you suggested.

MABEL. What did you have to eat?

VONNIE. I had fried chicken and Eddie had roast chicken.

MABEL. Isn't the food good?

VONNIE. Delicious.

MABEL. Did you introduce yourselves to Mrs. Nation?

VONNIE. Oh, yes. I told you that.

MABEL. That's right. I guess you did.

VONNIE. Remember I told her we were friends of yours and she said what a lovely refined couple you were and that everyone in Harrison missed you and couldn't wait for you to move back.

MABEL. Wasn't that sweet of her to say so. Then what did you do?

VONNIE. Well, then we took the loveliest walk around town and out to look at the lovely old homes and then we went to the drugstore for ice cream and then it was time to take the train home. And who was on the train but that woman. I saw Eddie kind of looking at her and I thought to myself you better not go to sleep again, there is something suspicious about her.

(JACK *wakes up.*)

JACK. Mabel?

MABEL. What?

JACK. What time is it?

MABEL. Nine o'clock.

JACK. Wake me up at ten, so I can get ready for bed.

MABEL. Why don't you go to bed now?

JACK. It's too early to be in bed.

MABEL. Well, you're sound asleep, you might as well be in bed. (*He closes his eyes and goes back to sleep.*) How do you know that is the woman he is seeing?

VONNIE. He told me. He said he was seeing the woman he met on that Sunday on the train to Harrison. (*She begins to cry.*)

MABEL. Now, Vonnie, you have to be brave and strong.

VONNIE. I know. I try. (*She cries again.*) Oh, Mabel. He asked me for a divorce.

MABEL. He what?

VONNIE. He asked me for a divorce.

MABEL. I don't believe you.

VONNIE. Well, he did.

MABEL. When?

VONNIE. This morning at breakfast.

MABEL. Oh, I can't believe it. I just cannot believe it.

VONNIE. May God strike me dead if it isn't true.

MABEL. Don't you give it to him. Don't you dare give it to him. Do you hear me?

VONNIE. Yes.

MABEL. Don't you dare give it to him.

VONNIE. Oh, I'm so humiliated. What if people back in Monroe found out my husband had asked me for a divorce. Oh, dear God. I can hardly face the day. I don't sleep at nights. I toss and turn.

MABEL. What about him?

VONNIE. Oh, he sleeps like a baby. He no sooner hits the pillow than he's asleep.

MABEL. The dirty dog. I'd kill Jack. I'd take a butcher knife and run it through his heart if he did something like that.

VONNIE. No you wouldn't either.

MABEL. Yes I would.

VONNIE. Oh, no.

MABEL. I certainly would. I wouldn't care if they hung me for it.

VONNIE. No you wouldn't either. You'd do just like I am doing. Sit here and cry.

MABEL. Oh, I guess I would. Did you ever find out the woman's name?

VONNIE. Yes, I did. He told me yesterday. Rachel . . .

MABEL. Rachel. Rachel what?

VONNIE. I don't know. That's all he said. Just Rachel.

MABEL. And she's from Harrison?

VONNIE. Oh, yes. Born and raised there. She works here in Houston, of course. . . .

MABEL. Rachel? My God, it is driving me crazy. I can't think who it can be. Rachel. Oh, my God. Yes. I bet it's Rachel Miller.

(*She gets a phone book.*) Here. Rachel Miller. She lives in the Heights. Oh, the she-devil.

(EDDIE *comes in.*)

EDDIE. Do I have a wife over here?

VONNIE. Yes, you do.

EDDIE. Stay and visit as long as you like. I just wanted you to know I was home. . . .

MABEL. Sit down and visit for a while.

EDDIE. No, I can't. I'm tired. Jack is asleep?

MABEL. He's been asleep. Ever since supper. (*She goes over and shakes* JACK.) Jack, wake up. Eddie is here.

(*He opens his eyes and sits up.*)

EDDIE. You shouldn't have done that, Mabel. Go on back to sleep, Jack.

JACK. No, I'm awake now. What time is it?

EDDIE. Nine-thirty.

JACK. Just getting home from work?

EDDIE. Yes.

JACK. I wouldn't like to work at nights. I like my shift.

EDDIE. I still work in the daytime.

JACK. Nights too?

EDDIE. Nights too.

JACK. Don't kill yourself.

EDDIE. Hard work never harmed anybody. Are you going home with me, Vonnie, or will you stay for a while?

VONNIE. I'm going to stay.

EDDIE. Good night.

JACK. Good night. (*He goes.*)

VONNIE. Mabel, tell Jack.

MABEL. Tell Jack what?

VONNIE. All about Eddie and how he's been behaving.

MABEL. I thought you didn't want him to know.

VONNIE. No, I've changed my mind. I want him to know. Jack, he's not working nights. How can he stand there and lie like that when he knows I know where he has been? Mabel, tell him.

JACK. I know all about it.

MABEL. What do you know all about?

JACK. What Eddie is up to.

VONNIE. How do you know?

JACK. Eddie told Cameron Russell about it, and Cameron told me.

VONNIE. Oh, I'm so humiliated. Who is Cameron Russell?

JACK. One of the men that works with us.

MABEL. The dirty dog.

JACK. Who's a dirty dog?

MABEL. Eddie.

JACK. Oh, I thought you meant Cameron Russell.

VONNIE. Was he shocked?

JACK. Sure.

VONNIE. Were you?

JACK. No. Nothing shocks me anymore.

MABEL. The dirty dog. Do you know who the woman is?

JACK. Yes.

MABEL. Who is it?

JACK. I don't think I'd better say.

MABEL. I know who it is, anyway. Rachel Miller.

JACK. You're wrong. It's Rachel all right, but it's not Rachel Miller.

MABEL. What Rachel is it then?

JACK. I don't think I should say. I'm not really sure. It's all just hearsay. I might give the name of a completely innocent person.

MABEL. Oh, you make me sick.

VONNIE. I'm going home. Good night.

MABEL. Good night. (JACK *has gone back to sleep.*) Jack. Jack. What Rachel is it?

JACK. I'm not going to tell you so stop nagging me.

MABEL. All right, don't tell me, Mr. Closemouthed. I'll take the train tomorrow into Harrison and I'll stay there until I do find out. I'll get the name of every Rachel that ever lived there and has moved to Houston.

(VONNIE *comes back in.*)

VONNIE. I found out. It's Rachel Gibson.

MABEL. Rachel Gibson. Oh, my God. I can't believe it. Why, she's a churchgoer and she's always acted so pious. How did you find out?

VONNIE. I asked Eddie and he told me. He said he loved her and couldn't live without her.

MABEL. He didn't.

VONNIE. Yes he did.

MABEL. Did you hear that, Jack?

JACK. What?

MABEL. What Vonnie just said.

JACK. No.

MABEL. Rachel's last name is Gibson. And Eddie just told Vonnie he loved her and couldn't live without her.

JACK. Loved who?

MABEL. Rachel Gibson. Did you ever hear of anything like that?

JACK. Oh, he'll get over it.

VONNIE. Well, I'll never get over it. I'll go to my grave with the memory of all this.

MABEL. Rachel Gibson. I saw her at Munn's shopping just last week. I called to her and she waved and said she couldn't visit as she had a lot to get done.

VONNIE. I wonder if she's in the phone book.

MABEL. Let's see. (*She gets the phone book and looks for her name.*) Yes sir. Here she is.

VONNIE. Call her up.

MABEL. Call her up?

VONNIE. Yes.

MABEL. What for?

VONNIE. Just to see what she'll say.

MABEL. All right. (*She goes to the phone. She asks for a number.*) Hello, Rachel. This is Mabel. Mabel Votaugh. Your old friend from Harrison. Ever since I saw you the other day in Munn's I've been meaning to call you. You what? Oh, I'm so sorry. (*She hangs up.*) I woke her up, she said. Out of a sound sleep. The sneaky thing. She sleeps and you don't.

VONNIE. What did she sound like?

MABEL. Oh, you know. Just ordinary . . .

VONNIE. Is she from a nice family?

MABEL. Nice enough. I've certainly never heard of any of them behaving like this before.

VONNIE. Is she older or younger than me?

MABEL. Younger.

VONNIE. How much?

MABEL. I'd say three years.

VONNIE. I'm going to call her up.

MABEL. What are you going to say to her?

VONNIE. I'm going to tell her flat out in no uncertain words to leave my husband alone. What's the number?

MABEL. Lehigh 1087.

(VONNIE *gives the number to the operator. She puts the phone down.*)

VONNIE. The line is busy. I bet I know who she's talking to.

MABEL. Who?

VONNIE. Eddie. (*She picks up the phone. She gives her own number. She puts the phone down.*) Yes. I knew it. Our line is busy too.

MABEL. How do you know he's talking to her?

VONNIE. I just know it. He never talks on the phone.

MABEL. He called you in Monroe, you said.

VONNIE. Once in six weeks. Excuse me. (*She leaves.* MABEL *asks the operator for a telephone number.*)

MABEL. Mr. Long. Jack said he met you on the street and you told him about Annie. I just want you to know how sorry I am. I was telling my friend Vonnie about it and she said she would like to write her and I would too, and in time pay her a visit. Oh, I see. Oh, all right. Yes. I understand. (*She hangs up. She looks over at* JACK. *He is asleep. She goes over to him. She shakes him. He opens his eyes.*)

JACK. Is it ten o'clock?

MABEL. Not quite.

JACK. What did you wake me for?

MABEL. I talked to Mr. Long.

JACK. Who is that?

MABEL. Annie Gayle's husband.

JACK. Oh.

MABEL. He said they didn't want anyone writing Annie or going to see her at present.

JACK. Who was going to see her?

MABEL. I was thinking about it. (VONNIE *enters.*) Was he on the phone?

VONNIE. Not when I got there. He was getting ready for bed.

MABEL. Are you going to call her now?

VONNIE. Who?

MABEL. Rachel Gibson.

VONNIE. No.

MABEL. Why not?

VONNIE. Oh, I don't know. I just don't want to. I think it would demean me to do something like that. It would put me on her level.

MABEL. I agree.

VONNIE. Harlot.

MABEL. Jezebel. What we should do is write her pastor and tell him what is going on. In Harrison when Mr. Lewis, who was president of the bank, was having an affair with that married lady, someone wrote his minister and told him what was going on and the minister called up Mr. Lewis and said he was coming over to pray with him.

VONNIE. And did he?

MABEL. Yes, he did.

VONNIE. And did it do any good?

MABEL. No, I'm afraid it didn't, but then some of the bank trustees heard about his behavior and went to him and told him if he didn't stop his carrying on he would have to resign as president of the bank.

VONNIE. And then what happened?

MABEL. He had a nervous breakdown. I called Mr. Long about an address for Annie. He said they didn't want anyone getting in touch with her at present.

(VONNIE *gets up.*)

VONNIE. I'm going home.

MABEL. Are you tired?

VONNIE. Mortally.

MABEL. Maybe you'll sleep tonight.

VONNIE. I hope so, but I doubt it. Good night.

MABEL. Good night. (VONNIE *leaves.* MABEL *looks over at* JACK.) Jack.

JACK. Yes.

MABEL. How long have you known about Eddie and that woman?

JACK. Oh, a day or so.

MABEL. Poor Vonnie. It's gotten her down. She has no fight in her at all. I would fight, you know. If I even heard of your doing anything like that. I would take on you and the woman. Why, I'd take a butcher knife and stab you in the heart. I told Vonnie I would, and I meant it too. Even if they hung me for it. Jack. Did you hear what I said? And I mean it too. Every word of it. (*He is asleep again. She looks over at him.*) Jack. Jack. (*If he hears her, he doesn't answer. She sighs and looks out the window. He opens his eyes.*)

JACK. What time is it now?

MABEL. Ten o'clock. One minute after.

(*He gets up.*)

JACK. I'm going to bed. Good night.

MABEL. Good night. What time are you getting up in the morning?

JACK. Five o'clock.

MABEL. Oh my God, that's so early.

JACK. You don't have to get up.

MABEL. I'll get up. I always like you to have a good breakfast.

JACK. I don't want you to get up. I want you to sleep. I can fix my own breakfast.

MABEL. Jack, do you know what you can give me for Christmas?

JACK. What?

MABEL. You can get me a piano. I miss playing.

JACK. All right. (*He starts away again.*) Good night.

(VONNIE *comes in.*)

VONNIE. Oh, I'm so glad you're not in bed. I don't have a single Coke in my house. I hope you're not out.

MABEL. No, I have some.

VONNIE. Can you loan me three?

MABEL. Yes, I can. (*She goes.*)

JACK. Eddie in bed?

VONNIE. Sound asleep.

JACK. I'm going to bed too. Good night.

VONNIE. Good night. (*He starts away.*) Jack.

JACK. Yes?

VONNIE. Speak to Eddie. Tell him to come to his senses.

JACK. Oh, I can't do that, Vonnie. I can't get mixed up in that. That's between you and Eddie. But he'll get over it.

VONNIE. When?

JACK. Sooner or later.

VONNIE. You really think so?

JACK. Yes.

(MABEL *comes in with bottles of Coca-Cola.*)

VONNIE. Jack thinks Eddie will get over this.

MABEL. I know. I heard him say that before. Do you want a Coke now?

VONNIE. Thank you.

(MABEL *opens a bottle and gives it to her. She opens one for herself.*)

MABEL. Do you want one, Jack?

JACK. No. I'm going to bed. Good night. (*He leaves.*)

MABEL. Good night.

VONNIE. Good night.

(MABEL *has a swig of her Coke.*)

MABEL. Mama doesn't like me to drink these. She's always telling me about Mr. Newsame who drank so many Cokes the lining of his stomach was eaten out.

VONNIE. Mercy. (EDDIE *comes in. He has his pajamas and a robe on.*) I thought you were asleep.

EDDIE. I had the light out, but I haven't slept. I'm out of cigarettes. Does Jack have any?

MABEL. I'll go see. (*She goes.*)

EDDIE. I want you to come back to the house with me.

VONNIE. Why?

EDDIE. I want to have another talk.

VONNIE. What about?

EDDIE. You know.

VONNIE. I'm not going to give you a divorce. I told you that.

EDDIE. Please.

VONNIE. I never will. Anyway, Jack says you'll get over it.

EDDIE. What does Jack know about it?

VONNIE. I'm only repeating what he said.

(JACK *comes out with* MABEL. *He is in pajamas and robe.*)

JACK. Do you smoke Camels or Chesterfields?

EDDIE. Chesterfields.

JACK. I only have Camels.

EDDIE. They will do me until I can get to the store in the morning.

JACK. Take this whole pack.

EDDIE. What will you do?

JACK. I have two more.

EDDIE. I can't believe how I've been smoking. I've been smoking over two packs a day.

VONNIE. That's too much.

EDDIE. I guess so.

VONNIE. How much do you smoke, Jack?

JACK. I don't just smoke cigarettes. I smoke a pipe too. And I'd chew tobacco if Mabel would let me. That's what I really enjoy.

MABEL. Well, you'll not do it. Not while you're married to me. If you are going to chew tobacco, you can just get yourself another wife.

VONNIE. Jack, I told Eddie what you said.

JACK. About what?

VONNIE. About his getting over . . . you know . . .

JACK. Well, I shouldn't have opened my mouth. None of it is any of my business.

(EDDIE *cries.*)

MABEL. Oh, Eddie. Poor thing.

EDDIE. I'm very confused. I've tried to live right all my life, to be good and do the right thing.

MABEL. Of course you have.

VONNIE. Jack says you'll get over it.

JACK. Keep me out of it, Vonnie. I think this should be just between you and Eddie.

VONNIE. Well, if prayer does any good, he'll get over it. I pray night and day that he does.

JACK. Can you see the clock from where you're sitting, Mabel?

MABEL. Yes. Ten-twenty.

JACK. My God, that's the latest I've been up in I don't know when.

VONNIE. And God usually answers my prayers. So I'm just going to keep on praying and I know He won't let me down this time.

(*They sit in silence as the lights fade.*)

Spring Dance

(from *The Roads to Home*)

The sense of homelessness becomes specific and personal in *Spring Dance*. In this play more than in either of the other two in the *Roads to Home* trilogy Horton Foote demonstrates that the loss of rootedness is finally a psychological issue. Going away from home and coming home again are both powerful needs, mythic patterns of attachment and freedom. Both rely on a set of assumptions and shared values that order human experience. When "home"—that grounding force larger than the individual and more enduring, whether religion, the family, work or whatever—is stripped away, identity itself is threatened. What begins in *A Nightingale* as a general sense of rootlessness, and grows into an overwhelming confusion of propriety and motive in *The Dearest of Friends*, becomes in *Spring Dance* the horror of the loss of self.

As the title suggests, in *Spring Dance* Annie is surrounded by images of renewal and order with which, sadly, she cannot connect. She wants to smell the chinaberry blossoms as a sign of spring and the cycle of the seasons. But, as she later admits, she is never sure of the evidence, she can never trust the patterns of natural life. So April is cruel to Annie. She is also surrounded by dancers and would-be dancers. In *Spring Dance*, as in Foote's other work, dancing is an ideal experience where the exuberance and movement of the present is wedded with the form and tradition of the dance itself. Passion and order are combined in the ritual of the dance which surrounds Annie but never is able to include her in its graceful rhythms. Because she cannot connect with these forces, Annie, like the other inmates, loses a sense of the past, of her place and time in the life process. She cannot, as she says, "keep everything straight and clear."

Healing, a basic concern in nearly all Horton Foote's work, is again crucial in *Spring Dance*. As Annie explains, "We want to get well don't we—for the sake of our loved ones and ourselves." But there is less chance for a return to health here than in the other plays because in Foote's work healing comes only after a character learns to see his or her relation to the world more clearly, whether more happily or not. Naturally, as the world becomes more formless and chaotic, identity becomes more elusive, for in Horton Foote's dramas one's identity is never discovered separate from other people and places. In *Spring Dance* Annie and her fellow inmates can only discover who they are by recognizing their connections to the enduring patterns around them, an increasingly difficult process in Harrison, Houston or Austin. For Annie, the pain of loss and desertion are too great, and so repeatedly she chooses fantasy over the frightening give-and-take of genuine attachment.

Spring Dance

CAST

Annie Gayle Long   Cecil Henry
Dave Dushon   Greene Hamilton

Place: Austin, Texas
Time: Spring, 1928

A section of an enclosed garden adjoining a ballroom-auditorium where a dance is being held. It is early evening of a mild spring night. The garden is a simple one but well kept. There are a few flowers and flowering trees in bloom.

ANNIE GAYLE LONG *is seated on a garden bench. Near her is* DAVE DUSHON, *in his late twenties. An orchestra is heard in the ballroom, a small orchestra, playing dance music.*

ANNIE *and* DAVE *can see the ballroom and dancers from where they are sitting. Only* ANNIE *from time to time looks in at the dancers.* DAVE *stares up at the night, or down at the ground, never at the dancers.*

ANNIE. It's a lovely night for a dance, isn't it? Everyone seems to be having such a good time. I haven't danced in so long I bet I've forgotten how. Did you ever like to dance? What good times we had at our dances at the opera house. Remember? (*She looks around at the garden.*) It's been a lovely spring, hasn't it? Last night I woke up and I thought for sure I smelled chinaberry blossoms, which are my favorite spring flowers. This morning at breakfast I asked if anyone knew if there were chinaberry trees in our gardens here, and no one knew, so when I finished breakfast I went over all the grounds looking for chinaberry trees, but I couldn't find any. Anyway, I no longer smell them. I smell Cape jessamine and roses and magnolias but no chinaberry blossoms. (*She glances at the dancers.*) Greene is going to the dance. He is getting all dressed up for it. His mother sent him black patent leather dancing shoes to go with his dress suit. He seems very happy. (*A pause. She listens to the music.*) The orchestra isn't always in proper tempo, is it? I think a waltz should be a little more marked for the dancers. (*She looks back at the dancers, hums a little of the waltz as she watches. She points towards the dancers.*) Look. There's Greene. He's dancing. I can't quite tell who he's dancing with. I believe it is Mabelle what's-her-name from I forget where. The one who says she was born on a plantation called Sycamore. Oh, look. Greene is a very graceful dancer. Very, very graceful. (*The music ends. We hear couples clapping. She claps.* DAVE *has not looked up once.*) I love to see people happy, don't you?

(CECIL, *a man in his forties, comes in.*)

CECIL. Annie, would you like to dance?

ANNIE. Thank you, but I can't. Thank you so very much for asking me, but I'm married, you know, and I have two children.

CECIL. I'm married too. But there can be no harm in our dancing together. Lots of people out there that are dancing are married, but it doesn't prevent them from enjoying dancing.

ANNIE. I think I'd better not, thank you. My husband, I'm sure, would be very upset if I did.

CECIL. Oh, well, I wouldn't know about that. It all seems harmless to me, but you know your husband better than I do, certainly. (*A pause.*) May I sit and visit for a while?

ANNIE. Yes. Mr. . . .

CECIL. Cecil . . . Henry . . .

ANNIE. Oh, yes, of course. My doctor says I'm not to apologize, but just frankly say at the present time I seem to forget names. And other things too. But forgetting them is not as embarrassing as forgetting names. (*She turns to* DAVE.) Mr. Cecil Henry. Mr. Dave Dushon. (*She looks back at* CECIL.) We came from the same town. Harrison. Forty miles from the Gulf of Mexico as the crow flies. I watched him grow up.

CECIL. I thought you lived in Houston?

ANNIE. I did. I lived in Houston after I married. I was born in Harrison. Where are you from, Mr. Henry?

CECIL. Please call me Cecil. Waco.

ANNIE. Do you have children?

CECIL. Four.

ANNIE. I have two.

CECIL. I'm to be released in another month they tell me.

ANNIE. I hope to be released soon too. Dave is going away on a visit next month to Harrison. He'll stay for a month with his parents.

CECIL. (*To* DAVE.) Then will you come back here?

ANNIE. Then he will come back here. He understands perfectly everything you say to him, but he doesn't care to talk.

(*The three sit in silence. The music begins again.*)

CECIL. My wife wants a divorce. I'm not going to give her one. I don't have to. I'm well. I'm cured. I'm getting out in a month. (*A pause.*) Do you think I should give her a divorce? After fifteen years of marriage? I've always been a good provider until I got sick. It's nobody's fault, you know, if you get sick.

ANNIE. No.

CECIL. Here's the letter from my wife asking for a divorce. Do you want to read it?

ANNIE. No.

CECIL. It would upset you?

ANNIE. Yes.

CECIL. You have a good husband?

ANNIE. Oh, yes.

CECIL. Loyal?

ANNIE. Yes.

CECIL. Are your children with him?

ANNIE. No. With my mother.

CECIL. My children are with my wife. She has poisoned their minds against me. They have not written me once. (*To* DAVE.) Are you married?

ANNIE. No, he's not.

CECIL. How long has he been here?

ANNIE. Five years. Except for the month, usually in the summer, when he goes back to Harrison for a month's visit.

CECIL. Has he never married?

ANNIE. No.

CECIL. How old was he when he came here?

ANNIE. Eighteen. I was living in Houston at the time, but a friend wrote to tell me he had been brought here. I believe he was away at college and went home for the Christmas holidays when they noticed he had not spoken a single word all that vacation. And to my knowledge he hasn't talked since.

CECIL. How long have you been here?

ANNIE. Two years.

CECIL. Two years?

ANNIE. Yes. (DAVE *takes a letter from his pocket and hands it to her.*) This is a letter from his mother. He knows I like to read them, because they're always full of news about my old friends in Harrison. No one from there writes me any longer. You see, all my close friends have married and moved away.

CECIL. Don't your mother and husband write you?

ANNIE. Yes. Every day. But they no longer live in Harrison, so they don't know what's going on there.

CECIL. How long have you been here?

ANNIE. Two years. (*A pause.*) Will you excuse me while I read the letter? (*She gets up and moves toward the light spilling out of the auditorium. While she reads,* CECIL *takes out his letter again and hands it to* DAVE.)

CECIL. Do you want to read my wife's letter?

(DAVE *makes no move to take the letter, so* CECIL *begins to read it himself.* GREENE HAMILTON *comes in. He has on an old-fashioned tux and he walks as if his shoes hurt him.*)

GREENE. Annie? (*She looks up from the letter and sees him.*) How do I look?

ANNIE. You look very handsome.

GREENE. Thank you. I've been dancing.

ANNIE. I saw you. You're a very graceful dancer.

GREENE. Thank you. I had to stop. My new shoes were hurting my feet.

ANNIE. That's just because they are new. They'll stretch out in time and you'll get used to them.

CECIL. What size shoe do you wear? Wait a minute. Let me guess. I'd say eleven.

GREENE. Eleven and a half.

CECIL. Let me see your shoe and I'll see if you have the right size. I know my shoes. I used to work in a shoe store.

GREENE. I don't dare take them off. I'm afraid I can't get them back on. I had a rough time trying to get them on earlier.

CECIL. Are you married?

GREENE. No.

CECIL. How long have you been here?

GREENE. I don't remember, if I did remember I'd forget.

ANNIE. His father is a doctor. If I had lived in Harrison when I had my babies, he would have delivered them. His mother, Miss Molly, sent the shoes for the dance to go with his dress suit. Greene goes home next week.

CECIL. For how long?

GREENE. A month. Unless . . .

CECIL. Unless . . .

GREENE. You know. Something upsets me. Sometimes I get upset easily. Not lately I haven't been upset.

CECIL. Maybe you're getting better.

GREENE. Maybe.

CECIL. I'm leaving for good in a month. I'm married and I have four children. My wife has just written me asking me for a divorce. It has upset me greatly. Here is the letter she wrote me. Would you care to read it? (GREENE *takes it.*) How would you answer a letter like that? We've been married fifteen years. I was an excellent provider until I got sick. (CECIL *sees* GREENE *holding the letter but not reading it.*) Did you read the letter?

GREENE. No.

CECIL. Why didn't you read it?

GREENE. Because it might upset me. I don't want to get upset. If I get upset, I won't be able to go home on a visit, although I always get upset anyway while I'm there.

CECIL. What upsets you?

GREENE. I don't know. I just get upset. I come from a very large family. My father is a doctor. My oldest brother is a lawyer. My sister is a successful Houston businesswoman. I have two younger brothers both finding themselves. I'm the nervous one. (*He points to* ANNIE.) She's nervous too, and she cries a lot, but I don't cry. I'm just nervous.

ANNIE. I haven't cried all week. I've been very calm and happy all week.

GREENE. Yes, you have.

CECIL. I asked her to dance.

GREENE. She won't dance. She's married.

CECIL. I'm married, and I'm willing to dance. A lot of married people in there are dancing.

GREENE. I'm going to dance. (*He starts away.*)

CECIL. Excuse me. I think I will too. (*He follows* GREENE *into building.* ANNIE *listens to the music.* DAVE *falls asleep.* ANNIE *sees this.*)

ANNIE. Don't go to sleep on me, Dave. Please, please, Dave. (*She shakes him. He wakes up.*) Let's talk. Did you read your mother's letter? It was very interesting. Mr. Henry Vaughn died at sixty-eight. That came as a shock. Or was that in the letter? Maybe it was in another letter. Laura Vaughn is expecting her first child. She is my very best friend. But there is one thing in that letter that is not true, and you must write her at once and tell her. My husband, Mr. Long, is not remarrying. That's quite impossible, because he is still married to me. Will you write and explain that to your mother? And if you don't, please give me permission to write for you, for I'm sure she did not mean it unkindly, and I'm sure she would be the first to want such a story corrected. (*A pause.*) Dave, how long have you been here? (*A pause, as if she expected* DAVE *to answer. He doesn't, of course.*) I told Cecil you have been here five years, and that would make you twenty-three—wouldn't it? (*Again she waits for an answer before continuing.*) Oh, yes. Because I remember distinctly you came here at eighteen. But what is confusing me is that I just this instant remembered that yesterday was your birthday, and someone, maybe Greene, said that you were now twenty-eight. And if that is so, and you came here at eighteen, you have been here ten years instead of five. (*A pause.*) How long have I been here? I told Cecil two. Or is it four? Have I been here four years instead of two? If it's four my little girl was six when I left, so she would be ten and he would be eight. If . . . (*A pause.*) This is what makes me nervous, extremely nervous. I try to keep everything straight and clear. But then these doubts begin and I don't remember anything correctly. Not how long you have been here, or I have been here. (GREENE *enters.*) Greene. Greene. Greene. (*She runs to him. He holds her. She is trembling.*) Greene. Greene. Greene. Do you remember how long Dave has been here?

GREENE. Ten years?

ANNIE. How long have I been here?

GREENE. Four years.

ANNIE. Four years. (*A pause.*) You're sure?

GREENE. Yes.

ANNIE. Of course, that's right. Now I remember. It was raining when my mother brought me here, and I asked at once to see the two of you, and I was told both of you were away visiting your parents. When you came back they took me to see you, and I had to tell you who I was, because neither you nor Dave recognized me. Remember?

GREENE. Sometimes, I remember.

ANNIE. Sometimes I remember . . . I remember my little girl is ten and my little boy is eight. I spent last Christmas with them. Of course, I did. I remember . . . (*A pause.*) I remember . . . Which Christmas was it? Was it this Christmas, or last? What year is this?

GREENE. 1928.

ANNIE. Did you know Mr. Henry Vaughn is dead?

GREENE. Yes.

ANNIE. Did he just die?

GREENE. No.

ANNIE. When?

GREENE. Last March.

ANNIE. Last March? A year ago?

GREENE. Yes.

ANNIE. And do you know if Laura Vaughn has had her baby?

GREENE. Yes.

ANNIE. When?

GREENE. Right after her father died. My father delivered the baby. . . .

(ANNIE *takes* DAVE's *letter again and begins to read it.*)

ANNIE. When was this letter written? (*A pause.*) When was it written? (*A pause.*) There is no date on it. (*A pause.*) I forget so much.

GREENE. And I forget . . .

ANNIE. But you know, I felt a certain suspicion even as I was reading the letter that I had heard this before. That's encouraging, isn't it? You remember, Dave, in discussing the letter with you and its news I was not sure if I had read about Mr. Henry Vaughn in this letter or another letter. It was in this letter, but still I felt somehow I may have heard it before, so when you said to me Mr. Henry Vaughn has been dead a year it wasn't a total surprise. That's encouraging, isn't it? (*A pause.*) There is a lot I don't want to remember, of course. (*A pause.*) But I do remember all the same. (*A pause. She looks at them.*) Mr. Long and I are divorced. I remember that now. They told me at Christmas. Mama and Brother told me when he didn't come to Christmas dinner. They sent the children for a walk with the nurse, and they told me. But which Christmas was it? Was it this Christmas, or last Christmas or the one before? I remember, whichever Christmas it was, she told me we had been divorced for six months. My mother has the custody of the children. She is their legal guardian. She insisted on that, she said, before consenting to the divorce. (*A pause.*) Then I suppose it is true Mr. Long is marrying again, and there will be no need, Dave, to write your mother to correct the rumor. (*A pause.*) But if that is written last March then I suppose he is married already. (*A pause. To* GREENE.) Mr. Long was my husband. I don't suppose you ever met him. I forget how long we were married. He was always, always, always, very kind to me and very patient. . . . I met him in Houston. We had gone there to live after the death of my father. . . .

(*A pause. The music begins again.*)

GREENE. Would you care to dance with me?

ANNIE. No, thank you kindly. I'm tired. I'll rest a while and watch you dance. (*He starts away.*) Greene. (*He pauses.*) When do you leave?

GREENE. Tomorrow.

ANNIE. I thought in a week.

GREENE. No. Tomorrow.

ANNIE. Would you be kind enough to take this note with you? (*She opens her purse and takes out a folded note.*) And give it to your father and ask him please, in the name of charity and our old and dear friendship, to see that Mother receives it. I don't think they allow her to receive the letters I've been sending from here, and it is imperative that she get this message from me. . . .

GREENE. All right.

(*She hands him the note. He puts it in his pocket.*)

ANNIE. Thank you. (GREENE *starts away.*) Greene. (*He pauses.*) When does Dave leave?

GREENE. Tomorrow.

ANNIE. Tomorrow? I thought in a month.

GREENE. No. Tomorrow.

ANNIE. Do you leave at the same time?

GREENE. I don't know. My parents come for me at seven.

ANNIE. In the morning?

GREENE. Yes. I don't know what time his parents will come for him. (*He starts away again.*)

ANNIE. Greene. (*He pauses.*) If I don't get to see you before you leave tell everyone in Harrison hello for me.

GREENE. I don't see anyone when I go to Harrison. Except for my mother and my father.

ANNIE. What do you do when you are there?

GREENE. I sit on the porch and rock and rest so I won't get nervous. When people come up to the porch I go to my room and shut the door. (*He leaves.*)

ANNIE. Dave, I wonder if Laura Vaughn's baby was a boy or a girl? I must write and tell her how happy I am for her. She waited quite a while before she was finally married. She went to Mexico on a two-month trip, with her cousin Laura Weems, the year I was married. Laura Weems has never married. And some people think she never will. I surely hope you find a nice girl someday, Dave, and when you're feeling better, you will marry and have children. I'd be lost without my children. (*A pause. She opens her purse and gets another note.*) I want you to take this note with you tomorrow and promise me you'll give it to your mother and ask her please to see that my mother gets it. I know that my mother has not been receiving my messages. (DAVE *makes no move to take the note. She doesn't press it on him.* ANNIE, *reading the note.*) "My dearest mother and brother: I want to come home and see my children. I know I shall be better and not be nervous if I can only do that." (*She looks at* DAVE.) I miss my children. How long have I been gone? (*She folds the note up and puts it in her purse again. They sit in silence, listening to the music.* CECIL *comes back in.*)

CECIL. Your friend Greene won't be going home tomorrow after all.

ANNIE. Why?

CECIL. He got nervous, right on the dance floor. He was dancing with a young lady when the music stopped, but he wouldn't stop dancing and the young lady became hysterical and they had to separate them and take him back to his room.

ANNIE. Let's hope he will be all right by the morning. His mother and father will be here to get him at seven.

CECIL. Annie, would you care to dance?

ANNIE. No, thank you. I told you that before. I'm old-fashioned. I don't believe a married lady should dance with anyone but her husband.

CECIL. And I respect that. I would feel the same way if I were married.

ANNIE. I thought you were married.

CECIL. No.

ANNIE. Were you never married?

CECIL. Oh, yes. But my wife died some years ago. I think I get confused about time, so I don't remember exactly how many years ago. I do know I went home for the funeral. She had a very large one. She was very loved and respected in our town.

ANNIE. What town was that?

CECIL. Ennis. A little town in Northeast Texas.

ANNIE. Oh, yes. . . . (*A pause.*) Ennis. Not Waco?

CECIL. No. I am not familiar with Waco. I have driven through it once or twice is all. Her death was very sudden. It came as a terrible shock to us all. She was known for her charity and good works.

ANNIE. Were there children?

CECIL. No . . . I'm sad to say. (*A pause.*) It's a nice dance. Isn't it?

ANNIE. Oh, yes.

CECIL. Everyone seems to be enjoying themselves.

ANNIE. Oh, yes. They seem to be.

CECIL. Do you mind if I sit here for a while and visit?

ANNIE. Certainly not. (*He sits. They listen to the music.*) Do you smell chinaberry blossoms?

CECIL. No. Do they have an odor?

ANNIE. Oh, yes. The loveliest most delicate fragrance. I thought for a moment I smelled them. I wasn't sure.

CECIL. I smell Cape jessamine. (*A pause.*) I believe you said you were married?

ANNIE. Oh, yes.

CECIL. If you're married where is your wedding ring?

ANNIE. I lost it. My husband is replacing it next week. It's our anniversary.

CECIL. You were married in the spring?

ANNIE. April sixth.

CECIL. I was married in the winter. (GREENE *comes in carrying his shoes.*) Are you calm again?

GREENE. Yes.

CECIL. I guess the dancing was too much of a strain. Why do you carry your shoes?

GREENE. My feet hurt.

CECIL. What size do you take? Eleven?

GREENE. Eleven and a half.

CECIL. Let me see your shoes. (GREENE *hands them to him.* CECIL *examines them.*) They shouldn't be hurting you. It's eleven and a half. Maybe your foot has grown since the last time you had it measured. When do you leave for your visit home?

GREENE. I've been. I just got back yesterday.

CECIL. (*Pointing to* DAVE.) When does your friend leave?

GREENE. He's been too. And he just returned yesterday.

CECIL. Did you have a good time?

GREENE. Oh, yes. Quiet. I didn't do much. I just sat on the front porch. They've paved the road in front of my house, and there are a lot of cars driving by now. (*To* ANNIE.) I gave your letter to my father and he gave it to your mother and she said to tell you she would see that you got home for a visit.

ANNIE. When?

GREENE. Soon.

ANNIE. Did she say how my children were?

GREENE. Yes. She said they were all well. She said they missed you and sent their love. (*The dance music begins again.*) If I could get my shoes on I'd go dance again. (*He tries, but he is unable to.*) But I can't.

(ANNIE *covers her face with her hands.*)

CECIL. Annie is crying. Is she unhappy?

GREENE. Nervous.

CECIL. What can we do?

GREENE. She'll be all right.

CECIL. When is the next dance scheduled?

GREENE. In the fall.

CECIL. And then at Christmas.

GREENE. And then again in the spring.

CECIL. One year we had a Valentine's Dance. Remember?

GREENE. No.

CECIL. Do you remember, Annie?

ANNIE. Yes. My husband, Mr. Long, came down from Houston for it especially. He brought me a lovely dress, white net with red Valentines stitched all over it. He said he was my Valentine and I was his. Forever. He wanted to come for the spring dance, but he couldn't get here—business.

CECIL. I'm sorry. It's a lovely dance though, isn't it?

ANNIE. Oh, yes. A very lovely dance. One of the loveliest I do believe. Although I still feel Mr. Long will surprise me and come to the dance.

CECIL. That would be a lovely surprise.

ANNIE. Oh, yes. I've had many pleasant surprises like that in my life. Many.

(GREENE *gets his shoes on.*)

GREENE. Now I can dance again. (*He leaves.*)

CECIL. Excuse me. (*He leaves. The music begins.*)

ANNIE. (*To* DAVE.) Greene is dancing again and so is Cecil. (*A pause.*) Can you see them? (*A pause.*) Mr. Long is not coming, you know. I don't know why I said that, to keep up appearances, I suppose. But I know now, in my heart, he will never come again. And my children and my mother and my brother, have they all deserted me? Certainly not. I'll not permit thoughts like that, for then I'll despair and never get well and we want to get well don't we—for the sake of our loved ones and ourselves.

(GREENE *comes in.*)

GREENE. May I intrude?

ANNIE. Certainly. You are always welcome. Isn't he, Dave?

GREENE. Dave? Dave Dushon from Harrison?

ANNIE. Yes.

GREENE. And you are?

ANNIE. Annie, Annie Gayle Long.

GREENE. Oh, yes. And will you be staying for a while?

ANNIE. Yes. I suppose I will—for a while . . .

(*The music is heard again. They listen as the lights fade.*)

Blind Date

Blind Date bears many resemblances to *The Dancers,* written by Horton Foote nearly thirty years earlier. Here again an overbearing older person wants to control a youngster's social life. As before, two young people are thrown together against their wills. And, as in *The Dancers,* there is a happy ending—of sorts. Felix and Sarah Nancy, like Horace and Mary Catherine, find their own way. Both plays affirm that young people will be all right if left to their natural instincts.

The Dancers was largely about the families of Horace and Emily; only in the last scenes did we see the interaction between Horace and Mary Catherine. *Blind Date,* on the other hand, introduces Felix quite early; consequently, there is much more dialogue here between him and Sarah Nancy than between the two youngsters in the earlier play. However, the suggestion that Sarah Nancy and Felix may be compatible after all comes very late in this play and is much less developed than is the young couple's relationship in *The Dancers.* Also, *Blind Date* focuses on a single family, while *The Dancers* is complicated by the intrigue of the elders in two families.

The conflict in this play is not, as it is in *The Dancers,* between families. Surprisingly, it is not really between the generations either. Rather the problems in *Blind Date* grow from Sarah Nancy's refusal to accept the traditional role of a woman. Dolores explains to Sarah Nancy that girls should be "peppy," should smile for the boys and, above all, should be "gracious" no matter what the situation. But, as Dolores knows all too well, Sarah Nancy is sarcastic and blunt. Instead of being sweet to Felix, she responds to his attempts at humming by proclaiming that "he can't carry a tune." And that one comment is not enough for Sarah Nancy. When Felix and Dolores insist on Felix's abilities as a hummer, then ask Sarah Nancy for a pleasant feminine inter-pretation of the situation, she lets Felix have it with both barrels:

> If you can sing, a screech owl can sing. . . . I'd rather listen to a jackass bray than you sing. You look like a warthog and you bray like a jackass. . . . You are a stinking warthog and I wish you would go on home so I could listen to Rudy Vallee in peace.

Sarah Nancy believes, as does Dolores's husband, Robert, that it is better to be "honest than gracious." In this play, as in all Horton Foote's work, authenticity between people is a basic vir-tue. The comedy—and the drama—here stem from the fact that this saving honesty is less acceptable in women than men, girls than boys. Sarah Nancy is a joy because she is able to ignore the mystique that put Dolores "on two beauty pages" but left her less than honest in her relationships. In fact, the mutual admission by Felix and Sarah Nancy that they are not conversationalists is possible only because they level with each other earlier on. A young woman capable of telling a young man that he is "dumb" or "stupid" is more trustworthy, *Blind Date* suggests, than one who is gracious all the time. True intimacy comes from honesty, not the illusion of sweetness.

Blind Date was first produced on the same program as *The Man Who Climbed the Pecan Trees* at The Loft Studio in Los An-geles in 1982. It was directed by Peggy Feury. The play's first New York production was at the HB Playwrights Foundation in July 1985, under the direction of Herbert Berghof.

Blind Date

CAST

Robert Henry	Dolores Henry
Sarah Nancy	Felix Robertson

Place: Harrison, Texas
Time: 1928

The living room of ROBERT *and* DOLORES HENRY. *It is empty.*
ROBERT *comes in. He is a lawyer and has a briefcase, several newspapers, a package of purchases from the drugstore. He drops all these on the sofa and takes his coat off, throwing it over a chair. He calls: "Dolores." There is no answer. He kicks his shoes off and calls: "Children." Again no answer. He goes to the radio and turns it on. He gets one of the newspapers and spreads it around the room as he looks through it. He calls again: "Dolores, I am home." A voice calls back: "She's not here."*

ROBERT. (*Calling.*) Where is she?

SARAH NANCY. (*The voice—calling.*) Yes.

ROBERT. Where?

SARAH NANCY. She took the children to a friend's to spend the night.

ROBERT. Where are you?

SARAH NANCY. In my room.

ROBERT. Did your aunt say when we were having supper?

SARAH NANCY. We've had supper. We ate with the children.

ROBERT. What did you have?

SARAH NANCY. Peanut butter and jelly sandwiches.

(*He is depressed by that. He goes to the window and looks out. He goes to the radio and turns it off. He sees two college yearbooks on a table. He goes and picks them up to look at them when his wife* DOLORES *comes in.*)

ROBERT. Where is my supper?

DOLORES. What?

ROBERT. Where is my supper? Do you know what time it is? I'm starved. I have been here at least half an hour.

DOLORES. Have you forgotten our conversation at breakfast?

ROBERT. What conversation?

DOLORES. Oh, Robert. I told you to eat uptown tonight.

ROBERT. I don't remember that.

DOLORES. I told you I was not going to fix supper tonight.

ROBERT. I don't remember a single word of that.

DOLORES. You were looking right at me when I told you. I said I was giving the children peanut butter and jelly sandwiches at five-thirty, and at six-thirty after their baths I was taking them over to Hannah's to spend the night so they would not be running in and out of here while Sarah Nancy was entertaining her date.

ROBERT. Does Sarah Nancy have another date?

DOLORES. Yes. Thank God. I told you that too this morning.

ROBERT. If you did I don't remember.

DOLORES. Of course not. You never listen to a word I say. Oh, if I live through this I'll live through anything. (*Whispering.*) Don't you remember my telling you this morning that at last I had arranged another date for her? After trying desperately for three days?

ROBERT. No.

DOLORES. Well, I did. And I hope this one turns out better than the last time. I talked to Sister late this afternoon. She is just beside herself. "You know suppose," she said, "she takes it into her head to insult this date too." "Sister," I said, "I refuse to get discouraged. I did not get on the beauty pages of the University of Texas and the Texas A&M yearbooks on my looks alone. It was on my personality. And that can be acquired." Don't you agree?

ROBERT. I guess.

DOLORES. I wasn't born a conversationalist, you know. I can remember being as shy as the next one, but I gritted my teeth and forced myself to converse, and so can Sarah Nancy. Don't you agree?

ROBERT. I guess. Who did you get her a date with?

DOLORES. Felix.

ROBERT. Felix who?

DOLORES. Felix Robertson.

ROBERT. Is that the best you could do? My God.

DOLORES. My God, yourself. I have been calling all over town all week trying to arrange dates for the poor little thing, and you know very well I had absolutely no luck. Not a one wanted to come over here until I called Felix Robertson. I finally called Sister two days ago I was so depressed and had a frank talk with her. I explained the situation to her and she said it was nothing new. She said every time a boy has come around they don't stay long, because Sarah Nancy either won't talk or is very sarcastic. She wants me to have a frank talk with her before Felix gets here and try and help her improve her disposition and I said I would. But it's not so easy to do, you know. I have been worrying over how to talk to her about all this all afternoon. And I almost have a sick headache.

ROBERT. What about supper?

DOLORES. What about your supper? What about it?

ROBERT. I forgot about eating uptown and I'm tired and I don't want to go back out. Is there anything to eat in the kitchen?

DOLORES. My God, Robert. I don't know what's in the kitchen. I feel this is a crisis in my niece's life and I really haven't had time to worry about what is in the kitchen. (*A pause.*) And don't start pouting, Robert.

ROBERT. I'm not pouting.

DOLORES. Yes, you are. I know you very well.

ROBERT. Well, my God, how much longer is this going on? Ever since your niece has been here all you've done is worry about her.

DOLORES. I tried to explain to you. (*She looks at the room.*) Oh, look at this room. I spent all afternoon cleaning it. (*She starts to pick up his shoes, his coat, etc.*)

ROBERT. I'll do that.

DOLORES. Just take them all out. I need to be alone now with Sarah Nancy.

(*He goes. She fixes pillows on the couch and rearranges a few chairs about the room, all the while singing in a bright, happy manner. After a moment she calls:* "Sarah Nancy." *She gets no answer and she calls again:* "Sarah Nancy, Sarah Nancy, I don't want to hurry you, but it's almost time for your date to be here." *Again, no response from* SARAH NANCY *and she is about to leave the room when* SARAH NANCY *appears. She is as doleful looking as* DOLORES HENRY *is cheerful.* DOLORES *gives her a bright, determined smile, which* SARAH NANCY *does not return.*)

DOLORES. Well, you do look sweet. Is that a new dress?

SARAH NANCY. Oh, no.

DOLORES. Well, it's new to me. It's very becoming. It has a lot of style. That's what I always look for first in my clothes, style. (SARAH NANCY *gives no reaction.*) Now, precious lamb, let me tell you a little about the young man who is coming to see you tonight. I don't know whether you remember meeting him or not, but he says he met you at Louise Davis's swim party as you were the only one that didn't want to swim. He is Felix Robertson. (SARAH NANCY *groans.*) What's the matter, dear? Do you remember him?

SARAH NANCY. I remember him.

DOLORES. That's nice. He felt sure you would. Why do you remember him?

SARAH NANCY. Because he kept slapping me on the back and asking me how I was.

DOLORES. He is a very sensitive boy. He was just trying to make you feel at home. And he is, as I'm sure you could tell, from a lovely family. His mother and your dear mother were girlhood friends. Now, difficult as it is for me to do, I feel I have to discuss a few things with you, Sarah Nancy, before Felix arrives. I think, dear, you have to learn to be a little more gracious to the young men that come to see you. Now I am extremely puzzled why my phone hasn't been rung off the wall since you've been my guest, but I think last night I was given a clue. Sam and Ned, those two boys that called last week, told their mother you were extremely hard to converse with. Boys, you know, need someone peppy to talk to. (SARAH NANCY *rolls her eyes.*) Now don't roll your eyes, darling. You know I have your best interest at heart. I want you to be just as popular as any girl here. But to accomplish that you have to learn to converse.

SARAH NANCY. I don't know what to talk about.

DOLORES. I know. I know. I called up your mother this very morning and told her all this, and she said that always seemed to be your trouble. When boys come around, you can't think of things to say. (*She goes to desk and opens a drawer and takes out a list.*) So I sat down and made a list of topics to talk about. And I thought before Felix got here, you and I could go over it, and you could memorize them and then you would always be sure of making conversation. All right, dear?

(SARAH NANCY *doesn't answer.* ROBERT *enters.*)

ROBERT. Excuse me.

DOLORES. Robert?

ROBERT. How much longer are you going to be?

DOLORES. Why?

ROBERT. Because I am starving, that's why.

DOLORES. Did you look in the icebox?

ROBERT. I looked in the icebox.

DOLORES. Well . . .

ROBERT. The ice has all melted.

DOLORES. Well, maybe you had better ride over to the icehouse and get a block of ice.

ROBERT. I will after I've eaten. I'm hungry.

DOLORES. All right. Just be patient. I won't be long with Sarah Nancy.

ROBERT. Honey, I'm starved.

DOLORES. I know you are starved. You have told us that a thousand times. Honestly, I'm not deaf. And I'll be out there as soon as I can, but Felix will be here any minute and Sarah Nancy and I have to go over some things first. Now excuse us, please. (*He goes.*) Now where were we? Oh, yes. I was going over my list of things to talk about. (DOLORES *picks up her list and begins reading.*) One: Who is going to win the football game next Friday? Two: Do you think we have had enough rain for the cotton yet? Three: I hear you were a football player in high school. What position did you play? Do you miss football? Four: I hear you are an insurance salesman. What kind of insurance do you sell? Five: What is the best car on the market today do you think? Six: What church do you belong to? Seven: Do you enjoy dancing? Eight: Do you enjoy bridge? (*She puts the list down.*) All right, that will do for a start. Now let's practice. I'll be Felix. Now. Hello, Sarah Nancy. (*A pause.* SARAH NANCY *looks at her like she thinks she's crazy.*) Now what do you say, Sarah Nancy?

SARAH NANCY. About what?

DOLORES. About what? About what you say when someone says hello to you, Sarah Nancy. Now let's start again. Hello, Sarah Nancy.

SARAH NANCY. Hello.

DOLORES. Honey, don't just say hello and above all don't scowl and say hello. Smile. Hello, how very nice to see you. Let me feel your warmth. Now will you remember that? Of course you will. All right, let's start on our questions. Begin with your first question. (*A pause.*) I'm waiting, honey.

SARAH NANCY. I forget.

DOLORES. Well, don't be discouraged. I'll go over the list carefully and slowly again. One: Who is going to win the football game next Friday? Two: Do you think we have had enough rain for the cotton yet? Three: I hear you were a football player in high school. What position did you play? Do you miss football? Four: I hear you are an insurance salesman. What kind of insurance do you sell? Five: What is the best car out on the market today do you think? Six: What church do you belong to? Seven: Do you enjoy dancing? Eight: Do you enjoy bridge? Now we won't be rigid about the questions, of course. You can ask the last question first if you want to.

SARAH NANCY. What's the last question again?

DOLORES. Do you enjoy bridge?

SARAH NANCY. I hate bridge.

DOLORES. Well then, sweetness, just substitute another question. Say, do you enjoy dancing?

SARAH NANCY. I hate dancing.

DOLORES. Now you don't hate dancing. You couldn't hate dancing. It is in your blood. Your mother and daddy are both beautiful
dancers. You just need to practice is all. Now . . .

SARAH NANCY. Why didn't you get me a date with Arch Leon? I
think he's the cute one.

DOLORES. He's going steady, honey, I explained that.

SARAH NANCY. Who is he going steady with?

DOLORES. Alberta Jackson.

SARAH NANCY. Is she cute?

DOLORES. I think she's right cute, a little common looking and
acting for my taste.

SARAH NANCY. He sure is cute.

DOLORES. Well, Felix Robertson is a lovely boy.

SARAH NANCY. I think he's about as cute as a warthog.

DOLORES. Sarah Nancy.

SARAH NANCY. I think he looks just like a warthog.

DOLORES. Sarah Nancy, precious . . .

SARAH NANCY. That's the question I'd like to ask him. How is
the hogpen, warthog?

DOLORES. Precious, precious.

SARAH NANCY. Anyway, they are all stupid.

DOLORES. Who, honey?

SARAH NANCY. Boys.

DOLORES. Precious, darling.

SARAH NANCY. Dumb and stupid. (*She starts away.*)

DOLORES. Sarah Nancy, where in the world are you going?

SARAH NANCY. I'm going to bed.

DOLORES. Sarah Nancy, what is possessing you to say a thing like that? You're just trying to tease me.

SARAH NANCY. Oh no I'm not. (*She starts away.*)

DOLORES. Sarah Nancy, you can't go to bed. You have a young man coming to call on you at any moment. You have to be gracious. . . .

SARAH NANCY. I don't feel like being gracious. I'm sleepy. I'm going to bed.

DOLORES. Sarah Nancy, you can't. Do you want to put me in my grave? The son of one of your mother's dearest friends will be here at any moment to call on you, and you cannot be so rude as to go to bed and refuse to receive him. Sarah Nancy, I beg you. I implore you.

SARAH NANCY. Oh, all right. (*She sits down.*) Ask me some questions.

DOLORES. No, dear. You ask me some questions.

SARAH NANCY. What church do you attend?

DOLORES. That's lovely. That's a lovely question to begin with. Now I'll answer as Felix will. Methodist.

SARAH NANCY. That's a dumb church.

DOLORES. Sarah Nancy.

SARAH NANCY. I think it's a dumb church. It's got no style. We used to be Methodist but we left for the Episcopal. They don't rant and rave in the Episcopal church.

DOLORES. And they don't rant and rave in the Methodist church either, honey. Not here. Not in Harrison.

SARAH NANCY. Last time I was there they did.

DOLORES. Well, things have changed. Anyway, you're not supposed to comment when he answers the questions, you're just supposed to sit back and listen to the answers as if you're fascinated and find it all very interesting.

SARAH NANCY. Why?

DOLORES. Because that's how you entertain young men, graciously. You make them feel you are interested in whatever they have to say.

SARAH NANCY. Suppose I'm not?

DOLORES. Well, it is not important if you are or not, you are supposed to make them think you are.

(ROBERT *enters.*)

ROBERT. Dolores.

DOLORES. What?

ROBERT. The children are on the phone.

DOLORES. What do they want?

ROBERT. They want to talk to you.

DOLORES. Ask them what they want. Tell them I can't talk now.

(SARAH NANCY *is looking at the yearbook.*)

SARAH NANCY. How did you make the beauty page at two colleges?

DOLORES. Personality. I always knew how to keep a conversation going.

ROBERT. Dolores.

DOLORES. Yes.

ROBERT. They say they won't tell me what they want. They'll only tell you.

DOLORES. All right. (*She goes.*)

SARAH NANCY. Did you go to college with Aunt Dolores?

ROBERT. We met the year she graduated.

SARAH NANCY. She was beautiful.

ROBERT. I guess she was.

(DOLORES *comes in.*)

DOLORES. They forgot their teddy bears. I said you would bring them over.

ROBERT. They're nine and ten years old. What do they want with teddy bears?

DOLORES. They still sleep with them. You know that.

ROBERT. Well, I'm not driving anywhere with two teddy bears for two half-grown children.

DOLORES. Why are you being so difficult?

ROBERT. I am not difficult. I am hungry and tired. I worked hard all day.

DOLORES. Well, I didn't exactly have a ball today myself, mister. If I find you something to eat will you take those teddy bears over to the children?

ROBERT. All right. I'll be the laughingstock of the town, but I'll do it.

(*She goes.*)

SARAH NANCY. How do you get on a beauty page?

ROBERT. Well, you have to be pretty to start with I guess. I think a committee of some kind looks the girls on campus over and makes recommendations and I guess they have judges. But I really don't know. You'll have to ask your aunt that.

SARAH NANCY. How did you meet Aunt Dolores?

ROBERT. At a dance. I think. Yes, I think it was at a dance the first time I met her. And I asked her for a date and six weeks later I popped the question.

SARAH NANCY. What does that mean?

ROBERT. What?

SARAH NANCY. Popping the question.

ROBERT. You know. I asked her to marry me. (SARAH NANCY *makes a face.*) What are you making a face about?

SARAH NANCY. I don't know. I sure hope nobody pops a question to me.

ROBERT. Well, they will someday.

SARAH NANCY. Who?

ROBERT. Some boy or other.

SARAH NANCY. I don't know any boys.

ROBERT. Of course you know some boys.

SARAH NANCY. Not any I'd want to pop the question to me.

(DOLORES *comes in.*)

DOLORES. I opened a can of chile and a can of tamales and sliced some tomatoes. Will that do you?

ROBERT. Thanks. (*He goes.*)

SARAH NANCY. Any of the dumb boys I know try popping a question to me, I'll kick them in the stomach.

DOLORES. What in the world are you talking about, honey? (*The doorbell rings.*) There he is. Now quickly, let me see how you look. (*She forces* SARAH NANCY *to stand up.*) Oh, pretty. (SARAH NANCY *sticks out her tongue.*) Oh, Sarah Nancy. (DOLORES *goes to the door and opens it.*) Come in, Felix. (FELIX *comes in.*) How handsome you look. I believe you two have met?

FELIX. Yes.

SARAH NANCY. What church do you attend?

FELIX. What?

SARAH NANCY. What church do you attend?

FELIX. Methodist.

DOLORES. (*Jumping in nervously.*) Sarah Nancy is an Episcopalian. She is very devout. Felix is very devout too, you know.

SARAH NANCY. Who is going to win the football game on Friday?

FELIX. We are.

SARAH NANCY. Why?

FELIX. Because we are the best team.

SARAH NANCY. Who says so?

FELIX. Everybody knows that. Do you like football?

SARAH NANCY. No.

FELIX. No?

SARAH NANCY. No.

FELIX. Do you like . . . ?

SARAH NANCY. I hate sports. I like to read. Do you like to read?

FELIX. No.

DOLORES. Well, you know what they say, opposites attract. (*She laughs merrily.* FELIX *laughs.* SARAH NANCY *scowls.*) Well, I'll stay and visit just a few minutes longer and then I'll leave you two young people alone. How is your sweet mother, Felix?

FELIX. O.K.

DOLORES. Your mother and Sarah Nancy's mother and I were all girls together. Did your mother tell you that? My, the good times we used to have together.

FELIX. Do you have a radio?

DOLORES. Yes, over there.

(*He goes to the radio and turns it on.*)

FELIX. Do you want to dance?

SARAH NANCY. No, I hate dancing. What church do you belong to?

DOLORES. You asked him that before, Sarah Nancy honey, remember? He said he was a Methodist and I said you were an
Episcopalian.

SARAH NANCY. Oh. (DOLORES *finds a way to get behind* FELIX *and
she begins mouthing a question for* SARAH NANCY *to ask.*) What do
you do?

FELIX. What do you mean?

SARAH NANCY. For a living.

FELIX. Right now I'm in insurance. But I'm leaving that. Not
enough money in it. I'm going to be a mortician.

SARAH NANCY. What's that?

DOLORES. An undertaker, honey.

SARAH NANCY. How do you get to do that?

FELIX. You go to school.

SARAH NANCY. What kind of school?

FELIX. A mortician school.

SARAH NANCY. Oh, who teaches you?

FELIX. Other morticians.

(DOLORES *begins to subtly mouth another question to her;* SARAH
NANCY *continues to ignore her, so* DOLORES *finally gives up.*)

DOLORES. I'm going now and leave you two young people alone
to enjoy yourselves. (*She goes. He goes to the radio and moves the
dial from one program to another.*)

FELIX. There is nothing on I want to hear. (*He turns the radio off.
He sits down and, smiling, looks at* SARAH NANCY.) Having a good
time on your visit here?

SARAH NANCY. It's okay.

FELIX. Let's play some games. What games do you like to play?

SARAH NANCY. I never played any.

FELIX. Never played any games?

SARAH NANCY. No.

FELIX. All right, I'll teach you one. How about ghosts?

SARAH NANCY. Ghosts?

FELIX. It's the name of the game. You start a word to be spelled and the one that spells a word is a third of a ghost. Get it?

SARAH NANCY. No.

FELIX. Well, maybe it isn't too much fun with just two playing. I know, let's see who can name the most books of the Bible. I'll go first. (*He doesn't wait for her to comment and he begins to rattle off the books of the Bible.*) Genesis, Exodus, Leviticus . . . (*He closes his eyes as he thinks of them and he takes it all very seriously.* SARAH NANCY *stares at him as if he is insane. When he gets to Daniel she slips quietly out of the room and is gone by the time he begins the New Testament. He is not aware she is gone.* ROBERT *comes in.* FELIX *is so concentrated he doesn't see him.* ROBERT *looks at him as if he is crazy, shakes his head in disbelief and leaves the room.* FELIX *is unaware of any of it. He says the names very fast as if speed were part of the game, so fast in fact that the names should not always be distinct. When he finishes, he opens his eyes.*) How did I do? I think I got every one. (*He looks at his watch.*) I did it in pretty fair amount of time too. Now let's see what you can do. (*He suddenly becomes aware she is not in the room. Calling.*) Sarah Nancy. (*He is puzzled by her disappearance and is about to go to the door leading into the rest of the house to call her when* ROBERT *comes in with two teddy bears.*)

ROBERT. Hello, Felix. (*They shake hands.*) What's new?

FELIX. Not a whole lot.

ROBERT. You're looking well.

FELIX. Thank you, sir. (ROBERT *starts out the front door.*) Excuse me. Do you know where Sarah Nancy is?

ROBERT. No I don't, son.

FELIX. She was here a minute ago. We were having a contest to see who could name the most books of the Bible.

ROBERT. Who won?

FELIX. I don't know. She was here when I started, but when I finished and opened my eyes she was gone.

ROBERT. Just sit down and relax. She'll be back.

FELIX. Yes sir.

(ROBERT *goes out.* FELIX *sits down.* DOLORES *comes in looking stricken.*)

DOLORES. Felix, Sarah Nancy has sent me out to apologize to you and beg your forgiveness. She has been stricken, suddenly, with a very bad sick headache. She's suffered from them, she says, since childhood, and the worst of it is the poor darling never, never knows when they will strike. She says she was sitting here listening to you rattle off all the books of the Bible and having one of the liveliest times of her life, when her attack began. She is just heartbroken, the poor little thing. She slipped out not wanting to disturb you, to take an aspirin, hoping to find relief for her headache, so she could resume the lovely time she was having with you, but she got no relief from the aspirin, and she says now the only relief are cold packs on her head and total, total silence. She is quite stricken, poor sweet thing. Too stricken to even come and say good night. "Whatever will Felix think of me?" she said. "Why, precious darling," I reassured her, "he will most certainly understand." I know you do. Don't you?

FELIX. Oh, yes ma'm.

DOLORES. How is your sweet mother?

FELIX. Just fine, thank you ma'm.

DOLORES. And your daddy's well?

FELIX. Oh, yes ma'm.

DOLORES. Tell your mother and daddy hello for me.

FELIX. I will. (*A pause.*) They said when I came over here to say hello for them.

DOLORES. Thank you. (*A pause.*)

FELIX. Well, I guess I'll be going on home.

DOLORES. All right, Felix.

FELIX. Tell Nancy Sarah . . .

DOLORES. Sarah Nancy.

FELIX. Oh, yes. Sarah Nancy. Tell her I hope she feels better.

DOLORES. I will.

FELIX. Tell her I said all the books in the Bible in under ten minutes, and if she thinks she can beat that to call me up and I'll come over and time her.

DOLORES. I'll tell her that.

FELIX. Well, good night again.

DOLORES. Good night to you, Felix dear. (*He goes.* DOLORES *sighs. She begins to turn the lights off when* SARAH NANCY *comes out.*) What are you doing out here, Sarah Nancy?

SARAH NANCY. I want to listen to the radio.

DOLORES. You cannot listen to the radio. You can be seen from the street if you sit in this room listening to the radio. I told that boy that you were mortally ill with a sick headache and you cannot appear five minutes later perfectly well and sit in the living room and listen to the radio.

SARAH NANCY. I want to hear Rudy Vallee.

DOLORES. You will not hear Rudy Vallee and run the risk of someone seeing you and telling Felix about it. What possesses you? I ask two lovely young men over last week and you refuse to speak to either of them all evening. I ask this sweet, charming boy over tonight and you walk out of the room while he is saying the books of the Bible. Well, I tell you one thing, I will not ask another single boy over here again until you decide to be gracious. And I know you can be gracious, as gracious as any girl here. Anyone with the lovely mother you have can certainly be gracious. (ROBERT *enters.*) Oh, you gave me such a start. I thought you were Felix. How were the children?

ROBERT. All right.

DOLORES. Did you tell them to behave themselves and to mind Hannah and to get to bed when she told them to?

ROBERT. No.

DOLORES. Why not?

ROBERT. Because it would have done no good. They were all running around like a bunch of wild Indians. They weren't any more interested in those teddy bears than I am. Did Felix pop the question to you, Sarah Nancy?

SARAH NANCY. No. And if he had I'd have knocked his head off.

DOLORES. What's all this about popping questions?

ROBERT. I was telling Sarah Nancy how we met and after six weeks I asked you to marry me.

DOLORES. Six weeks? It was three months.

ROBERT. Six weeks.

DOLORES. I only went out twice with you in the first six weeks. We didn't start going steady until our third date. You took me to a tea dance at your frat house and you asked me to wear your fraternity pin and I said I had to think about it, as I wasn't in the habit of just casually accepting fraternity pins like some girls I knew.

(*The door opens and* FELIX *enters.*)

FELIX. Excuse me. I left my hat.

DOLORES. Oh, Felix. Isn't this remarkable? I was just about to go to the phone and call you and tell you that Sarah Nancy had completely recovered from her headache. You hadn't gone five minutes when she came out and said the aspirin worked after all and where is Felix and she was so distressed that you had gone that she insisted I go to the phone and see if you wouldn't come back which I was about to do. Isn't that so, Sarah Nancy?

(SARAH NANCY *doesn't answer.*)

FELIX. Did Mrs. Henry tell you I said all the books of the Bible in under ten minutes?

DOLORES. Yes, I did. Didn't I, Sarah Nancy? (SARAH NANCY *doesn't answer.*) And she was so impressed. Weren't you, Sarah Nancy? (*Again no answer from* SARAH NANCY.)

FELIX. Want to hear me do it again? You can time me this time.

SARAH NANCY. No.

FELIX. Want to play another game then? How about movie stars?

DOLORES. That sounds like fun. Doesn't it, Robert? How do you play that?

FELIX. Well, you think of initials like R. V., and you all try to guess who I'm thinking of.

SARAH NANCY. Rudy Vallee.

FELIX. No, you give up?

DOLORES. I do. I never can think of anything. Can you think of who it is, Robert?

ROBERT. No.

FELIX. Do you give up, Sarah Nancy?

SARAH NANCY. No. (*A pause. There is silence.*)

FELIX. Now do you give up?

SARAH NANCY. I'll die before I give up. (*Again silence.*)

DOLORES. Honey, you can't take all night. It won't be any fun then. I think there should be a time limit, Felix, and if we don't guess it . . .

FELIX. (*Interrupting.*) Give up?

SARAH NANCY. No.

DOLORES. Let's have a five-minute time limit. (*She looks at her watch.*) Five minutes is almost up.

FELIX. Give up?

SARAH NANCY. No.

DOLORES. Time is up. Who is it?

FELIX. Rudolph Valentino.

DOLORES. Rudolph Valentino. Imagine. Now why couldn't I have thought of that? Isn't that a fun game, Sarah Nancy honey? Why don't you pick some initials?

SARAH NANCY. O. B.

DOLORES. O. B. My. O. B. Can you think of an O. B., Felix?

FELIX. Not yet.

DOLORES. Can you, Robert?

ROBERT. No.

DOLORES. My, you picked a hard one, Sarah honey. O. B. Can she give us a clue?

FELIX. Yes. You can ask things like is it a man or a woman.

DOLORES. Is it a man or a woman?

SARAH NANCY. A woman.

DOLORES. A woman. My goodness.

SARAH NANCY. Give up?

DOLORES. I do. Do you, Felix?

FELIX. Yes. Who is it?

SARAH NANCY. Olive Blue.

FELIX. Olive Blue. Who is she?

SARAH NANCY. A girl back home.

FELIX. She's not a movie star.

SARAH NANCY. Who said she was?

FELIX. Well, goose. They're supposed to be movie stars.

SARAH NANCY. You're a goose yourself.

DOLORES. Sarah Nancy.

SARAH NANCY. It's a dumb game anyway.

FELIX. Well, let's play popular songs.

DOLORES. That sounds like fun. How do you do that?

FELIX. Well, you hum or whistle part of a song and the others have to guess what it is.

DOLORES. Oh, grand. Doesn't that sound like fun, Sarah Nancy? (*Again no answer from* SARAH NANCY.) Why don't you whistle something, Sarah Nancy?

SARAH NANCY. I can't whistle.

DOLORES. Well, then hum something.

SARAH NANCY. I can't hum either.

FELIX. I'll hum and you all guess. (*He hums.*) Can you guess?

DOLORES. I can't. Can you, Robert?

ROBERT. No.

DOLORES. Can you, Sarah Nancy?

SARAH NANCY. No, but I never will be able to guess what he hums, because he can't carry a tune.

DOLORES. Well, I don't agree at all. I think Felix has a very sweet voice.

ROBERT. Then how come you can't tell what he's humming?

DOLORES. Because I didn't know the song, I suppose.

ROBERT. What was the song, Felix?

FELIX. "Missouri Waltz."

ROBERT. Don't you know the "Missouri Waltz" when you hear it?

DOLORES. Yes, I know the "Missouri Waltz" when I hear it. Hum something else, Felix. (*He hums another tune. Again very flat.*) Now what's the name of that, honey?

FELIX. "Home Sweet Home."

ROBERT. "Home Sweet Home." My God!

(DOLORES *glares at* ROBERT.)

DOLORES. Oh, of course. It was on the tip of my tongue. All right, Sarah Nancy honey, it's your turn.

FELIX. No, it's still my turn. I keep on until you guess what I'm singing.

SARAH NANCY. How are we going to guess what you're singing when you can't sing?

FELIX. I certainly can sing. I'm in the choir at the Methodist Church. I'm in a quartet that sings twice a year at the Lions Club.

SARAH NANCY. If you can sing, a screech owl can sing.

DOLORES. Sarah Nancy, honey.

SARAH NANCY. I'd rather listen to a jackass bray than you sing. You look like a warthog and you bray like a jackass.

FELIX. Who looks like a warthog?

SARAH NANCY. You do.

FELIX. I'm rubber and you're glue, everything you say bounces off of me and sticks on you.

SARAH NANCY. Warthog. You are a stinking warthog and I wish you would go on home so I could listen to Rudy Vallee in peace.

FELIX. Don't worry. I'm going home. I didn't want to come over here in the first place but my mama bribed me to come over here. Well, a million dollars couldn't make me stay here now and two million couldn't ever get me here again if you were here. (*He leaves.*)

DOLORES. Oh, my God. I have never seen such carrying on in my life. Sarah Nancy, what am I going to tell Sister? She will take to her bed when I report this. Absolutely have a breakdown.

SARAH NANCY. I'm sorry. I'm not going to lie and tell some old fool jackass they can sing when they can't.

ROBERT. I agree with Sarah Nancy. He can't carry a tune at all.

DOLORES. Nobody asked your opinion.

ROBERT. Well, I'm giving it to you whether you asked for it or not.

DOLORES. And I don't want to hear it. How can you expect Sarah Nancy to learn to be gracious if we don't set an example?

ROBERT. I didn't tell her not to be gracious. I just told her that I agreed with what she said about his singing. I'm being honest. If that's ungracious, all right. I'd rather be honest than gracious.

DOLORES. That's all right for you. You're a man. But let me tell you right now I didn't get on two beauty pages by being honest, but by being gracious to people. But I'm whipped now and worn out. I've done all I can do. I can do no more. (*She leaves.*)

ROBERT. I guess your aunt's a little upset.

SARAH NANCY. I guess so. Do you mind if I listen to Rudy Vallee on the radio?

ROBERT. No.

(*She turns on the radio. She turns the dial.*)

SARAH NANCY. What time is it?

ROBERT. Almost ten.

SARAH NANCY. Shoot. I missed Rudy Vallee.

ROBERT. Well, you can hear him next week.

SARAH NANCY. I'll be home next week.

ROBERT. I'm going to go see to your aunt. Will you be all right?

SARAH NANCY. Sure.

(*He goes. She gets the yearbooks. She looks at one and then at the other.* FELIX *comes in.*)

FELIX. Where's Mrs. Henry?

SARAH NANCY. I don't know.

FELIX. I told my mama what happened and she said I owed Mrs. Henry an apology for speaking like I did. I told her what you said to me and she said it didn't matter how other people acted, I had to remember that I was a gentleman and that I was always to act in a gentlemanly fashion. So tell Mrs. Henry I'm here and I want to apologize. (*She goes. He sees the yearbooks. He looks at them.* SARAH NANCY *comes in.*) Did you tell her?

SARAH NANCY. No. I couldn't. She's gone to bed. She has a sick headache.

FELIX. (*He points to the book.*) She was pretty, wasn't she?

SARAH NANCY. Yes she was.

FELIX. You don't sing any better than I do.

SARAH NANCY. I didn't say I did.

FELIX. And you're never going to be on any beauty pages, I bet.

SARAH NANCY. I didn't say I would.

FELIX. Don't you care?

SARAH NANCY. No.

(*There is silence. An uncomfortable silence. He closes the yearbook.*)

FELIX. I can't think of a whole lot to talk about. Can you?

SARAH NANCY. No.

FELIX. Your aunt is quite a conversationalist. It's easy to talk when she's around.

SARAH NANCY. I guess. (*A pause. Silence.*)

FELIX. Do you mind if I stay on here for a while?

SARAH NANCY. No.

FELIX. I told my mother I'd stay at least another hour. If you get sleepy, you just go on to bed. I'll just sit here and look at these yearbooks.

SARAH NANCY. I'm not sleepy.

FELIX. You want one of the yearbooks?

SARAH NANCY. Thank you.

(*He hands her one. She opens it. He takes one and opens it. After a beat they are both completely absorbed in looking at the yearbooks. They continue looking at them as the light fades.*)

The Prisoner's Song

More than any other play in this collection, *The Prisoner's Song* divides the people of Harrison, Texas, into the haves and the have-nots. For example, Mae and Mrs. Estill, who have to struggle, discuss the parties held by other women who live in comfortable affluence. Mrs. Estill summarizes her point of view for Mae:

> What these women spend on parties would make your head swim. I swear they sit up nights thinking of ways to spend money in order to outdo each other. I bet they've got enough food over there to feed this whole town for a week.

This class division is not, of course, just among the women of Harrison. John is turned down for a filling station job because, as a white man, he might be able to leave to improve himself. Blacks and Mexicans, who work without hope, get such jobs. Worst of all, Mr. Wright's promises to help John are false, for the rich need not be responsible to the less well off. The politics of the workplace in *The Prisoner's Song* is neither pretty nor fair.

But, as in other Horton Foote plays, these realities are not examined in isolation. In Foote's work social injustice is one form taken by a more general injustice that is an irreparable part of the human condition. In *The Prisoner's Song* social problems are symptoms of problems of intimacy, which are the burden of people of all classes. For example, Luther Wright uses his power in the community, his influence peddling, to manipulate John and Mae. His wealth allows him to get close to Mrs. Estill and Mae in ways less fortunate men could not. But these abuses are explained in the play as the futile efforts of a broken and bitter man. Like his wife, Luther has never recovered from the death of their daughter, Mary Martha. His pseudo-friendships with other wealthy men and his sentimental attachments to younger women express what a character in another Foote play calls "the endless inward chant." Luther is stuck in the grieving process, trapped, like the prisoner in the song, in a cage of narcissism. In *The Prisoner's Song* the rich also have their reasons, and love, even when it fails, is always more powerful than privilege.

John, at the other end of the social ladder from Luther, is similarly handicapped by personal ghosts that keep him from others. Like other modern businessmen that Horton Foote has created, Mae's husband is energetic and resilient, even thoughtful. But all his willfulness is shallow; his optimism is forced. And his vision is flawed. Like Brother Vaughn in *The Orphans' Home Cycle*, John's frantic activity, all his powers of positive thinking, cover a deep sense of irresponsibility and failure. Here is a man running from his own emotions. Under his slick exterior is a boy terrified by his own weakness, his alcoholism, that dogs him as much as Mary Martha haunts Luther Wright. Most telling is John's dislike of Flatonia and Livingston, the old places that represent the past.

The two ways of living in Horton Foote's dramatic world are represented in *The Prisoner's Song* by Livingston and by the new Harrison. In Mae's homeplace, as she tells Mrs. Estill,

> We still are waiting there every year to see what the cotton crop is going to do. If we have a good crop and it brings a good price, we feel rich; if the crop is a failure, or the price is low, we all feel poor.

Livingston, as its name suggests, is a place where the emphasis is on living. There seems to be a sense of shared interests and emotions there from which a community can grow. Not yet fractured by the new opportunism, Livingston is still a "we all" place. But Harrison, even by 1927, has been corrupted by oil, and the love of it, as Mrs. Estill describes:

> . . . when oil was discovered, and the people working for the oil companies moved in, everyone went a little crazy. Women began smoking and drinking in public. Why, girls who were raised here all their lives in a good Christian way, by good Christian mothers, began to get drunk at the dances, and the husbands and the wives began trading each other for other husbands and wives. And then everybody spending money every way they could. And that's all anybody could talk about was how much money this one's worth and how much that one's worth.

There is some Puritanical exaggeration in Mrs. Estill's words, but the theme is a repeated one in these plays. Money and tokens of external power are not the source of the peace and contentment so cherished by Horton Foote's characters. Like Chekhov, Foote dramatizes worlds in transition, and his sympathies are clearly with the more orderly and traditional ways which are fast dying out.

The Prisoner's Song was presented first by the HB Playwrights Foundation in New York City in July 1985, as one of three plays collectively called Harrison, Texas. (The others were The One-Armed Man and Blind Date.) The production was directed by Herbert Berghof.

The Prisoner's Song

CAST

Mae Murray	Bonny Estill
John Murray	Luther Wright

Place: Harrison, Texas
Time: Spring, 1927

MAE *and* JOHN MURRAY's *one-room furnished apartment.* JOHN *is there drinking coffee.* MAE *comes in.*

MAE. Good morning, my dearest.

JOHN. Coffee is delicious, my dear.

MAE. Thank you, John. (*She crosses to the bed and begins to make it up.*) Are you looking for work today, John?

JOHN. Yes. I have an extremely important appointment today, which indeed might lead in time to any number of things. (*He looks in the mirror, whistling.*) Do I look all right?

MAE. Oh, yes.

JOHN. Prosperous, I hope.

MAE. Oh, yes. (*He starts away.*) John . . .

JOHN. Yes, my dear.

MAE. I hate to bother you with this, but Mrs. Estill spoke to me again today and she said that she really had to have the rent before the week was out, or she would have to ask us to leave.

JOHN. Did she?

MAE. Yes.

JOHN. Did she indeed?

MAE. Yes, but you mustn't be angry with her. She was very nice about it. Most polite.

JOHN. Most polite?

MAE. Most polite.

JOHN. I'm glad to hear that.

MAE. I told her you were looking for work and you had some prospects.

JOHN. And what did she say?

MAE. She was delighted for you, she said, just delighted. She said she thought you had a great future ahead.

JOHN. Did she?

MAE. Yes.

JOHN. Well, that was damn nice of her.

MAE. I thought so. (*A pause.*) John . . .

JOHN. Yes, darling.

MAE. I hate to bother you about this but the money you gave me last week is all spent, and I have groceries to buy . . . and . . . (*She cries.*)

JOHN. Mae, what is it?

MAE. I'm worried. I'm so worried.

JOHN. Now why? Don't you believe in me?

MAE. Yes, I do. But I'm just wracked by worry. (*He goes to her.*)

JOHN. Now, now, Mae. We're going to make it.

MAE. But what will happen if you don't get a job before our money is all gone? (*A pause.*) How much money do we have left?

JOHN. Now you let me worry about that. I'll not have you worry your pretty head about such things. (*He sighs and goes and sits down.*)

MAE. Aren't you going on your appointment?

JOHN. Not now.

MAE. Why?

JOHN. I don't want to leave you discouraged and unhappy.

MAE. No. You go. If the appointment might lead to a job . . .

JOHN. Only in the future.

MAE. How far in the future?

JOHN. Five years or ten, after I've acquired executive experience.

MAE. Five years or ten!

(MRS. ESTILL, *the landlady, knocks at the door.*)

JOHN. Come in. (MRS. ESTILL *enters.*) Good morning, Mrs. Estill.

MRS. ESTILL. Good morning, John. You're wanted on the phone.

JOHN. Thank you. (*He leaves.*)

MRS. ESTILL. Believe it or not, Rita Darst is having a morning coffee, an afternoon bridge luncheon and a dinner party for couples tonight. She says she wants to get all her obligations over at once. I wasn't invited to any of them. Were you?

MAE. No.

MRS. ESTILL. Well, you're a stranger here. I'm sure she's never met you. Has she ever met you?

MAE. I don't think so.

MRS. ESTILL. They don't ask me though, because I haven't accepted invitations to parties in ten years. I'm in no position to pay back obligations like that. What these women spend on parties would make your head swim. I swear they sit up nights thinking of ways to spend money in order to outdo each other. I bet they've got enough food over there to feed this whole town for a week. They'll have ham, turkey, fried chicken, deviled eggs, potato salad, molded salad, God knows how many desserts. She'll send me a plate over afterwards, she always does, and I'll give you a taste.

MAE. Thank you.

(JOHN *comes back in.*)

JOHN. Thank you, Mrs. Estill.

MRS. ESTILL. Not at all.

JOHN. Well, good news! Good news!

MRS. ESTILL. Why don't you tell us what the good news is?! I'm gonna leave you two alone and I won't even listen through the keyhole. (*She goes. He continues.*)

JOHN. Thank God I didn't go for that appointment. Thank heavens we had our little talk and I stayed behind to comfort you.

MAE. Who was it, John?

JOHN. Your father.

MAE. My father?

JOHN. Yes, your father. Just as courteous as he could be. He asked how we were getting along and had I found work yet. I said no, but I was very hopeful, and he said he had set up an appointment with a friend of his, a Mr. Luther Wright.

MAE. Mr. Luther Wright?

JOHN. Yes. Do you know him?

MAE. I used to know him. His daughter went to Sullins with me and I met him several times when he came to see her there, but then she died right after she finished her sophomore year and I never saw him again. I remember now, at the time she said she lived near here, but I'd forgotten it.

JOHN. He has three houses now, your daddy said. One in Mississippi, one in Arkansas and one near here. Your daddy said he's been here a week and he's expecting a visit from me. He has vast interests, your daddy said.

MAE. Oh, vast? . . .

JOHN. Cotton, oil, cattle. . . . He's a man of untold wealth, your daddy said.

MAE. Oh, untold . . . (*A pause.*) What was his daughter's name? She was a sweet girl. She was plain, but very sweet, not a bit stuck-up in spite of all their money. (*A pause.*) Oh, what was . . . ? Mary Martha . . . Mary Martha Wright.

JOHN. Well, I tell you right now this is the break I've been ex-pecting. Many a night while you were asleep I'd get out of bed and stand here by this window and look out at this town and think to myself why have I come here. Will I ever be able to find a job here? But something, some little voice kept telling me, John Murray, don't panic. Don't panic. Rome wasn't built in a day. If you don't believe in yourself who will?

MAE. Did Daddy say what kind of a job he was going to offer you?

JOHN. No, and I pretended like I was indifferent. I pretended like I was getting offers every day for jobs. But you know it has to be something big. I hope it's in oil. That's a business I want to get to know. I do believe by the time I'm forty—I've always believed this, really—that I'm going to be a millionaire. That I'm going to have my own oil wells . . . and I do believe that before too long your father is going to be man enough to come up to me and shake my hand and say, "I owe you an apology. I was wrong about you. You're a fine man." (*A pause.*) Did you tell him I had stopped drinking?

MAE. No. Why?

JOHN. Because he said he'd heard I had. He said he'd heard that I hadn't had a drink in six months.

MAE. I didn't tell him that.

JOHN. I said it was eight months. (*A pause.*) It is eight months. Isn't it?

MAE. All of that. Did you ask about Mother?

JOHN. Yes. He said she was feeling fine. He asked how you were. I said you were fine.

MAE. Did he mention my sisters?

JOHN. No. (*He looks at his watch.*) I have to go. He said Mr. Wright would be expecting me this morning. (*He starts out.*)

MAE. John . . . Don't forget to leave me some money. (*A pause.*)

JOHN. Oh, sure. (*He reaches in his pocket.*) Will five dollars do you?

MAE. Yes. Thank you.

JOHN. I wish it could be more. Anyway, I feel today is a real turning point for us. I feel today something mighty good and wonderful is going to happen to your husband.

MAE. Oh, I think so too.

(*He kisses her. He leaves. She goes to the window and looks out. There is a knock on the door.*)

MAE. Come in.

(MRS. ESTILL *enters with a plate of food.*)

MRS. ESTILL. See. Didn't I tell you she'd send a plate over for me? Her cook just brought it over. Look at this. I hope you're hungry. It's more than I can eat in a month of Sundays.

MAE. I'm not very hungry. Thank you. I was at the window watching the guests. Everyone is certainly dressed up.

MRS. ESTILL. Aren't they? I'd hate to be their husbands, the way they spend money on clothes. It's the oil crowd that started it, you know. Oh, we had lots of parties before then, but when oil was discovered, and the people working for the oil companies moved in, everyone went a little crazy. Women began smoking and drinking in public. Why, girls who were raised here all their lives in a good Christian way, by good Christian mothers, began to get drunk at the dances, and the husbands and the wives began trading each other for other husbands and wives. And then everybody spending money every way they could. And that's all anybody could talk about was how much money this one's worth and how much that one's worth. You're from Livingston, aren't you?

MAE. Yes.

MRS. ESTILL. Is it the same in Livingston?

MAE. No. We still are waiting there every year to see what the cotton crop is going to do. If we have a good crop and it brings a good price, we feel rich; if the crop is a failure, or the price is low, we all feel poor. That's why my husband didn't want to go to Livingston to get established. He said he couldn't spend the rest of his life worrying about the weather and the price of cotton.

MRS. ESTILL. Was he from Livingston originally?

MAE. No. Flatonia. He had cousins in Livingston that he used to visit.

MRS. ESTILL. I've never been in Flatonia. It's near San Antonio, isn't it?

MAE. Yes ma'm. There is not much of anything there. They do some farming, but nothing like around Livingston. My husband sure doesn't like Flatonia. He says there is no future there whatsoever. Do you know Mr. Wright?

MRS. ESTILL. Mr. Luther Wright?

MAE. Yes.

MRS. ESTILL. Yes, I know him. I used to see him all the time, but he's not around here much anymore. His only daughter died here nine or ten years ago, and he has never spent a whole lot of time here since.

MAE. I knew his daughter.

MRS. ESTILL. Mary Martha?

MAE. I went to school with her at Sullins.

MRS. ESTILL. Wasn't it sad? She was a sweet thing. It made Mr. Wright very bitter, you know. He said at the time they could take his money and his oil wells and his cotton and his cattle, but just give him back Mary Martha. Well, that couldn't be done, of course. They have a big tombstone for her out in the graveyard, with a sculpture of her head on top of it and all kinds of verses from the Bible and poetry on the tombstone itself. You ought to go out and look at it one day before the summer is here and it gets too hot. Although the cemetery is never really too hot because of all those trees. Have you seen Mr. Wright since you've been here?

MAE. No. I had even forgotten he lived in Harrison. The good news was from my father. He called my husband to tell him to go see Mr. Wright about a job.

MRS. ESTILL. Well, he's got jobs. For sure. And I hope he gives your husband one.

MAE. I hope so too. Something tells me he will. My husband said he felt today was a turning point and I do feel that too. Oh, yes, I do. I do feel that too. (*She cries.*) Oh, goodness, excuse me. I don't know what has come over me. I guess it's all the excitement of my father calling and all.

MRS. ESTILL. I thought your father and your husband didn't speak.

MAE. They haven't in five years. That's why I was so surprised when he called and asked to speak to John. (*A pause.*) You see my husband used to drink. And my daddy didn't want me to marry him, but I did anyway and we went out to California to live. My husband had hopes of finding work on an oil crew, but then he got to drinking and the oil crew job didn't work out and we went on back to Flatonia to live with his family. But he and his daddy couldn't get along, and I was going to have a baby then and I went to Livingston to have it. And the baby was born dead, and the night he was born they couldn't find my husband because he was on a drunk, so when they did find him and he had sobered up, my father asked him to leave the house, and he did and I left too. I go back every summer to visit, without my husband, of course. So when my father called this morning it was a real surprise. An omen of happiness. My husband hasn't had a drink in eight months.

MRS. ESTILL. Oh, I think that is remarkable. You said your baby was born dead?

MAE. Yes. It was a boy. But I didn't name it. On its tombstone we just put Baby Murray. That was a sad time for us.

(*There is a knock on the door. She goes to answer it.* LUTHER WRIGHT, *55, is there.*)

MR. WRIGHT. Mae Murray?

MAE. Yes?

MR. WRIGHT. I'm a friend of your father's. Luther Wright.

MAE. Oh, Mr. Wright, of course. Forgive me for not recognizing you. Won't you come in? (*He enters.*)

MR. WRIGHT. Hello, Bonny.

MRS. ESTILL. Hello, Luther. I didn't know until just now you all were acquainted.

MAE. I don't know if you remember, Mr. Wright, but I went to school with your daughter.

MR. WRIGHT. Did you? Bless your heart!

MAE. We met once when you came to school to visit Mary Martha.

MR. WRIGHT. Did we? Oh, my goodness. So you knew Mary Martha?

MAE. Oh, yes sir.

MRS. ESTILL. Have a piece of fried chicken, Luther? Rita Darst sent it over to me, so I know it's good.

MR. WRIGHT. Thank you. It looks good. (*He takes a piece.*)

MRS. ESTILL. I was telling Mae I would hate to be the husbands of the women here, the way they spend money.

MR. WRIGHT. Well, money is made to be spent, Bonny.

MRS. ESTILL. It is if you have it, Luther.

MR. WRIGHT. Well, there is something in that, of course, Bonny.

MRS. ESTILL. Will you have another piece of chicken before I go?

MR. WRIGHT. Thank you, no.

MRS. ESTILL. A piece of cake?

MR. WRIGHT. No. Thank you. (*A pause.*) Well, maybe I will have a piece of cake. (*He takes it.*) Now take it out of here before I eat it all. It is good. (*She laughs and goes.*) You know we lost Mary Martha.

MAE. Yes sir. I was very sorry when I heard it.

MR. WRIGHT. It about killed me. My wife too. To tell you the truth, I don't think she ever has gotten over it. (*A pause.*) How long have you been married, young lady?

MAE. Six years.

MR. WRIGHT. Any children?

MAE. No sir. We had a little boy that was born dead. I didn't name it though. On its tombstone we just put Baby Murray. That was a sad time for us.

MR. WRIGHT. My goodness. Mary Martha was our only child. We took a little fourteen-year-old Mexican boy that was raised on our place and Mary Martha had treated like a pet before she died and we educated him, and did what we could for him, but he's trifling and a disappointment to us. Where is your husband?

MAE. Well, he went someplace I thought to find you. He didn't tell me where. My daddy called him and said he wanted him to go around to see you.

MR. WRIGHT. Oh, well, maybe that's how it was. Your daddy told me where you were living and I thought I'd just come on over here.

MAE. Yes sir. I guess my husband went out to your house.

MR. WRIGHT. No, I expect he went to my office. I keep an office in town. Don't worry about it. The girl that works for me will tell him where I am. (*A pause.*) When Mary Martha died I said to my wife, "Mama . . . they can take everything I have. My oil wells, my cotton, my cattle, if they will just give us back Mary Martha." "Well, that is not going to happen," she said. "She is gone and nothing will bring her back. It's the Lord's will," she said. "Why is it the Lord's will?" I asked. "That's not for us to know as of this time," she said. "Someday it will be revealed to us and we will understand." . . . And I guess I will, someday. I don't now, and that's for sure. I mean, I didn't ask for any of this good fortune, you know, that people say has come to me. Luck brought it to me. One day a man came up to me and said, "You have, we think, oil on your land. We want to drill and find out." And I did. God knows I did. I went to bed one night a poor man and woke up the next morning a rich one. And I've prospered ever since. I don't know how, I'm not shrewd, I don't study over it, I don't worry over it. I just prosper. A man with three daughters came up to me the other day and said, "How come you are so rich and I hardly have a dime?" and I said, "How come you have three daughters and mine was taken from me?" Well, that stopped him. "That's something to think about," he said. One night Mama and I was talking and I said maybe I had sinned in some terrible way, and that's why Mary Martha was taken. "Maybe we both have," she said. "Not you," I said, "you don't know the meaning of the word." "How do you know what is and what isn't in my heart?" she said. "Well, I guess that's right," I said, "but if you have sinned enough to have Mary Martha taken from us, I would be mighty surprised. Now I'm a man. Everybody knows we're naturally more sinful." "In what way?" she said. "In all ways," I told her. But still I don't know what I done to have had this happen. Whatever it was, I think in all fairness I should have had some warning, don't you? (*A pause.*) Nice glass. Where'd you get it?

MAE. It was here when we moved in.

MR. WRIGHT. Todd Landry, you know, is as rich as I am, but he don't mind telling you how he got rich. He thinks it's all right, but I don't. He got rich by taking advantage of ignorant nigras. When he heard the oil company was leasing my land, he went right quick to all the nigras that had lived anywhere near mine and signed them to leases for practically nothing. They made nickels out of it and he made millions. One of them tried to kill him when he found out what he done, but Todd shot and killed him first; he drove all out in the country and all over freedman's town with that man's body in the back of his truck as a warning to the others if they tried anything. None of them did.

(JOHN *comes in.*)

MAE. Oh, John. Mr. Wright came here looking for you.

MR. WRIGHT. (*Extending his hand.*) Luther Wright. We've been having a lovely talk. She knew Mary Martha. Did you know Mary Martha?

JOHN. No sir.

MR. WRIGHT. We put up a lovely tombstone for Mary Martha out in the cemetery. It's a work of art, if I do say so myself. People come from miles around to see it, you know!

MAE. Do they?

MR. WRIGHT. From miles around. Would you like to ride out now and see her tombstone?

MAE. Oh, yes, I would. Wouldn't you, John?

JOHN. Yes I would but I don't know that I better today. I have an appointment that could in time lead to a very important executive position and I feel therefore, under the circumstances . . .

MR. WRIGHT. Who are you seeing?

JOHN. A gentleman that has connections out at the Texas Gulf Sulphur Company.

MR. WRIGHT. They're all Northerners, you know. The whole bunch of them are Northerners. They bring in their own kind. They'll never hire you, unless as a laborer. Every executive out there is from up north someplace. And that just burns me up. The whole thing is run from Wall Street. They're stealing us blind. Taking all our resources and sending the money right back up to New York City and Wall Street. You're wasting your time, son, with those Yankee thieves. You come on out to the cemetery with us and look at Mary Martha's tombstone and then I'll send you over to see some friends of mine with connections in the oil business. And between me and my friends we'll find you a good job, so don't worry about a thing.

JOHN. Yes sir. Thank you.

MAE. Is Mrs. Wright here with you? I remember so well meeting her too at Sullins.

MR. WRIGHT. No, Mama didn't come with me on this trip. To tell you the truth she doesn't like to come here at all anymore. Too many memories of Mary Martha, she says. Mary Martha was born and raised on our farm at the edge of town. She lived there with us for sixteen happy years until she went off to Sullins. To tell you the truth, I don't go out there much anymore myself. When I come back here to do the little business I have to do around here I just stay out at the Magnolia Hotel and I eat my meals in town. Like I told Mama, I don't enjoy rattling around in that big old house of ours out in the country. And it is big. Fourteen rooms. We had the house Mary Martha was born and raised in taken down and this new one put up in its place the year Mary Martha first went off to Sullins. We didn't tell her a word about it. Thought we'd surprise her with it when she came home from college that summer. Well, it surprised her all right, she just broke out crying when she saw it and said she didn't like it at all, and she wanted her old house back. Well, Mama and I were heartsick, let me tell you, that she didn't like it. Anyway, she got sick that summer and the new house was the house she died in. I thought for a while of trying to build back the old house as a kind of memorial to Mary Martha, but I couldn't for the life of me remember how it looked exactly and neither could Mama, so we gave up on that. I'm going to call Mama tonight and tell her I met a sweet friend of Mary Martha's and she'll be so happy about that.

(*He starts out. They follow as the lights fade. The lights are brought up. It is later the same day.* MAE *is there. There is a knock on the door.*)

MRS. ESTILL. (*Offstage.*) Oh, Mae, you're back.

MAE. Cats and dogs—it's raining cats and dogs.

(MRS. ESTILL *enters.*)

MRS. ESTILL. John called and he said to tell you he would be later than he thought as he had to see about a job.

MAE. I hope he gets it. I do so hope he does.

MRS. ESTILL. Is this a job with Luther?

MAE. No. A friend of his in the oil business.

MRS. ESTILL. He has friends all right. The rich all do. Did you have a nice time with him?

MAE. Just lovely. First we drove out to the cemetery to see Mary Martha's tombstone and in spite of what you had told me, I wasn't prepared for it, and neither was John, I am sure. Why, it is huge! On the top, you remember, is this marble bust of Mary Martha, and Mr. Luther kept saying, "Isn't it just like her?" and I said yes, but to tell you the truth, I didn't think it was like her at all, because Mary Martha was sweet, but she wasn't pretty, not a bit, and this lady on the top of that tombstone is ravishingly beautiful. And you remember on every side of that tombstone they have marble benches and that's a good thing because you can sit while you read all they have written on the tombstone; they practically have the whole Bible up there plus the words to "The Prisoner's Song," which he said was Mary Martha's favorite song. He said she sang it all the summer she was dying. He asked me if I sang and I said I did and then he asked me if I knew "The Prisoner's Song," and I said I did. He asked if I would sing it for him and I did and then he began to cry and it was the saddest thing in this world. And we would have been there yet, I guess, but I stepped by mistake into a bed of red ants and got stung, and so he took us back to his car, talking about Mary Martha the whole time. John finally got the subject around to his introducing him to some friends about a job and he wrote out the name of a man and told John he was very rich and very important and would surely help him. So we let John off in town and he said he wanted to drive me out to the country to the house that he built for Mary Martha and that she didn't like. And so we went out there and it is big. They have a nigra couple taking care of it, and we went inside and it's furnished like a palace, and he took me into the room where Mary Martha died. He explained that everything was just as it was when she left and that as long as he lived nothing in that room would ever be touched, and then he cried and cried and he said he missed his daughter so, and that he was lonely and he did appreciate my taking so much time with him and that while he was here on business would I go for a ride with him every afternoon and I said I would love to. Then he asked if he could take me and John out to dinner tonight. And I said why, I thought that would be lovely, but I would have to ask John.

MRS. ESTILL. Can I ask you for a favor?

MAE. Of course.

MRS. ESTILL. Would you sing "The Prisoner's Song" for me? I think I'd like to learn to sing it.

MAE. Oh, sure. (*The phone rings.* MRS. ESTILL *goes to answer it.* MAE *looks at herself in the mirror, singing.*)

"If I had the wings of an angel
Over the prison walls I would fly
And I'd fly to the arms of
my poor darling . . ."

(JOHN *comes in.*)

MAE. Oh, I've had the loveliest time.

JOHN. Well, I haven't. Thank you very much. I have had a rotten time.

MAE. What happened?

JOHN. I have been humiliated and insulted and I am in a fury. That old jackass taking us out to that cemetery in the hot sun, while we had to hear him read every damn verse on that tombstone and making you sing "The Prisoner's Song" in the middle of a cemetery, getting stung by vicious red ants and the old bag of wind talking about all the rich friends he had who would help me.

MAE. I thought your phone message was you had gone to see about a job?

JOHN. Oh, yes. I went to see about a job all right. I went to see this fellow he sent me to, I had to wait for an hour while he talked on the phone about God knows what, and then he asked what he could do for me. I explained that Mr. Wright had sent me to see him about a job and he said, "What kind of a job?" and I said working for an oil company was I believe the kind of job he had in mind for me. I was about to say in an executive capacity, but before I could get those words out, he said, "You go here," and he wrote something on a piece of paper and handed it to me. He said, "Tell him Jack Davis sent you," and I thanked him. I went outside and looked at the paper and it said, "Cary Heath, Magnolia Filling Station," and that made me suspicious but I decided to go over anyway. So I went over to see Mr. Cary Heath and he asked me what I wanted and I said I was sent there by Jack Davis, and he said, "What for?" and I said, "About a job," and he said he had no job for me. The only job he had at present was for a nigra or a Mexican since it paid so little he couldn't really offer it to a white man, and I said, "What does it pay?" and he said, "Eight dollars a week." He said even if I wanted it he wouldn't give it to me, because I would only stay until I could find something better and a nigra or a Mexican wouldn't be able to find anything better so they would have to stay.

MAE. Honey, I'm sure Mr. Wright . . .

JOHN. Mr. Wright. He's a bag of wind. He's self-centered like all the rich. All he wants to do is talk about that Mary Martha. Well, I don't want to see him again. I don't want to hear about Mary Martha and his trouble and his rich, influential oil friends. And I don't know what the hell I'm going to do. I might as well level with you. We're almost broke. We have fifteen dollars left. I am so desperate I almost begged that filling station man to give me the eight-dollar-a-week job. But I didn't and I wouldn't. Not if I have to take you back to Flatonia and ask my dad to take us in again. (*She is crying.*) Now don't cry, Mae. That doesn't help.

MAE. I know that. But I'm so disappointed. I was hoping everything was going to turn out so well. Mr. Wright seems so nice, and sincere and interested. . . . I'm sure there has been a mistake of some kind. A terrible mistake.

(*There is a knock on the door.* MAE *goes.* LUTHER WRIGHT *is there.*)

MAE. Oh, Mr. Wright. I didn't expect you so soon. John just got here and I haven't had a chance to ask him about our having supper together.

MR. WRIGHT. That's not why I've come. I've come to apologize to John. To personally apologize. I was going to call Mama and tell her what a lovely time I had with you all today and before I put in the call I thought I'd call Jack Davis and find out how your interview went and Jack Davis said he had gotten his wires mixed up and sent you over to the Magnolia Filling Station, but the opening was for a nigra or a Mexican, but he said he would keep you in mind for the future. (*Offers drink.*)

MAE. No, he doesn't drink anymore!

JOHN. Mr. Wright . . . I'm not interested in being a filling station attendant. I am interested in the oil business, and in the exploration side. . . . I am interested in an executive position. (*He leaves.*)

MR. WRIGHT. That young man is upset, isn't he?

MAE. Yes sir. He's had many a disappointment. He has not been able to find work in many years.

MR. WRIGHT. I know. Your daddy told me all about it. He says you've pawned a fortune in jewels to keep you going. Are they all gone?

MAE. Yes sir.

MR. WRIGHT. Well, I've got friends. I'll find him a job.

(JOHN *comes back in.*)

JOHN. I apologize for my rudeness.

MR. WRIGHT. I was telling Mae, I'll find you a job. I have influence here, you know. Friends . . . Many connections.

JOHN. I need a job now. If you can speak to your friend Jack Davis, I will take that eight-dollar-a-week job.

MR. WRIGHT. That's been taken. A nigra applied right after you left and they gave it to him. A nice, humble one, Jack said. I know him, Calvin Croom, raised around here. Has eight children. Don't you worry. Me or my friends will find you a job and it won't be for no eight dollars a week either. Fifteen or twenty to start or I won't let you take it. I told this little lady's daddy I would help and I will.

JOHN. Thank you. How soon do you think that will be?

MR. WRIGHT. What?

JOHN. You or your friends will find me a job. How soon?

MR. WRIGHT. You never can tell about things like that. It might be tomorrow. It might be next week or next month. The important thing is the right job.

JOHN. Oh yes, certainly. The right job.

MR. WRIGHT. It could be in oil, or in the mercantile business or working at the gin or the bank.

JOHN. A week, or a month . . .

MAE. Or a day. You said it could be a day, didn't you, Mr. Wright?

MR. WRIGHT. It could be, you never know. I have wonderful

friends here. All fine, upstanding Christian men, who have influence. You met one today . . . Jack Davis. He's in oil. God
knows how many wells he's got. Almost more than me. When he
signed his first lease he couldn't write his own name. Had to sign
that first lease with an X. But he learned to write soon enough.
Then there is Frank Douglas, he is president of the bank, who is
a fine, educated man, and owns a little of everything around
here. Garrett Watson owns cotton gins, oil wells; Ludie Taylor,
who doesn't own anything, but knows everybody that does. I'm
getting hungry. Are you folks hungry?

MAE. John, Mr. Wright asked us to have supper with him. I said
I would have to ask you first.

JOHN. Thank you. I would like to go.

MR. WRIGHT. Before we go could I ask you to do me one favor,
young lady? Would you sing "The Prisoner's Song" for me one
more time?

MAE. Yes sir.

MR. WRIGHT. (*To* JOHN.) That was my daughter Mary Martha's
favorite song. She sang it all that summer before she died.

JOHN. Yes sir. I remember your saying that.

MR. WRIGHT. And when she wasn't singing it, she was playing it
on the Victrola. She had nine or ten records of it. She said her
dream was to have a record of John McCormack singing it. She
wrote him a letter asking if he would consider singing it, but he
never answered her to my knowledge. Let's call Mrs. Estill to
come in here so she can hear you sing.

MAE. All right. (*She goes to the door; she calls:*) Mrs. Estill. Mr.
Wright would like you to join us, please.

MR. WRIGHT. When I call Mama and tell her about how beautifully you sing this song that Mary Martha loved so much I bet
she is going to want to take the next train down here to hear you
herself.

(MRS. ESTILL *comes into the room.*)

MRS. ESTILL. Did you get your job, John?

JOHN. No.

MR. WRIGHT. We're going to find him one though. One of these days. A good job too. Now sit down here beside me, Bonny. I want you to hear Mae sing "The Prisoner's Song." That was Mary Martha's favorite.

MRS. ESTILL. That's what Mae was telling me.

JOHN. Mr. Wright . . .

MR. WRIGHT. Yes sir?

JOHN. What were the names of those men again?

MR. WRIGHT. What men?

JOHN. The ones you are going to speak to about a job for me.

MR. WRIGHT. Oh, yes. All fine, upstanding men. Salt of the earth. Bonny knows them all. Jack Davis, he's in oil. God knows how many wells he's got. Do you have any idea how many wells he has, Bonny?

MRS. ESTILL. No. And I doubt if he does either.

MR. WRIGHT. Frank Douglas, Garrett Watson and Ludie Taylor.

MRS. ESTILL. I think they all have oil interests of some kind. If they don't own wells outright they own shares. Don't they, Luther?

MR. WRIGHT. Oh, yes. All fine men. Good friends of mine. Do anything for me. Just like I would for them. Now sing us that song, young lady.

(MAE *stands up. She sings.*)

MAE. (*Singing.*)

"Oh, I wish I had someone to love me,
Someone to call me my own . . ."

(MR. WRIGHT *and* MRS. ESTILL *listen appreciatively, but* JOHN, *only half listening, is thinking of his real chances of finding a job as the lights fade.*)

The One-Armed Man

In one way *The One-Armed Man* is a typical Horton Foote play; like his other work, it has a rigorous sense of historic time and place. Here the action is even predicated on two historical moments. The first is local and contemporary. As C. W. Rowe notes, the unifying presence of cotton is being replaced by the divisive fever for oil. The other historical force will come from outside Texas the following year. That, of course, is the Great Depression. So here again Foote uses an exact and, as much as his art will allow, authentic time frame. This drama of the work-place is located in a cotton gin in Harrison, Texas, in the summer of 1928.

But these are about the only ways *The One-Armed Man* is typical of Foote's work. This play is fascinating because it is so unusual in style and theme. It is one of the writer's shortest and most elliptical plays, and yet it also changes tone as do few other Foote pieces. At the beginning a simple, nearly quaint, natu-ralistic play, *The One-Armed Man* ends as almost pure psychologi-cal and symbolic theater. Most different from Foote's other work, though, is the intense drama of the play. For minutes which seem like hours, McHenry holds a gun on C. W. at the front of the stage; the audience is forced to confront a murder that is acted out before their eyes. For a playwright known as a master of understatement, this is a remarkably cruel play.

The One-Armed Man shows that in Horton Foote's most recent plays the social issues are less hidden in the fabric of the stories. Here feelings of impotence and rage, based on injustice, become a driving force, a motive, in the play. And at one point the depersonalization of the machine age is offered as an explanation of McHenry's violence. Previously sublimated anger over the loss of a more communal and pastoral life is visible and active in *The One-Armed Man.*

But, like Foote's earlier work, this play should not be read as a political allegory. As the imminent murder of Pinkey dramatizes, McHenry's revenge is too indiscriminate to be considered a moral force in the play. In *The One-Armed Man* Horton Foote makes the political issues a symptom of a more pervasive malady: the loss of fellow feeling that accompanies the breakdown of community. C. W. Rowe isn't so much an evil boss as an unwitting agent of this social decay. Like John in *The Prisoner's Song* and Phil in *The Land of the Astronauts*, C. W. lives with enthusiasm and resilience, but also with a tragically flawed vision. His businessman's ethic of growth, abundance and thrift hides a destructive paternalism; he substitutes a simplistic, Horatio Alger view of life for genuine empathy. McHenry and C. W. are not just employer and employee, owner and victim; they are carriers of the same disease.

In the end, *The One-Armed Man* is more religious, even visionary, than it is political. It is rather like a Protestant version of "A Good Man Is Hard to Find." Like Flannery O'Connor, but in his own voice and style, Horton Foote has imagined a time when command has replaced compassion, when force and control have replaced love. But Foote's world is even darker than Flannery O'Connor's. Here there is no epiphany, no desperate bargaining and no radical spiritual dimension that can call these characters home. The cornerstone of Horton Foote's faith has always been the strength of empathy and compassion. When that kind of personal and social power disappears, as it does in *The One-Armed*

Man, only beasts will be born in Bethlehem—and prayer will be impossible.

The One-Armed Man was first presented in July 1985 by the HB Playwrights Foundation in New York City, as one of three plays collectively called *Harrison, Texas.* The production was directed by Herbert Berghof.

The One-Armed Man

CAST

C. W. Rowe   Pinkey Anderson   Ned McHenry

Place: Harrison, Texas
Time: Summer, 1928

An office in a cotton gin. The manager of the cotton gin, c. w.
rowe, *in his early fifties, is behind his desk. There are various
photographs around the room of* c. w. *with staff heads and digni-
taries, and a stalk of cotton is tacked on the wall. He is working
at his desk and is surrounded by letters and papers. There is a
knock on the door.* c. w. *(calling):* "Come in." pinkey anderson *enters.* c. w. *continues with his work.* pinkey *stands by the
door.*

c. w. Pinkey, look out the window and see how many cotton
wagons are in the gin yard.

(pinkey *looks out the window.*)

pinkey. Seven.

c. w. How many bales have they ginned so far today?

pinkey. Fifteen.

c. w. They might as well leave it to rot in the field the prices
they're paying. If it were my cotton I would store it until the price
goes up again. Tell anyone that asks you that my advice is to
store the cotton for a year if necessary.

pinkey. What if they don't have a place to store it?

c. w. Tell them to rent space.

pinkey. Do you think cotton will ever hit forty cents a pound
again like it did in 1912?

C. W. Might. This country is on a curve of prosperity. Anything might happen. The way they are discovering oil in this county, someday you might look out in the gin yard and see oil wells. I had a dream the other night . . . (*A noise is heard in the outer office.*) Is that somebody out there?

PINKEY. Yes. That's what I came in to tell you.

C. W. Who is it? (PINKEY *pantomimes a man with one arm.*) Oh, my God. Get rid of him.

PINKEY. I can't get rid of him.

C. W. Yes, you can. Use your wits. Tell him I'm very busy.

PINKEY. I told him that.

C. W. Then distract him some way. This is the height of the cotton season.

PINKEY. I can't fool him anymore. Oh, see him and get it over with. He's harmless.

C. W. He may be harmless, but how would you like it if a man came in here every other week asking you to give him his arm back?

PINKEY. He soon leaves after that. All you have to do is to say you haven't got it, and he leaves.

C. W. Well, I don't want to do that anymore. Tell him I said to go away.

(PINKEY *leaves.* C. W. *goes back to his work.* PINKEY *comes back in.*)

PINKEY. He insists on seeing you. He says he won't leave until he does.

C. W. Oh, my God, I swear I think he's crazy. (*A pause.*) Tell him I know what he wants. Tell him I haven't got his damn arm and tell him if he doesn't stop worrying and driving me crazy I am going to call the sheriff and have him arrested.

PINKEY. Yes sir. (*He starts away.*)

C. W. Wait a minute. Forget about saying that. He always leaves after I offer him five dollars. (*He takes a bill out of his pocket.*) Here, give this to him, but tell him if I hear of his getting drunk like he did on the last five dollars I gave him, it will be the last he ever gets from me. (PINKEY *starts out.*) And Pinkey . . . (PINKEY *pauses.*) Tell him he doesn't have to come back here anymore asking about his arm. Tell him I'll send five dollars every week up to Christmas as long as I hear he stays sober. (*He starts away.*) Oh, by the way. Jeff Lyons was here this morning when you were uptown for coffee—and incidentally, you were gone over an hour. I know because Jeffrey waited at least an hour here for you, and an hour is too long to be away.

PINKEY. Yes sir. (*He starts away.*)

C. W. Hold your horses, Pinkey. He left you a bill. (*He gets the bill and hands it to* PINKEY. PINKEY *puts it in his pocket.*) He calls you "dearie." Why does he call you that?

PINKEY. That's what my wife calls me. Jeffrey Lyons is a member of my Boy Scout troop, and when they heard my wife calling me that, they started calling me that too.

C. W. Well, I think that's a lot of foolishness. Ask him not to call you that anymore when he comes around here. It doesn't sound dignified. (*He starts out.*) Pinkey.

PINKEY. Yes sir.

C. W. He told me the bill was three months old.

PINKEY. Yes sir.

C. W. How much is it for?

PINKEY. Eight dollars.

C. W. Eight dollars?

PINKEY. Yes sir.

C. W. My God, you haven't been able to pay back eight dollars in three months? (*A pause.*) How many bills do you have?

PINKEY. Quite a bit.

C. W. What do you mean quite a bit?

PINKEY. Three hundred dollars.

C. W. Three hundred dollars. That's a fortune now for someone in your position. How in the name of God did you ever get that much in debt? I pay you a decent salary here, I think. I mean, I know you can't get rich on it, but you should be able certainly to live comfortably with a wife and only one child on forty dollars a week. At Christmastime you get a turkey and a fifteen-dollar bonus. How much is your house rent?

PINKEY. Twenty-five dollars a month.

C. W. Cut out the cigarettes. That would save you quite a bit. How many packages a day do you smoke?

PINKEY. Two.

C. W. Two too many. All right, two packages of cigarettes a day, twenty-five dollars a month for rent. Where does the rest go?

PINKEY. There's food and clothes. A man has to eat, you know.

C. W. Do you have your own garden?

PINKEY. No sir.

C. W. That's another extravagance. Grocery stores rob you blind. I grow my own food, at least I hire a nigra to do it. I pay him two dollars a week and he can take home any of the vegetables we can't use. Do you belong to any fraternal organizations?

PINKEY. No sir.

C. W. I know you're not a member of the Lions Club.

PINKEY. No sir.

C. W. Or the Chamber of Commerce.

PINKEY. No sir.

C. W. I belong to them all, and I contribute personally to my church. I drive a car, and my wife drives a car, and I still save money every month.

PINKEY. Yes sir.

C. W. I am only able to take five hundred dollars a month out of the business, you know. Of course you know that. You keep the books.

PINKEY. That's three hundred more than I do.

C. W. Yes, but I'm an executive. I run the oil mill and the cotton gin. You're only a bookkeeper. I have to be a leader in this town. I pay dues every month to the Lions, the Chamber of Commerce, I'm the third most generous giver to the Baptist church. I own my own home which I paid three thousand dollars for in cash. I go day and night. I am past president of the Chamber of Commerce, past president of the Lions Club, and its present tail twister. I teach the men's Bible class at the Baptist church, I am deacon of the church, a member of the choir, helped to start a building and loan association and am an officer in the White Man's Union.

PINKEY. Yes sir, I know, sir.

C. W. And you are three hundred dollars in debt. Not me.

PINKEY. Yes sir.

C. W. I owe not a penny in this world.

PINKEY. Yes sir.

(*There is another noise outside.*)

PINKEY. I better get out to him. (PINKEY *goes.* C. W. *goes back to work at his desk.* PINKEY *comes back in.*)

C. W. And I'd like to say further, there is no excuse for a man to be in debt in this great little town of ours. Nature endowed us with abundance. We have cotton land that is as fertile as anything in the Valley of the Nile. We have rice fields, oil, sulphur. I have a vision for this beloved town and county of ours, and you need a vision in life, Pinkey.

PINKEY. Yes sir. I'm sure, but the McHenry boy . . .

c. w. What about him?

PINKEY. He said he won't leave until he sees you.

c. w. Did you give him the five dollars?

PINKEY. Yes sir. He said he didn't want it. He wants to see you.

c. w. My God. I guess I'll have to see him to get rid of him. Well, I might as well get it over with. Send him in here.

PINKEY. Yes sir. (*He starts out.*)

c. w. First give me back the five dollars.

PINKEY. Yes sir.

(*He gives him the money, then goes.* MCHENRY, *21, comes in. His left arm has been severed at the elbow, and only a stump is left.*)

c. w. Hello, son. (*No answer.*) How are you today? (*Still no answer.*) Well, you certainly seem to have recovered nicely from your accident. Home again? (*Still no response.*) I don't smoke cigarettes. You can get one though from Pinkey if you'd like a cigarette. He smokes two packs a day. I've been lecturing him about it. He can't afford two packs a day. He owes everybody in town. Of course, he has an extravagant wife, and he's spineless, no backbone. He just lets her spend like she was the wife of a millionaire, which she certainly ain't. (*A pause.*) Well now, I was telling my wife Billie Joe the other night, I said the thing I hated most of all about . . . what is your first name again, son? I always get you McHenry boys mixed up. (*A pause.*) Now let's see. Don't tell me. I believe you're Ned. Isn't that right? Ned? I said, "Billie Joe, what I hate the most about Ned's accident is that I had to let him go from his job at the cotton gin." I don't sleep nights worrying about letting you go, son. But like I said to Billie Joe, there is just no way in the world we can use a one-arm man on a cotton gin. All that machinery is dangerous enough for a man with two arms. Why, shoot, you ought to certainly know about that. (*A pause.*) Well, I guess Pinkey told you this is a busy time of the year for me; it will get busier and busier all through September, as we have a bumper cotton crop, so I would appreciate it so much if you would take this five dollars now and excuse me, and I asked Pinkey to tell you that you needn't come back here anymore as every week I am going to . . . (MCHENRY *takes out a gun.* C. W. *sees it, but tries to ignore it.*) I'll send five dollars over to your house every week from now to Christmas, but I do hope you will not use it for whiskey, but for nourishing food. (MCHENRY *lifts up the gun.*) Of course, if you want to use it for whiskey it would sadden me, but that is your entire business. (*He gets up. He's even more cheerful now.*) So, now, son, if you'll excuse me and let me get on to my work, I will give you the five dollars for this week in advance.

MCHENRY. I don't want your damn five dollars.

C. W. You don't?

MCHENRY. No, keep your goddamned five dollars. Give me my arm back.

C. W. Now, son. Talk like a sane man. Take the two five-dollar bills.

MCHENRY. I said keep your goddamned bills. Give me back my arm.

C. W. How in the world am I going to do that?

MCHENRY. You figure that out.

C. W. How can I figure that out?

MCHENRY. That's your problem. Tell your damn machinery to figure it out. It took it. Chewed it up.

C. W. Was that my fault? I have had nigras working here for years that can't even read or write and none of them ever lost so much as a hair of their heads. When I was in Russia showing the Bolsheviks how to run a cotton gin . . . Did I ever tell you about the time I went to Russia, son? I spent a year there. (*He goes to the wall and takes down a picture.*) Here I am with the Bolsheviks teaching them about cotton gins. (MCHENRY *doesn't even glance at the picture.* C. W. *is becoming extremely nervous. He puts the picture on the desk.*) I got a Russian hat still someplace around here. (*He opens desk drawer looking for it.*) If I can find it, I'll make a present of it to you.

McHENRY. I don't want no damn Russian hat.

C. W. Give you a Russian hat and ten dollars and five dollars every week until Christmas.

(McHENRY *moves down with the gun.*)

McHENRY. Give me back my arm.

C. W. Son, be reasonable. I can't do that. You know I can't do that, son.

McHENRY. Don't call me son.

C. W. Say, I meant no offense, Ned.

McHENRY. Don't call me Ned.

C. W. What can I call you then?

McHENRY. Knub.

C. W. Why in the world would I want to call you that?

McHENRY. Call me Knub.

C. W. Why in the name of God?

McHENRY. Because that's what they call me now in the pool hall.

C. W. Well, then stay out of the pool hall.

McHENRY. I work in the pool hall. That's the only work I can get as a one-armed man.

C. W. Well, that surely upsets me. I hate to hear of you going into a pool hall, much less working there. Now sit down and let's talk this over like reasonable men. Let me call Pinkey and have him go to the corner for Coca-Colas. (*He starts for the door. McHENRY stops him with the gun.*)

MCHENRY. I don't want any goddamned Coca-Colas. I want my arm back.

C. W. My God, son. Talk sense. I'd sure give you back your arm if I could. How in this world can I do that? Use your head. Use your . . .

(MCHENRY *raises the gun and* C. W. *backs into the room.*)

MCHENRY. The day I lost my arm I begged them not to cut it off. I said, "For God sakes don't cut off my arm. Kill me first." "It's already gone," they said. "We have to cut off what's left." "Where's my arm?" I said. "Mixed up in somebody's bale of cotton," they said.

C. W. Well, that's how it goes, son. My oldest boy had his toe froze off while he was over in France fighting the Germans, but he don't let it get him down, not Delbert. He's a fine boy. He's an example to us all. Why, Whitney Taylor lost a leg in a hunting accident, but that doesn't keep him from getting around. He rides horseback every day just like other men. Thomas Edison is deaf as a post and look at all he's done in spite of his handicap.

MCHENRY. I heard yesterday at the pool hall you said whoever got the bale of cotton with my arm chopped up didn't get much.

C. W. I didn't say that. Who said I said that?

MCHENRY. That I probably ruined the cotton and that whoever it was you will give them their next bale free.

C. W. I didn't say that. Whoever said I said that is a liar.

(MCHENRY *moves closer with the pistol.*)

C. W. (*In terror now.*) Knub.

MCHENRY. Mr. Knub.

C. W. Mr. Knub.

MCHENRY. Mr. Knub please.

C. W. Mr. Knub please.

MCHENRY. Mr. Knub please sir.

c. w. Mr. Knub please sir.

McHENRY. Mr. Knub in the name of God, please.

c. w. Mr. Knub in the name of God, please.

McHENRY. Mr. Knub in the name of God, please sir.

c. w. Mr. Knub in the name of God, please sir.

McHENRY. Please what?

c. w. Please don't kill me.

McHENRY. Mr. Knub sir.

c. w. Mr. Knub sir.

McHENRY. Mr. Knub sir, please don't kill me.

c. w. Mr. Knub sir, please don't kill me.

McHENRY. Get on your knees. (c. w. *gets on his knees.*) Pray.

c. w. Our Father . . .

McHENRY. Louder.

c. w. (*Loud.*) Now I lay me down to sleep. I pray the Lord my soul to keep.

McHENRY. Not that one. The other one.

c. w. Our Father . . .

McHENRY. Louder . . .

c. w. Pinkey . . .

McHENRY. Why do you want Pinkey?

c. w. To go for the Coca-Colas. I am very thirsty . . .

McHENRY. You don't need any Coca-Colas. Pray . . .

c. w. Our Father . . .

McHENRY. You said that.

c. w. Now I lay me down to sleep . . .

MCHENRY. I told you I didn't want to hear that one.

C. W. Our Father . . .

MCHENRY. You said that.

C. W. I can't remember the rest of it. Our Father . . . Our Father . . . (*He screams.*) Pinkey . . . (*He runs towards the door. Again* MCHENRY *stops him with the gun.*) I tell you what, I think all this has affected your mind. You are not yourself. I think we'd better get you to a doctor, and I'll pay for it. And I tell you what else—I bet I can find you some kind of a job again around here at the gin. What do they pay you at the pool hall? (*No answer.*) Whatever it is I certainly bet I can do better. If they pay you twelve a week I'll make it fifteen. I could make you night watchman. I always figured we needed two of them anyway. (*A pause.*) I remember it now. I remember the Lord's Prayer. Now I lay me down to sleep. I pray the . . . I'm sorry. I got that wrong. I got mixed up again. Our Father which art in heaven. Hallowed be thy name. . . .

MCHENRY. Give me back my arm.

C. W. Our Father which art in heaven, hallowed be thy name, thy kingdom come, thy will be done on earth as it is in heaven. . . .

(MCHENRY *shoots him. He slumps over. He is killed.* PINKEY *comes in. He looks in horror at what has happened.*)

MCHENRY. He wouldn't give me back . . . (*He sees* PINKEY. *He raises the gun.*) Pray . . .

PINKEY. Yes sir. (*A pause.*) How in the hell does it go? My God, how does it go? You killed him. Why did you kill him? (MCHENRY *moves toward him.*) I'm gonna pray. I'll think of something. Our Father . . . which art in heaven. Our Father. Hallowed be thy name. Our Father. Hallowed be thy name. Our Father . . . Our Father . . .

(*He is crying.* MCHENRY *is pointing the gun at him as the lights fade.*)

The Road to the Graveyard

Horton Foote has said that the seeds for this play go back to the early 1950s, and it is easy to find echoes here of his earlier writing. As before, the family house is changing from the site of a staid existence to a less orderly place:

> It has once been a fine, well-built, one-story house, with enormous high ceilings. The wallpaper, once of excellent quality and design, is now faded and stained. The furniture is dark and old looking, and trees seem to shade all light from the room.

Once again there are problems of class and race as the family confronts the possibility that Sonny might marry the Cajun Bertie Dee, a "common woman." And, as in many of Foote's plays of the 1950s, Lillie is a controlling mother who wants everyone to appreciate India's sacrifice and who stands ready "to put . . . out of our lives forever" those who, like Ben, leave in search of their own identity. This is a "going away" drama in the same vein as *Only the Heart*, *The Old Beginning* and *The Midnight Caller*.

From these elements Foote has fashioned one of his darker plays. Outside the Hall household Stanley Campbell appears as another desperate, confused climber of pecan trees. Inside the home Lillie's pursuit of imaginary rabbits is a funny and terrible reminder of the emotional isolation that is the subject of *The Roads to Home*. As in the trilogy, so in this play the psychological disorientation is a symptom of a wider social disruption. Here Lyda and India are victims of the changing roles of women. Not prepared for the world of work, they are trapped in their homes as caretakers for their aging parents. Brought up only to care for others, Lyda worries about whom she will cook for when her mama and papa are dead.

The Road to the Graveyard, like many of Foote's plays, is about the family in transition. Two of the Hall children, Ben and Roberta, have joined the exodus to larger cities like San Antonio, Waco and El Paso. They have severed their ties to the homeplace in order to search for "fine" clothes, cars and houses. The place they have abandoned is no Eden either. Beneath the eccentric, comic surface of the remaining family lies a debilitating neurasthenia. Headaches, upset stomachs, high blood pressure, muscle twitches and skin rashes are epidemic among the Halls and their neighbors. Caught between their inherited dreams of wealth and leisure (in the old plantation society) and the bitter present reality of hard work and poverty, the Halls and Darsts long for any semblance of "normal life." Once the regenerative cycle of the family order is broken, the center will not hold.

Most unsettling is the paralysis that lies behind the compulsiveness and hysteria of the action. Those who should be going away are compelled to repeat stifling rituals of pseudo-order; those who have gone away show no signs of returning. The family, which ideally nurtures the mythic needs to leave and come home, cages the inhibited children and banishes the adventurous ones. Sonny, the product of this loss of healthy roles and direction, is left to suffer "sick headaches" and to half promise, half threaten that he will bring his friend over to meet the family. Unlike Foote's typical plays of the 1950s, no reconciliations or decisive actions are made. In *The Road to the Graveyard*

Sonny cannot find the emotional flexibility or the courage to act against the rising tide of inwardness.

The Road to the Graveyard was first presented by the Ensemble Studio Theatre in New York City in May 1985. The production was directed by Curt Dempster.

The Road to the Graveyard

CAST

India Hall   Tom Hall
Lyda Darst   Lillie Hall
Sonny Hall

Place: Harrison, Texas
Time: 1939

The action takes place in the dining room–sitting room of the HALL *home. It has once been a fine, well-built, one-story house, with enormous high ceilings. The wallpaper, once of excellent quality and design, is now faded and stained. The furniture is dark and old looking, and trees seem to shade all light from the room.*

A small, bird-like woman is seated, sewing. It is INDIA HALL, *the oldest daughter. She is small and pitifully thin, with a long, sharp nose and abundant hair piled up on her head. She is nearing fifty, but her face has no quality of age, or anything except thinness. Her eyes are bright and she walks with an exaggerated hurriedness.*

A WOMAN *calls from the front door:*

WOMAN. (*Calling.*) India. India.

(INDIA *jumps up from her chair when she is called.*)   ·

INDIA. (*Calling back.*) Ye-e-es?

LYDA. It's Lyd.

INDIA. Come on in. I'm back in the dining room.

(LYDA DARST *comes in the door. She is also thin, but taller. She has a red, frantic face, and her hair is bobbed. It looks uncombed, as if she had been running in a full wind. She screams when she talks.*)

LYDA. I just had to come over here to get some rest. The whole family's over there and they're fighting. They're fighting just terribly.

(INDIA *giggles as a young girl might when hearing a gossipy story of intrigue.* LYDA *sits nervously in a rocking chair.*)

LYDA. It's one of the worst fights I've ever witnessed. And the Lord knows I've witnessed some fights in my time. I fought with them for two hours and I had to leave. I can't fight like I used to.

INDIA. (*Giggling.*) My goodness.

LYDA. Mama is red in the face and got to choking and I had to nearly put my arm out of joint knocking her on the back. The others were too busy fighting even to notice she was about to fall out. We take her to the doctor to get her high blood pressure down and they come over and fight and raise it up again.

INDIA. My gracious, what are they fighting about?

LYDA. (*Screaming.*) You know. Anything. I don't know what they're fighting about. They just love to fight. I don't know. They never know.

INDIA. (*Giggling.*) I declare. Is Alberta there?

LYDA. I tell you they're all there. All of them. Alberta and Sharon started it. Sharon demanded to know what was in that book Alberta's husband is writing.

INDIA. What book?

LYDA. Didn't you know he quit his business to write a long, historical novel? Sharon thinks it's about our family. Alberta said she wouldn't know, as she'd never read a book and didn't intend to read one now, but that if it were about our family, it wouldn't be complimentary about some of them. Sharon said she took that as a personal insult and wanted to know what was in the book. Alberta said to ask her husband. That was two hours ago. When I left they were fighting over whether I worked the Mescan help too hard.

INDIA. (*Giggling.*) Well, don't shout, honey. We're not fighting over here.

LYDA. I'm so nervous. I wish they'd all go home. Alberta's been visiting two days and I feel a hundred years old already. She can't sleep at night, and she wakes me up at three in the morning to go riding with her. Ever since she heard of Stanley Campbell gettin' drunk and climbin' the pecan trees in the courthouse square at four in the morning she's afraid she'll miss something. I ask her what does she do in Port Arthur when she can't sleep. She says ride. Well, I told her I wish she'd go back there and ride. If she doesn't go soon I'm gonna be dead for sleep. I tell you it's not fair. I have to nurse Papa and Mama. They don't. They just drop in when the spirit moves them and cause confusion, and make more work for me. Then when they leave, Mama and Papa are so wound up and excited they always have sinking spells. (*She has worked herself up to a pitch of excitement. She is nearly screaming now.*) How is your mama?

INDIA. Pretty well.

LYDA. How's Mr. Hall?

INDIA. Pretty well. His leg is gettin' worse. I know what's wrong with that though. I told him at supper last night. I said, "Papa, if you don't stop worrying over that war news I'm gonna throw the radio out of the house."

LYDA. How's Sonny?

INDIA. Fine.

LYDA. Romance still going on?

INDIA. I suppose so.

LYDA. Well, he'll never marry a common woman. I was sittin' in the drugstore havin' a Coke and he came in with her. He didn't see me sittin' there until they had ordered their drinks. He looked so embarrassed when he saw me. He just blushed all over. (*A pause.*)

INDIA. Lyd, I'm worried. I'm very worried. If he marries I don't know what we'll do.

LYDA. Sonny will never marry a common woman. Mark my words he'll never marry a common woman. We've been through this before and he's never done it and he never will. (*A pause.*) Sonny will never marry a common woman. (*A pause.*) Where is Miss Lillie?

INDIA. She's napping. I tried to take a nap but I couldn't sleep. We were preserving this morning and it wore me out. When I get too tired I can't get my rest.

LYDA. What were you preserving?

INDIA. Figs.

(MR. HALL *comes in the door. He is a lean, erect man in his seventies.*)

MR. HALL. Hello there, Miss Lyda. How are you?

LYDA. Hello, Mr. Tom. I'm pretty good.

MR. HALL. How's your papa?

LYDA. Papa's not well, Mr. Tom. At least he wasn't well this morning. I guess by tonight he'll be terrible. The children are all over there again fighting. I guess Mama's blood pressure will go up to a hundred and ninety.

MR. HALL. (*His leg twitching violently.*) A hundred and ninety?

INDIA. She's exaggerating, Papa. Don't get nervous. (*He starts toward the radio.*) Where are you going?

MR. HALL. (*Pretending not to hear.*) Where's Mama?

INDIA. Napping. You sit there and leave her alone. (MR. HALL *continues toward the radio.*) Don't turn that thing on, Papa. I won't have you getting upset about the war. What can you do about it? Nothing.

MR. HALL. I want to hear the five o'clock news, Sister.

INDIA. No sir.

MR. HALL. I tell you it's a terrible thing, Miss Lyd.

LYDA. What, Mr. Hall?

MR. HALL. This war.

LYDA. I had to stop reading about it. It got me too nervous. I couldn't get the news on the radio if I wanted to. Mama has serials on all the time.

MR. HALL. Sister . . .

INDIA. I'm not going to let you turn the radio on, Papa, so stop asking me.

MR. HALL. Please, Sister. Just this once.

INDIA. No sir. (*A pause.*) Where's Sonny? Didn't he drive you home?

MR. HALL. No ma'm.

INDIA. Why? He knows I don't want you walkin' too much.

MR. HALL. He wasn't ready to come home, so I came on.

INDIA. Do you mean to tell me he let you walk all that way from town?

MR. HALL. Now listen here, young lady. You can stop me from listening to the radio, but you can't stop me from walking from town when I want to.

INDIA. Oh yes I can.

MR. HALL. Well, you can't.

INDIA. I can. I have to nurse you when you get sick. Please, have some consideration for me. I have the house to take care of; four people to do all the cooking for; Mama . . .

LYDA. Where's your cook?

INDIA. Gone.

LYDA. Where's she gone to?

INDIA. I don't know. She just hasn't come to work in two days. I'm real sorry. Mama was used to her and had gotten fond of her. Mama loved to have her comb her hair.

MR. HALL. Nobody's gonna stop me from walkin' from town.

INDIA. Be quiet, Papa. (*A pause.*) What time did Sonny say he'd be here for supper?

MR. HALL. He said not to wait supper on him.

LYDA. Sonny will never in this world marry a common girl.

INDIA. Is tonight lodge night?

MR. HALL. I don't know.

INDIA. American Legion?

MR. HALL. I don't remember.

INDIA. Has he got a date with Bertie Dee Landry?

MR. HALL. My heavens, Sister, the boy's grown. I don't know, I'm sure.

INDIA. Well, I know you both do your best to keep it from me when he does. If you want to see him throw his life away on a Cajun . . .

MR. HALL. She's no more Cajun than I am.

INDIA. Her name is Lesant and she comes from Louisiana. If that doesn't make her a Cajun then I don't know what does.

LYDA. Sonny will never in this world marry a common woman. (*A pause.*) I wish I could get a job. (*She is screaming again.*) I'd let them come here and nurse two old people and see how they like it. I'd let my sisters see how they'd like scrubbing and standing over a hot stove all day like I have to do. I would. I'd walk right off that place. I'd leave them nursing Papa and Mama.

(INDIA *giggles. She twists a strand of her hair back and forth.*)

MR. HALL. Miss Lyd, you know you'd never have a moment's

peace unless you were seein' to them yourself. I remarked to your papa the other day, he couldn't buy, with all the money in the world, the attention that you give to the two of them. He agreed.

LYDA. What I want to know is what was wrong with you all?

MR. HALL. Who are you referring to, Miss Lyd?

LYDA. You and Mama and Papa and Miss Lillie. Whatever was in your minds? (*She is screaming now.*) Why didn't you drive us out of the house and make us learn something to support ourselves by?

INDIA. Let me tell you, working would be a pleasure after all I have to do every day.

LYDA. Who's gonna take care of me when they're gone? Nobody. Who's gonna take care of India and myself after all our years of service to our families? Sonny may take care of her, but I'd rather starve than depend on my sisters. I'll get no more thanks from them for nursing Mama and Papa than the Mexicans. Do you appreciate that, Mr. Hall?

INDIA. I wouldn't mind anything if our house wasn't smack on the road to the graveyard. Papa, I wish you'd speak to Mr. Burtner. Looks like sometimes he could use another route for his old hearse. Harrison's gettin' so big there are almost two funerals every day.

MR. HALL. Yes'm. (*He shakes his leg. From another room* MRS. HALL [MISS LILLIE] *screams.*)

LILLIE. (*Screaming.*) Sister. You sister.

INDIA. There's Mama. Excuse me. I'll have to help her dress.

LYDA. I told India we sat and rocked on the front porch and didn't learn anything to make a living and life passed us by. It just passed us by.

MR. HALL. Well, in yours and Sister's day young ladies weren't supposed to work.

INDIA. Some girls did. Some girls learned to teach or to type.

MR. HALL. Nice girls, Miss Lyda?

LYDA. Yes sir. Nice girls. Very nice girls. Pride's fine if you can afford it, but like I told Mama and Papa, why in heaven's name didn't they teach me, they couldn't afford it.

MR. HALL. You're a mighty good cook. I think that's an accomplishment.

LYDA. (*Shouting.*) Who'll I cook for? That's what I'd like to know. Who'll I cook for when Mama and Papa are dead? (MR. HALL *sneaks over to the radio.*) Who'll I cook for? I broke out in a rash worrying about that the other night. Who'll I cook for, Mr. Hall? Who'll I cook for? Answer that one if you can. That's like being a schoolteacher with no school.

(*She is rocking her chair back and forth, violently.* MR. HALL *has turned the radio on very low. He is straining to listen.* INDIA *comes in with her mother,* MISS LILLIE.)

INDIA. Lillie dear, there's Lyd.

LILLIE. Good afternoon, sweet Lyd. You're lookin' mighty pretty and fresh today. Gonna sit on the front porch and flirt with the young men?

LYDA. (*Snorting.*) Miss Lillie!

LILLIE. I know you young girls.

LYDA. Young? Honey, I've turned into a witch and a scarecrow.

LILLIE. I've often told Sister, of all the Darsts I thought you had the most style and were the prettiest.

LYDA. I don't feel pretty, Miss Lillie. I feel like my head is about to burst open. I think I've caught Mama's high blood pressure.

LILLIE. And how is Lady Mother?

LYDA. If she lives through today, Miss Lillie, nothing can kill her. I'll vow to that. They're all over there fighting.

LILLIE. (*Laughing. Her laughter is soft and girlish.*) I'll say. Fighting doesn't mean a thing to your family. (*A pause.*) Sister, where's Sonny?

INDIA. Papa walked from town.

LILLIE. Answer my question. Where is Sonny?

INDIA. I don't know, Mama. Ask Papa.

LILLIE. It's near suppertime. He should be home. When will you children learn that your strength will go if you neglect eating good nourishing meals?

INDIA. Papa?

MR. HALL. What?

INDIA. I hear you have the radio on. Turn it off.

MR. HALL. Now, Sister.

INDIA. Turn off that radio, Papa. You'll have another spell.

LILLIE. Who all's comin' to the party?

LYDA. (*Screaming.*) What party? My God, I'm not dressed for any party!

LILLIE. The tea party. You silly thing.

INDIA. (*Giggling.*) Lillie dear, there's gonna be no party. It's almost suppertime.

LILLIE. Sister, someday I'm gonna surprise you and invite everybody in town to a party. I'm gonna fill the house with people and you won't be ready for them. You should always be ready for company in the afternoon. When I was running this house we were always ready for company in the afternoon. Cokes and cakes and coffee. Cheese straws and watermelon pickle.

INDIA. People had more time in those days. Anyway, no one comes to see us, so what's the sense of slaving in a hot kitchen?

LILLIE. Sister ought to go out more, Lyd. I nag Sister all the time about going out of the house more. She's got no appetite and she has no color. That's from staying shut up in the house all the time.

INDIA. All right, Lillie dear.

LYDA. It's the truth. They appreciate you more when you go and do. We ought to take the day off and go to Houston.

LILLIE. I wish she would take a trip. She always enjoys it so when she goes. She went to visit some of our kinfolks in Victoria several times and she had the best time.

LYDA. Victoria? When did you go to Victoria, India?

INDIA. You remember those three summers in '16, '17 and '18.

LYDA. Oh.

LILLIE. She still talks about it, so I know she had a good time. Sister, please take a trip.

INDIA. I can't afford it, Mama.

LILLIE. She can't afford it. We'd have to be millionaires before you'd think you could afford it. The children are all educated. Sonny and Mr. Hall make nice salaries.

INDIA. Papa can't work, Mama.

LILLIE. What's wrong with him?

INDIA. He had a stroke, now you remember?

LILLIE. India's always been too conscientious. It doesn't pay to be so conscientious. While the other girls were out dancing, she was home studying.

INDIA. That's because I was a slow study. I always had to work hard for what I got.

LILLIE. Thurman was the student in our family.

INDIA. Sonny was twice as bright as Thurman. He just never had his opportunities. He was too busy earnin' the money for Thurman to do on, and be ungrateful on. (*A pause.*) If I had it to do over again I wouldn't be so worried about A's and B's. I know I was a goose to sit home and study while other girls had a good time.

LILLIE. (*Suddenly reaching into the air.*) Ooh! Look at that pretty little rabbit. (*She pulls out of the air an imaginary rabbit. She holds it in her lap stroking it.*) See my bunny rabbit. (*She reaches again.*) Ooh, the air's just full of them!

INDIA. (*Giggles.*) Mama.

LILLIE. Where's Mr. Hall?

INDIA. Sittin' right over here. Papa, speak to Mama so she'll know you're here.

MR. HALL. Hello, Miss Lillie.

LILLIE. Hello, Mr. Hall. How was town today?

MR. HALL. Just fine, Lillie.

LILLIE. I declare. What would men do if they couldn't go to town every day? What in heaven's name do they find to talk about all the time, standing on those street corners?

(*The phone rings.* INDIA *goes to answer it.*)

LYDA. If that's for me, say I'm not here.

(INDIA *goes and comes back.*)

INDIA. That was Alberta. She said she saw you slip over here and she wants you to come back. They are all starving to death and what about supper?

LYDA. What about supper? The idea. The nerve. They can fix their own supper. (*She gets out of her chair.*) I'm eating at the drugstore tonight.

INDIA. You can eat with us.

LYDA. No ma'm. I'm too nervous. I'm gonna have to ride to calm my nerves down.

INDIA. You'd be welcome. We have plenty.

LILLIE. Sister, why don't you go for a spin and cool yourself off?

INDIA. No ma'm. I have to get supper.

LILLIE. She never gets out of the house. It makes me feel so bad Sister never gets any pleasure.

(LYDA *starts out of the room, screaming as she goes.*)

LYDA. If anybody calls say I'm goin' for a long ride. They better cook for themselves. If they wait for me to come home and cook they'll surely starve. (*She is out the door.*)

LILLIE. Well, it's not serious. . . .

INDIA. Shh, Lillie dear, she might hear you. (*A pause.*) Papa.

MR. HALL. Dammit, India, I've got the radio off.

INDIA. I'm not worryin' about the radio. Where's Sonny? (*He sulks and doesn't answer.*) You heard me. Where's Sonny?

MR. HALL. Sister, I told you, I don't know. He's a grown man. If I would ask him where he was off to, he very likely would tell me none of my business.

INDIA. Did he tell Mr. Reavis he wasn't buying stock in his picture show?

MR. HALL. I don't know.

INDIA. Today was the day for him to decide yes or no, wasn't it? (MR. HALL *doesn't answer.*) Yes or no, wasn't it?

MR. HALL. I believe so, Sister.

INDIA. When is he gonna tell Mr. Reavis he's goin' to start his own picture show? (MISS LILLIE *has fallen asleep and is snoring very gently.*) Mama. Lillie dear. No napping. I'm gonna feed you soon. (*She gently shakes her.*) Lillie dear. If you sleep now, you won't sleep tonight. (MR. HALL *tries to slip out of the room.*) Papa. I see you. Now you come back here and answer me about Sonny. He tells you everything. Did he see Mr. Reavis and tell him he wasn't goin' to buy into that picture show? (MISS LILLIE *snores again.*) Woo hoo. Lillie dear. Woo hoo . . . (LILLIE *wakes up suddenly. She grabs into the air.*)

LILLIE. Ooh. Catch that rabbit.

(INDIA *grabs the air.*)

INDIA. Here. I've caught him, Lillie dear. (*She hands the imaginary rabbit to her mother.*)

INDIA. Papa, did Sonny . . . ? (*He shrugs his shoulders, flaps his leg, pretending he doesn't know the answer.*) Don't pretend you don't know, Papa. I know perfectly well you do. You may not know whether he went out with Bertie Dee Landry or not, but you surely know if he told Mr. Reavis he was starting his own picture show.

MR. HALL. I don't know, Sister. I didn't ask him.

INDIA. Well, all right, Mr. Close Mouth. I know how I can find out. I'll just call Mr. Reavis and ask him.

MR. HALL. Now looky here, Sister, your brother would be furious if you did anything like that. This is strictly business. (*A pause.*) Personally, I'm against his takin' the risk of his own business.

INDIA. You're afraid of the risk. Of course you are. You've no gumption. That's why you never bought land for fifty cents an acre you could sell now for twenty-five dollars. Well, I'm gonna make Sonny have some backbone. He is gonna do it. My Lord, to listen to you all that poor boy should slave at that picture show the rest of his life for Mr. Reavis. And for what? For nothing?

MR. HALL. He don't work for nothing. He's getting two hundred and twenty-five dollars every month.

INDIA. And if I hadn't nagged and nagged for five years he'd still be gettin' two hundred.

MR. HALL. Well, he's now willin' to give him a percentage of the profits.

INDIA. A percentage of the profits? After eighteen years, a percentage of the profits?

MR. HALL. He's done a lot on that money. That money helped send Thurman through school.

INDIA. That and Mama and I working our fingers to the bone trying to cut down here. You helped too. You were working then.

MR. HALL. He bought all of Roberta's trousseau. . . .

INDIA. What Mama and I didn't sew.

MR. HALL. I know you worked hard, Sister. We all worked hard. You can have a cook in the kitchen right now, though. Sonny said you should have . . . (*His leg flaps pathetically.*)

LILLIE. Sister, my rabbit got away.

(INDIA, *half distractedly, grabs the air.*)

INDIA. Here, Mama.

LILLIE. What's that?

INDIA. Your rabbit.

LILLIE. That's not my rabbit. It's under the china closet. I can see the little devil from here.

INDIA. Shh, Mama.

LILLIE. Sister, get me my rabbit.

INDIA. I don't know where it is, Mama.

LILLIE. I told you. Under the china closet.

INDIA. All right, Mama. (*She stoops and grabs under the china closet.*)

LILLIE. And don't be cross. (*She brings the imaginary rabbit to her mother.* MISS LILLIE *accepts it and sits silently stroking it. A pause.*)

MR. HALL. We've always gotten along somehow. I don't say Sonny didn't tell Mr. Reavis he was going to start his own picture show. I only say it's his business, Sister. I don't think you should nag him so much about it.

INDIA. I have to nag him, Papa. I have to nag him.

LILLIE. Now look here, Sister, don't sass your papa. I'll send you to your room if you do.

INDIA. Shh, Mama.

LILLIE. And don't shh me.

MR. HALL. It's all right, Lillie. She meant no offense.

LILLIE. I can't help it if she didn't. I've never allowed the children not to have respect for their elders. Nobody has been sweeter and kinder to them than their parents. But I'll always demand respect. Children don't appreciate it if you let them run all over you. That was the trouble with Ben. Sonny always had respect for our wishes and Ben didn't. You see where that led to. He married that girl and we had to put him out of our lives forever.

(INDIA *is crying. A pause.*)

MR. HALL. Don't cry, Sister. If you cry Lillie gets upset.

INDIA. I know, Papa, what you all think of me. I know you all think I'm an old interfering nag.

MR. HALL. I said nothing of the kind.

(LILLIE *has gone back to sleep.*)

INDIA. But somebody, Papa, has to consider the future. You can't work anymore.

MR. HALL. I could if you'd let me.

INDIA. And fall out again in the heat and be in bed for two months for me to nurse? I don't want you to work, Papa. You should take it easy. We have to think of the future. Sonny has to take a chance.

MR. HALL. It's not fair to Sonny. He ought to have some kind of life for himself. I hate to be a burden this way.

INDIA. Who's gonna take responsibility here if Sonny doesn't? The one we scrimped and saved for to get to college? Oh, no. He hasn't written us for six months. Roberta? Her husband can hardly support her and two children.

MR. HALL. Ben's doing well. He wants to help. He writes to Sonny and begs to help.

INDIA. Well, he won't help. Mama wouldn't have it.

MR. HALL. Sister.

INDIA. While I live I won't have it. Out of respect to Mama I'll never have us take anything from Ben.

MR. HALL. Sister. Sister, please, don't be so hard . . .

INDIA. We all vowed to Mama we'd never let him help us. I feel sorry for Sonny. I know why he doesn't want to take his money and start a picture show. I know where he is right now, Papa. You aren't foolin' me one minute. It's that woman. He didn't speak to Mr. Reavis and he probably has a date with that woman. I know. I know. I know every time he goes out with her.

MR. HALL. Don't be hard on him, Sister. He's a grown man. . . .

INDIA. I know, Papa, I feel sorry for him. I only wish it was someone I could feel was our equal. . . .

MR. HALL. She's a clean-livin' woman. She's good and steady. . . .

INDIA. She's tried to trap him.

MR. HALL. Sister.

INDIA. I know she's tried to trap him. Well, she may get him. Then God help us. That's all. God help us. What will he do? Bring her here?

(LILLIE, *waking up.*)

LILLIE. Bring who here?

INDIA. Do you think I could stay here if that happened? Or Mama? Do you think Mama could live here with that woman?

MR. HALL. As far as I can tell, she's a nice girl.

INDIA. Girl? Woman. She's three years older than I am and I'm a year older than Sonny. I know what she does. Yes sir. Rain or shine she goes to the picture show twice a day. Nobody likes the picture show that much.

MR. HALL. She works mighty hard, all I can see. I don't see how she has all that time to go to picture shows like they say. She clerks eight hours a day.

INDIA. She's wrapped you around her finger with one of her smiles.

LILLIE. The whole town is trembling for fear Sonny will marry beneath himself.

MR. HALL. Now don't worry, Lillie.

LILLIE. I do worry. I want him here where we can watch him. Everybody is terrified he will marry beneath himself.

INDIA. Shh, Mama. Here's a rabbit to love.

LILLIE. I don't want a rabbit. I want Sonny. Mr. Hall, I want the children home on time for their meals. I told you and told you. Don't we have Ben for an example before us day and night? I tell you it's terrible. The way they tell me these women run after the men these days. When I was a girl we didn't even show our ankles, and now they show off everything and wear perfume besides.

(SONNY *comes in the door. He is a man in his late forties. He is small and gentle. He looks worried and concerned.*)

INDIA. Hello, Sonny. Mama was wondering where you were. I'll get supper right on.

LILLIE. I expect all my children on time for their meals.

MR. HALL. Hello, Son.

(INDIA *goes toward the kitchen.*)

LILLIE. Come sit by me, Son, and catch rabbits for me. The room is full of them.

INDIA. I'll have supper in a hurry.

SONNY. I won't stay for supper, Sister.

INDIA. Did you see Mr. Reavis?

SONNY. Yes. Didn't Papa tell you?

INDIA. Papa doesn't tell me anything.

SONNY. I decided to take him up on his proposition.

INDIA. Oh.

SONNY. I'm buying a sixth interest in the Gem.

INDIA. Oh.

SONNY. It seemed wise. As he said, if we start a war against each other, the chains will move in.

INDIA. What chains?

SONNY. The moving picture chains.

INDIA. Oh.

SONNY. It seemed the wisest thing to do. I just don't see how with all my responsibilities I could take a chance on starting my own picture show.

(*A pause.* INDIA *gets up excitedly.*)

INDIA. It just burns me up. That's all. Eighteen years. Eighteen years you have kept that damn place going. A sixth interest.

SONNY. Well, he has problems that we know nothing about. He tries to be fair. I know he tries to be.

INDIA. Eighteen years. Rain and shine. Ten hours a day.

SONNY. Sister . . .

INDIA. You and Papa are just alike. You've no gumption. You let people push you around and take advantage of you. That is what you do. If it weren't for my nagging you'd never have taken the operator's course, you'd probably be takin' up tickets. . . . (*A pause.*) Well, it's your life. But anyone with as much as you have to offer . . .

SONNY. I know, Sister. (*A pause.*) Sister, Papa . . . Lillie dear . . .

(MR. HALL's *leg shakes violently.*)

MR. HALL. Yes, Sonny?

SONNY. I don't know whether you all know it or not, but I've been goin' with a pretty girl, I mean a girl pretty steadily. . . . I'd like you all to meet her. . . .

LILLIE. No woman's comin' into my house. No woman that wears perfume and goes to the picture show twice a day to catch a young man. I like women with modesty. I didn't court Mr. Hall; Mr. Hall courted me.

SONNY. Mama.

MR. HALL. No, Lillie. (*A pause.*)

INDIA. When do you want to bring her over, Sonny?

SONNY. Tonight.

INDIA. Tonight?

LILLIE. She won't get in my house. When she comes in out I go.

INDIA. Shh, Mama.

SONNY. I've been putting it off. I think it's time now to bring her over. We're having supper together, and after supper I thought I might bring her by. Sister, I don't know whether Papa has told you yet . . .

INDIA. Papa never tells me anything.

(MR. HALL's *leg twitches.*)

SONNY. I'm thinking about getting married.

(INDIA *breaks out crying.*)

MR. HALL. Now, Sister.

INDIA. I'm sorry. I'm sorry.

LILLIE. What's Sister crying about?

MR. HALL. Shh, Lillie dear. Sister's just gotten nervous.

LILLIE. Did she take her quinine?

INDIA. It isn't that I don't want Sonny to marry. I do. I want him to have a happy normal life. But what's to become of us?

SONNY. I thought after we were married we might take the front room. (*A pause.*)

INDIA. What's to become of me, Sonny?

SONNY. You will stay here with us.

MR. HALL. This is a big house. We've had more than that living here.

SONNY. Bertie Dee will keep right on working. . . .

INDIA. And am I to cook? Am I to always do the cookin' and the cleaning? Not that I mind. I'll stand by Mama and Papa while I have a breath of life left in me, but I'd like it understood . . .

SONNY. I want you to have a woman here to help you.

(LILLIE *is crying.*)

INDIA. Shh, Mama.

LILLIE. Something's happening you all aren't telling me.

INDIA. Lillie dear, you hear every word we say.

LILLIE. But I don't understand. I don't understand too well anymore. . . .

INDIA. Explain to her, Sonny. . . .

SONNY. Lillie dear, you know I'm a grown man.

LILLIE. I've told everybody. Sonny is as devoted to me as if . . . well, as if . . . he was another India.

INDIA. Mama, Sonny is trying to explain something.

LILLIE. I've been blessed with two children out of five that have done for us and given to us. . . .

SONNY. Listen to me, Lillie dear. . . .

LILLIE. And soon I'll be dead, and Mr. Hall will be dead, and I can rest in peace knowing that you will always take care of Sister.

INDIA. I'll be all right, Mama. Don't worry about me. (*She is crying again.*)

LILLIE. Sister deserves to be taken care of. She has done without and scrimped and saved and given to the family and denied herself. The others had opportunities and went off for themselves, but Sister you might say has kept us all going, and Sonny you mustn't ever forget it.

SONNY. Mama . . . I . . .

LILLIE. If you forget it, I couldn't rest in my grave.

MR. HALL. Lillie, the boy is trying to tell you . . .

LILLIE. I know what he's trying to tell me. Ask him if he remembers who didn't go out of this house except for a Coke. Saved her nickels and dimes to help him go off for a course to learn how to operate a motion picture machine. Who did, Sonny?

SONNY. I know, India did, Mama.

LILLIE. And the rest have forgotten, but don't you forget. She had ambitions for you all, and took what your papa made and squeezed it until all of you had some way to take care of yourselves; all except India. She never had any young men come calling, because she never had time. She was too busy doing for us all. Now they've all forgotten it. All except you, Sonny boy.

SONNY. Mama . . .

LILLIE. Let's just forget about it now and eat our supper.

INDIA. I can't eat. I just can't eat a thing. (*She is sobbing and has to leave the room.*)

MR. HALL. Lillie dear, you've gotten India all upset.

LILLIE. India is a jewel and a treasure and they've all forgotten. Even you, Mr. Hall.

MR. HALL. Now, Mama . . .

LILLIE. Even you.

(MR. HALL's *eyes fill up with tears. His leg shakes. He hides his face so his tears can't be seen. There is a pause.* SONNY *has his face covered with his hands.*)

LILLIE. Now I want you to go to her, Sonny. Go to your sister and tell her not to cry.

SONNY. Mama . . .

LILLIE. Go to her. Go to her and tell her never to fear. You won't desert her.

SONNY. Mama.

LILLIE. Go on, Sonny. Go on. Don't disappoint your mother. . . . (A pause.)

(MR. HALL's leg twitches quietly. A Mexican orchestra can be heard, in the distance, playing a waltz. The screen door slams. LYDA enters.)

LYDA. Oh, hello, Mr. Tom. Where's India?

MR. HALL. Lyin' down, Miss Lyd. Won't you come in?

LYDA. I couldn't eat. I tried three drugstores. Every time I sat down they'd call me on the phone.

MR. HALL. Yes'm.

LYDA. My sisters livin' in their fine homes in San Antonio and Waco and El Paso. My sisters with their cars and their children and their fine clothes. . . . You'd think they could cook a meal.

LILLIE. Mr. Hall, when was the last time we heard from Roberta?

MR. HALL. Last week.

LILLIE. And Thurman?

MR. HALL. Six months ago.

LILLIE. Where is Thurman's letter? I've forgotten what he said.

MR. HALL. You know what he said. He said he was fine and doin' well with his job.

LILLIE. Where is the letter?

MR. HALL. I thought you had read it, Miss Lillie. I tore it up.

LILLIE. I have all the letters he wrote from college.

MR. HALL. Yes'm.

(LILLIE nods her head and closes her eyes.)

LYDA. Did you have your supper?

MR. HALL. No, India got a sick headache and had to lie down.

LYDA. I know what they are. I get them at least once a week.

MR. HALL. I'm not so hungry. We'll just have to wait until she feels better.

LYDA. Yes sir. I think I'll go sit on the porch and get out of your way.

MR. HALL. You're never in our way, Lyda. You're just like one of our own family.

LYDA. Thank you, Mr. Tom. Tell India I'm on the porch if she wants to come talk after supper.

MR. HALL. Yes'm.

(*She goes out of the room. The screen door can be heard slamming.* MR. HALL *goes to the radio and sneaks it on, softly.* LILLIE *is gently snoring.* SONNY *comes in. He looks depressed and forlorn.*)

SONNY. She's all right.

MR. HALL. Sister?

SONNY. Yes sir. She says she's all right.

MR. HALL. Fine, Son.

(SONNY *starts out of the room. He pauses.*)

SONNY. Papa . . .

MR. HALL. It'll be all right, Sonny.

(SONNY *turns and goes out. The screen door is heard to slam.* INDIA *comes in. She has changed her dress and smoothed her hair and powdered her face.*)

MR. HALL. I thought it better if I let her sleep, India. I'll stay up with her tonight if she can't sleep.

INDIA. Yes sir.

MR. HALL. I just have the radio on listening to some organ music. I thought you wouldn't mind my listening to a concert.

INDIA. Yes sir. (*A pause.*) Sonny has gone to have supper with his friend.

MR. HALL. India, I'm so sorry . . . I . . .

INDIA. That's all right, Papa. I want Sonny to marry and have a normal life. Could you fix supper for you and Mama? I don't feel so hungry. I hate to play off but the sight of food would kill me right now.

MR. HALL. Certainly. Miss Lyd's out on the gallery.

INDIA. Take Mama out in the kitchen if you will, Papa, I don't want this room to get all messed up. Sonny is bringing his friend by to see us later this evening.

MR. HALL. Miss Bertie Dee?

INDIA. Yes sir.

MR. HALL. All right. Lillie dear will want to put on a fresh dress to meet her. I'll dress up a little bit too.

INDIA. Don't you know her?

MR. HALL. Yes'm, but I mean to welcome her into the house.

INDIA. Yes sir.

MR. HALL. Miss Lyd's out on the gallery.

INDIA. Yes sir.

MR. HALL. Why don't you go out there and rest? (*He gently shakes* LILLIE.) Lillie dear. Wake up.

LILLIE. Where's Sonny?

MR. HALL. He'll be back directly. Let's go out to the kitchen for supper.

(*He helps her up and they walk out to the kitchen.* INDIA *walks around the room. The screen door is heard to slam.* INDIA *starts, fixes her hair.* LYDA *appears.* INDIA *seems relieved.*)

INDIA. Oh . . . I thought it was . . .

LYDA. India, anything wrong? Sonny passed me on the porch and he didn't speak. I could feel nothing but gloom.

INDIA. We had a scene. Mama . . . well, don't say anything to anybody but it looks serious this time.

LYDA. This is the thousandth time I've heard you say it looks serious this time.

INDIA. This time it does. (*A pause.*)

LYDA. The air was nice on the porch. I was countin' lightnin' bugs. The air was filled with lightnin' bugs. I used to love so to chase lightnin' bugs when I was young. Yes sir, we just sat and rocked and life passed us by. (*The waltz can be heard again.*) Listen to the music. Wonder where the dance is?

INDIA. Sounds like a Mexican dance to me.

LYDA. I declare. Want to go 'round and see? They have them behind the jail, I hear. Old Phillipe gives them. He's up to everything, that Mexican, hot tamales, watermelons and dances. When I get his age I'm just goin' to give up. (*A pause.*) This is one of my ridin' nights. I can tell the way my nerves are jumping. I bet I ride tonight until four or five in the morning. Would you like to ride with me? (*A pause.*) I know what you're thinkin' about. I refuse to get excited. Sonny has too much breeding. He's not goin' to marry a common girl. I told you a long time ago he picked that type to go with so he'd never have to marry.

INDIA. He's never invited them to the house though.

LYDA. (*She gets excited and her voice rises.*) Bertie Dee Landry. Sonny will never marry her. Sonny will never marry a common woman. No. Well, he better hurry up and do something with her, or the town's goin' to have a blind woman on its hands, as many times as she goes to the picture show to get an excuse to talk to him. (*A pause.*) Well, we can sleep in peace nights.

We've stood by our parents. (*A pause.*) Your house is always so cool.

INDIA. I know. Sometimes I wish we could get a little more sun.

LYDA. Your front room gets sun.

INDIA. Yes, my bedroom gets sun all morning. Our house needs paint so badly.

LYDA. Not as much as ours. Well, that's the price of being poor. I said to Papa the other day, I said, "What was wrong with you and Mr. Tom? When you came here as young men you could buy land, all the land you wanted for a dollar an acre." . . .

INDIA. Fifty cents.

LYDA. Fifty cents. Did they buy land? No. Now you can't talk about it for less than five hundred.

INDIA. Papa was never a businessman. He never thought it would be worth anything.

LYDA. Papa had it, Lord knows. But he couldn't hold on to it. Well, we've got our houses. That's something.

INDIA. Yes. (*A pause.*)

LYDA. You can smell the Cape jessamine out in the graveyard.

INDIA. They smell nice.

LYDA. Cemetery has grown so much.

INDIA. I swear I think Mama would get well if we didn't live on the road to the graveyard. All those funerals upset her.

LYDA. Did I tell you I went to Nina's funeral last weekend?

INDIA. No.

LYDA. She had a real big funeral. All the old-timers were there. People I hadn't seen in years. The Pridgeons were there. Remember the Pridgeons? They came all the way from Corpus. They've gotten so prosperous. You can just tell by lookin' at them.

INDIA. It looked like a big funeral. (*A car stops.*) Did you hear a car stop?

LYDA. Yes.

INDIA. Look out and see if it's Sonny and that woman.

LYDA. Now this is your house. Let her know it from the start.

(INDIA *cries.*)

INDIA. I have to excuse myself. I can't go through with it.

LYDA. Come back here and sit down. I'm ashamed of you. Are you gonna let any Cajun woman make you run in your own house?

INDIA. She's so bold. I hate her because she's so bold. (SONNY *comes in. He is alone. There is a pause.*) Hello, Sonny. Forget something?

SONNY. No. (*He turns to go out of the room.*)

INDIA. Where's your friend? (SONNY *doesn't answer. He starts in the house.*) Where's your friend, Sonny?

SONNY. I'll have to bring her over another time. I have a headache. My stomach got upset because of my headache.

INDIA. Couldn't you eat any supper?

SONNY. No.

INDIA. I've told you until I'm tired that if you wore your glasses all the time you wouldn't have any headaches. (SONNY *goes inside without answering.*) He never listens to a thing I say.

LYDA. Didn't I tell you not to get excited? Sonny will never marry a common woman. Mama was remarking that same thing this morning.

(MR. *and* MRS. HALL *come out.*)

MR. HALL. Who slammed the screen door?

LYDA. Sonny.

MR. HALL. Did he bring his friend?

INDIA. No.

(MR. HALL *goes inside.*)

LILLIE. Sonny's such a good boy.

(*The town hall clock strikes nine.*)

LILLIE. Nine o'clock on the dot. He's such a good boy. He knows I like all the children in the house by nine. He's never given me a moment's worry in my life.

(MR. HALL *comes back in.*)

MR. HALL. Sonny's stomach is upset.

INDIA. He said he had a sick headache.

MR. HALL. I could hear him throwin' up.

(INDIA *gets up.*)

INDIA. I wonder if I could do anything.

MR. HALL. I'd leave him alone, Sister.

INDIA. Yes sir. Poor thing. He won't wear his glasses. I've told him and told him about wearing them. Eyestrain gives you headaches. (*A pause.*) Did you ask him about his lady friend?

MR. HALL. Yes I did, but he wouldn't answer.

INDIA. He wouldn't answer me either.

(*A pause. They all rock.*)

LYDA. Sonny will never marry a common girl. Never in this world.

(SONNY *comes out.*)

MR. HALL. Gonna sit with us, Sonny?

SONNY. I think I will.

INDIA. How's your headache, Sonny?

SONNY. It's a little relieved.

MR. HALL. Sister thinks you should wear glasses.

SONNY. Yes sir. (*A pause.*)

LYDA. Yes sir. I bet I ride all night tonight. When I'm nervous I just have to ride all night.

(*They sit in silence. Dance music is heard.*)

INDIA. Mama, hear the dance music?

LILLIE. I hear. I could never teach Mr. Hall to dance so he really enjoyed it. . . . I was the belle of many a ball.

LYDA. That's what Mama says. She says Miss Lillie was always very popular.

LILLIE. The thing I remember about your mama was her suit of hair. I think it was the most beautiful suit of hair I've ever seen. (*A pause.*) Catch me a rabbit, Son.

(SONNY *grabs into the air.*)

SONNY. Here you are, Lillie dear.

INDIA. That's a waltz. I love to hear Mexicans play a waltz. I declare you can hear it as plain as if it were in the next room. (*A pause.*)

SONNY. I'll bring my friend over to meet you next week.

MR. HALL. All right, Son.

INDIA. Yes sir. Just as plain as if it were in the next room.

(*They all sit listening to the dance music as the lights fade.*)

The Land of the
Astronauts

The Land of the Astronauts is the most contemporary portrait of Harrison in this volume of short plays. In the spring of 1983 the small town is "fast turning into a bedroom town." It is evolving into a suburb of Houston, a place that feels akin to the Space Program and cheers for the Astros.

Even as Harrison moves uptown, this play echoes earlier ones about the old Harrison. *The Land of the Astronauts* begins, like *The Chase*, in a sheriff's office, though now it is a woman—Loula Kerr—who enforces the law. Lorena's situation, that of a woman left with her daughter while her husband wanders, is very similar to Georgette's in *The Traveling Lady*. Like Will Thornton in *The Oil Well*, Mr. Taylor holds to his dream of getting rich, here with a patent rather than an oil well. And Phil Massey's life seems very close to that of Henry Thomas in *The Traveling Lady*; Phil acts out the dislocation hidden behind Henry's lies and evasions.

But *The Land of the Astronauts* is hardly a nostalgic look at Harrisonians lost in the chaos of suburbia; it is a present-tense play about the false idols of our times. The play opens with Loula going to her television set to complain that she "can't hear a word anybody says when that's blasting away." This breakdown in communication, and the loss of intimacy it implies, breeds a deadening vicariousness in the new generation in Harrison. The local obsession with the astronauts—the celebrities and heroes of the moment—is a symptom of the formulaic, placeless 1980s. Comfortable with the alienation, the clean, neat distance between private and public experience, the new Harrisonians long for a Houston-of-the-mind, an antiseptic heaven. As Mabel Sue has explained to her teacher, Phil (and many others like him) looks yearningly to some place "far, far away" where there are no tensions or conflicts, where everyone is kind and good and true.

The problem with all this utopian imagery, according to the play, is that it denies the full reality, the depth, of human experience. Phil runs away from Harrison in hopes of avoiding the dark, messy realities of intimate living; his astronaut paradise, he says, "will be beautiful . . . not like here." Consequently, he can never develop the compassion and empathy that grow from a sense of shared humanity. He is an earnest, caring, hard-working man who tries to love his family. But he is unwilling to accept the limitations and inequities of the fallen human nature. Like far too many people, Phil wants to escape, to "go up into space and leave this earth and all its troubles and frustrations behind."

Even religious experience, which should be built on compassion and understanding, can become trivialized into the pursuit of "proper" baptism. Those who, like Buster, follow Phil's first impulses make religion into another trendy lifestyle to be put on like a new set of clothes. As he offers Phil the religion he is "trying," Buster would do well to learn the moral of Phil's story. When Phil finally declares that he is "an astronaut and . . . [he is] lost," he is confessing that, in Foote's view, the pursuit of the land of the astronauts, and the perfectionism it is built on, is ultimately destructive to the essential human need for acceptance and closeness.

Life, as Horton Foote envisions it, is never easy. It requires an amazing courage to rediscover one's past, make peace with life and face death. Without courage, deep and satisfying love is not possible. Even with courage, intimacy is hard to find and difficult to maintain. But as burdensome as life can be, the search for meaning in Foote's plays is never served by shiny new images of false peace and contentment like those represented by the Astronauts and the Astrodome.

Foote writes, by his own description, to discover and in some cases to recover a sense of order. Writing is a quest for self-knowledge, identity and meaning, here expressed by Phil's postcard inscribed "Guess who?" *The Land of the Astronauts* is a funny but troubling play about the ease with which that quest can be cheapened and distorted in the homogeneous, escapist society we are building for ourselves. In Foote's vision, the only satisfying journey is a perilous, mysterious and burdensome one. *The Land of the Astronauts* is a reminder that the religions we imagine for ourselves need to be practical, earthbound. It is a cautionary tale about the need for immanence before transcendence.

The Land of the Astronauts was first presented by the Ensemble Studio Theatre in New York City in May 1988. The production was directed by Curt Dempster.

The Land of the Astronauts

CAST

Loula Kerr
Lorena Massey
Buster Duncan
Rusty
Kathleen
Bertie Dee Taylor
Mrs. Taylor
Mr. Taylor
Son Taylor
Mabel Sue Taylor
Mr. Henry

Lila
Bernice
Young Boy
Miss Sitter
Drunk (Crosby Davis)
Woman Prisoner (*voice only*)
Carl
V. O. Conklin
Deputy Kelly
Phil Massey

Place: Harrison, Texas
Time: Late spring, 1983

The lights are brought up on the sheriff's office. The office is on the ground floor of the jail. It is well equipped for a small town and quiet at the moment. A woman in her mid-forties sits beside a desk reading a newspaper. A television is on in the corner of the room. The woman, LOULA KERR, *glances from her paper now and then to look at the television screen, watches for a second and then goes back to reading again.*

LORENA MASSEY, *32, enters. It is obvious from the way she enters the room that her contact with sheriffs and their offices has been slight.*

LOULA, *busy with her paper, does not notice her at first.* LORENA *stands for a moment looking at* LOULA, *and every now and then glancing at the television set. Then she takes another step or two into the room.*

LORENA. Excuse me.

(LOULA *still doesn't hear her.* LORENA *moves in even closer to* LOULA *and speaks louder, trying to be heard over the television.*)

LORENA. Excuse me.

(*This time she gets* LOULA's *attention and* LOULA *rises up out of her chair, puts her newspaper down and goes over to the television set and turns it off.*)

LOULA. I can't hear a word anybody says when that's blasting away. Are you looking for the sheriff?

LORENA. Yes ma'm. I am.

LOULA. I'm the sheriff.

LORENA. Yes ma'm. I know that.

LOULA. Well, you must live around here. Most strangers that come into the jail are surprised when I announce that I'm the sheriff.

LORENA. I read about it in the paper when your husband died and they appointed you the sheriff to fill out his term.

LOULA. He died sitting right in that chair, bless his sweet heart. (*She shakes her head in regret.*) I wasn't with him at the end, I'm sorry to say. I was off playing bridge when he left us. (*She sighs.*) Of course, the boys that were his deputies and now are mine don't let me hardly lift a finger, you know. I just mostly sit here and take calls. And try to look busy and hope in some way to make myself useful, and to earn the handsome salary the good people in this county are paying me. (*She opens a desk drawer.*) I have a gun in here in the desk and I can shoot it too, if I have to, but I hope I never have to. No, my deputies insist on doing all the work. They don't want me to stir from this chair. They're all fine boys—two of them were sitting right beside my husband when he had his attack. They said he was sitting here just as normal and happy, and all of a sudden over he went. "He had a smile on his face," they said. "Don't tell me that just to make me feel good." "No," they said, "he had a smile on his face as God is our witness." "Well, that's the way I want to go," I said, "with a smile on my face."

LORENA. Sheriff—lady—I—I—

(BUSTER DUNCAN, *a deputy, 30, enters before she can finish her sentence.*)

LOULA. Hello, Buster, did you get it settled?

BUSTER. I tried to. Don't know if I did or not.

LOULA. Well, if anybody can settle it, you can. Buster is our level-headed one around here. Nothing gets him upset, does it, Buster?

BUSTER. Not if I can help it.

LOULA. Have a seat, honey. Buster, pull up a chair for the lady.

(BUSTER *does so and then he sits down.*)

LOULA. What's your name?

LORENA. Lorena Massey—lady—Sheriff—my husband went to Houston and I can't find him and I am worried. Because, you see—

LOULA. Is that so? Well, we'll get to all that in a minute. First I have to get you to answer a few questions. For our records. You see we have to keep careful records.

LORENA. Yes ma'm. But you see my husband—

LOULA. We'll get to your husband in a minute, darling. But we have our priorities here and we have to stick to how things should be done. Isn't that right, Buster?

BUSTER. Yes ma'm.

LOULA. You see, I can't have anyone pointing a finger of criticism at me and saying she's not being sheriff like it should be done.

LORENA. But I'm worried, you know. You see I think—

LOULA. All right, little lady, all right. We'll get to what you think in a minute.

LORENA. Yes ma'm.

LOULA. Married or single?

LORENA. Married. You see it's my husband—

LOULA. I know. I know. But these are just questions we're duty-bound to ask. You say you have lived here for a while?

LORENA. Five years.

LOULA. There was a time, Buster, when I knew everybody, black or white. Not now.

BUSTER. That's because we are fast turning into a bedroom town. A lot of people living here work in Houston now. They take whole truckloads of workers into Houston to work every day.

LOULA. Well, if I had to travel sixty miles to work, I think I'd find me another job.

BUSTER. Work isn't all that easy to get around here and the pay is better in Houston.

LOULA. Have you seen all those fine new houses out at the lake? Most of them are rich Houston people.

LORENA. I've heard that too. A couple of years ago when my husband and I were first working for his brother at the restaurant . . .

BUSTER. Did you work in that café behind the river bridge?

LORENA. Yes sir, two and a half years.

BUSTER. I knew I seen you before.

LORENA. Yes sir, I remember you used to come into the restaurant.

BUSTER. I did and I do. I haven't seen you there for a while.

LORENA. No sir. I don't work there now. Anyway, one day a man came into the restaurant, all excited, and said, "Guess what, Phil?" That's my husband's name, Philip Carlson Massey, everybody calls him Phil though. "Guess what, one of the astronauts has bought him a big, fine house out at the lake and he'll be commuting between here and the Space Center." Well, my husband got so excited there wasn't any holding him, you see he's crazy about the astronauts, always wanted to be one in his heart. I think that's why he agreed to come and work with his brother in the restaurant, because his brother said Harrison was next door to the Space Center. Of course, when we got there we found out that wasn't exactly the truth, we were forty miles away, but this man said the astronaut didn't mind the distance at all and was coming here to live.

LOULA. Which one?

LORENA. The man never said, he just said an astronaut. Anyway, it turned out not to be true. It was some official over at NASA, but not an astronaut. But he knew the astronauts though, because he came into the restaurant to eat one day and my husband went up to him and asked him if he did, and he said yes, he knew them all and that they were just as nice as they could be and just as plain as you and me. And he drew a map for my husband to show us where different ones lived. And every Sunday afternoon my husband and I and our little girl would ride over and look for their homes. We saw Alan Shepard once too, just as plain.

LOULA. You did?

LORENA. Yes, and Phil said to our little girl, "There is Alan Shepard, he has been to the moon and back"; and she waved to him and he waved back and said "Hi!" . . .

LOULA. He said "Hi"?

LORENA. He sure did. Just as plain as I'm talking to you. And he smiled when he said it too. He's the one he always wanted to go to the moon with, my husband said. He's always wanted to be an astronaut; he said he would give twenty-five years off his life to be one. "Well, put that out of your mind," his brother said. "You can never in this world be an astronaut. You only went to the freshman year of high school." "I can go to the junior college here at night and take courses." "You would not last a day out at the junior college," his brother said. But he paid no attention at all to that and he started going to the junior college. He was out there every night it was open and he got a high school certificate in less than six months; they never had seen anybody so motivated, his teachers told him, and he was just about finishing his freshman year of college when he and his brother had a fight.

LOULA. What did they fight about?

LORENA. Well, one thing and another. His brother said he was half doing his work at the restaurant, because he stayed up all hours of the night studying and couldn't work anything but the breakfast and dinner shifts.

LOULA. What did he study?

LORENA. Oh, everything he could. English and math and science. Anyway, his brother said he would have to cut out the lessons or quit the restaurant and so he quit! Next day his brother came over to the hotel where we live and he asked him to come back; but my husband said he thought he'd been at the restaurant long enough and was going into Houston to find work—and he did.

LOULA. Why didn't you and your little girl go with him?

LORENA. We couldn't afford that—you see I have a job here at the fruit market. And I thought I'd work on here until he found a job in Houston and we could join him there.

LOULA. I see.

LORENA. And besides, my little girl is in dancing school here in Harrison. She loves tap dancing and her recital was to be in a month and we both knew she would just die if she had to leave before then. So me and the baby stayed at the hotel.

LOULA. Which one?

LORENA. The Colonial Inn. I work there an hour or two a day in exchange for their watching my little girl when she's home from school. They let her come down to the lobby and do her homework, or play with her dolls, or tap-dance until I get home. And our little girl loves being in the hotel. Everybody is so friendly

there. It is just one big, happy family, and they are always asking
her to do one of her tap dances for them. One of the ladies is
always calling her Eleanor Powell. "Who in the world is that?"
my little girl asked me. "She is a lady dancer that used to be in
the movies," I told her.

LOULA. I remember Eleanor Powell. I used to go to the movies to
see her.

LORENA. Well, I don't think I ever saw her in a movie, but I saw
her two times on TV. Somebody told me the other day she is real
religious and teaches Sunday School.

LOULA. Bless her heart! Has your husband found work in
Houston?

LORENA. No, not yet.

LOULA. How long has he been there?

LORENA. A month and four days. He was coming here to visit
the week before last, but his car broke down and he couldn't
make it; and I wrote him and told him not to worry about that,
but to be sure and get here this weekend even if he had to walk,
as Mabel Sue had her recital this Friday night, but yesterday the
letter I wrote him telling him that was returned and I called the
boardinghouse where he was staying. And someone answered
the phone that couldn't half speak English and I couldn't understand her and she couldn't understand me either. But this morning I called him again, and the landlady answered and she said he
had left there a week before and had left no forwarding address,
and didn't say where he was going. And so I called his brother
and he hadn't heard from him either. I waited another day and
then when I hadn't heard anything, I decided that I better get
over here.

LOULA. I really hope he's all right, but as we know, Houston is a
wicked city—a wicked city.

BUSTER. Does he have any relatives beside his brother?

LORENA. No sir.

BUSTER. Do you have a picture of him?

LORENA. (*She opens her purse and gets out pictures.*) This was taken when we first met, and this was taken on our wedding day, and this was kind of blurred—but it was taken by me two years ago.

BUSTER. Does he still look like that?

LORENA. Yes sir.

BUSTER. How old is he?

LORENA. Thirty-five.

BUSTER. Height?

LORENA. About five feet eleven.

BUSTER. Weight?

LORENA. About a hundred and sixty pounds. He is nice looking. At least I think he is. . . .

BUSTER. Color of his eyes?

LORENA. Hazel.

BUSTER. Hair?

LORENA. Brown, dark brown.

BUSTER. Straight or wavy?

LORENA. Wavy.

BUSTER. What kind of clothes would he be wearing?

LORENA. Well, he has a dark blue suit when he goes out looking for a job. Otherwise, he just wears, you know, blue jeans or khakis and work clothes.

BUSTER. All right. Miss Loula and I will get to work on this.

LORENA. Thank you.

BUSTER. We'll be in touch right away with the Houston police. But tell you what I think. I don't think anything bad has happened to him.

LORENA. You don't?

BUSTER. I think he has moved to another boardinghouse and just forgot to tell you. And you'll be hearing from him soon.

LORENA. I wouldn't be surprised if you are right. Anyway I certainly hope you are. He knows about our little girl's dance recital on Friday and he knows she was counting on his being there.

BUSTER. And I bet that's what will happen. He'll just ride up there and say that he moved, not thinking you would write him and the letter be returned and you'd be worried.

LORENA. Oh, no. He couldn't have thought that, because when he left he said, "Lorena, you know how I hate to write worse than poison and we can't afford phone calls, but promise me you will send a postcard every other day at least, so I will know how you and the baby are making out."

BUSTER. Oh, well, that's different then.

LOULA. He'll turn up. Don't worry. I say always try and look on the bright side.

BUSTER. I can find you at the fruit market or the hotel if I need you?

LORENA. Yes sir.

(*The lights fade as she gets up to go. The lights are brought up on a section of a small restaurant.* RUSTY, *43, the owner, is standing by the cash counter with* KATHLEEN, *30, a waitress. He is checking slips. The restaurant is empty except for the two of them.*)

RUSTY. We sold ten more specials today than yesterday.

KATHLEEN. Ten more?

RUSTY. Yes.

KATHLEEN. What's the special tomorrow?

RUSTY. Fried oysters.

KATHLEEN. Thank God I'm not the cook. I hate frying oysters. The only thing that's worse is frying chicken.

(LORENA *enters.*)

LORENA. Hello, Rusty.

RUSTY. Hello, Lorena.

KATHLEEN. Hello, Lorena.

LORENA. Hello, Kathleen. You didn't hear from Phil today, did you?

RUSTY. No, but Kathleen got a postcard from him this morning, she thinks.

LORENA. You did?

KATHLEEN. I guess it's from him. It isn't signed. It was a picture of some astronauts on something down at the Space Center and on the back he just wrote "Guess who?"

LORENA. "Guess who?"

KATHLEEN. Yes.

LORENA. That's all?

KATHLEEN. That's all.

RUSTY. Did you go to the sheriff like I told you to?

LORENA. I just came from there.

RUSTY. What did they say?

LORENA. Well, the lady sheriff . . . Loula . . .

RUSTY. Miss Loula . . .

LORENA. Yes. She seemed real concerned at first. She said Houston is a wicked city, but the deputy named Buster didn't seem at all worried. He says he just moved and forgot to tell me.

KATHLEEN. I bet he's right.

RUSTY. I think he is too. Tell Mabel Sue I'm coming to her recital on Friday.

KATHLEEN. So am I. I'm going to clap my hands off when she dances.

RUSTY. I'm closing the restaurant early so we can get there as soon as the doors are opened and get us good seats.

LORENA. Phil said he was coming too.

RUSTY. Then you know he's going to be there.

LORENA. I sure hope so. Do you have the postcard you got from Phil?

KATHLEEN. No, I left it at my boardinghouse. I'll bring it over to you later if you want to see it.

LORENA. No, that's all right. (*A pause.*) He said what again?

KATHLEEN. "Guess who?"

LORENA. Uh huh. "Guess who?" So long.

RUSTY. So long.

(LORENA *leaves.*)

KATHLEEN. Wonder where he is?

RUSTY. God knows.

KATHLEEN. Maybe he's gone to the moon.

RUSTY. Maybe so.

KATHLEEN. He'll turn up.

RUSTY. I know.

(*The lights are brought up on the reception desk in the lobby of the Colonial Inn. The lobby is small, old-fashioned but clean, with two chairs at the far end and a screen which hides a small upright piano.*

BERTIE DEE TAYLOR, *35, is at the desk. In a corner of the lobby*

MABEL SUE, *12, is tap-dancing.* SON, BERTIE DEE'*s husband, 38, is near her looking at a paper.* MR. *and* MRS. TAYLOR, SON'*s mother and father, in their late sixties, enter.*)

BERTIE DEE. Mother Taylor, I'm short seventy-five dollars in my cash drawer. You and Daddy Taylor didn't take out any money without a slip accounting for it, did you?

MRS. TAYLOR. Not me. Did you, Daddy?

MR. TAYLOR. No, Mother. I did not!

BERTIE DEE. Now you are both sure?

MRS. TAYLOR. I'm sure.

BERTIE DEE. Well, you have done it in time past.

MRS. TAYLOR. When?

BERTIE DEE. Many a time, Mother Taylor. Son is my witness.

MRS. TAYLOR. Not me.

BERTIE DEE. Well, you have so! Hasn't she, Son?

MRS. TAYLOR. Well, it's our money.

BERTIE DEE. I'm not disputing that. I know it's your money and your hotel. But we have to have a system else I can't keep these books straight.

MRS. TAYLOR. I need a hundred dollars now, please.

SON. A hundred dollars! What for, Mama?

MRS. TAYLOR. I just need it.

SON. Why, Mama? You know the hotel is not doing all that well.

MRS. TAYLOR. It's an emergency.

SON. It's always an emergency it seems to me.

MRS. TAYLOR. Rebekah's children need some dental work.

SON. Well, can't Rebekah's husband pay for it?

MRS. TAYLOR. No. She just called to say they are short this month. (SON *gives a cry of pain.*)

BERTIE DEE. Are you okay, Son?

(*He gives another cry of pain.*)

BERTIE DEE. Did your back go out again?

SON. It did. It did.

BERTIE DEE. (*Calling.*) Stop that tap-dancing now, Mabel Sue honey. (MABEL SUE *does so.*) I think I'd better try to get you upstairs, Son. Daddy Taylor, you stay here please and watch the desk.

MR. TAYLOR. I will.

MRS. TAYLOR. I'll help too. Lean on us now, Son.

SON. Oh, Mama. Watch it! Be careful!

(*The three slowly make their way out of the room.*)

MABEL SUE. Can I tap-dance now?

MR. TAYLOR. If you want to, honey. (*He goes to the cash drawer and takes out money. She goes back to tap-dancing.* BERTIE DEE *comes back in.*)

MR. TAYLOR. How is he?

BERTIE DEE. Well, we got him on the bed. Mother Taylor is staying with him. Lorena will be here before too long to relieve me and I will be able to sit with him. You can go on now if you want to.

MR. TAYLOR. I'll rest for a while. Guess who called me on the phone just before I came down, Bertie Dee?

BERTIE DEE. Who?

MR. TAYLOR. Professor Autry.

(MABEL SUE *has stopped tap-dancing and comes to listen to them.*)

BERTIE DEE. Who is that?

MR. TAYLOR. Who is that? You mean you don't know who Professor Autry is?

BERTIE DEE. I do not.

MR. TAYLOR. He was only the smartest superintendent of schools we ever had here.

BERTIE DEE. Well, he hasn't been superintendent of schools since I've been here.

MR. TAYLOR. I guess not. He lives in Louisiana now. He called me long distance.

BERTIE DEE. What for?

MR. TAYLOR. He wanted to know where he could buy another of my pecan crackers. His was lost or stolen. (A pause.) Well, I do think my luck will change one day, I do think that. And I am not going to be so trusting next time. I am going to be wary of my business associates. When I invented my pecan cracker, a very wise man and a good friend came up to me and said, "Before you show your pecan cracker to another soul, I want you to promise me that you will get a patent for it. I want you . . ."

BERTIE DEE. Daddy Taylor, I have heard all this about your pecan cracker a million times.

MR. TAYLOR. Well, I was just bringing it up to make clear to you that I would never repeat the mistake of trusting an invention of mine again in unscrupulous hands. Never! I still think if my pecan cracker had been handled properly, merchandised and advertised, why I would have made a fortune for my family. Professor Autry just said to me he couldn't understand why no more were being made. "Answer me that," I said, "and you will unravel a mystery." Professor Autry said you should go to your friends and form a new corporation and begin again the manufacturing of your pecan cracker. "But you don't understand," I said, "the patent was stolen from me." "You'll invent something yet," he said, "that will make a fortune. Your friends all have faith in you." "Thank you," I said.

(*He goes off to the dining room.* BERTIE DEE *looks at* MABEL SUE *and shakes her head in dismay.* LORENA *comes in.*)

LORENA. I'm sorry I'm late.

BERTIE DEE. That's all right. Catch your breath. What did the sheriff say?

LORENA. She said it would turn out to be some kind of misunderstanding.

BERTIE DEE. That's what I think. He'll come up here the night of the recital and be surprised you're worried at all.

LORENA. I guess so. Kathleen, the waitress at Rusty's Restaurant, got a postcard from Phil, she thinks, this morning. It was a picture of some astronauts, she said, and on it was written "Guess who?"

BERTIE DEE. Why did she think it was from him?

LORENA. I don't know. She just did.

BERTIE DEE. Did you see it?

LORENA. No. She'd left it in her room.

(MABEL SUE *comes up to her mother. They embrace.*)

MABEL SUE. Mama, play my recital piece for me so I can practice my dance.

LORENA. Oh, honey, I've got to relieve Bertie Dee now so she can have some time off. She's been here all day.

BERTIE DEE. I can wait a few more minutes. Go ahead. I'll watch you.

LORENA. Well, all right.

BERTIE DEE. The piano is still out here. We had it moved out here to make extra room in the dining room last week when we had the Lions banquet and I've never moved it back. It's behind that screen.

(LORENA *removes the screen. She goes to the piano.*)

BERTIE DEE. How did you learn to play the piano, Lorena?

LORENA. My mother taught me. I was the only child she had and she played every Sunday at our church. I don't know who taught her.

BERTIE DEE. I would have given anything in this world if I had practiced when I took lessons as a girl.

(LORENA *begins to play a dance tune.* MABEL SUE *begins her tap routine. When she finishes,* BERTIE DEE *applauds.*)

MABEL SUE. Thank you.

BERTIE DEE. Is her costume finished yet?

LORENA. No, I'll get it done tomorrow.

MABEL SUE. Mr. Son's back went out again.

LORENA. Oh, I'm sorry, Bertie Dee. What caused it?

BERTIE DEE. W-o-r-r-y! (*She goes to the desk.* LORENA *and* MABEL SUE *follow after her.* BERTIE DEE *gets her purse.*)

BERTIE DEE. "You're a fool, Son," I said. "Your family don't appreciate it. You've just been killing yourself for nothing." (*She starts out.*) I'll be back in an hour. (*She goes upstairs.* LORENA *and* MABEL SUE *go behind the desk.*)

MABEL SUE. Who don't appreciate it, Mama?

LORENA. Mr. Son's mother and father and his sisters, I think she means.

MABEL SUE. Miss Bertie Dee told me that no one in the family takes any responsibility for the least thing but Mr. Son. She says his mama and daddy are extravagant and his sisters and their husbands come here and put up and don't pay a cent. They're going to lose the hotel if they are not careful. They are going to end up in the poorhouse. (*A pause.*) Will they, Mama?

LORENA. What?

MABEL SUE. Lose the hotel and end up in the poorhouse.

LORENA. I don't think so. I hope not.

(MR. HENRY *enters. He is 45.*)

MR. HENRY. Good evening.

LORENA. Good evening, Mr. Henry.

MABEL SUE. How's the stock market today?

MR. HENRY. Pretty fair, young lady. (*He passes through.*)

LORENA. How do you know about the stock market?

MABEL SUE. That's what Miss Sitter always asks him when she sees him. He's sweet on Miss Sitter and she is sweet on him.

LORENA. How do you know that?

MABEL SUE. Miss Bertie Dee told me. She says it's worrying them all to death. Mr. Son and her mother and father don't approve of him. Miss Bertie Dee says part of her feels sorry for Miss Sitter because she's never had a beau before and has always seemed so lonely. Does she seem lonely to you, Mama?

LORENA. I guess.

(*The phone rings.* LORENA *answers it.*)

LORENA. Colonial Inn. Yes. Oh, I see. Well, in about an hour. Oh, I see. All right. Thank you.

MABEL SUE. Who was that?

LORENA. That was the lady sheriff over at the jail. They have something to tell me about Daddy.

MABEL SUE. What?

LORENA. She said she didn't want to tell me over the phone.

MABEL SUE. Why?

LORENA. I don't know why. (*She goes to the phone and dials.*) Hello, Bertie Dee. I hate to ask you this, but do you think Sitter or Mr. Taylor could come down here and watch the desk for a few minutes? They have some news about Phil over at the jail and they won't tell me over the phone. I'm gonna die if I have to wait an hour to hear what it is. No, I don't want you to come down. I want you to get your rest. Just ask Sitter or Mr. Taylor, please, and tell them I won't be any longer than I can help. Thank you. (*She hangs up the phone.* MR. HENRY *comes back through the lobby.*)

MR. HENRY. Good evening.

LORENA. Good evening.

MABEL SUE. How's the stock market, Mr. Henry?

MR. HENRY. Fine, thank you. (*He goes out.* MABEL SUE *turns on the radio, gets some music and starts to tap.*)

LORENA. Not for a while, honey, please.

(*She turns the music off. Two older women,* LILA *and* BERNICE, *hotel residents, come into the lobby and go towards the stairs.*)

LILA *and* BERNICE. Evening.

LORENA. Evening.

LILA *and* BERNICE. What is on the menu for supper this evening, do you know?

LORENA. No ma'm. We haven't eaten yet. The dining room won't be open for another fifteen minutes.

(*The two ladies go up the stairs. A* YOUNG BOY *brings in a stack of newspapers and puts them on the desk and starts back out.*)

YOUNG BOY. Hello, Mabel Sue.

MABEL SUE. Hello.

(*He goes out the door again as* SITTER, *45, tall, thin and nervous, comes into the lobby from upstairs and crosses over to the desk.* MABEL SUE *sees her before* LORENA *does.*)

MABEL SUE. Hello, Miss Sitter.

(LORENA *sees her then.*)

LORENA. Hello, Sitter. I am sorry to trouble you.

SITTER. It's no trouble. I hope everything is all right. Houston is such a big and wicked place these days. I wish Phil would come on back here where it is nice and quiet and everyone knows each other. You tell him that when you see him.

LORENA. I will.

MABEL SUE. How is Mr. Son feeling?

SITTER. He's still not too well. But he always recovers, sweetheart. It just takes time. Bertie Dee is with him now. She is a good, sweet, loyal wife. And he is blessed there certainly.

LORENA. I'll be back as soon as I can. Come on with me, Mabel Sue.

SITTER. She can stay with me if she likes. I always enjoy her company.

LORENA. Well, if you don't mind. She hasn't had her supper yet, and I would hate for her to miss it.

SITTER. I don't mind at all.

(LORENA *kisses* MABEL SUE *good-bye.*)

LORENA. I'll be back as soon as I can. (*She goes.*)

SITTER. How was school?

MABEL SUE. Fine.

SITTER. What did you learn today at school?

MABEL SUE. A lot of things. Miss Emerald Greene is our homeroom teacher and she had been down to the Space Center over the weekend, and she had a lot of pictures and she showed them to us, and I said I had been there too, a lot of times, with my mama and daddy, and once I saw Alan Shepard and I waved to him and said "Hi!" and he waved back. She said I was a very lucky girl. And she said we were all lucky that this part of the country had been chosen to train the astronauts, and that should make us all very proud that we live on the Gulf Coast.

SITTER. And we certainly should be proud.

MABEL SUE. And I told her that my daddy is always telling me stories about the land of the astronauts and it wasn't on the Gulf Coast of Texas, but it was someplace far, far away where he said we would all go someday on spaceships just like we drive around in cars today. And there would be plenty to eat there and no troubles, and everybody would be kind and happy. And she said that sounded more like heaven to her.

SITTER. Who did?

MABEL SUE. Miss Emerald Greene, our homeroom teacher.

SITTER. Oh, yes.

MABEL SUE. Would you like to go to the moon someday?

SITTER. No, honey. The very thought terrifies me. Indeed . . . the very thought.

MABEL SUE. My teacher says everybody should ask their mother and daddy to take them to the Space Center and see the sights. She said we were very lucky to be living in the land of the astro-nauts and should all take advantage of it as much as possible.

SITTER. Did she? Well . . .

MABEL SUE. My teacher said it would make her so happy if one of the boys in our class were one day chosen to be an astronaut. She said she prayed every night for that.

SITTER. Well, now . . .

MABEL SUE. I saw Mr. Henry tonight.

SITTER. Did you?

MABEL SUE. I asked him how the stock market was.

SITTER. Did you? What did he say?

MABEL SUE. Fine. Thank you.

SITTER. I hope so for his sake. He could stand a little encourage-ment, I think. He's from the North, you know. New York City. A Harvard graduate. Brilliant, he is. Reads the *New York Times* and the *Wall Street Journal* every living day of his life. Subscribes to them, you know. Mama says he just does it to put on airs and show he is better than anyone else. And she gets in a fury every time he writes to the *Houston Post* and they print one of his letters. He had a brilliant letter in there last week about taxes, you know. Oh heavens, it's always something. He's down here, you know, trying to unravel some land left to him and his sister by their father. But bless his heart it is so complicated. His sister is very unreasonable and the state is claiming unpaid taxes and boundaries are in dispute. Mama says she thinks he's making the whole thing up. She doesn't think there is any land. "Why, Mama," I said, "why would he come all the way down here and make up something like that?" "To get free room and board," she said. Free room and board? He pays his way, even though I have to admit he's late every now and then. He always finally pays.

(MR. HENRY *comes in.*)

MR. HENRY. Hello there, Miss Sitter. Have they got you working?

SITTER. For a little while until Lorena gets back. Do you want to go to have your supper now, Mabel Sue?

MABEL SUE. No ma'm. I'm not hungry yet.

(LILA *and* BERNICE *come back in.*)

LILA. Dining room open now?

SITTER. Yes ma'm. I think so.

MR. HENRY. Yes it is, ladies.

BERNICE. What's on the menu?

MR. HENRY. Mashed potatoes, mustard greens, lye hominy and pork chops.

LILA. Oh, lovely.

BERNICE. And what is for dessert?

SITTER. Peach cobbler.

LILA. Oh, lovely. Peach cobbler.

BERNICE. How is your land coming along, Mr. Henry?

MR. HENRY. Oh, it's very complicated, ladies. Sometimes I get discouraged, I must confess.

LILA. You mustn't get discouraged, Mr. Henry.

SITTER. That's what I tell him. Did you see the letter to the editor he had published in the *Houston Post?*

BERNICE. No.

SITTER. Yes. All about our taxes.

BERNICE. Mercy! Isn't he smart!

LILA. Of course he's smart. He's a Harvard graduate. You have to be smart to be a Harvard graduate.

MABEL SUE. I'm hungry, Miss Sitter.

SITTER. Well, go on and eat your supper then, darling.

BERNICE. We'll join you, darling.

(*They go out to the dining room.*)

SITTER. You better go eat your supper, Mr. Henry.

MR. HENRY. I'm not hungry now, thank you. I'll just stay here and visit with you if you don't mind.

SITTER. No, I don't mind. I don't mind at all. It's been warm today, hasn't it?

MR. HENRY. Yes, it has.

SITTER. Does it get warm in New York City?

MR. HENRY. Oh, yes.

SITTER. And cold too. I know. I don't think I'd like all that snow. (*The phone rings.*) Excuse me.

(*She goes to answer the phone as the lights fade. The lights are brought up on the jail office.* LOULA *is at her desk.* BUSTER, *handcuffed to a* DRUNK, *comes in.*)

BUSTER. Book him, Miss Loula. He tried to cut a man.

LOULA. Crosby Davis. Right?

BUSTER. Right. You have all the facts in there on him somewhere already.

LOULA. I know.

(*The* DRUNK *mumbles something that is incoherent.* BUSTER *throws a long knife on the table.*)

BUSTER. That's the knife I took off him.

(*The* DRUNK *struggles, trying to get to his knife, but he is too drunk to put up much of a struggle.*)

DRUNK. Now I tell you . . . mister . . .

BUSTER. Watch your mouth, there is a lady present.

DRUNK. I see her. She looks just like my sweet old mother. I wasn't gonna cuss in front of her. . . . I'd just as soon cuss in front of my mother as her. Please sir, give me back my knife!

BUSTER. When you are sober.

(*He takes him out of the room. A* WOMAN *is heard singing a hymn in one of the cells.* CARL, *32, a deputy, comes in.*)

CARL. Buster brought in another drunk?

LOULA. Yes.

CARL. How many drunks have we locked up tonight?

LOULA. Three.

CARL. That lady drunk going to sing all night?

LOULA. I guess so. When she's not singing, she's preaching.

CARL. What is she preaching about?

LOULA. I don't know. I can't understand her. Sounds like she's speaking in tongues.

(BUSTER *comes back in.*)

BUSTER. He went to sleep the minute he lay down on the cot in his cell.

(LORENA *comes in.*)

LOULA. Oh, howdy you do. Come on in. We didn't expect you this soon.

LORENA. I couldn't wait. I want to know what you've heard.

LOULA. Buster was the one took the message.

BUSTER. Yes'm. We got a call from the police over in Baytown. They said they got a call from somebody saying there was a man in town talking kind of strange and asking directions to the Space Center and saying he was an astronaut that had lost his way, and he was a close friend of Alan Shepard, so the police met the man that called and he pointed this fellow out, and when they tried to talk to him he put up an awful row and they had a real struggle to calm him and get him over to the jail so they could ask him a few questions. By the time they got him into the jail he was calmed down, it seems, but he wouldn't answer any of their questions. He wouldn't tell them who he was, or where he came from, or what he wanted, and so they searched him and found a wallet on him that had your name and address in it, and they asked him who you were, but he wouldn't answer that either, so they called us here to see if I knew who you might be, and I said I thought you were his wife, and I asked what the man looked like and he said he had dark, curly hair and hazel eyes and was five foot eleven and wore khakis. So I said it might be your husband and I would send for you and see what you thought. So they said when you got here, if it was your husband, maybe you could talk to him and get him to cooperate with them.

LORENA. Yes sir.

BUSTER. Do you think it's your husband?

LORENA. Yes I do.

BUSTER. Would you like to speak to him?

LORENA. All right.

(BUSTER *takes the phone. He dials.*)

BUSTER. Officer Kirby. I have the lady here now and she believes it is her husband, and she would like to try speaking to him. All right. Thank you. (*He turns to* LORENA.) He is going to bring him to the phone. (*He hands her the phone.*) The officer will have him on the phone in just a minute.

(*The* WOMAN *upstairs begins to sing again.*)

LOULA. Carl, go upstairs and ask that lady to stop singing for a little. Tell her we need a little quiet right now.

(CARL *goes.*)

LORENA. (*Into phone.*) Thank you. (*A pause.*) Hello. Hello. Phil? Can you hear me? This is Lorena. Can you hear me? How are you? Why don't you speak to me, Phil? At least say hello. (*A pause.*) I got worried about you, Phil. My last letter to you was returned last week and I called your landlady. (*A pause.*) Phil? What's wrong, honey? Why are you crying, darling? Is there something wrong, Phil? (*A pause.*) Phil? Phil? (*A pause.*) Yes sir. No sir. He wouldn't say a word. Yes sir, I feel sure it is my husband. His name is Phil. Yes sir. That's right. Phil Carlson Massey. Yes sir. That's him all right. Yes sir, that's right, he has two back teeth missing. Yes sir, I heard him crying. No sir, I've never known him to cry before. Not even when his mama died. No sir. Yes sir. I sure will some way. Tell him I'll get there as soon as I can. (*She hangs up the phone.*)

LORENA. I know he's my husband. He had two of my letters on him addressed to Philip Massey, so he's bound to be my husband. He wouldn't talk to me either. He just began to cry. The officer said I could come for him and he would let me bring him home.

BUSTER. Do you have a car to go and get him?

LORENA. No sir. I sure don't, but I'll get one some way.

(CARL *comes back in.*)

CARL. That lady preacher says she's going to take her clothes off. She says she is the Whore of Babylon.

LOULA. I'll Whore of Babylon her. Buster, you go up there and tell her to keep her clothes on. Tell her there are men up there in them other cells.

BUSTER. Carl, you do it. I'm going to take the rest of the night off and drive this lady to get her husband.

LORENA. You don't have to do that. I can find some way.

BUSTER. I want to do it.

LOULA. And I think it's a good idea myself. But go speak to that lady preacher first and tell her not to take her clothes off. You know if anybody can get her to mind, you can.

BUSTER. I'll try. (*He goes upstairs.*)

LORENA. Do you mind if I call the hotel and let my little girl know where I'm going?

LOULA. No, help yourself.

LORENA. Thank you.

(*She takes the phone and dials as the lights fade. The lights are brought up on the hotel lobby.* SITTER *and* MR. HENRY *are there.* SITTER *is reading his palm.*)

SITTER. My. Oh, my. Fascinating.

MR. HENRY. What do you see?

SITTER. I see money.

MR. HENRY. Lots of money, I hope.

SITTER. Oh, a great deal.

MR. HENRY. Fine. Splendid. Splendid.

SITTER. And I see a very long life.

MR. HENRY. And what about my land? What do you see about my land?

SITTER. Well—now—oh—yes—

(BERTIE DEE *comes into lobby.*)

BERTIE DEE. Lorena not back yet?

SITTER. No, she called and said something unexpected had come up and it would be another two hours.

MR. HENRY. Miss Sitter is telling my fortune.

BERTIE DEE. I don't believe in all that.

MR. HENRY. You don't?

BERTIE DEE. No, not a bit of it. I went to a fortune-teller three times and the exact opposite happened to what she prophesied.

SITTER. Bertie Dee only believes in practical things.

BERTIE DEE. That is right.

MR. HENRY. Miss Sitter, would you like to go for a little walk?

SITTER. Why, yes. Are you ready to take over, Bertie Dee?

BERTIE DEE. Yes.

SITTER. How is Son feeling?

BERTIE DEE. He's still very uncomfortable.

SITTER. Poor Son.

BERTIE DEE. Mr. Henry.

MR. HENRY. Yes?

BERTIE DEE. Your rent is due again.

MR. HENRY. I'm well aware of it, Miss Bertie Dee. I'll have a check for you soon. I'm expecting one any day now.

(SITTER *and* MR. HENRY *leave.* BERTIE DEE *goes to the door and watches them.* MABEL SUE *comes in.*)

MABEL SUE. Mama went to get Daddy over in Baytown.

BERTIE DEE. What's he doing in Baytown?

MABEL SUE. I don't know.

BERTIE DEE. Has old Mr. Henry been here talking to Sitter ever since she's been here?

MABEL SUE. Uh huh.

BERTIE DEE. She's such a fool.

MABEL SUE. Why?

BERTIE DEE. Because she is. But don't you ever say I said that.

MABEL SUE. I won't.

BERTIE DEE. He's just stringing her along if you ask me. She told her mama she's hoping he'll ask her to marry him. "Well, Mother Taylor," I said, "has he asked her to marry him?" "Not yet," she said, "but I don't sleep half the night for fear he will." "Well, just go on to sleep," I said, "and stop worrying. He'll never ask her. One day we're going to all wake up and he's going to be gone, leaving us with a big unpaid board bill." But don't you ever say I said that.

(*She goes to the books as the lights fade. The lights are brought up and we see* LORENA *and* BUSTER *in a car. They are on their way to get* PHIL.)

LORENA. Were you born here?

BUSTER. Yes I was. Born and raised. Except for the time I was in the army. Where were you born?

LORENA. On a farm. The other side of Conroe. Well, it had been a farm. It wasn't much of one when I was born. By that time there were rumors all around about putting the new airport on

that side of Houston and my daddy said there was no use in killing himself farming when Houston would be coming out that
way before you could turn around good and this farm would be
worth all kinds of money. So he went to the bank and borrowed
some money on the farm so we could live in style until he could
sell it for the price he thought it was worth.

BUSTER. How much did he think it was going to be worth?

LORENA. Oh, I don't know. One day he would say a hundred
thousand and the next five hundred thousand or a million. But
my mama took sick and had to have all kinds of operations and
that took all the money he borrowed and the bank wouldn't loan
him any more, and then Mama died and the bank took over the
farm and Daddy and me moved into Conroe and I met my husband. We married and had the baby and his brother wrote him to
come to Harrison and work for him. Said that it was next door to
the Space Center and my daddy argued that Conroe was just as
close, but my husband said he felt sure his brother knew what he
was talking about, and maybe he knew something that we didn't,
and so we came on to Harrison, and it turned out his brother was
wrong on all accounts, and that Conroe was every bit as close to
the Space Center, but we were here and there was nothing we
could do about that and the pay was good and so we stayed.

BUSTER. What happened to your daddy?

LORENA. Well, a year later Henry Lawes Hyde, who is kin to us
some way on my daddy's side, phoned to say he found him dead
on his farm the bank now owned. He had taken a tent out there
and was living in the tent when he died. He's buried back in
Conroe beside Mama. Phil took me and the baby there last year
to see if their graves were being taken proper care of. We went by
our old farm. They have turned it into an industrial park. There
are all kinds of buildings on it now. Daddy was right. "God
knows what the bank sold it for," Phil said. (*A pause.*) Is Baytown near the Space Center?

BUSTER. Yes, it is. We'll pass by it on our way. I wonder if we're ever going to have a man up in space again. The Russians have them up there all the time.

LORENA. When we put the man on the moon, I thought there would be noplace we couldn't go. Phil didn't either. "We're all going to be living up there one day," he said. "I hope to goodness we don't trash it up, the way we do down here." Did you ever think about being an astronaut?

BUSTER. No, I don't even like to fly in aeroplanes. That's the only thing I didn't like about the army. They moved us every place on an aeroplane.

LORENA. I don't think I would like to be an astronaut either. They are going to send a lady up there you know, one day. They're training her right this minute, Phil says, at the Space Center. I saw Alan Shepard once.

BUSTER. I know. I heard you say that.

LORENA. At least, Phil says it was. To tell you the truth I didn't think it was at all, but I let on like I thought I did. One day Phil said, "Now that they have a Catholic astronaut and are training a woman and a black man to go up in space, maybe the next thing," he said, "is that they will send up a family." "A what?" I said. "A family. A father, a mother and a little girl. And that would be us." "Who?" I said. "You and me and the baby," he said. But he was only teasing, of course. Not about himself. He wasn't teasing about that. He wanted to try for it the worst way. He studied night and day although he said all the time he knew it was foolish and it could never happen to him. "Then why are you killing yourself going to school?" I said. "I don't know," he said. "Maybe if I can only get enough education, there is something that I can do to be part of the Space Program." And then he would talk forever about the Space Program and the future and the land of the astronauts in which he said, if not our children, then our children's children would be living one day.

BUSTER. (A pause.) Would you like a little music?

LORENA. All right.

BUSTER. Would you mind listening to some religious music?

LORENA. Why, no.

BUSTER. I'm going with a girl that is very religious. I never have been, so I'm trying to catch up. (*He gets a program of hymns. They listen for a beat.*)

LORENA. Where does your girl live?

BUSTER. In Harrison.

LORENA. What's her name? Maybe I know her.

BUSTER. Edith Tolliver. Do you know her?

LORENA. No, I don't.

BUSTER. Were you ever baptized?

LORENA. Yes.

BUSTER. I wasn't. At least, not in the proper way according to Edith.

LORENA. Which way is that?

BUSTER. In the river. Moving water.

LORENA. Then I don't guess she would call me baptized either. I just had water sprinkled on my head.

(*They are quiet, listening to the music as the lights fade. The lights are brought up on the office of the Baytown jail.* DEPUTY KELLY *is there on duty.* V. O. CONKLIN *enters with a suitcase.*)

V. O. Howdy do. I'm V. O. Conklin.

KELLY. Yes sir. What can I do for you?

V. O. I have a suitcase here that I seen a man put down in a bus station, and so after I thought he had forgotten it and I picked up the suitcase I went hurrying after him hollering "You left your suitcase," and he said he didn't want it no more. He said he would be wearing a spacesuit from now on. "Well," I said, "I sure don't want it," and I took it back to the bus station. But the man working there said it sounded suspicious to him and he sure didn't want it and he said I should bring it to you.

KELLY. Thank you.

(LORENA *and* BUSTER *enter.*)

BUSTER. Are you Kelly?

KELLY. Yes.

BUSTER. This is Mrs. Massey. She's here to get her husband.

KELLY. Oh. Yes. Is this his suitcase, lady?

(*She looks at it.*)

LORENA. Why, yes, it is.

V. O. A man left it in the bus station. I ran after him and tried to give it to him, but he said he didn't want it anymore as he was wearing a spacesuit from now on.

(LORENA *has opened the suitcase.*)

LORENA. That is his all right.

V. O. Well, I'm glad I brought it over. I'll say good night to you folks.

KELLY. Good night, sir.

(V. O. *leaves.*)

KELLY. Have a seat, lady, and I'll get your husband.

BUSTER. Thank you.

(*He and* LORENA *get chairs.* KELLY *goes out of the office. They wait in silence. The* DEPUTY *comes back in.*)

KELLY. I'm sorry. He says he has no wife and won't come. (*A pause.*) Are you sure it's your husband?

LORENA. I can't be dead sure unless I see him.

BUSTER. Show him your pictures.

(*She shows him the pictures of* PHIL.)

KELLY. Yes ma'm. That's him. You want to come talk to him? Maybe you can get him to go with you.

LORENA. All right.

(*He starts away. She follows after him as the lights fade. The lights are brought up in a jail cell.* PHIL *is there dressed in khakis and staring into space.* LORENA *and the* DEPUTY *come up.* PHIL *does not see them, or if he does, shows no sign of recognizing her.*)

LORENA. (*Whispering.*) That's my husband.

KELLY. Would you like to be alone with him?

LORENA. Yes sir.

(*The* DEPUTY *unlocks the cell.* PHIL *still does not look at his wife. The* DEPUTY *starts away.*)

KELLY. I'll be in the office.

LORENA. Yes sir. Thank you.

(*He goes. She goes into the cell.* PHIL *still doesn't look at her.*)

LORENA. Phil— (*He continues not looking at her.*) Don't you know me? I'm Lorena, Phil. Lorena. Your wife. Mabel Sue sends her love to you. Her recital is Friday night. You remember? That's why I got so worried when the letter I sent you was returned. I thought now what if Phil with all he has on his mind has forgotten Mabel Sue's dance recital and doesn't come. (*A pause.*) Phil— Do you hear me? I'm talking to you, honey. Please look at me. I've come here to take you home with me. A nice young man from the sheriff's office in Harrison drove me here to get you and he will drive us back to the hotel. He's going with a girl that's very religious, he says, and he played hymns on the radio and he—

PHIL. I'm an astronaut and I'm lost.

LORENA. What, honey?

PHIL. I'm an astronaut and I'm lost.

LORENA. What, honey?

PHIL. What, honey? Is that all you can say to me? What, honey?

(*She cries. A pause.*)

PHIL. I'm sorry. I'm sorry. I mean no harm. Not to you or anybody. I'm weary and I'm tired and I'm discouraged, but I mean no harm.

LORENA. Phil . . .

PHIL. I'm thirty-five. Sweet Jesus. Tired and discouraged and thirty-five.

LORENA. Don't be discouraged, darling. Things will work out all right. I know.

PHIL. I'm tired and discouraged and I can't pretend any longer. I work in a restaurant and I go to school at night. Day after day. Year after year. And nothing happens. I go to Houston to look for work and nothing happens and nothing is going to happen and I want something to happen. Is that too much to ask? I want something for once to happen to me. I am tired of reading about things happening to other men. I want something to happen to me. Why can't I go up into space and leave this earth and all its troubles and frustrations behind?

LORENA. Well, even if you went, you would have to come back down sometime, or you would die. Come on home with me now. Baby is going to be in her dance recital Friday night like I told you. Don't you want to see her? It would break her heart if you didn't come to see her dance.

PHIL. All right. (*He starts out of the cell. He pauses.*) But answer me one thing and answer me logically and then I'll come home with you. Why can't I be an astronaut? They are human beings, aren't they? Just like me. They walk and talk. Have wives and children. (*A pause.*) Don't worry. I'm going. I know the answer to that. (*A pause.*) I'm tired. I'm tired. I work and work and get nowhere and I'm tired.

LORENA. Of course you are. (*A pause.*) Rusty said you could have your job back at the restaurant anytime you wanted it and you could go to night school as much as you wanted and he would never in this world say a word. . . .

PHIL. Thank you. That is kind of Rusty. (*He is composed now. They start out. He pauses.*) Not ten miles away, this minute perhaps, men are being trained to go up into space, and even if they finally never get to go, still they are being given the chance.

(*A pause. They continue on as the lights fade and are brought up in the jail office.* KELLY *and* BUSTER *are there.* LORENA *and* PHIL *come in.*)

LORENA. Buster, this is my husband, Phil.

BUSTER. Pleased to know you.

(*They shake hands. He picks up the suitcase.*)

LORENA. Buster is going to drive us to Harrison.

PHIL. You know, I think I came here on the bus. I wonder where I left my car.

LORENA. I expect you left it in Houston?

PHIL. I guess I did.

(*They start out.*)

KELLY. Good luck to you.

LORENA. Thank you, and thank you for all your kindness.

KELLY. That's all right.

(*They leave.* DEPUTY KELLY *turns on the radio. He picks up a newspaper.* V. O. *comes back in.*)

V. O. Officer?

KELLY. Yes sir.

V. O. That man leaving with the lady. He's the one I tried to give the suitcase to. He said he didn't want it.

KELLY. I know. He's just a little mixed up.

v. o. He's not in the Space Program, is he?

KELLY. No.

v. o. I didn't think so. Good night.

(*He goes as the lights fade. The lights are brought up on the car again.* PHIL *and* BUSTER *are in the front.* LORENA *is in the back seat asleep.*)

BUSTER. The little lady is asleep. She must have been tired. (*A pause.*) I was telling your wife that the girl I'm engaged to is very religious. (*A pause.*) She won't marry me until I'm baptized in the proper way. Have you been baptized?

PHIL. Yes.

BUSTER. In the proper way?

PHIL. Depends on what you call the proper way.

BUSTER. She says according to the Bible you have to be immersed in running water—a river, or a sea, I guess, or the ocean or the Gulf would do it. As long as it's running water. (*A pause.*) Are you an Astro fan?

PHIL. I watch them sometimes on television.

BUSTER. I like to ride in and see them play at the Astrodome. I love the Astrodome. Have you ever been there?

PHIL. No.

BUSTER. That's the Space Center we're passing.

PHIL. I know.

BUSTER. The Astros were named after the Astronauts.

PHIL. I know that. (*He begins to cry.*)

BUSTER. Is there something wrong, fellow? Did I say something wrong? If I did, I meant no offense I can assure you.

PHIL. I work hard. In the name of God, we all work hard. Someday . . . (*A pause.*) Someday, there will be an end to this. I hope someday. (*Again, he is composed.*)

BUSTER. Maybe you should try religion. I'm trying it. My fiancée says it will bring me peace of mind.

(PHIL *doesn't answer. They ride on in silence as the lights fade. The lights are brought up on the lobby.* MABEL SUE *and* BERTIE DEE *are there.* LILA *and* BERNICE *come in.*)

MABEL SUE. How was your supper?

LILA. Lovely.

BERNICE. I don't care for peach cobbler.

LILA. I love it.

BERNICE. We're sorry about Son's back.

LILA. Oh, yes. We are so sorry. Please tell him we are sorry.

BERTIE DEE. I will. I will. Thank you.

BERNICE. Good night.

BERTIE DEE. Good night.

LILA. When is your recital, sweetheart?

MABEL SUE. Friday.

BERNICE. Friday. We'll be there.

(*They leave.*)

MABEL SUE. She calls me Eleanor Powell.

BERTIE DEE. Who does?

MABEL SUE. Miss Lila.

(MR. *and* MRS. TAYLOR, BERTIE DEE'*s in-laws, come out of the dining room.*)

MRS. TAYLOR. We sent up a plate to Son.

BERTIE DEE. Thank you.

(MR. TAYLOR *goes to the cash register, opens it, takes out some money and shuts the cash drawer.*)

BERTIE DEE. Daddy Taylor, did you remember to put in a slip for the cash you took?

MR. TAYLOR. Oh, no. I did not. I am sorry. (*He gets a fountain pen and a piece of paper, writes out an amount and then puts it back in the cash drawer.*)

BERTIE DEE. You know I can't keep the books properly unless everyone that takes cash out of the drawer remembers to put a slip in the drawer for the amount you take out.

MRS. TAYLOR. I always do.

BERTIE DEE. No you don't, Mother Taylor.

MRS. TAYLOR. Don't I? I thought I did.

BERTIE DEE. No. And didn't we have this conversation once today?

MRS. TAYLOR. Yes, we did.

BERTIE DEE. And Sitter never puts in a slip.

MRS. TAYLOR. Well, you know Sitter is inclined to be scattered. Have you seen her? She wasn't in her room.

BERTIE DEE. She went walking with Mr. Henry.

MRS. TAYLOR. Did she? You know, I think she forgot to eat sup-per again. I inquired in the dining room if she had been in for supper and they said no.

MR. TAYLOR. We're going to visit the Clarks in case anyone needs us.

BERTIE DEE. All right.

(*They leave. She opens the cash drawer to look at the amount they have taken out.*)

BERTIE DEE. Well, child, now you have witnessed what upsets Son and keeps his back out of place. We were both working in Houston and had lovely jobs when his aunt, who was quite rich and owned this hotel, died and left the hotel and her jewels and some cash, they would never tell us how much, to them, and they called up Son and said nothing would do but we would have to give up our jobs and move here and they would let us take charge of the hotel. And they said it would be a gold mine. Well, it might be, but what they didn't tell us was that his three sisters and their husbands and children would be coming here anytime they wanted and put up on us, eat us out of house and home, go into the cash drawer and take out what they want without even bothering to write a slip, and that his mother and father and Sitter would live here permanently, not hardly lift a finger to help us any way.

(SITTER *and* MR. HENRY *come in.*)

BERTIE DEE. Did you see your mama?

SITTER. Yes.

BERTIE DEE. She was worried that you hadn't eaten your supper.

SITTER. I know that. We're going to eat now.

BERTIE DEE. I thought you had eaten, Mr. Henry.

SITTER. No, he has not eaten.

(*They go out.*)

BERTIE DEE. Well, don't take my head off, lady. I don't care if he never eats again.

(LORENA *and* PHIL *stand just outside the lobby area.* BERTIE DEE *has gone back to work on her books and* MABEL SUE *reads a book and they are not aware of* LORENA *and* PHIL.)

PHIL. I remember now what happened to my car. I sold it. (*A pause.*) It broke down in Houston and when they told me what it would cost to fix it there was no way in this world I could afford it, so I asked them how much they would give for it, and they gave me fifty dollars. I have twenty-five left. (*A pause.*) I'm going to make all this up to you. I'm going to swallow my pride and go back to work at Rusty's and I'll be sensible now and we'll save our money. (*A pause.*) What will we tell Mabel Sue?

LORENA. We won't tell her anything except you have decided to come back here and live.

(*They go into the hotel lobby.*)

BERTIE DEE. Well, look who's here. Welcome home.

PHIL. Thank you.

LORENA. I hope she hasn't been too much trouble.

BERTIE DEE. No, she's a lot of company. I tell her all my secrets. Don't I, sugar?

MABEL SUE. Yes ma'm. (*She has gone to her father and he embraces and kisses her.*)

MABEL SUE. I'm going to be in a dance recital Friday night, Daddy. Are you going to be here?

PHIL. I sure am.

BERTIE DEE. Have you eaten anything? The kitchen is closed but I can go out there and scare up something I bet.

LORENA. Thank you. We stopped for a hamburger on our way back here. Come on, honey. Say good night to Bertie Dee.

MABEL SUE. Good night, Miss Bertie Dee.

BERTIE DEE. Good night.

LORENA. And thank you for all your kindness.

BERTIE DEE. That's all right.

(SON *comes creeping into the room from the stairs, stooped over because of his back and holding on to the wall.*)

BERTIE DEE. Son. My heavens, what are you doing down here?

SON. I was losing my mind cooped up in my room all by myself. Nobody to talk to. (*He starts across the room slowly and painfully.*)

PHIL. Here, Son. Let me help you. (*He goes to him and takes him by the arm and leads him across the room.* MABEL SUE *and* LORENA *watch them.*)

BERTIE DEE. Why didn't you watch television?

SON. I'm sick of television. Sick to death of it.

BERTIE DEE. Well, I guess so. (PHIL *has gotten* SON *as far as the desk.* BERTIE DEE *gets a chair for him.*) I was just fixing to watch a little television now that things have quieted down for the night.

SON. Can we watch the Astros?

BERTIE DEE. No we cannot. I don't want to watch any baseball games.

(PHIL *helps* SON *into a chair.*)

SON. Thank you, Phil.

PHIL. That's all right. (PHIL *starts towards* MABEL SUE *and* LORENA.)

SON. Did you hear the Harrison Bank and Trust Company had been sold?

PHIL. No.

SON. Yes, I heard today a Houston bank bought it. They say they have an astronaut on the board of directors of the Houston bank, and they say he'll be down every now and then to greet the cus-tomers. So we'll get a look at him.

(PHIL *doesn't comment.* LORENA *and* MABEL SUE *leave, and* PHIL *goes after them. A pause.*)

BERTIE DEE. Did they say what astronaut?

SON. No.

BERTIE DEE. I hope it's Alan Shepard. I still think he's the cutest of them all. It can't be John Glenn. He's a senator up North someplace. Alan Shepard has always been my favorite.

SON. I liked the one that was killed.

BERTIE DEE. Oh, yes. What was his name?

SON. I don't remember that. (*He whispers.*) Where was he?

BERTIE DEE. (*Whispering.*) Search me.

(*The lights fade and are brought up on the hotel bedroom of* PHIL *and* LORENA. *They enter and turn on a light. There is a single bed, a double bed and two chairs and a table.*)

MABEL SUE. Show Daddy my costume, Mama.

(LORENA *goes to a closet and brings out her dance costume.*)

MABEL SUE. Isn't it pretty?

PHIL. Yes it is.

LORENA. It's not quite finished yet. I still have some work to do on it.

MABEL SUE. Do you want me to try it on?

PHIL. Sure.

(MABEL SUE *takes off her dress and puts the costume on.*)

PHIL. That's beautiful, honey.

LORENA. Doesn't she look pretty in it?

PHIL. I think so.

MABEL SUE. Want to see the tap routine I'm doing in the recital?

PHIL. All right.

(MABEL SUE *does her tap routine. When she finishes,* PHIL *and* LORENA *applaud.*)

PHIL. That's wonderful. (PHIL *sits in a chair.* MABEL SUE *gets in his lap.*)

MABEL SUE. Daddy . . .

PHIL. What, honey?

MABEL SUE. Tell me a story.

PHIL. All right. What do you want to hear?

MABEL SUE. About the land of the astronauts.

PHIL. Well, let's see. The land of the astronauts will be beautiful, of course, not like here. A beauty we have never seen before and perhaps can't even imagine, and the people living there . . . (*He pauses.*)

MABEL SUE. The people . . .

PHIL. Will be happy all the time. Day and night. They will have no petty cares, no worries. They will have abundance all around them. They will be good and noble and kind.

(LORENA *hums a hymn.*)

LORENA. That's one of those religious songs I heard in Buster's car tonight. They're catching. I can't get this one out of my head. Buster says he is marrying a girl that is very religious.

MABEL SUE. Who is Buster?

LORENA. He's the nice man that took me in his car to get Daddy.

(*A woman can be heard crying. They listen.*)

MABEL SUE. That's Miss Sitter crying. We hear her often at night in her room crying. Don't we, Mama?

LORENA. Yes.

PHIL. Why is she crying?

MABEL SUE. We don't know. Do we, Mama?

LORENA. No. I guess she's unhappy.

PHIL. Poor soul. (*A pause.*) The land of the astronauts is verdant and lovely.

MABEL SUE. What does that mean—verdant?

PHIL. Green. Lush. Fertile.

MABEL SUE. Like here?

PHIL. Like nothing we have ever seen before or imagined. The land of the astronauts is peaceful and there are no cares and no worries.

MABEL SUE. Miss Sitter has stopped crying.

LORENA. Yes, she has.

MABEL SUE. And one day we'll all go to the land of the astronauts. Won't we, Daddy?

PHIL. Yes, I suppose we will someday. And if not me and your mama or you, then your children certainly.

LORENA. I wonder which one of the astronauts will come here to the bank.

PHIL. I wonder. (*A pause.*)

MABEL SUE. Why are you so quiet, Daddy?

PHIL. I'm just thinking, honey.

MABEL SUE. About the land of the astronauts?

PHIL. Yes, I guess so, honey, in a way.

(*The lights fade.*)

Selected One-Act Plays of
HORTON FOOTE
has been set in Goudy Old Style
by G & S Typesetters,
printed & bound by Braun-Brumfield and
designed by Whitehead & Whitehead.
Photographs on front of cover/dustjacket
are by Keith Carter.